EXALTED SECRETS OF BRILLIANT MINDS

How to Arouse Intelligence and Climb the Mountain of Greatness
Like the "Chosen" Few According to the Wisdom of Age
(#2 of Hints of Wisdom Series)

WISDOM J.O.Y. MAKANO

America Star Books

© 2014 by Wisdom J.O.Y. Makano.
All rights reserved. No part of this book may be reproduced, stored in a retrieval system or transmitted in any form or by any means without the prior written permission of the publishers, except by a reviewer who may quote brief passages in a review to be printed in a newspaper, magazine or journal.

First printing

This publication contains the opinions and ideas of its author. Author intends to offer information of a general nature. Any reliance on the information herein is at the reader's own discretion.

The author and publisher specifically disclaim all responsibility for any liability, loss, or right, personal or otherwise, which is incurred as a consequence, directly or indirectly, of the use and application of any contents of this book. They further make no representations or warranties with respect to the accuracy or completeness of the contents of this work and specifically disclaim all warranties including without limitation any implied warranty of fitness for a particular purpose. Any recommendations are made without any guarantee on the part of the author or the publisher.

America Star Books has allowed this work to remain exactly as the author intended, verbatim, without editorial input.

Softcover 9781611028201
PUBLISHED BY AMERICA STAR BOOKS, LLLP
www.americastarbooks.com

Printed in the United States of America

TABLE OF CONTENTS

INTRODUCTION..15

PART ONE *THE PHILOSOPHER STONE* 25
CHAPTER I *ANATOMY OF ATTAINMENT* 25
CHAPTER II *ANATOMY OF DESIRE* 39
CHAPTER III *DETERMINATION*..60
CHAPTER IV *THE HIGHEST KNOWLEDGE OF
   GREATNESS* 125

PART TWO *THE ROYAL SECRET*..137
CHAPTER V *HARMONIOUS FEELINGS* 137
CHAPTER VI *GOVERNING FEELINGS*................................153
CHAPTER VII *VIRTUES* 163
CHAPTER VIII *THE LAND MINE OF VIRTUES*..................184
CHAPTER IX *THE SOLAR PLEXUS* 200
CHAPTER X *AROUSING THE SOLAR PLEXUS* 210
CHAPTER XI *HARMONIOUS BREATHING*.........................221

PART THREE *THE ELIXIR OF INTELLIGENCE*....................248
CHAPTER XII *INTELLIGENCE AND THE SOURCE OF
   INTELLIGENCE* 250
CHAPTER XIII *THE COURAGE PILLAR*..............................289
CHAPTER XIV *THE LOVE PILLAR*.....................................306
CHAPTER XV *THE TRUTH PILLAR (INTEGRITY)* 339
CHAPTER XVI *THE SILENCE PILLAR* 351
CHAPTER XVII *THE ATTENTION PILLAR*..........................370
CHAPTER XVIII *THE SELF-CONFIDENCE PILLAR*..........421
CHAPTER XIX *THE ACTION PILLAR*..................................459
CHAPTER XX *THE HUMILITY PILLAR*...............................484
CHAPTER XXI *THE PHILANTHROPY (CHARITY) PILLAR* 501
CHAPTER XXII *THE PERSISTENCE PILLAR* 517

Mama wa Africa, naku abudu!
Femme Africaine, je t'adore!
African Mother, I adore you!

To all Mothers and Daughters of the African Seed wherever dispersed — to you who are our true Heroines and Goddesses in the tongue of the Hallowed Forerunners of our Kind and by the Grace and Will of the Great Architect of the Universe, the Supreme Creative Power of all that was, is, or will ever be and the Causeless Cause of existence; to you who are the Great Symbol of our life beyond life; to you who have kept the flames of hope, courage, resolve, and resilience of the Motherland alive despite the heartless, destructive, and almost devilish leadership and management of its sons — this fruit of my life and humble handiwork of my heart, head, hands, wholeheartedly and lovingly I dedicate.

A THOUGHT OF GRATITUDE

Here, now and forever, in all humility and gratitude, I bow my head, salute, and pay back a small installment of the eternal debt I will never be able to repay in full to the three luminaries of my path of life, my beloved elder brothers — **our pioneer,** the late **Fataki Telesphore Makano; his successor, Doctor Sheria Christophe Makano; our family strategist, the Engineer George Mboko Ya Makano**—for being such great lamps of undimmed light for me and benchmarks for my formal educational journey and risk-taking attitude in life. Without your pioneering and unbendable desire to go as far you could with your education despite all the hardships you faced, pulling along with you those you held dear and near, and without your unconditional brotherly love to lend hands to and uplift your often failing, falling down, and troubling little brothers behind you, this series of *"Hints of Wisdom"* would have been not only impossible to achieve but even to think of. Brothers, thank you from the bottom of my heart for unfailingly carrying on the DREAM of our Father **Makano Sr** and our Mother **Laliya Oropa Abala Makano,** whom I know and feel are reading the pages of this work from better dimensions of life.

A thought on completion of
EXALTED SECRETS OF BRILLIANT MINDS

Genesis 28:16-17 writes: "16 Then Jacob awoke from his sleep and said, "Surely the LORD is in this place, and I did not know it." 17 He was afraid and said, "How awesome is this place! This is none other than the house of God, and this is the gate of heaven." January 3rd, 2014, an hour or two before I retired for the day, exactly two days after I had shipped the final product of this book (or so I thought) to the book review agency for further examination and appreciation; I came across on www.TED.com these three magnificent talks by Angela Lee Duckworth, Simon Sinek, and Elizabeth Gilbert respectively: www.ted.com/talks/ angela_lee_duckworth_the_key_to_success_grit.html www.ted. com/talks/simon_sinek_how_great_leaders_inspire_action.html http://www.ted.com/talks/elizabeth_gilbert_on_genius.html.

As I finished watching these incredible talks for the first time, I looked at my wife and loudly screamed with genuine and overwhelming spontaneous humility: "Mama! Mama! I just wrote the magic formula of acquisition of the mysterious power we call intelligence and I did not know it." I say this not with a slight sense of arrogance whatsoever but humility in the purest form a human being is capable of feeling. Why did these three talks cause me to scream so joyfully? I will leave it to you to watch them (if they are still available on the web) and read the book to figure out for yourself the reason.

Without exaggeration whatsoever, the magic formula of acquisition of the mysterious power we call intelligence is really what is in this book. But do not take my word for it; let your own experience or application of the laws herein explained prove it to you. And please note that when I say "magic formula," I do not mean when one says "Abracadabra!" and "Bingo!"

Money, cars, clothes, all your needs and wants fall from the sky or manifest without any consciously sustained constrictive mental and physical effort on your part. Far from that! I mean the knowledge and wisdom to accomplish with one's own feelings, thoughts, and actions whatever one effectively sets his/her mind on.

This psycho-mythological definition of intelligence, which I hope will alter and enhance the traditional understanding and most importantly aid the acquisition of that mysterious power we call intelligence, is the finest masterwork of the trinity of my feelings, thoughts, and deeds; my heart, head, and hands thus far; and I offer it to the world with the purest love of my heart, truest humility of my being and ecstasy beyond description.

In here, again, I hope the reader will find that oftentimes outwardly perilous yet Golden Inner Path to the Schoolroom of Self-Knowledge; the only place where fear, doubt, selfishness, and all other destructive vices are forever conquered; and the Dynamic Wings for the mind to fly to the edges and to the Heart of the Universe in quest of the Greatest Good or the constructive way of life, which alone can free our Home Planet from its stubborn ills and clenches of hatred, hunger, poverty and restore to all prosperity, health, and happiness in everlasting peace and harmony.

This piece of work is really as awesome as the resting place of Jacob, the master key of the gateway to incredible achievements, and I am not exaggerating anything here. Seriously! Like some of my shortsighted and ego-driven critics, if you are skeptical and feel that I am unworthy of authoring such a book, take a deep breath and then relax because you I may be with you myself. To this moment, like all good writers, I still do not believe that I, a mere student of life, a self-confessed talentless person, an apprentice grit-driven thinker and doer, a person labeled with all kinds of shortcomings, could possibly be the author of a wonderful book. While I am out of words to describe my feelings of accomplishment in this work, I sincerely hope

www.makanologos.com

Exalted Secrets of Brilliant Minds   11

the reader will not take my word for it but will put every claim in this work to an honest test before rendering any judgment whatsoever.

Now that the student is ready and the Teacher is in, let the class begin! ENJOY THE JOURNEY! Lovingly, humbly, and joyfully I AM Wisdom Joseph Ombe Ya Makano, Portland, Oregon, United States of America, 97233; January 4th, 2014; 10:14 AM PST.

ADDENDUM

Points to Ponder

You are about to step into a field of ENLIGHTENMENT. But before you dare to step in, I encourage you to ponder the quotations given below, then relax, ponder, and relax, ponder again, and then proceed joyfully and cheerfully if you wish to harness the finest from your search:

"If you want your children to be intelligent, read them fairy tales. If you want them to be more intelligent, read them more fairy tales." Albert Einstein

"It is for this reason that to sensitive souls, the souls awakened to the Presence of the Spirit, the immanence of the God-Presence becomes in all the secret haunts of nature an abiding fact ever present to their consciousness. Therefore, these enlightened ones see more, hear more, feel more, and receive more from intimate association with nature than those average folk whose chief characteristics are their gregariousness, their obtuseness to blatant noise, and their love of excitement—often indeed, their acute horror of being alone. They are afraid of the mystery of life which in silence knocks on the door of consciousness,—afraid because it has been clothed in terror when it should be radiant with beauty." Ella A. Fletcher, *The Law of the Rhythmic Breath*, page 250

"When you pursue for greatness, don't expect others to support you. You'll represent the courage, strength, and vision they don't yet have." James Arthur Ray

INTRODUCTION

Triumph! What a glorious word! Its sound alone vibrates with a sense of grandeur and a desire to live an unforgettable life. The prospect alone of becoming triumphant in one's endeavor almost magically transports one to a higher dimension of life by kindling flames of joy that have eluded the human mind since the end of timelessness. No sane person can spend a lifetime without ever thinking about or trying to triumph in his undertakings. It is man's relations with his undertakings and social performance that mostly determine whether he lives a life of weeping and mourning or a life of excitement and fulfillment.

However, a vast majority of men, well over ninety percent, wish (underscore *wish*) their undertakings had produced better results; thus it is led by the three to five percent who feel they have earned the right by virtue of their triumphant performance, or so it seems. But when you look deeper, you will find that even among the three to five percent who may be exteriorizing their feeling of triumph, a good portion of them are not really triumphant, for real success is more subtle than most of us think of it. Some may be successful in their undertakings but miserable failures in their family and social lives. Based on this premise, one can safely assume that fewer than two percent of the population at any time can broadly and comprehensively claim triumph in life. No science, religion, or philosophy has ever claimed the superiority of two percent of the human population in talent, intelligence, or wisdom over the ninety-eight percent of their fellow men to whom happiness becomes even more elusive with every sunrise and sunset. While people of weak character, intellect, or aptitude never attain success, surprisingly enough, a huge number of people of good character, strong mental power, and aptitude fail massively as well.

A quick read of a recent article on intelligence from the online version of *Forbes* magazine—"Intelligence Is Overrated: What You Really Need To Succeed" at http://www.forbes.com/sites/keldjensen/2012/04/12/intelligence-is-overrated-what-you-really-need-to-succeed/(accessed June 18, 2012)—will give the reader an effective glance at what I hope to discuss in detail to at least satisfy the average seeker. I call your attention to this article for two simple reasons: first, because it was published almost two years after the manuscript of this book was finished and ready for review and editing; and second, because it gave me confidence that the theme presented in this work is extremely useful because it aims to remove the illusion from the general public's conception about what many wrongly call *intelligence* and the effect of this misconception on the performance of our daily duties.

Even if we are all sometimes pessimistic, I think you and I can agree that at least a tenth of people everywhere are of good character, intellect, and aptitude in their endeavors. Of course, there is no scientific evidence to support this theory, but it is probably true, because if a good portion of people were not somewhat good morally and mentally, ours would not be a livable planet but a completely chaotic jungle.

If those characteristics were the prerequisites of success, the world today would have at least 700,000,000 (seven hundred million) very successful people (as this book is being written, governmental and nonprofit organizations estimate Planet Earth is currently home to more than seven billion people). It may be very simple to prove that there are not six hundred million genuinely happy people on this Earth, at least not in our lifetime with all the evidence of a growing world prison population, tyranny, dictatorships, pseudo-democracies, poverty, backdoor political deals, terrorism, wars, riots, diseases, drug trafficking, unbalanced justice, civil unrest, widespread hunger, etc. So if good character, mental power, and extraordinary talent (bear in mind, the opposite of these

Exalted Secrets of Brilliant Minds   **17**

characteristics makes the odds of triumph negative or worse, if there is anything worse than negative) are not the prerequisites of success, what are? Why do so few people attain genuine happiness in life?

These questions and more will be the focus of this work. I will explore how everything we need to triumph is inside ourselves and how looking for our solutions outside knocks us deadly blows that usually leave us hopeless for a very long time, if not a lifetime. I will look at how the so-called realities are but the illusions and dreams of our senses that distract us unnecessarily, as we unfortunately discover too late in life when those remorseful questions keep popping up in our heads: "If I had it to do all over again…?" "Had I known this…?" etc. "It is never too late," a wise person consoles him/herself.

Teaching younger generations the lessons of life we have learned so they can do better where we fell short is what has kept mankind slowly but surely marching forward, improving life with every passing and coming generation and age. Mankind moves on at the speed of a turtle when it could literally be moving at a much higher speed if we only knew how to from the get-go. I will try to explore and analyze how some of our fellow men — who come into the world as naked as we did and with the same five senses and body parts as the rest of us; who breathe the same air we do; who have the same blood color and walk on the same ground; who eat, work, and sleep like you and me — exert tremendous power to the point we respect and fear them like fire.

I will take no credit for any of the truths herein laid out, as none of them is my own invention but rather the wisdom of sages of old. I have simply dedicated my precious time and energy to search for these truths, and I have strived to put them together from some of the very ancient tales, mythologies, and books with the hope that they may be useful to someone with the desire, determination, and strength to roll the wheel of the Earth a little bit faster toward the harbor of happiness. Thus I

www.makanologos.com

will not need to break new ground because the truths treated here may appear new to some readers who may be betrayed by the dreams of their senses. But these truths are in fact self-created and all creating, and they are as old as the universe itself.

I may just be the instrument through which you are reminded of them, at least physically, but believe me, I am neither the true author nor the inventor. However, I will let you take pleasure in finding out who is. Nevertheless, I will put together fragments of information that you may have seen or heard (or thought you have seen or heard) here and there, a sort of one-stop shopping of very precious ideas that took people—apparently small-bodied people but of unbendable self-confidence, such as Napoleon and Bill Gates—to the pinnacle of their careers. I will strive to show how people of unbendable faith, strong self-confidence, heroic courage, and attentive mind, yet who are also lovers of silence, become leaders and heroes of men in time and space.

Like you, the many readers of this book, I am human with weaknesses and obstacles to conquer. And of course, I am still dreaming to climb the mountain of greatness myself like the chosen few. Thus, the possibilities of falling short in satisfying readers' expectations are real, and I am the first to acknowledge it. One thing I can say with no uncertainty is this: if everything else in this book happens to be of no value to you; if this book does not serve as your owner's manual toward your goal; if nothing else, one thing I certainly hope it will do is serve as a very effective morning star or compass along your journey to the mountaintop of greatness.

Wherever you are going, as long as you are honest with yourself, look and study with your inner eyes and mind, and utilize your head, heart, and hands to get the results of your truest desires, this book will not let you down. And if you hold it with both your heart and hands, it will be one of your best companions ever. Thus, my promise to you, the reader,

www.makanologos.com

Exalted Secrets of Brilliant Minds   **19**

whom I owe satisfaction, is this: if I fall short in meeting your expectations, one thing I am positively confident of is that if you attentively study this work, you will seize what you need to do in order for life to dare and trust you with the keys of the universe and secrets of the Gods.

At least that much is guaranteed for a true seeker who earnestly studies the teachings of this book. If your reading is not for mere leisure, if you are not on the simplistic adventure of fault-finding but rather an actual search of elusive secrets and mysteries of life, I believe you will find here a solid springboard for imagination and creativity that will propel you as high as you want to climb on the mountain of greatness and overcome any obstacles that may keep you from writing your name among the self-chosen few. If you are looking for effective tools of inner and outer labor for expansion and enhancement of life in your corner of the universe, I predict you will not be disappointed. If you are looking for results, products of labor and not handouts, I trust you have found your way. If your aim is to put the discipline of human spirit to the test and see what it can do for you, you will be amazed how your heart will be caught in the fire of joy and happiness untold.

Another thing I can pledge with certainty is that you will not discover in this work (I apologize in advance if this disappoints you) the magic, wonderment, or beauty of *INACTION*, implied or otherwise. If there is such a thing as alchemy of inaction, I confess my ignorance because I have never had a desire to know or seek to understand it; therefore, I cannot relate it to the reader or associate myself with it in any shape or form. This is even truer because I have never had any intention to proclaim it, silently or otherwise, to anyone. It would be pure folly on my part and complete wickedness of the worst form to even try to mislead people in this way.

Reading this book will be more like a tour of a cold and dark planet, no light to lighten the path, no water to cheer up life, no heat to warm up the body, no air to breathe or to supply oxygen

www.makanologos.com

to those who believe in getting something for nothing—those who want the prize but refuse to pay the price of effort in all its forms, including physical, mental, and spiritual, and those who believe, even the slightest, in the power of supernatural manifestations to influence mankind's evolution. Do not get me wrong—I believe in God and all His manifestations, as you will discover in this book. But I do not believe whatsoever that God will ever drop coins in the hands of a believer or open a large bank account for someone who prays to death without action.

In here, there will be great disappointments or bitter pills for those who refuse to acknowledge the power of their own feelings, thoughts, and actions. Folks who do not believe the power of their own hearts, the most strategic locations from where all success must be planned and quite frankly executed, will find nothing interesting here. While the head and the hands are two major factors of triumph in climbing the mountain of greatness, the heart must be the center or the sun around which all other elements orbit.

As we all know, no rational person would give keys to his or her most intimate dwelling to an unworthy person, much less to a stranger, or reveal his or her secrets to a person who has not yet earned confidence and trust beyond the reach of doubt and fear. So as you read this book, in the deepest chamber of your true being, keep asking yourself, *Why should life trust me with the keys of the universe and the secrets of the Gods that raise the daring few to the top of the mountain of greatness?* If you ask yourself with true, deep desire for answers, you will benefit enormously from this book, and your search elsewhere will be made less cumbersome, more enjoyable, and more beneficial; otherwise, this book, like many others of similar focus, will be just another mystery novel that happened to fall in your hands.

After thoroughly and attentively reading this book with a deep desire to understand what is in the lines and between them, the reader, I hope, will gain some of the choicest wisdom and knowledge from the Higher Power. Truly attentive readers will obtain the keys of the universe and discover the secrets of the Gods that ancient philosophers spent lifetimes painstakingly seeking the world over. All men who wrote their names on the wall of time—including Moses, Aaron, Joshua, Socrates, Plato, Alexander the Great, Mohammed, Columbus, Napoleon, Cromwell, Washington, Lincoln, Gandhi, Martin Luther King, and now Nelson Mandela, etc.—have used these same powers but in different manners and for different purposes.

While Jesus may have been ambiguous about other things or may have kept the pearls from the masses, He was never vague about the source of His power. He was very frank and straightforward about it. You will recall that He never took credit for any of His astonishing miracles; instead, He gave credit to the Father in Him (the Higher Power within all of us), as He told anyone who would listen:

"Believest thou not that I am in the Father, and the Father in me? The words that I speak unto you I speak not of myself: but the Father that dwelleth in me, he does the works. Believe me that I am in the Father, and the Father in me: or else believe me for the very works' sake" Jesus said, John 14: 10-11 (KJV).

Jesus called the Higher Power *Father*; scientists call it *energy*; religions call it *God, Guardian Angel*; in metaphysics and New Age teaching, it is called *Universal Mind, Life, or Intelligent Substance, "I AM Presence"*, etc., and those who want to stay on the sidelines of religious conflicts call it the *Great Architect of the Universe*; Hebrews call it *Ehyeh asher Ehyeh, Ein sof, Keter, YHVH, or Shekhinah,* translated as *I AM that I AM or the CROWN* in English. You too can name it what you will as long as you truly believe and comply with its desires. Notice, Jesus gave all credit back to the Father! Well! That is because giving credit to the source of achievements, as Jesus did and all great Masters of life do, is the name of the game, is the technique that triggers the quick triumph of what would have otherwise taken a long

www.makanologos.com

time. It is what the pros (truly obedient and knowledgeable students of the truth) learn to do unconsciously and effortlessly.

I will elaborate more about the Higher Power throughout this book in many different ways. For now, as you prepare to absorb what may possibly change your life forever, I want you to know that there has never been a special human being. We all have the same access to this Power that no human vocabulary can do justice to describing accurately. This Power, like the sun or the air we breathe, is, all things being equal, accessible to all of us, whether you are at the White House, Vatican Palace, or Buckingham Palace, or at a remote village in Micronesia, India, or Africa. You and I also have the same power those great men of olden days and today had or have, the Higher Power that was used billions of years ago, for it is ageless and still exists today with its qualities.

The beauty of life is that you do not have to be overtly religious but simply divine in your own heart. You need to have noble goals and believe in the life in you to have the same power as life in the highest and furthest realms in the universe. If you are willing to use this power constructively, then nothing else will matter. This Higher Power is evident throughout nature. It is the same power that makes the plants grow, that makes a mere seed dropped into the ground feed generations of humans and other species; it is the same power that enables a small bug or a germ to develop effective defensive and protective mechanisms against unmatchable powers of the environment.

Attempting to destroy, limit, restrain, misuse, or deny the expression of this Higher Power is what religions call *sin*, but it is in fact what causes pain, suffering, diseases, poverty, failure, and all kinds of unhappiness and unwelcome consequences. Instead of the word *sin*, I prefer to say *the misuse of energy*. This book aims to present the qualities that will enable, if used correctly, the Higher Power to express itself through you, to the extent you allow and cooperate with It. As the fiat on the Egyptian Sphinx decrees, "To Know, to Dare, to DO, and to

www.makanologos.com

be Silent." I will strive to show how and why reaching the mountaintop of greatness in life, as the chosen—or better yet the daring—few do, is work to be done with intellect enlightened by study, an uncheckable audacity, an unconquerable will, and an incorruptible discretion. "We are instructed," as one great writer put it, to "listen and learn...search and discover, for to know the mysteries is to stand face to face with God." Let's begin unearthing the Exalted Secrets of Brilliant Minds.

PART ONE

THE PHILOSOPHER STONE

CHAPTER I

Anatomy of Attainment

Some of the most difficult questions to answer are also the most essential to understand if we are to comprehend life and the role we are to play in order to live an abundant life. Some of those questions are; *was the cause made for the effect or the effect made for the cause? Were children made for parents or parents for children? Was the ocean made for the fish or fish for the ocean? Was the universe made for its inhabitants or its inhabitants for the universe? Was the beginning made for the end or the end for the beginning?* Good answers to those questions can help you understand whether life is an endlessly straight line or a circle with each of us its true center. For now, I will not suggest or dare to answer these questions here; however, I hope that clues dropped along the way will enable you to answer each of them for yourself to your own satisfaction.

For now, let me say this: The cause gives meaning to the effect and vice versa; parents give meaning to children and vice versa; the ocean gives meaning to fish and vice versa; the universe gives meaning to its inhabitants and vice versa; the beginning gives meaning to the end and vice versa. Thus, whether the cause was made for the effect or the beginning for the end or vice versa, it is all so that the ball of life and existence may roll endlessly and smoothly. The work of the universe in which we live is always in progress, and it may or may not have been made for us.

Man was not made to be carried by work but to carry the work of the universe forward to keep the ball of life rolling endlessly. Any attempt to reverse the onward march of that work or even to slow it down has never been made without dire consequences or penalties. A wise man never swims against the current of a mighty river but with it; hence, he arrives not only safely but faster as well. Therefore, the key to climbing to the mountaintop of greatness is thus knowing and working with the laws of life that surround us. There is almost no choice here — we cannot avoid working with the laws of the universe to find peace. We either work with them enthusiastically or become pitilessly crushed.

In all probability, we were made for the universe and not the other way around. We must comply with the demands and the unbiased laws of the universe rather than hope and wait for the universe to comply with our often selfish and unfettered desires. These laws of the universe, like the sun, are no respecters of man, and they shine on kings as well as commoners, the high priest as well as the parishioners. And like the rain, they fall on the kings and their subjects, on the high priests and their followers, the rich as well as the poor, the young and the old indiscriminately.

The universe is not simply an empty space, as the illusion of humans seems to suggest. It is in fact a set of laws that must be obeyed — and obeyed faithfully — in order to bear constructive results. If they are disobeyed, they inflict serious consequences. This is the first and foremost exalted secret of brilliant minds, and anyone who thinks he or she is here to be served by the universe is like a train or a truck speeding in the wrong direction at full speed. Once you know the business of the universe in general, it will be much easier to define your own in order to comply with the universe around you. Thus,

www.makanologos.com

the wise and smart thing to know, first, is the business of the universe.

Even though man was made for the universe, the universe is not an ungrateful master, for it pays back its workers in the same currency it was served with. If you serve it with enthusiasm, it will pay you enthusiastically; if you serve it pessimistically, so will it pay you back. Thus, the first law of climbing the mountain of greatness is to serve the universe and to serve it well and happily, or as the Christian Master put it:

But seek ye first the kingdom of God, and his righteousness; and all these things shall be added unto you. Matthew 6:33 (KJV)

As well, when you comply with the laws of the universe, the universe turns and serves you beyond your wildest imagination. This is not religion, philosophy, or metaphysics; it is a scientific law. Everything being equal, when a farmer does his job well, the harvest is always astonishing; the best players rarely lose the game; dedicated students have the best odds of success, etc. "A worker is worthy of his wages" is common sense.

Now, what is the business of the universe? The answer to this question is the source of all religious conflicts and numerous wars in history. There is no one answer, certainly, for the question surpasses the understanding of the human mind. Religious monologues are certainly beyond the scope of this book; however, one thing I can say with deep conviction is that you are as close as the human mind can be to the truth if you believe that the business of the universe is the beautiful, harmonious, and permanent expansion of life. Your contribution to that goal is what results in what we call happiness. Attempting to swim against the current of rivers of the universe results in a life of failure, pain, suffering, and all kinds of misery. How then to comply with the expansion of life and obey the laws of the universe? Is it obeying the Ten Commandments as prescribed by Moses? Probably, but again, that is what this book is all about—what to do to gain that very

www.makanologos.com

important favor, the ability to climb the mountain of greatness that every human heart, soul, and mind craves.

One more thing before moving on: most of us are very confused when we are told to obey the laws of the universe. For many people, the first thing that comes to mind regarding the concept of the universe—erroneously, of course—is the blue-covered empty space with unreachable horizons. But verily, the universe that is called to our attention in this book is our own life, and complying with it is to comply with the very laws of the universe—nothing more, nothing less. Let's go back to the Christian Master for illustration to my Christian readers. Didn't He say, *"The kingdom of heaven is within you"*? Just check Luke 17:21. Got it? In his gigantic work *The Masks of God*, Joseph Campbell, speaking of ascension, said that Jesus went into the world within because there is no place up where Jesus could have gone to.

You do not need to be a weatherman to predict when or if it will be sunny or rainy, or a NASA scientist to find evidence of life in outer space. All you need is to know the laws that govern your own life. And I mean your individual life, because if peace, justice, happiness, and harmony are good for you, they are certainly good for the rest of your fellow men; if they are bad for you, then examine yourself and your motives. All the qualities needed to expand life are in you manifold. That is why, as the Greek masters taught, self-knowledge is the sole qualification for receiving the keys of the universe and the secrets of the Gods. All the possibilities and potentialities for transforming the universe for better or worse are lodged inside you. But make no mistake—the universe is not so naïve to let anyone destroy or even slow down its cherished, ever-ongoing work. It mercilessly inflicts pain and misery on whomever entertains destructive desires.

Genesis and many other myths around the world tell us that man is an image of God. True, but going one step further than just image is a major step in knowing oneself. Rather than see

www.makanologos.com

yourself as an image of God, see your *inner self* as God because you truly are, God being the sum of everything. God is energy and everything is energy, and so are you. Let's try to make it easier to understand and less religious. Affirming to yourself that you are God does not mean that you're the object of worship by the mass. It simply means all the qualities that are in God are in you as well, just as a drop of water has the same composition as all the water in the oceans, lakes, and rivers. If a drop of water is unlike the ocean, then man is unlike God as well. Just because some drops of water are in the mud, it does not make them less water than the water of a spring. This isn't determined by your belief or knowledge; it is a truth unaffected by your ignorance. For that matter, it has been there from the beginning of time, waiting for you to just acknowledge it in order to enjoy its benefits. This acknowledgement transforms your whole *self*. It stimulates previously dormant divine powers that make your being and bring you in harmony with the whole, therefore making your task of climbing the mountain of greatness easier. Of course, just acknowledging may not be sufficient; the secret is to feel, to think, and to act as a man or woman on a divine mission (not religious mission but divine or constructive mission.)

Before proceeding, I feel compelled to issue a dire yet very necessary warning and a heartfelt disclaimer. The world, or this home planet of ours, is not an easy or safe place to live in for either good or bad people. Life here is sometimes damned if you do, damned if you do not. It is safe for neither criminal nor righteous just yet, and it is even deadlier for those who dare to challenge the status quo. Thus, if you do not feel you have a divine or constructive mission from the very bottom of your heart, a special message from the Great Ones, and unless you have a genuine calling to prophesize and are willing to accept the fate of all prophets, true or false, who have come before you, please do not go around in public and chant, *"I am God, I am this, or I am that."* If you do, do it at your own risk,

www.makanologos.com

not at the counsel of this author. In his book *The Masks of God: Occidental Mythology,* my "teacher," the master mythologist Joseph Campbell, writes:

The female mystic Rabi'a al-Adawiya of Basra seems to have been the first to employ in her writings the imagery of wine, as "divine love," and the cup, as "the filled soul or heart," which became subsequently a typical trope of the mystics of Islam. The Persian Abu Yazid (Bayazid) of Bistan (d. 874 A.D.) carried the image to an absolutely Indian conclusion when he sang: "I am the Wine-drinker, the Wine, and the Cupbearer!" "God speaks with my tongue and I have vanished." "I came forth from Bayzidness, like a snake from its skin. Then I looked. And I saw that lover, beloved, and the love are one; for in the world of unity all can be one." "Glory to me!"

Compare the Indian Ashtavakra Samhita, of approximately the same date: "Wonderful am I! Adoration to myself!...I am that stainless Self in which, through ignorance, knowledge, knower, and the knowable appear!"

Such excitement was permissible, even normal, in India; in Islam, however, dangerous. And so it came to pass that when the next great mystic in the line, al-Hallaj, uttered what, anywhere else would have been recognized as a mystic truism, "I am God...I am the Real," he was crucified. The model of the mystic life for Hallaj was Jesus, not Mohammed; and his concept of the way (as we learned from his fable for moth) was, through suffering, surrender (pages 449-450).

"I am God..." and all kinds of affirmation must be uttered in the temple of silence in your own heart, in a low breath in the privacy of your dwelling, and, if occasion requires it, audibly only in the environment of like-minded people. I also believe it is very wise to heed the counsel of Matthew 6:6 *But thou, when thou prayest, enter into thy closet, and when thou hast shut thy door, pray to thy Father which is in secret; and thy Father which seeth in secret shall reward thee openly.* Now my heart is clean, my mind is at peace, and my soul is in harmony with both. Let's proceed.

www.makanologos.com

The attention of the reader is strongly called here to always remember throughout this book that whenever the name of God is mentioned, the author does not refer to a Specific Being in the sky—the God of the Jews, Christians, Muslims, Buddhists, Hindus, or anything of the sort—but to the Highest Ideal and Supreme Law of the universe, or the Inner and Higher Self of every one of us. This point cannot be made clear enough. And of course, the reader is absolutely free to imagine God in his/her own comprehension and understanding. But always remember that by *God*, the author in this work simply means the Highest Ideal and Supreme Law that is Master of the universe, or the Inner and Higher Self of every one of us. This cannot be emphasized strongly enough. Not that the Gods of the Jews, Christians, Muslims, Buddhists, or Hindus are not Gods, because they are in the minds of their believers. However, this work is not about what divides us; rather, it is about what unites us, what makes us *out of the many, one;* **NOT what makes us different from and opposite to one another.** Here, God is the Highest Quality that is unique and changeless in all of us. Anything else may be imagined to suit or please the reader's feelings and thoughts as dictated by his or her own free will. Now let's carry on.

Here is where working smart and working wisely make an obvious difference. You know very well that it is not those who work two or three jobs who make the most money. It is a well-known fact that hard workers work for the smart ones, and the smart workers are employed by the wise ones. "*C students often own the business that B and A students work for,*" said James A. Ray. Why do you think that is the case? Easy—hard work is a product of the physical body; smart work is a product of the intellect, where human ideas are processed; and wise work is a product of the mind, which is the seat of inspiration; and inspiration, as the ancient sages believed, is a product of the stars and the Gods. In other words, wise work is a product of intuition, and intuition is inspired by the Higher Power; thus,

www.makanologos.com

it requires minimal human processing besides attention and silence. We will come back to this point in subsequent chapters.

Those who see themselves as kings in their inner kingdoms have from the starting line an insurmountable advantage that makes the competition look like a turtle racing against the gazelle. In their hands are swords that will take them to battle after battle, invincibly victorious in all their constructive undertakings. Recognizing one's own powers is like a healthy and well-trained athlete competing against an unhealthy and untrained one. Acknowledging and staying in touch with the Kingdom (inner powers) within are the prerequisites of greatness. Acceptance of the artificial separation of man from God or denying the godliness of man is the beginning of all troubles.

No man who is in touch with his Inner or Higher Self can know a scant failure. Mindfulness of the true nature of man, which is one with God, is the beginning of success in all undertakings. There is really a very good reason, beyond the grasp of average minds, why ancient Greek sages proclaimed, "Know thyself and thou shall know all the mysteries of the Gods and of the universe." No man who deeply believes to be a God of math, physics, business, or prosperity and acts likewise (fearlessly, doubtlessly, and selflessly) can ever fail to understand the laws that govern those areas of life. "I AM God of math!" "I AM God of physics!" "I AM God of business!" "I AM God of prosperity!" Those decrees or affirmations may sound ridiculous to the ear and mind of the unlearned, but when accompanied by feelings, thoughts, and actions, they are the game-changer codes in the game of life.

Fortunately, in much of the modern world, so-called *blasphemy* is no longer an offense punishable by crucifixion or a legal offense at all. Some religious zealots and spin doctors may twist the words of the Bible, but that does not put a dent in the truth, and if their twisting does anything, it is to keep the meek even meeker and the ignorant more clueless. Psalm 82:6

www.makanologos.com

states, "I have said, Ye are Gods; and all of you are children of the most High"; and John 10:34 correctly and clearly quotes Jesus answering nonbelievers by saying, "Is it not written in your law, I said, Ye are Gods?"

You would think that Jesus, being Jesus, would put an end to the dispute over the natural divinity of man, but those whose lack of knowledge — or those whose interests are served by placing God at an unreachable distance like a celestial orb rather than the real engine and energy that runs our lives and without which man would not move a finger or an eyebrow — will call these statements an abomination.

The knowledge of the natural divinity of man is paramount. It can never be emphasized strongly enough because without it, the deadliest enemies of man — fear, doubt, anger, selfishness, irritation, ignorance, judgment, self-distrust, discouragement, etc. — overtake him and destructively run him, forever keeping exalted secrets of brilliant minds out of reach.

On the other hand, striving to feel, think, and act as an extension, tool, or open door to the world of Higher Powers helps keep negative qualities from entertaining or influencing your mind, thoughts, or actions, and it brings in faith, courage, self-confidence, gratitude, fearlessness, understanding, joy, freedom, happiness, and many more qualities without which climbing the mountain of greatness is the grandest of all illusions. Well, this may sound too good to be true for many people, but again, there is a reason why many people do not know the secrets of brilliant minds, much less make it to the top of the mountain of greatness.

The mastery of life, the manipulation of the laws of life, has never been accidental; it is a product of conscious effort acquired by trial and error through faith, courage, self-confidence, and persistence — the four points of the square of success. I say conscious effort because, to paraphrase Joseph Campbell, consciousness is life. Nothing is done without life, and better and great things are done with consciousness.

www.makanologos.com

Believe you are God because you are. Feel, think, and act like it, then wait and see how not only will your fellow men come from every corner of the world at the right time and the right place to help you, but so will invisible and cosmic helpers. Belief in the natural divinity of man—feeling, thinking, and acting like it—is what is meant by *thrice-greatest Hermes Trismegistus* when he said, "As above, so below" and "As the beginning, so will be the end."

Ignoring or denying this mighty truth serves no one's best interests. God does not bestow his favors based on pity or flattery. Making Him look like an outer-space orb, a faraway angry old man, a simultaneously merciless and merciful man, or a chief prosecutor of the republic of universe does not persuade Him a bit. But knowing you are a part of Him and allowing Him to manifest his wonders through you (the open door) sways Him to make you immortal in the hearts of your fellow men. Those heroes of old whose names are still in our hearts today did not do it differently.

The knowledge you are reading is a privilege only few people have received throughout the history of man. Even today it is being proclaimed by many wise men, but very few have ears to hear. This is truly a great time to be alive, a fantastic moment to be present on planet Earth. A little more than 200 years ago, seekers of the truth traveled hundreds of miles just to apply for entry into schools of knowledge without guarantee of being accepted. Since the mid-nineteenth century, great writers have spilled untold amounts of ink, but very few people have had the eyes to read the truth revealed to us by those who sacrificed their all to get access to this inestimable treasure. Today, in the comfort of our homes, with a remote control or computer mouse in our hands, we can easily find this teaching on television or on the World Wide Web. In ancient times, it was spoken only metaphorically in ultra-secret schools of self-knowledge, leaving students to decipher it for themselves. It was never authorized to be revealed to the public except in parables or

www.makanologos.com

Exalted Secrets of Brilliant Minds   35

in a cleverly coded language. Socrates was condemned to a hemlock-based drink for attempting to reveal it to the younger generation. "Socrates' pursuit of virtue and his strict adherence to truth clashed with the current course of Athenian politics and society…He was, nevertheless, found guilty of corrupting the minds of the youth of Athens and sentenced to death by drinking a mixture containing poison hemlock," according to Wikipedia (http://en.wikipedia.org/wiki/Socrates, accessed September 2010).

The Christian Master could speak of this truth only in parables to keep the undisciplined masses from gaining a clue, and even so, his fate is well known. It is widely believed that Jesus taught two of his most trusted students—his mother, Mary, and John the Beloved—this truth in unambiguous language. Joan of Arc was burned at the stake for claiming excessive power (Divine guidance) when she was nineteen years old after being tried by an ecclesiastical court. Years after her death, she was found innocent, declared a martyr, beatified in 1909, and later canonized in 1920; she is one of three patron saints of France. Alexander the Great used this truth to conquer the world. Columbus traveled not a road less but never traveled on his way to the discovery of the New World using the same power; George Washington and Abraham Lincoln did not use anything different. All great men and women whose names stand tall forever have used this same power. Of it, Genevieve Behrend wrote, "To get good results we must properly understand our relation to the impersonal power we are using. It is intelligent, and we are intelligent and two intelligences must co-operate."

Fasten your seat belt—we are heading where the rubber meets the road, and I want you to remember Behrend's quotation. It will serve you well down the road. For now, just bear in mind that two intelligences must cooperate, but rest assured that cooperation is for mutual interest through mutual love and respect regardless of the inclusion of one in the other. Just as potable water from the river mixes just fine with that

www.makanologos.com

of the salty ocean water, and just as cement teams up just fine with solid rock, so do small and big intelligences blend. Two similar forces never oppose one another. It is the law of nature for a higher power to strengthen a lower power, the bigger to provide for the smaller. Torrential rains strengthen small rivers. Now, do not fool yourself here. There is more than just admitting your natural divinity features. It may be tempting to think that once you have the keys of the universe and secrets of the Gods, then let the party begin.

Not so fast. There is more. "Knowing thyself" is not just a beginning; it is a beginning on a very strong footing. Just because you have the key to your house or office does not mean you are in it. To be in your house, you have to open the door and set your feet in. Just because you are in your office or home, does it mean you are doing what you are supposed to be doing? If you have an office, try to go in there, just relax, and do nothing. I guarantee you, you will be fired, and if you are self-employed, your days in business will be numbered.

Energy or God is forever active, forever expanding. Even the Christian Master had to work in carpentry and teaching not just for a living but for the expansion of life and his own growth as well. Alexander the Great, Napoleon, and George Washington had to lead their troops in the field. Columbus had to sail and sail right. In this same perspective, Behrend continues the above statement, saying:

We must not fly in the face of the Law expecting it to do for us what it can do through us; and we must therefore use our intelligence with knowledge that it is acting as the instrument of greater intelligence; and because we have this knowledge we may and should cease from all anxiety as to the final result.

It is absolutely ludicrous to think that knowledge can free man from work when work is truly the mission of man on Earth. "Knowledge is power," said the magnificent Francis Bacon, but with its power, knowledge can never free you in a thousand years without action. The easiest way to lose all consideration of respect in society is to underestimate the value of work. If society does not look up to a person who does not value work, why should the universe do otherwise? The only time man is barely exempted from the burden of work is when his days here on Earth are in twilight or when one is understandably incapacitated by illness. Just as society does not tolerate sluggish people regardless of education, the universe, the Universal Mind, energy, or God does not cooperate with them. The Universal Mind or God is almighty, uncreated and creator of everything. God, the Universal Mind, is consistently seeking an open door to manifest in the world of actions, and He can do that only through men and other earthly creatures. Man does not do anything; in fact, everything is done for him through Him. Man's part is simply to direct the energy given him in positive (hopefully) or negative direction, and according to the choices he makes, he reaps joy (reward) or pain (punishment or, rather, the reminder to open the door correctly).

Man craves happiness, and only success in whatever he does can bring it to him. In order for that to happen, you must allow the Universal Mind to not do it for you but through you. The only thing that justifies the presence of man in the universe is the construction of the temple, the infinite temple of joy. While God can do it alone, the law of the universe obliges our conscious and willing participation if we are to enjoy the fruit of our labor. Harmony, the mother of progress, has to be sustained by all of us. Success doesn't just come; it is the product of conscious, methodical cooperation with the laws of life.

But first things first. If you want to acquire a brilliant mind, it is important to know the sources of all achievements, the philosopher stone. It is crucial to understand that success has never been given to man out of curiosity or for sensual gratification. It comes from a specific source for a specific purpose through a specific effort. The great temple of life is a house of harmony and happiness, and your happiness is a big

www.makanologos.com

part of it. The universe cares a great deal about your happiness, the harmony among your feelings, thoughts, and actions. Even on the physical plane, it is not enough to build a house and then relax; if you do, it will collapse before long.

The universe is not only in the business of expanding life; it is also in the business of maintaining what has already been built, and it can do so only with those who believe in the powers that have been deposited in their beings. This is the source of greatness, and without the knowledge of what is there, nothing in this book matters. The first order of greatness is self-knowledge; this is really the philosopher stone. I have no better words to express it. Now that you know what very few know, now that you know the source of all greatness, now that you know where to find the keys of the universe and the secrets of the Gods, it is time to know what to do to open the door, step inside, and cause the universe to bestow upon you all its favors, to build the temple of happiness in your corner of the universe.

www.makanologos.com

CHAPTER II

Anatomy of Desire

"Follow your bliss…What inspires you? What makes your brain light up? Find it and feed it." James Arthur Ray

How many sane people do you know who would go on a trip not knowing at least the direction, approximate distance, and name of the location of their final destination? I can see you scratching your head. I can almost anticipate a series of questions popping up in your head. Let's just ask the easiest and most obvious one — is it even possible? *"Of course, it is not!"* would be a suitable answer.

Anyone who would pack his belongings and travel in a direction and location yet to be specified in his mind cannot and should not be taken seriously. Society expects very little if any accomplishment at all from this kind of person. Even a refugee running from war or persecution who may not have had time to say goodbye knows at least that he/she is going to a place of safety. The most reliable thing that explorers and navigators carry in their sometimes mind-boggling adventures is not food or water. While food and water are critical, the compass that shows the direction of the journey, believe it or not, is the most important equipment in their hands. Ask an experienced sailor and he will tell you that even in the middle of the ocean, there are alternatives that can save his life should he run out of food, water, or even the ship itself. Cuban dissidents who sometime dare to cross the ocean on a tube to the USA do not hang onto their food and potable water but to their mirrors that can reflect the light and give patrolling United States Coast Guard boats the direction to the location of their whereabouts.

Such is the power of desire. It is inner work that aims to project the end product of an activity before its undertaking and throughout the process. Unless the desire is clear, no mind can become brilliant; thus, climbing a mountain of greatness would be utterly impossible. Even Archimedes, who almost instinctively discovered pi, knew what he was after. He may not have known how to get there, but deep inside, he knew "it," his desire, before screaming, *"Eureka, I have found it!"*

While writing your desire down on a piece of paper is a good way to keep it in focus, thoroughly knowing its details is practically indispensable. As you may already be aware of or as you will find out in the coming chapters, nothing happens without action. Action, of course, is the practical externalization of thoughts and feelings.

We live in a world of duality. If there is "in," there must be "out"; if there is "north," there must be "south"; if there is "center," there must be "circumference"; if there is "multiplication," there must be "division"; and if there is "externalization," there must be "internalization." Desire is not simply the picture of the final outcome of an activity but the inner work that leads to the end product. A successful farmer is not the one who sees the beautiful harvest and the money that comes with it but rather the one who sees the harvest and all the details that show the way to the harvest. A great engineer or architect is not the one who has a beautiful picture of a luxurious mansion, but rather one who, along with seeing the picture of the end product, sees the details that lead to the construction of that house. Most people who see the image of their desire never accomplish it, but those who dream their desires happening in the minutest detail, step by step, not only eventually see their dream come true, but it happens in less time and with less effort than anticipated.

Knowing the specifics of your desire helps you anticipate the possible obstacles that may occur down the road, therefore enabling you to prepare accordingly and avoiding any discouragement that may cause you to abandon what would otherwise be a worthy cause. Another benefit of knowledge of

www.makanologos.com

the specifics of your desire is to help keep your two feet here on Earth. You can stop building castles in Spain and start building them where you are with what you presently have, not where you want to be with what you want to have. The nature of man has proved that any desire is achievable as long as it is realistic according to your ways, means, and effort. This is by no means discouraging you from thinking big; far from it, for anything big is done one small step at a time. It is simply a reminder of the function of the laws of nature. You will agree with me that Ford Motor Company, Microsoft, Wal-Mart, and other big companies were not built with the billions of dollars and hundreds of thousands of employees that they have today but by one or two people well armed with the details of their desires and who lived to see not just the full realization of their desires but that beyond their wildest imagination.

I want you to dream big, but I also want you to be practical, for practicality is accommodation to or cooperation with the Universal Mind. Let me illustrate this important thought. Imagine you are a qualified U.S. citizen and you are your school's student president at Washington State University, but your dream is one day to become president of the United States of America. What is the likelihood of success? Running progressively for political offices, maybe you start for city council, then for mayor or state senator, then governor or U.S. senator, then eventually for POTUS (president of the United States); or going from student president to running for president of the United States? Think about it.

Have you ever wondered how the four-wheeled carriage, now called a car, is an outgrowth of a two-wheeled carriage once pulled by a horse? No wonder vehicle strength is still called *horsepower* when the former engine, the horse, is long forgotten. Think about it. Such is the power of specified desire when carefully worked inside; it comes out as a force of nature that few minds can comprehend. Desire is always a work of inspiration. Etymologically from Latin, *inspiration* means *being breathed into by God.* So the more breath you let God breathe into you, the more life and power you will get.

The clearer the details you have about your desire, the more likely your desire will successfully come to life. In most cases, it is not a matter of dreaming big or small but dreaming clearly. If you blindly dream to be a lawyer or a doctor but ignore the requirements of passing in elementary and high schools, you probably will never get there. If your desire is to be an army general but you are blind to the discipline required to be a recruit or a good soldier, your chances of attaining a generalship will not just be low but infinitesimal.

In the Old Testament, we are told that God is jealous. This characterization of God is supported by the very first of the Ten Commandments that the Bible says God gave Moses on Mount Sinai. I believe this to be the truth, nothing but the whole truth — not because God is really jealous in the human sense of the term but because the notion is supported by nature. Naturally, man cannot walk two paths at the same time to reach a destination; even animals that have twice as many feet as we do can walk only one way at the same time to reach their destination.

At different times, man can reach many destinations, but he can reach only one destination at a time. It is the same with desire. A desire that is to be accomplished must be the sole preoccupation of your thoughts, feelings, and actions whenever it is its rightful time for those activities. A desire must be so intense to the point that it occupies your whole intellect and mind. In his book *The New Psychology*, Charles Haanel writes the following story:

The story is told of a student placing himself under the tutelage of a sage. The sage seemed indifferent and careless in his work of advancing the student. The student complained to the sage that he was not being taught. The sage said, "Very well, young man. Follow me." He led him over the hills, through the valleys and fields, and out into a lake into deep waters. The sage then plunged the student beneath the water and held him there until all other desires of a young man were concentrated into the one all-important desire, namely air. Finally, when nearly dead for want of breath, the sage lifted him up and said, "Young man, what did you want most when you were under the water?" The young man replied, "Air, air, air." Then his teacher said, "When you want Wisdom as bad as you wanted the air you will get it," (page, 23).

A deep understanding of your desire is attained by a deep love that you have for it. The more you love your desire, the more it will reveal itself to you. If you love your desire to the point of being capable of giving your whole being to it or going the extra mile for it, very likely you will achieve it. Love is the most powerful force in the universe, and light is its greatest influence (more on love in Chapter Fourteen.) If you love your desire dearly enough, the light of your love will shine on it, giving you its clear view in time and space. The deep love of your desire opens up your inner sight to clearly see what it takes to achieve it. When nothing else on the face of the Earth matters but your desire, then if the intellect fails you, intuition will forcefully intervene and reveal the truth about it; invisible helpers or the Gods will come, if necessary, to your assistance by not working for but through you as well as through your fellow men and other means of their choice.

Just as it is imperative for a farmer to plant seeds in the ground before harvesting crops, it is absolutely required for anyone who wants to live a happy life to self-impregnate with a desire. If a farmer depends primarily on the quality of his seeds for a better return, a quality desire is a secret of brilliant minds and a seed for a successful climb to the mountaintop of greatness. Desire is a personal thing; you have to determine what it is for yourself. No matter what people say, you must choose a desire for yourself simply because no one knows the quality of feelings and thoughts that thrill your heart better than you.

While desire is by itself one wing of success, alone it is not enough to push you to the top of the mountain of greatness.

www.makanologos.com

Now, you can tell me that we all have desires, but are we all entitled to success? Of course, yes! We are all entitled to success, but the question is why on Earth so few really succeed. A part of the answer to this question can be found in the previous pages, but this being the main question of this work throughout the book to the last page, I will always come back to it to add more light for better clarification and understanding of how to hit that elusive target called success. From that perspective, I want to direct your curiosity to one thing that may have been going on around you frequently but unnoticed by you. It is said, "Well-mannered women do not make history." Indeed, well-mannered people rarely reach their dreams.

This is not to say that those who climb the mountain of greatness are lawbreakers and immoral people and that you should be one. Not at all. It is to say that successful people take their action to the very edge of the law, exploiting it to the maximum, sometimes bending but never breaking it. (I will not intentionally go deeply into this point, for it is exactly the subject of my fourth book, *Emancipated Intelligence*.) They love their desire to risk everything very much because of the accomplishment it can provide. They may not be politically correct in the eyes of the multitudes but rather of the law. Their actions are understood by reading the disclosures veiled in fine print that multitudes of people do not bother to read. They are constantly looking for loopholes in the law and social contracts. Notice I said *loophole*, which *Oxford American Desk Dictionary and Thesaurus* defines as "evading a rule, etc. without infringing it." ("Emancipated intelligence triumphs by cunning," as Levi would say. Read the legends of Hebrew patriarchs Abraham, Jacob, David etc. to get a glimpse, but do not get ahead of yourself. My book *Emancipated Intelligence* [manuscript in progress] will have plenty, including stories of modern-day patriarchs for you to chew on.)

Successful people love their desire like we all love the air we breathe. They love their desire for a life spent on the periphery of the law and moral codes. They are not immoral nor are they lawbreakers, but they are incredibly and stubbornly bigger risk-takers than most people. They drive in the fast lane at the maximum legal speed limit with all the risks of crossing the line at the right place at the right time. They act lawfully and morally but mostly strategically in everything they do to fulfill their desires. A desire has to be deeply esteemed if it is to be realized. A desire is like a jealous lover; it does demand your total attention, and in some cases it demands your life as well in order for it to materialize. And unless you are ready and willing to give in to its demands, you may never see its realization reach the light of the day.

Desire is one of the strongest forces of nature. When we have it, we are not always able to explain why or how we acquired it, but amazingly we do everything in our power to accomplish it. When a desire is genuine and strong, many times there are profound underlying causes; some *personal* desires are tools used by Mother Nature (God or the Universal Mind) to bring the good fortune that is to be given to mankind in general and not necessarily for individual needs. Like sex, many times when people engage in pursuing desire, it is usually for personal satisfaction, but through that personal pleasure, the wheel of evolution runs forward, which of course was not the intention of the actors.

You will notice that people or animals do not engage in sex activities for fear of extinction of their species or for hope of its protection, for that matter. For thousands and thousands of generations, the continuity of genes and species has gone on through the satisfaction of personal needs. Therefore, it is imperative to choose your desire carefully because its impact may last longer than you may have imagined. Desires are seeds of continuity planted in us by invisible forces for their own purposes. Those who understand and comply with the deeper underlying causes of their desires are the ones who not

www.makanologos.com

only climb the mountain of greatness with ease but also more importantly find genuine happiness in their accomplishment.

Nature bountifully rewards those who obey its laws, those who want to be the channel of expression of its desires. As you will be reminded throughout this book, your desires are primarily the desires of nature; in fact, you are simply a tool through which nature carries out its mission because you are a part of nature itself. For its own purpose, nature — the source of infinite supply — provides each human many and sometimes different desires, but it is your duty to choose which one is more important to you and give it your whole attention. To nature, you are like a hunting dog that captures prey for its owner, and as a gesture of gratitude, you get compensated a nice meal, a warm house to sleep in, and a few pats on the back and head; or you are like a camel that carries both its owner and heavy load across the desert and gets plenty of water and decorative dressing as compensation at the end of the trip.

People who choose constructive desires and pursue them with unshakable determination are the ones who climb the mountain of greatness. Life is an enjoyable game (not easy but enjoyable regardless of hurdles) for people with positive desires. Destructive desires not only will never get you anywhere on the ladder of greatness, but they will also get you in hot water. Guess what? All over the world, nothing keeps governments busier than building prisons and literally running the lives of people with bad desires. Law enforcement is the face of governments all over the world. Assuming the legends of the Bible, Qur'an, and other sacred books are factual, we are told people of bad desires here on Earth will spend a good deal of their afterlife in fire while those of good desires will spend it in happiness forever.

That should tell you that positive desires pay and negative desires damn. A negative desire makes both men and spirits unattractive while a positive desire makes them attractive. Anyone with a constructive desire never climbs the mountain

www.makanologos.com

of greatness alone; there are always powerful, invisible helpers' hands and eyes that protect, watch over, and assist a fearless, self-confident, determined, faithful, and selfless person, a sincere student of self-knowledge. People or invisible hands are never attracted to negative and destructive desires, at least not in the long term. Even charismatic people who end up doing evil deceive the world by casting aside the sheepskin afterward and showing their true wolf skin; otherwise, they could never have attracted even their own relatives, let alone their neighbors. A positive desire is like a bright star that shines on people's paths all the way to the destination.

I don't want this to sound easier than it really is. Having a constructive desire alone is no guarantee of greatness. While a positive desire is a huge step forward, it is just that—a huge step and nothing more. It is not a finish line. Countless people with magnificent desires live and die without even coming close to fulfilling any of them. That is because all men may be created equal, but not all constructive (or otherwise) desires are created equal. There is one desire that is above the rest, which almost with certainty guarantees the fulfillment of all others. "Talk is easy," but "action is everything." Action leads to results, quality action leads to quality results, and bad action leads to bad results. That is the bottom line. To desire easy things may be comforting, but to desire meaningful things is the secret of greatness.

A person who is serious about achieving his desires must first be willing to take on the most important desire of them all, and that is the control of willpower in order to get in contact with his or her Inner or Higher Self through self-discipline. When one is able to control his willpower, he increases his chance of success. Success in controlling willpower guarantees the success of all other desires because it compels you to think right, feel good, and act effectively, or keep on keeping on until the result is imminent. Keep on keeping on, seeking the best— that is the test of willpower. Those who succeed in achieving

www.makanologos.com

their desires without complete control of their willpower live in constant fear of losing their hard-won wealth or fame. They live a cosmetic life addicted to all kinds of drugs, painkillers, and lies, with a relentless lack of inner peace and true happiness.

Masters of their willpower fear nothing, for they know they can repeat their success at will anytime, whereas those who have little control of their own willpower live in constant fear, which sometimes leads them to drugs, alcohol, and unhappy lives despite what they project to the outside world. You must take care of yourself first, and there is no better way to take care of yourself than taking care of your willpower, the real engine of life.

While following your desires assures no safety, discouragement is the mortal enemy of greatness or any achievement, for that matter, and it is the mother of all suffering. People who begin something then quit never achieve anything. They are like those who, instead of stepping on the snake's head, step on the tail. What happens afterwards? It strikes back, and so pain continues.

Like thoughts and feelings, desires are self-created; man is simply a magnet that either attracts or repulses them as they float from the nothingness. Constructive desires are simply life's attempts of to fully express or expand itself for its own purposes. Destructive desires are a counter-power that delays the expansion of life. Man positively contributes to the expansion of life by choosing constructive desires. While the achievement of both constructive and destructive desires may generate pain and suffering in the process, ultimately the constructive ones are the essence of greatness.

The amazing thing about life is that no man is too weak to accomplish a desire that has absolutely captivated his heart and attention. In other words, a desire that has completely won an individual's heart, head, and hand; faith, reason, and deed; and feelings, thoughts, and actions eventually comes to life regardless of seeming difficult circumstances, as long as actions and commitment keep in step with love and reason. It is for this reason that ancient sages believed that life never gives anyone a desire that he or she cannot successfully carry out. If you are an avid reader of self-help literature, you may have noticed that all gurus of success techniques profess that the secret of success is not doing what you can but doing what you love, what you enjoy doing, what delights you, what thrills your heart regardless of apparent obstacles in the way. The desire of life is that it wants us to know ourselves and the world around us better so we can do what we love most in order to be more successful.

Those who are satisfied doing what they can rather than what they love and enjoy may be talented, geniuses, or well educated, but they have a very high likelihood of failure, for talent, genius, or education is never an adequate predictor of greatness, or mere success in life, for that matter. Greatness is never a product of what one can do but rather of what one loves and enjoys best regardless of the pain and hardship that come with it. Let me say this more clearly: loving and joyful actions alone produce greatness, for as you will see later on in subsequent chapters, only love and joy sustain determination, which is the most fundamental ingredient of achievement.

When you choose to do what you can, you are simply limiting yourself to what you are really able to do. You are blocking the ability of the powers of the universe to channel themselves through you to manifest whatever they may intend to bring from the invisible to the visible. You are submitting the powers of your Big Self to the powers of your small self. We are here to do things with love, in love, and for love's sake in order to produce happiness, which is the real engine of life, but we often choose to do what we can rather than what we love and enjoy because of fear and doubt of the magnificent powers that lie dormant in us. Many times, usually unconsciously, we choose to do what we can rather than what we truly love for selfish reasons. We choose to do the easy things that are maybe

www.makanologos.com

good for ourselves rather than the harder things that are good for the whole community. That is, of course, consciously or otherwise, a violation of Higher Laws. Remember, ignorance of the law is never the basis of innocence.

When you submit your higher powers to lower powers, you are violating the law of the universe, and because these laws can never be violated without penalty, the price you pay, of course, is failure. The fullness of human ability comes about by doing what brings ecstasy to the heart. As frightening as the word may be to many, greatness is not the art of doing the impossible or extraordinary, but rather the art of doing what you enjoy and love most. It does not matter what you love as long as it is a positive addition to the life of your fellow men. It may be cooking, singing, preaching, politics, volunteering, chemistry, writing, or rocket science — anything you love doing and believe will improve life in general. Pablo Picasso is famous not for just painting but painting with love of his work. George Washington is famous for fighting the British not with hate but love for his country. Hitler, Stalin, Saddam Hussein, and many other villains of history are infamous not just for wars but also for fighting and leading people with hate.

Speaking of love, of all the countless powers that exist, none comes close to the power of love. Love is the most dominant power above and below. Light (understanding or illumination) and harmony (smooth performance) are its most immediate influences. When you love something to the near exclusion of all else; when you focus your complete attention on something; when you seek something with undivided insight, light, or understanding; illumination will shine upon it so that you can locate it, attract it, and enable yourself to gain better knowledge of it. Genuine love and joy have a magnetic power that makes understanding what the heart craves highly possible. The imperative of doing what you love most cannot be overstated. As the greatest power in the universe, love, through light, will illuminate you. Light will shine upon whatever you deeply love. Both your inner and outer eyes will see it in the greatest detail, your intellect will think of it clearly, your heart will feel passionate and joyful about it, and your hands will act on it easily with time the more you love it.

What is desire? *The Oxford American Desk Dictionary and Thesaurus* defines it as longing or craving, yearning, passion, hunger, and thirst. What happens when you are hungry or thirsty? Don't you go out to find food or a proper beverage to satisfy your hunger and quench your thirst? Do you take substitutes for food or proper liquid? Try a substitute for food or beverage the next time you are hungry or thirsty and see what will happen to you. Life will feel empty rather than half full, leaving you with a lingering mood of misery. When you love and hang onto your desire as a drowning man loves and hangs onto a life jacket, a lightbulb in your head will suddenly turn on and show you where everything you wish to know is. Thus, the power of love brings things to us with reasonable effort on our part. Love is what many call the Law of Attraction.

Chapter Fourteen, "The Love Pillar: The mother of all virtues," will have more to say about love, but let's pave the way. Love does what no other power can do. It softens our pains; it wipes our tears; it transforms enemies; it reconciles fire and water; it brings the invisible into the visible; it brings a teacher and a student onto the same dimension; it keeps the dead and the living in touch forever; it keeps orbs peacefully dancing around the sun; it does the unbelievable; it does miracles. If love can make Venus come to the aid of the Earth; if love can make the sun delightfully illumine systems of worlds; then love can certainly allow your desire to manifest itself with genuine effort on your part. All great sages of old have advised to have a strong desire if you really want to climb the mountain of greatness. No one can measure the strength of desire, but loving a desire is measurable through determination and mental and physical efforts. Here is what James Ray in his book *Harmonic Wealth* writes about the strength and love of desire:

www.makanologos.com

There will always be the price to pay. There will always be sacrifice. There will always be a price for the prize, yet interestingly enough, when you're living the life you choose and following your calling, the sacrifice doesn't feel like sacrifice, it feels like a gift... (page 286) Fall in love with someone or something and pursue this passion with a single eye. When you fall in love so completely that you give yourself totally to something, that's when your heart is open and the consciousness of Christ and Buddha is flowing through you. It doesn't matter what it is, but you must immerse yourself completely to it. It could be Jesus, Buddha, Krishna, a mate, or your career, but it's that truly inspired state you're after," (page, 287).

To measure the strength of your desire, measure your love for it. To measure the love you have for your desire, measure the level of determination and attention you give to it. How much time and effort would you avail to have it happen? What would you give up for it? Ask yourself these and more questions honestly, in a soul-inquiring way. Question yourself, and you will know unmistakably whether your desire is worth pursuing. One thing must be made clear—everything that comes or will ever come to you will always come through you. Unless you have a desire and love your desire strongly, you will confuse the "Giver," the universe, and certainly you will probably get only the crumbs of what you want, if you get anything at all.

Similarly, regardless of the brilliant installation of electrical wires in your house, regardless of the sophistication of your home or cellular phone, unless they are connected to the main source of electricity or communication (dam, generator, satellite, or otherwise), your house will never have electrical light and your phone will never connect you with the people you would like to stay in touch with. Our desires are manifested thanks to the attention we give to them. Attention is what connects you with the source of all things. Love is to your desire what the connection to the source of electricity or communication is to

www.makanologos.com

your house or phone. The bad news is that without attention, we achieve very little, if anything at all. The GOOD news is that when the love of a desire is strong, our attention sometimes acts regardless of will. Yes, it requires double the power to pay attention to your desire and love it strongly. Humans being humans, unnecessary things sometimes distract us. But should you fail to pay attention to your desire as you would like, at least give it your sincerest love, and your weakness somewhere else may be taken care of, forgiven, or substituted by other alternative powers of the life.

Constructive desire is imperative.

Love is power. It is the most highly charged power of life. When charged with genuine love, desire becomes as powerful as dynamite. It is people with highly love-charged desires who leave indelible marks on the world. In her book *The Game of Life and How to Play It*, Florence S. Shinn writes, "Desire is a tremendous force, and must be directed in the right channels, or chaos ensures." History is full of misguided people with destructive desires who brought nations to near-total ruin, greedy people who brought giant companies to their knees, evil leaders who forced their followers to mass suicide, and on and on we can go.

Desire, as I said earlier, is not a creation of man. Stars are the only factories of desires, as the Romans concluded. Life attempts to express itself through man, and it is absolutely impossible to find a person who is without desire. While we all have our desires, positive or negative, only positive ones lead to real greatness. Greatness in life comes to us in different packages, diverse ways, and means of doing things. There is no specific method of greatness, and even knowledge of successful methods is no guarantee. Life being life, what worked for Joe may not work for Jane or Bob and vice versa. What may have been a winning method for Bob and Mary may be a losing formula for Joel and Jane and vice versa. Sometimes being at the right place at the right time is all you need. Even though there is no "one size fits all" formula, there is a misleading "one size fits all" method to greatness, and that is to wander from your desires. "Never let me wander from my heart's desire" is an affirmation that Florence S. Shinn gave her students, not necessarily so life can sustain their attention or help them to focus on their desire, but so they can keep themselves reminded that wandering from their desire has one and only one outcome—failure.

In all professions, the ability to focus on a target can get you almost anywhere. In the military, soldiers are classified as experts, sharpshooters, and marksmen according to how they stay focused on their targets. Greatness is not really as unpredictable as many of us like to believe. In fact, most people can predict the potential of their greatness by simply finding out how focused on their desires they are. Be the expert of your desire; stay close to it; see, feel, think, and act on it even incrementally. Eventually your mind will shine brilliantly as you gain better insight into what it is you would like to accomplish, and ultimately your Higher Mental Self or Invisible Helpers, Messengers of Great Ones, will put you at the right place at the right time.

The word *desire* is an English word whose origin, according to http://www.etymonline.com/index.php?term=desire (accessed September 2009), is from the Old French *desirer*, which is from the Latin word *desiderare*, meaning, "long for, wish for." The original sense is perhaps "await what the stars will bring," from the phrase *desidere*, "from the stars," from *sidus* (gen. *sideris*), "heavenly body, star, constellation." Did you notice these words: "from the stars...heavenly body, star, constellation"? In the best interests of the readers, let me repeat what I said earlier: Like thoughts and feelings, desires are not man-made creatures. They are self-created. They are simply given to man by the universe, or as the Romans thought, by the stars.

www.makanologos.com

Exalted Secrets of Brilliant Minds **55**

"Desire," Catherine Ponder, quoting Dr. Emilie Cady, wrote, "is God tapping at the door of your mind, trying to give you a greater good." Notice that the Romans said desire is from the "stars"; they called it "heavenly body." Cady said it is "God trying to give greater good." Either way, you do not make your desire. You are simply a harbor built to allow a ship to dock and properly unload its contents. The harbor never made a ship; all it does is let the ship come in and allow sailors to unpack whatever is inside. What happens if the harbor turns down the ship, if there is no other harbor at a reasonable distance, and the ship runs out of fuel? The most probable scenario is that the ship will sink and disappear. When you suppress your desires, you deny them an outlet or a passageway to the outer world. They probably withdraw to the inner world until someone is ready and able to accommodate them. It sometimes takes days, months, years, generations, or even eons before that same desire finds a receptive vessel. And that is how science, freedom, and other wonders of the modern day have come to us—in progressive increments as positive desires are accommodated by the free will of man, who is to provide the open door.

Sometime regardless of your consent, desires force their way out, violently or otherwise, but certainly with dire consequences. The Bible story of Jonah 1:1-17 may be a good example. I will not go further but will leave this as a mental exercise for the reader to find his or her own illustrations in real life. This happens when Mother Nature has chosen someone to express herself through, but that person gives in to fear, doubt, and selfishness. To avoid negative consequences of a frustrated desire that could not find its way out, it is wise to desire big so the desire can be expressed fully and completely. When you desire big, small desires come as a matter of consequence. When, for instance, you desire to be a medical doctor, it is guaranteed that a high school diploma will come way before clinching your MD credentials.

www.makanologos.com

Big desires are not for the faint of heart. The way to greatness can be frightening sometimes, and it must be pursued with great determination and endurance. While it opens a whole range of probabilities of comfort, it guarantees no happiness, safety, and security along the way. Greatness and happiness can be two different animals. You can live a completely joyful life of happiness in your heart and never reach the mountaintop of greatness, and you can live a life of greatness maybe in the eyes of the world and not live a life of happiness in your heart. Illustrations of this truth are countless. Incidents of the rich and famous who seek joy in illegal drugs and alcohol and politically powerful people who seek joy in sexual relationships outside of marriage should not be a surprise.

The reason I brought this point up here is that I really want to encourage you to desire big because when you desire big, you desire fully; you will allow everything that has the potential of making you great and happy to come out completely. Greatness is meaningless if it does not give you and those whose lives you touch happiness. Each individual will have his own span of life here on Earth. Therefore, while greatness is not measured by how long one lives, it definitely is measured by the amount of happiness in the hearts of others long after one is no longer on the scene or has passed on.

It would make no sense to desire to be a medical doctor without desiring to live the social and moral responsibility of an MD, desiring to be married but not willing to be a good spouse or parent, or desiring wealth but not willing to assume the responsibilities that come with it. The law of the universe is no respecter of man; it is as blind as the blindfolded Lady Justice, if you will. It is a snake; it bites a rock, tree, animal, or person who steps on its tail. Dare to desire big and right, and your greatness can be a vessel that will take you safely across the ocean of troubled water to an island of the chosen few.

How old is Rome, Jerusalem, or Damascus? Nobody really knows for sure. All we know is that they are very ancient cities.

www.makanologos.com

Exalted Secrets of Brilliant Minds   57

Well! Let's think of younger cities. How old is London, Paris, New York, Los Angeles, or Tokyo? No one really accurately knows how old even these relatively young and modern cities are. Many of them started as small villages either by indigenous people or conquerors and grew to what they are today. Let's assume that all are several hundred years old. Eternal City is Rome's nickname. But what do the Eternal City, Rome, and a much younger city like New York have in common? They are all still under construction and always will be.

"A great city is not built in a day," said sages of old. A potential great man knows this timeless teaching deep in his heart. Your desire is like a city in itself, or at least must be. That is constructive desire, for it never outgrows its missions. That is the power of a constructive desire. Our desires are sometimes influenced by events and people that we have no control over, but this should not be discouraging. Great people always prepare for the worst but fight for the best.

Greatness is not for the weak. Greatness is built out of a firm, determined, and dynamic desire. Life is a school of its own. We are not here on Earth for celebration or mourning; we are here to learn through experiences and get tested in everything we do. And the test of life is stronger than the inner powers that many of us are willing to put up. Life, of course, does not test us beyond our strength just as no competent teacher can test his students on a subject he had not covered previously. Life is not a different teacher. Just as in our conventional school, the more advanced you are, the tougher your test; and in the school of life, the more constructive you are, the harder your obstacles; the more destructive, the easier. In other words, it is always easier to destroy but harder to build.

Many people fail to reach their potential because they feel or act as if life owes them something. In fact, life owes nothing to anyone; instead, we owe life everything for what it has given us. It gives us air to breathe; it circulates our blood; it keeps us safe and healthy in our lives' most vulnerable moments while

www.makanologos.com

we sleep; it gives desires, feelings, and thoughts; and the list goes on—and all free of charge. Life does not even ask us to meet it halfway. All it asks of us is to clear the way for it to supply us with more of its love, wisdom, and power to fulfill our desires.

Once they clear their desires with the test of constructiveness, great people are firm, determined, and dynamic with their desire. They understand "easy come, easy go." They fight the evil of discouragement with all their teeth and nails—or life if need be. They understand that they are the rocks on which their desires are built, so they are dynamic and flexible in their feeling, thinking and acting to accommodate changes as the universe reveals more knowledge and abilities. They understand that vibrations of their feelings, thoughts, and actions may go a long distance in time and space to affect or be affected by those of others and come back to them on the same current to affect them positively or negatively. They know as you sow, so shall you reap. "And I if I be lifted up from the Earth, I will draw all men unto me," said the Christian Master (John 12:32). No life is ever lived without affecting or being unaffected by the lives of others, be it of a prophet, a king, or a beggar. No one has anything with which to do anything that affects him or herself but life in general. Every life inspires or is inspired by someone else's, somewhere or sometime. Unless you understand the magnitude of the firmness, determination, and dynamism of your desires, greatness will most likely be an elusive target for you.

Taking firmness, determination, and dynamism of your desires lightly can be a serious mistake. If there are only a few points from this book that should strongly impress you, this is one of them. The only distance between you and your desire's achievement is the intensity of your thoughts, feelings, and actions; these are the three points of a triangle of victory. When you understand everything you do for the fulfillment of your desire, you will conclude that accomplishment of your desire

www.makanologos.com

is nothing but your service to life. Your accomplishment is simply an expression of faith, trust, love, and confidence in life. It is a demonstration of what a man can do when life is used properly. The faith, trust, fearlessness, and love of life are what it takes to achieve greatness.

As this section of desire is coming to an end, I want to draw your attention to a few quick reminders you should always bear in mind. First, destructive desire will bring your own ruin sooner or later. Constructive desire is the basis of greatness. It has been so since the beginning of time, it is so now, and it will always be so until the end of time. Constructive desire is not simply the basis of great achievement; it is actually an urge from Life itself, and it is God wanting to express Himself through you, asking you to give sufficient obedience and harmony to pave the way to bring about His quick and powerful realizations. Destructive desire is a house divided against itself, built on the sand with no foundation, whereas constructive desire is a house built on a solid rock, God, that neither the winds of heaven nor the trembling of the Earth or the wrath of the sea can shake or destroy.

www.makanologos.com

CHAPTER III

Determination

If life were just about *"viva la musica!"* or *"à la santé"* all the time, the world would have countless kings, princes, billionaires, and maybe even gods. And I mean every word literally. Chaos would be the master of the universe. Thank God, it is not. We all desire to be rich; we all desire to be admired, to be adored, and to be everything good beyond imagination. This is not to imply that desire is a bad thing but rather to say that to reach a certain level of greatness, there are many obstacles that one must conquer. These obstacles are necessary to distinguish the weak from the strong. Unless you freely accept obeying the laws of nature, greatness may never be possible for you. Despite everything you may have read in many schools of life, the universe is in perfect harmony with itself, and nothing is broken here. We are not here to fix anything outside of ourselves but to adjust our own individualities or individual lives in alignment with the Higher Self in order to drive through the dreams of our senses or illusions safely to the destiny life wishes for each of us. Civilization—building roads, airplanes, trains, cruise ships, cars, computers, amusement parks, etc.; or even eating and sex, for that matter—is a great thing, although it is not the purpose of life. It is a way and means, a tool to inspire and prove self-knowledge to man and to enable him to discover the three pillars of wisdom, strength, and beauty of his Inner Self. Those readers who have read the first book of these series, *The Best Kept Secrets of Personal Magnetism*, will recall alignment of the body and the mind.

This adjustment is not physical, of course, but rather spiritual obedience of laws that typical, average men are either unaware of or neglect. Oh yes! The good news is that we all have desires! The strange news is that desires may just be the tip of the iceberg. They give a hint that unless you go deep inside the water, you will never know what it takes to climb the ladder of greatness, you will never discover the secrets of self-mastery, and you will never know the true beauty of life and what it has in store for you. Life, regardless of what many people may say or feel about it, is in perfect harmony with itself, and those of mankind who bring their feelings closer to the harmony that life exalts are the magnificent rulers of themselves and the rest of us.

Bringing your feelings closer to the harmony of life is not a physical exercise. It does not depend on your health or wealth. In fact, your health and wealth depend on it. A frail old or young person can do it better than an apparently healthy and wealthy middle-aged person. Why so? It is about obedience to the laws. Obedience to the law is more of an inside work than it is of outside. Even the laws of man must be obeyed or accepted inwardly before they can be complied with outwardly. Spiritual or natural laws are ninety-nine percent inside work and one percent outside. Those who obey these laws do it happily and with free will.

For hundreds of centuries, man believed that the world was flat, the Earth was the center of the universe, and all other orbs, including the sun and stars, circulated around the Earth. For a very long time, man also believed there to be an edge or a sea cliff beyond the shores. Those who dared to think differently either became outcast in society or simply lost their lives for opposing the view of the day. Not to say that the view of the day was merely political or religious; it was genuine but ignorant, of course. People and the culture of the day earnestly believed with all their hearts what they believed, and they silenced any voice that tried to contradict it.

Indeed, the lords of the day were successful in silencing the voices of the weak, but what they failed at was putting off the ever-burning flame of truth in the hearts of the determined ones who were willing to explore the truth and prove its veracity to

www.makanologos.com

the whole world. It is amazing what the world went through for what today we take for granted. It is not just philosophical ideas that were opposed by the establishment or society but also common ideas that had immediate impact on people's lives. For instance, in many people's minds, what we today call the automobile is an invention of the later nineteenth century and early twentieth century. What many people are not always conscious of is that the automobile is an outgrowth of the ages-old carriage that was pulled by horses and other animals, thus the term *horsepower*. I can go on and on listing how earnestness brought mankind to the point of instant messages around the world and the possibility of a man walking on three different continents in less than twenty-four hours.

That is the power of determination. It may have taken mankind millions of years to reach where we are today and maybe millions more to reach amazing wonders of the future that we can scarcely dream of today, but believe me, if you arm yourself with determination in your quest to realize your dream, there is no great obstacle you cannot overcome. Determination is a magnificent law of life that enables the invisible forces to trust man and work through him in order to make achievements possible. Determination is truly incredible, and nothing great has ever been accomplished without strict obedience to it. There is no single person who has ever achieved a great thing without determination. The pyramids of Egypt and the Great Wall of China are some of the works of indescribable determination. In his book *The God in You*, Robert Collier writes:

Three things educators try to instill in children are: First: Knowledge; second: Judgment; third: Persistence. And the greatest of the three is Persistence. Many a man succeeds without education. Many even without good judgment. But none has ever got anywhere worthwhile without persistence. Without a strong desire, without that inner urge which pushes him on, over obstacles, through discouragement, to the goal of his heart's desire. "Nothing in the world can take place of persistence," said Calvin Coolidge. "Talent will not. Nothing is more common than unsuccessful men with talent. Genius will not. Unrewarded genius is almost a proverb. Education will not; the world is full of educated derelicts. Persistence and determination alone are omnipotent. The slogan 'Press on' has solved and always will solve problems of the human race.

Wonder why James A. Ray is right when he said, "C students often own the businesses that A and B students work for"? Yes! Knowledge is important, no question about that. Yes! Education is important. Yes, good judgment is critical, and yes, talent is valuable. But all these are raw materials needed for success. We all have them to some extent, and while having more of them is desirable, they do not do much good unless they are backed by determination. It is by far better to have less talent, less knowledge, less education, and less judgment but have an unyielding determination than vice versa, because with determination you can create, increase, and perfect other qualities beyond imagination.

Greatness is more a product of an unwavering and tireless determination than it is of talent, education, or anything else. We have all heard countless stories of school dropouts who have gone on to do wonders. This is not to suggest that dropping out of school is a good idea but to warn you that counting on your education alone as your primary weapon of greatness is a great mistake. Determination can take you to the edge of greatness faster than few qualities can. Jean Paul Belmondo, a French actor, well-known poor student, went on to be one of the greatest French movie stars of the twentieth century. *"Chance comes to prepared minds,"* said Louis Pasteur. The truth of this statement can never be disputed. Consider the odds of winning a Powerball jackpot are one in 175,223,510 (www.powerball.com/powerball/pb_prizes.asp; accessed June 20, 2012), but only those who play always win it.

www.makanologos.com

Whether you believe it or not, we are surrounded by invisible helpers or friends of mighty power. Call them what you will. Some people are so aware of them and love them so immensely that they call them Masters of Light. They are popularly known as spirits, guardian angels, saints, gurus, spiritual elder brothers and sisters, etc. They are always ready and willing to help at any time, yet they do not intrude themselves in the affairs of men unless voluntarily and consciously invited. While they do not interfere with our free will or impose upon us what they know and feel is best for us, they sometimes help us whenever necessary regardless of our awareness of them or not. But nothing draws them out and motivates faster than our determination to do what is right and constructive. The Invisible Helpers use the All-seeing Eye of God for they are the All-knowing mind of God, since they stand for the Highest Ideal in the universe. If your sixth sense or third eye was to suddenly open or you inner light to shine your path, there is no better way of living life than pursuing your desire with earnest, sincere, and unbending yet rational determination.

Determination is a by-product of belief in yourself as the outlet of higher powers that govern life, belief in yourself such that no matter the obstacle, you will successfully finish what you started. A person who truly knows and believes in himself is literally a demigod or a true agent of better and higher powers. Just as man believes that God will come to his aid whenever possible, God also believes in a man who believes in himself to be His channel or co-creator here on Earth. Self-knowledge has been the subject of study in all true ancient schools and right-headed religions throughout time and space. The Greeks decorated the doors of their temples with the inscription *"Know thyself"* in order for the public to see and know the object of their study. However, behind the closed doors of the temples, they were engraving the prize of self-knowledge—*"and you will acquire the keys to the universe and the secrets of the Gods"*—for only earnest and worthiest seekers to see.

www.makanologos.com

Work is the most consequential activity of life, because through work, we discover and know ourselves better, and we ultimately understand God. Only through work do we learn the reality of life while enjoying its substance. A man who does not work misses all the juices of life. The poor and the rich all find the joy of life in work. Nothing under the sun is more pleasurable than the achievement of a task that was joyfully done because it really leads us to the discovery of ourselves, what we really are capable of being, doing, and having. Only through work do we become co-creators of life. The impression some financially less-fortunate people have about those who are financially fortunate is that they either do not work or they work very little. Nothing could be further from the truth. Honestly rich people actually work harder and smarter because many of them live in constant fear of losing their wealth, the fear of the possibility of needing the basics of life again. Thus, they work constantly to keep or upgrade their standard of living. On the other hand, some rich people dismiss the poor as lazy, but the fact is that rich people were once poor, and because of smart and wise work, they got where they are today.

Work is of such vital importance to life not because of what it provides materially but because of what it causes us on the spiritual level. All wise men I have had the fortune to read about have all listed fear, doubt, selfishness, and ignorance as the worst enemies of mankind. I know of no other way that these merciless enemies of man are overcome except through work and positive activity. Through work, man acquires knowledge, courage, self-confidence, and the spirit of charity. While work by itself is not the sole purpose of life, it causes self-knowledge by stimulating or arousing self-confidence, courage, knowledge, love, and all other virtues that are really channels to self-knowledge. Work, food, and sex are only doors that enable us to discover or rediscover, if you will, the SELF inside us — courage, faith, self-reliance, wisdom, strength, beauty, harmony, independence, and so on.

www.makanologos.com

Lazy people or those who are less enthusiastic about work rarely know their worth. They are most of the time ignorant, doubt- and fear-stricken, and most of all dependent on those who gained their independence through work. Thus, work stimulates virtues, and through parenting and appropriate companionship, sex stimulates love of fellow men, the basis of the Golden Rule. Food, on the other hand, stimulates inner qualities such as self-preservation. And can you guess what else? Did I hear you say the beautiful word spelled *w-o-r-k*? If you said that, you are *damn right!* This sends us back to all those qualities or virtues stimulated by work. And so goes life year after year, generation after generation, age after age, eon after eon, incarnation after incarnation (if you subscribe to the idea) until the Inner or Higher Self is fully revealed to all the human race without exception, as we all know and feel the secrets of the Gods and hold in our hands the keys of the universe. Thus, nature puts and uses everything around us, including work, food, and sex, not to satisfy the illusions of the world or the dreams of our senses but to lead us to acquisition of Self-Knowledge, which is the only way to everlasting *Nirvana, the kingdom of heaven, Shekinah, ehyeh-asher-ehyeh,* and is the only way total happiness is obtained.

Now the question is, what do you think keeps some rich people rich, and what propels some poor people to riches? Did I hear you say education, talent, or good judgment? If you said so, your answer is only partially correct. Here is the hard truth: only determination brings the reward of sincere work to fruition.

I do not need to tell you this, but I am sure you may have heard it countless times: *A quitter never wins, and a winner never quits.* What do you think keeps the winner pressing on? Determination does it. Determination demonstrates the value of your aspiration, passion, devotion, and belief in your own Self. Through your determination, the Gods bring your desire to fruitfulness. Determination alone can enable you to see and

www.makanologos.com

Exalted Secrets of Brilliant Minds 67

reach the heart of infinity and pick for yourself the choicest fruits from the tree of life at the center of its garden. Determination alone can stamp your heart with wisdom, strength, and beauty, the three points of the triangle of victorious achievement. A constructively determined person is a powerful person indeed; he is so powerful that he inspired the adage *"one with God is majority."*

You may think that "one with God is majority" means one who believes in an abstract God or at least one who professes his love of an abstract God, but indeed it is one who endures to bring the constructive desires of God within himself into outer manifestation regardless of apparent setbacks. He is with majority because sooner or later, one way or another, his cause will prevail. One determined person with God is majority because determination has the power of resistance and multiplication. He has the power to multiply the power of one manifold and to reduce the power of obstacle to nothing. Think about it, and you will agree that one determined person is more powerful than hundreds or even thousands who are not. Who do you think will win the competition between a team of less skillful but determined players and one of very skillful but less determined players? Why do you think countries with more natural resources and huge populations are not always the wealthiest ones? You would think India, Russia, Nigeria, Congo, and Brazil would be the world's economic superpowers.

Determination is a hand we stretch to or a bridge we build for invisible helpers or friends of mighty powers to cross from the heart of infinity to our points in the universe and render us the service we cannot do for ourselves and that only they can do. It is foolish to think human problems are solved by human effort alone. If that were the case, many of our problems would have been solved the human way, but the human way is always the way of confusion. Thank God we are smarter than that and that our planet is on track in its initiative in love. Greatness always comes in strict association with the Supreme Being, commonly

www.makanologos.com

known as God or the Highest and Purest Ideal beyond full understanding of human intellect — not simply the Infinite, the All-Pervading Principle of Life, but also the Individualized Mighty Presence of God in man and in the universe; not the abstract or the remote God but the Mighty Presence of the Supreme Law that is the reservoir and source or cause of radiations of courage, humility, self-confidence, wisdom, love, and charity in man. I adamantly say this because I strongly concur with these words of the brilliant Ella A. Fletcher:

"It is for this reason that to sensitive souls, the souls awakened to the Presence of the Spirit, the immanence of the God-Presence becomes in all the secret haunts of nature an abiding fact ever present to their consciousness. Therefore, these enlightened ones see more, hear more, feel more, and receive more from intimate association with nature than those average folk whose chief characteristics are their gregariousness, their obtuseness to blatant noise, and their love of excitement — often indeed, their acute horror of being alone. They are afraid of the mystery of life which in silence knocks on the door of consciousness, — afraid because it has been clothed in terror when it should be radiant with beauty," (The Law of the Rhythmic Breath, page 250).

While the God taught in our churches, synagogues, and mosques is a good start, I am talking not about the God who most of our religions many times fail to adequately describe but the God of the pre-religion pristine man, the Self God within us or the Supreme Law, the Cosmic Law, the Highest Ideal, the Inner and Higher Self of each one of us. This God — the Master within, the Deity of pristine man of the pre-religious world — is the God who imprints greatness in the mind and heart of man. He is the God who mingles with man/woman when he/she is determined to do what is constructive and selfless. Great civilization after great civilization has been built by higher powers or at least through their direction to mankind, and as soon as those great powers are ignored, civilization crumbles. Like great civilizations, individuals seeking for greatness have no other avenue but working in absolute cooperation with their Inner Self for selfless ends; otherwise, the search for greatness is futile.

In the Saint Germain Series of the Saint Germain Foundation, volume 3, page 262-263, the Master Saint Germain says to his students, "*This reminds us of the old, time-worn Statement: Seek ye first the Kingdom of Heaven, and all the outer things are added, or given into your use, under your command. That Kingdom is the 'Great I AM Presence,' the only Reality of you — who is the Owner and Giver of all created and manifested things...All greatness is depended on the 'I AM Presence,' and it is the governor of the form, or should be. In It is all strength, courage, and power.*"

Let me repeat myself here, for goodness' sake. When I say God, I do not necessarily mean the God of any religion or any particular sacred book. I do not mean the God of the west, east, south, or north; or the bearded Old Man in the sky. I do mean, however, the Supreme Law, the Cosmic Law of which Presence is in all of us and everywhere in the universe. More precisely, I mean the Deity of the pristine man of the pre-religion age that we knowingly or unknowingly all call God. I mean that God, the Giver of life, light, and laws; present everywhere; that God who is the Causeless Cause of all causes and effect; that God, the Great Architect of the universe who is Unknown and Indescribable in any human words.

The Inner or Higher Self holds the Divine Will that makes everything possible. This Divine Will is released only when man through physical (work or right actions) and mental (good feelings and thoughts) efforts consciously opens the door with determination to do what is right and constructive. Recall that *awakening below causes awakening above*. I strive to go deeper on this point later on in Chapter Four, for it is the humble opinion of this author that the reader who misses this point misses one of the most precious secrets revealed in this work and may not benefit much from what is in the rest of this book — not that the rest of this book is religious, because it is not, but because greatness is attained through the search for the Highest IDEAL or the Supreme LAW of the universe, and the Highest Ideal or Supreme Law is what founders of religions called God in order to keep the masses from drowning in unnecessary confusion. Through the search for the Highest Ideal or Supreme Law, everything is revealed to man, but the revelation from above comes only when man below yearns and consciously seeks for the truth. Again, the reader is reminded here that throughout this book, whenever the name of God is mentioned, the author does not refer to a specific being in the sky but to the Highest Ideal and Supreme Law of the universe or the Inner and Higher Self of every one of us.

The blending of Divine Will and human conscious determination for a constructive cause is the invincible formula of greatness. It was what took the great ones to the mountaintop of greatness, and it is the Exalted Secret of Brilliant Minds. The different methods of arousing intelligence that will be highlighted throughout this book will simply be its various manifestations. In history, you will find that all truly great people did not do it otherwise. Those who are bent on seeking the mysteries of greatness at any cost need to seek no further, for *THIS IS IT*. Just relinquish a fire of rational determination for a constructive cause, water it down a little bit with rationality and humility, and you automatically command the Divine Will to act. The pyramids of Egypt, the Great Wall of China, the Eurotunnel, the Suez Canal, the United States of America, and other wonders of the world were created with humble and rational human determination in association with Divine Will. Divine Will is nothing but a selfless and constructive cause, or the Causeless Cause.

If you still doubt, go read the founding documents of the United States of America. And if still you do not get a big enough dose of the truth to quench your thirst, then you may be looking for something else and not the secret that sharpens and causes brilliant minds to climb the mountain of greatness. Take

www.makanologos.com

Exalted Secrets of Brilliant Minds **71**

a look at these few words from one of the founding documents of the USA, the Declaration of Independence: *"We hold these truths to be self-evident, that all men are created equal, that they are endowed by their Creator with certain unalienable Rights, that among these are Life, Liberty and the pursuit of Happiness."* Can the famous *"In God We Trust"* on U.S. currency, from one cent to the biggest note, tell it better? Do you think that the "God Bless America" on bumper stickers and in national patriotic songs sung in churches and elsewhere is an accidental, fanatical, blind inscription of national feelings? Or is it a spark of light anonymously yet purposely dropped in the culture by the enlightened ones (whose only job was to steer the magnificent Vessel of the State upon an ideal course at all times and keep it safe against the destruction any storm may bring), who understood that for national greatness' sake, the government and the people must be grateful and aim for the highest of all Ideals, determined cooperation with God (Inner and Higher Self or the Highest Ideal and the Supreme Law of the universe), for goodness' sake?

Here, for your own reflection and enjoyment, are some American national songs aimed to stir national feeling in an individual and national determined cooperation with God (Inner Self) in personal and public endeavors. Hopefully you will find, as many have, the cry for greatness by mortal tongues of America pollinating the hearts of generations to come with the spirit of determination and the submission to the Almighty in order for the greatness of the country to bear fruit that will feed many over centuries to come.

But first this "American Pledge of Allegiance" directly from own heart, head, and mouth of the United States government: "I PLEDGE ALLEGIANCE TO THE FLAG OF THE UNITED STATES OF AMERICA AND TO THE REPUBLIC FOR WHICH IT STANDS, **ONE NATION UNDER GOD,** INDIVISIBLE, WITH LIBERTY AND JUSTICE FOR ALL." The Pledge of Allegiance received official recognition by Congress

www.makanologos.com

in an Act approved on June 22, 1942. However, the pledge was first published in 1892 in the *Youth's Companion* magazine in Boston, Massachusetts, to celebrate the 400th anniversary of the discovery of America and was first used in public schools to celebrate Columbus Day on October 12, 1892. The phrase "under God" was added to the pledge by a Congressional act approved on June 14, 1954. At that time, President Eisenhower said, "In this way we are reaffirming the transcendence of religious faith in America's heritage and future; in this way we shall constantly strengthen those spiritual weapons which forever will be our country's most powerful resource in peace and war."

http://publications.usa.gov/epublications/ourflag/pledge.htm Accessed 11/11/2013.

Now this:

America the Beautiful
By Katharine Lee Bates

O beautiful for spacious skies,
For amber waves of grain,
For purple mountain majesties
Above the fruited plain!
America! America! God shed His grace on thee,
And crown thy good with brotherhood
From sea to shining sea!

O beautiful for pilgrim feet,
Whose stern impassioned stress
A thoroughfare for freedom beat
Across the wilderness!
America! America! God mend thine every flaw,
Confirm thy soul in self-control,
Thy liberty in law!

www.makanologos.com

O beautiful for heroes proved
In liberating strife,
Who more than self their country loved,
And mercy more than life!
America! America! May God thy gold refine
Till all success be nobleness,
And every gain divine!

O Beautiful for patriot dream
That sees beyond the years
Thine alabaster cities gleam,
Undimmed by human tears!
America! America! God shed His grace on thee,
And crown thy good with brotherhood
From sea to shining sea!

<u>America Invincible</u>
By Clarence C. Birchard

We hail Thy Power and Majesty,
Ascended Host of Light!
Shine on our loved America,
And hold her in Thy Might
Shine on our loved America
And hold her in thy Might.
Pour over her Thy Golden Flame,
Enrich her in white;
Protect and bless her in Thy Name,
And hold her in Thy Light.
Protect and Bless her in Thy Name,
And hold her in Thy Light
America, the Shining One,
The Jewel burning bright!
Oh Crown her Living Light.
A Crown of Living Light

www.makanologos.com

America Invincible,
Triumphant in the Right!
Oh, lead her on to victory,
And crown her Land of Light,
Oh, lead her on to Victory,
And crown her Land of Light.

The foundation of the greatness of America on God is not an accidental act, blind faith, or mere luck. In fact, it was sought with the blood and sweat of lovers of the American Republic who were excellent students of esoteric mythologies, philosophy, and moral and religious history of all great real or mythical civilizations that ever existed or recorded. They understood very well that God (Higher Self) is the foundation of any great empire or power that ever existed on Earth. They were convinced that ignorance of or revolt against God is the beginning of the downfall of any civilization that ever existed anywhere. The tradition created by the founders of America to willingly submit the nation to God has never faded nor ceased to be sought despite all the talk of freedom and justice. Hence, never in the existence of America will a stupid and foolish atheist, ignorant of the power of the Higher Self, reach the pinnacle of the Unites States government. To keep the eyes open and ensure this does not happen, all keystone buildings or symbols of the US government have been and will always be dedicated to God.

In fact (and very few people know this), the three buildings in which the United States government makes its most important decisions—namely the Capitol, the White House, and the Supreme Court of the United States — were effectively dedicated to God. Virtually all fifty states' capitols were dedicated to God, as was every courthouse where God's loudest call for peace and justice on Earth is heard by aspiring, upright judges and hopeful impartial juries who make America a beacon of justice to the world. The most popular monuments in the United States—

www.makanologos.com

Exalted Secrets of Brilliant Minds 75

including the Statue of Liberty, the Washington Monument, the Lincoln and Jefferson Memorials, and Mt. Rushmore — were all dedicated to God. The world's first and America's flagship national park, Yellowstone National Park, was dedicated to God as well. And in the Gettysburg Address, under God, Abraham Lincoln officially, publicly, and unequivocally once more submitted, *"the government of the people, by the people and for the people, shall not perish from the Earth,"* to the will of the Higher Self of the nation.

After a long-lasting shadow of the cloud left by the catastrophic governance formula of Philip the Fair, France was finally sealed in the heart of light when the most inspired of her children raised her on the lightening pillars of Liberty, Equality, and Brotherly Love — brotherly love that had been expressed by the lips of the many but found in the hearts of the few; brotherly love that unifies time and space; brotherly love that aims below to mirror above; brotherly love that had been the dream of man; brotherly love that strengthens all and brings social justice; brotherly love that is the true cause of human progress; brotherly love best expressed by wishing every fellow countryman the same happiness or constructive way of life that one wishes for him- or herself; brotherly love that is the true illumination of the light of God in the heart of man from the city of light to the borders of their land.

Not to condone its predatory inclinations, but for a very long time, as the Earth rotates around its axis, the world rotated around England (in the golden days of the British empire) and found balance from her uncharacteristic nature, her amazing patience and the determination of her people gained from long education since some decisions were made early on in her political inception to face and march toward the light of God that never fails. In his book *The Power of Will,* published early in the twentieth century about England's almost divinely inspired peculiar mentality, Frank Channing Haddock, quoting William Matthews, wrote:

www.makanologos.com

And this same adaptive pursuit of the main thing has made Cromwell's and Carlyle's England the First Power in Europe. As William Matthews has said: 'The asthmatic skeleton' (William III.) who disputed, sword in hand, the bloody field of Landon, succeeded at last, without winning a single great victory, in destroying the prestige of his antagonist (Louis XIV.), exhausting his resources, and sowing the seeds of his final ruin, simply by the superiority of British patience and perseverance. So, too, in the war of giants waged with Napoleon, when all the great military power of the continent went down before the iron flail of the 'child of destiny,' like ninepins, England wearied him out by her pertinacity, rather than by the brilliancy of her operations, triumphing by sheer dogged determination over the greatest master of combination the world ever saw."

It was identically this that led, in American history, to the surrender of Cornwallis to Washington...To a Will of this sort defeats are merely new lights on reason, and difficulties are fresh gymnastics for development of colossal resolve, and discouragements are the goading stimuli of titanic bursts of energy (page 44).

And of course, the power of England's characteristics has not faded out. It is still with us and undoubtedly will be with many generations to come when you consider that the extent of the power of the English language's influence in the world is probably second only to the Holy Bible and other offshoot entities of the British Empire. Is there any question that some of the most powerful political bodies in the world such as the United States (U.S.) and the United Nations (U.N.) were either inspired or founded by the United Kingdom (U.K.)?

China's greatness has been episodic due to frequent interruptions of her submission to the Supreme Law, and the people of the ever-confused Russia will neither know nor taste the real fruit of freedom, justice, and prosperity until Russian way of life surrenders to the Supreme Law, the constructive way of life.

www.makanologos.com

Mother Africa, on the other hand, has been brought to its knees by the weakness of her spinal cord to stand up straight for herself, to face and let the light of her Higher Self shine through the hearts and heads of the land and her children, and to stop allowing vicious forces to impose diabolical use of black magic and sorcery of the worse kind in politics, commerce, and social life in general, which has generated a culture of fearfulness, self-destruction, selfishness, and heartlessness in political and spiritual leaders and their subjects.

Consequently, the people of Mother Africa have been enslaved by fear, hate, jealousy, greed, doubt, and, most unfortunately, self-mistrust and self-faithlessness for a very long time indeed. The worth of work, that instrument of stimulation of virtues and inner qualities, is either neglected or discouraged by the failure of payment of adequate wages to workers at almost all levels. This has been going on since our kings and high priests lost the *Codes of the Law of Laws, the Directive Intelligence of the universe, or the philosopher stone* due to overprotection, inadequate succession of the priesthood, and, most unfortunately, the misguided desire to assert or claim the freedom of their free will from the Divine Will.

With the loss of the *Codes of the Supreme Law*, we lost the *Point of Contact with Inner Deity.* As we lost the true *Point of Contact with Inner Deity*, wisdom was withdrawn from our kings, high priests, and leaders, and consequently we completely forgot the *Source of life, wisdom, and power.* The few priests who submitted their free will to the Divine Will migrated northward due to the hostility of their lands toward them, and with them went the seeds or germs of all civilizations ever recorded or known in the history of man anywhere on this planet.

All the miseries that Africa has ever known have been caused by and can be justified only by the apparent loss of the link with the man without and *Man Within*, the *I AM THAT I AM*, or the *Point of Contact with Inner Deity.* This Directive Divine Principle was dearly loved and worshiped by the wisest

www.makanologos.com

kings, judges, and priests of Egypt, Ethiopia and throughout Abyssinia long before Zarathustra, Melchizedek, Abraham, Isaac, Jacob, Moses, Nebuchadnezzar, Buddha, or Plato. We ceased to admire virtues, light, and truth, and with that, we lost courage, fearlessness, self-confidence, self-control, strength, and harmony, and we accepted enslavement by fear, blind submission, and doubt of our own Self. We acquired false hope and faith that God will fight our battles and free us from poverty, ignorance, the cult of personality, miseries, and domestic or foreign tyranny.

Hope is coming back; however, it has not arrived yet. It is on the horizon, like the mighty sunrays waiting for the passing cloud to clear up before lighting the sky, illumining the inner eyes, and charging the body of man with life and energy. Now Africans are finding that God is nowhere but within, and through our own determination, fearlessness, self-control, self-confidence, and courageous actions and the work of the trinity of our own hearts, heads, and hands, God shall fight our battles, but through us. There are no miracles but work. No man shall be above the law, and no leader shall be acceptable unless he or she leads virtuously. Hope is coming again. Indeed, the hope of glory is rising as the children of Africa are finding that the way out of their mayhem is to be in the light, and the only way to associate with God is through self-confidence, self-mastery, self-help, and self-knowledge. And the only way to demand God to act for us is to let Him act through us by way of the quality of our actions. As Africans are recalling that long-lost memory and are working hard to cast off the shadow of that ancient tragedy, Light is making inroads, illumining the land, hearts, heads, and hands of the people once more. They are becoming aware of their Inner and Higher Self as the doer and the only way to happiness in life and the afterlife.

It is, however, noteworthy to mention that the loss of the Point of Contact with Inner Deity is not a unique African experience. What is unique, perhaps, is that the African recovery of it has been a very slow and excruciating process, and even though other cultures are recovering faster, they have never fully recovered and never will recover fast enough to enable the light to illumine the complete solving of their problems.

Of course, all cultures of the world at some point in history go through the same experience in different forms, which is why human problems are almost identical everywhere: lack of full power over one's life; lack of wisdom to submit to the Supreme Law of the universe; lack of love of the Inner Self; lack of genuine happiness and harmony; inability to recognize and tap into the Inner power; lack of intelligence to erase poverty, wars, and crime, etc.

In the experience of the Hebrews, for instance, the Point of Contact was lost and found, lost and found, and lost and found again, but still they never fully apprehended it. In his book *The Work of the Kabbalist,* here is how Z'ev Ben Shimon Halevi explained how Jews came to apprehend the Point of Contact with Inner Deity:

"However, all have their origin in the knowledge that lies behind the Bible that was revealed to Salomon, given to Moses, and passed onto Abraham by Malchizedek. Beyond this point, it becomes the pure teaching as handed down from the first fully realized man called Enoch, whose name means the 'Initiated'. He became Metatron, the great Instructor of Mankind (page 29). (We will come back to Enoch, but for now, bear this in mind.)

Any surprise why theirs (Jews') seems to be the most complicated problem of them all? Their persecution occurred frequently and in widely different geographical locations, from East to West, South to North, yet they seem to be some of the most enduring people on Earth. Wonder why theirs is one of the most successful and amazing survival stories of the human race (mythological or not)? Surviving slavery in Egypt, captivity in Babylon, brutal Roman occupation in Palestine, expulsion in Spain, rampant discrimination in Europe, the Holocaust, pogroms, expulsions, mob attacks, etc.

www.makanologos.com

(read more here: www.simpletoremember.com/articles/a/ HistoryJewishPersecution), and coming out of each trial strengthened with more determination than before. Attempting to put in words the appearance and disappearance of the Point of Contact with the *Directive Divine Principle of the Universe*, Ernest Holmes, one of the greatest teachers of the twentieth century, carefully trying to explain this ancient mystery, wrote:

"Can you imagine a power so great that it is both an infinite presence and a limitless law? If you can, you are drawing close to a better idea of the way Life works. Most of the bibles of the world have said that all things are formed by Its word. This word has been called the **Secret Word**, *the* **Lost Word**. *It is said some of the ancients had a holy scroll upon which was inscribed the sacred and the secret name of Life. This scroll was supposed to have been put in an ark, in a chest, and laid away in a place which was called the Holy of Holies, the innermost room of the temple. What do you suppose was inscribed upon this sacred scroll? Just this: the words "I AM." Here is a concept of the pure, simple and direct affirmation of Life making everything out of itself. This is why most of the scriptures have stated that all things are made by the Word of God,"* (*The Art of Life*, page, 37)

And of this word "I AM," in his masterful work, *The Hero with a Thousand Faces,* on pages 267-269, Joseph Campbell writes:

"The Aged of the Aged, the Unknown of the Unknown, has a form and yet has no form," we read in a Cabala text of the medieval Hebrews. "He has a form where the universe is preserved, and yet has no form, because he cannot be comprehended." This Aged of the Aged is represented as a face in profile: always in profile, because the hidden side can never be known. This is called "The Great Face," Makroprosopos; from the stands of its white beard the entire world proceeds. "That beard, the truth of all truth, proceedeth from the place of the ears, and descendeth around the mouth of the Holy One; and descendeth and ascendeth, covering the cheeks which are called the places of copious fragrance; it is

Exalted Secrets of Brilliant Minds   81

white with ornament: and it descendeth in the equilibrium of balanced power, and furnisheth a covering even unto the midst of the breast. That is the beard of adornment, true and perfect, from which flow down thirteen fountains, scattering the most precious balm of splendor. This is disposed in thirteen forms...And certain dispositions are found in the universe, according to those thirteen dispositions which depend from that venerable beard, and they are opened out into the thirteen gates of mercies."

The white beard of Makroprosopos descends over another head "The Little Face," Mikrorposopos, represented full face and with beard of black. And whereas the eye of The Great Face is without lid and never shuts the eyes of The Little Face open and close in a slow rhythm of universal destiny. This is the opening and closing of the cosmogonic round. The Little Face is named "God," the Great Face "I AM."

The Pocket Encyclopedia of Masonic Symbols defines the Lost Word outwardly in slightly different terms yet with the same inner meaning. It says the Lost Word is:

The symbol of knowledge of God, immortality, hidden secrets of nature. Perhaps the most abstruse and most important symbol of Fraternity...The Lost Word is not a syllable or several syllables; "word" is here used as St. John used it: "In the beginning was the word, and Word was with God, and the Word was God. The Lost is not discovered..."Never may we find it here. You shall gaze through microscope and telescope and catch no sight of its shadow. You shall travel in many lands and far and see it not. You shall listen to all the words of all the tongues which all men ever spoken and will speak – the Word, the great secret, the unknowableness which the Great Architect sets before his children, a will-o'-the-wisp to follow, a pot of gold at the end of a rainbow. Never here is to be found, but the search for it is the reason of life.

Now back to Enoch. As the legend of Enoch goes, Enoch is the only man of the present age of mankind or the "iron age" ever known to have been transfigured permanently from manhood into angelhood without passing through the change

www.makanologos.com

called death. He is said to have been the grandfather of Noah and a seventh-generation descendant of Adam, the father of the human race according to biblical mythology. Enoch, a learned and a God-loving man, demanded that God show him the TRUTH. God (Higher Self), pleased by his unconditional obedience, decided to show Enoch the Codes of the Supreme Law. Thus He pulled up Enoch (as if by a vacuum) by the power of the sacred fire very high in the skies. While still there, God decided to reveal Himself to Enoch by showing him a lightning triangle with a golden inscription of His ineffable name above the cloud. When Enoch was let go back to Earth, he fell down deep in the Earth, where he built an underground temple of nine mausoleums beneath each other and dedicated it to God (his Inner and Higher Self.) He made a golden plate upon which he engraved the ineffable characters of the Codes of the Supreme Law of the universe. Upon the completion of this subterranean temple, he made a secure and secret opening through which he could go down and worship his Higher Self whenever necessary. No one else was permitted to visit the subterranean temple without grave consequences.

Even Enoch himself was not allowed to go in but once per year. Only a chosen few of his descendants who accepted to take an oath of secrecy, loyalty, and complete obedience were made aware of the existence of this top-secret sacred temple of God and the inestimable knowledge it contained. After the Great Flood that happened long after Enoch's transfiguration (he is said to have lived about 365 years) and the passing of his sons, the location of the temple and the KNOWLEDGE hidden in it were lost. Many centuries later, it was mysteriously recovered and passed (see the above Halevi quotation) to Joseph and Moses before disappearing again, only to be rediscovered again by the prophet Samuel, who passed it King David and David to his son King Solomon, then Solomon to the most trustworthy builders of the Temple of Jerusalem and from the builders of the Temple of Jerusalem to the earnest and most sincere truth

www.makanologos.com

Exalted Secrets of Brilliant Minds   **83**

seekers of today throughout the world. Whether this is how
the secret passed from Enoch to generations after him, no one
really knows for sure. However, in the Bible, there is clearly a
record of how this knowledge of the Codes of the Supreme Law
passed from Egyptian high priests to generations of Israelites
and the rest of the world. In his effort to trace something of an
origin and the passage of the Codes of the Supreme Law from
the Egyptian high priests from Moses to Aaron, from David to
Solomon and from Solomon to future generations, the Masonic
scholar John R. Bennett, relying mostly on the Bible and other
esoteric sources, in his book *The Origin of Freemasonry and
Knights Templar*, writes:

*Aaron, who was Moses' brother, of the tribe of Levites, by a
miraculous judgment, became the first high priest. Moses directed
that twelve rods should be laid in the Holy of the Holies of the
tabernacle, one for each tribe; the name of Aaron on one rod to
represent the tribe of Levi, and Moses said, "The man's rod
whom I shall choose shall blossom." On the next day these rods
were brought out and exhibited to the people, and while all the
rest remained dry and withered, that of Aaron alone dubbed and
blossomed and yielded fruit (Number xvii). Philo-Judaeus says
that "Moses was instructed by Egyptian priests in the philosophy
of symbols and hieroglyphics as well as in the mysteries of the
sacred animals." The sacred historian tells us he was "learned in
all the wisdom of Egyptians"; and Manetho and other traditionary
writers tells us that he was educated at Heliopolis as a priest, under
his Egyptian name of Osarsiph, and that there he was taught the
whole range of literature and science, which it was customary to
impart to the priesthood of Egypt. It is not strange, when he began
in the wilderness to establish a new religion, that he should have
given a holy use of the symbols whose meaning he had learned in
his ecclesiastical education on the banks of the Nile (pages 27-28).*

*In the year 1116 B.C., just before the battle of the Israelites and
the Philistines at Ebenezer, near Shiloh, the ark of covenant was
brought from Shiloh in the camp of Israelites to inspire them with*

www.makanologos.com

great courage and confidence, but the Philistines overcame them, captured the ark and carried it first to Ashdod, then Gath, and from there to Ekron. In the year 1115 B.C. it was returned by the Philistines from Ekron to the Israelites at Kirjath-jearim, a city of the Gibeonites situated about nine miles northwest of Jerusalem, and there placed in the house of Abinadab, a Levite, where it remained for seventy year before being conveyed to Jerusalem (I Sam. iv-vi). The tabernacle was taken again from Shiloh to Gibeon, but the exact time of its removal is not known. In 1 Chronicles xxi: 29, it states that the tabernacle of Moses was still at Gibeon (1017 B.C.). Again, in 2 Chron. i. 3-13, that the tabernacle still remained at Gibeon, and that Solomon went there to sacrifice before it, (page, 33).

In 1045 B.C. the ark of covenant, which was at Kirjath-jearim, was carried, under King David's instructions, to Jerusalem, where it was placed in the temporary tabernacle erected for its use. Here the priests performed their daily service until Solomon erected the temple, then the temporary or Davidic tabernacle was put away as a relic, (page 39) (N.b.: Quote is longer than usual as the book is now in the public domain.)

And on this very same point, Lloyd M. Graham, whose work *Deceptions and the Myths of the Bible* I hope to explore even more in the fourth book of these series, *Emancipated Intelligence*, takes a radical stance by going to the point of branding the writers of the Bible, from Moses down, as plagiarists who used ancient wisdom collected from different parts of the world to form a new religion. He goes even further by accusing the Western intellect and mind of naïveté for accepting Hebrew religious literature at face value. In the preface of his book, he writes:

Literally, the priestly account of Creation is but kindergarten cosmology, yet we have accepted it for two thousand years. This is because the Western man is incapable of abstract thought. All the metaphysical and cosmological knowledge Western man has, came to him from the East. The ancient Orientals were capable of such thought but not Western man, and this includes the Jews. In his metaphysical incompetency Western man puts the stamp of his own ego on everything, including the Creator. Now blinded by his own error, he cannot see that it is only that part of the race incapable of abstract thought that believes in his anthropomorphic creation. That part of him called Christian could not even create a God or religion for himself; it had to borrow these from the Middle Eastern Jews. And what did they know about other worlds and galaxies? They did not even know this world is round. How then could their cosmology be right?

In spite of their pretended intimacy with the Creator, the Jews never had great knowledge of things cosmic and metaphysical; they were plagiarists culling mythic artifacts they did not understand. In their day the wisdom-knowledge was lost and so they were but epigonists – "the unworthy descendants of mighty Homer," their own included. This brings us to another point that must be understood – a pre-religious age of enlightenment, and the loss of its knowledge.

Time was when man knew vastly about Causation and Creation than he does today – the Mythopoeic Age. We call its enlightened ones Initiates and their knowledge, The Ancient Wisdom. With reason uncorrupted by false theologies they were able to study Reality and arrive at Truth…Due to a change in the cyclic law that knowledge was lost; priests took place of the Initiates and religion of metaphysics, (pages, 2-3).

Many legends have been told about Enoch, be it in the Bible or elsewhere. But the closest thing to the truth about him is that Enoch was a native of the ancient empire and present-day Ethiopia, once known as Abyssinia. Some accounts suspect he came to Ethiopia from Atlantis as a survivor of the tragic sinking of the continent into the ocean. As a lad, he was very obedient to God, pleasing Him with his feelings, thoughts, words, actions, and consciousness. Consequently, God revealed to him the "Point of Contact with Inner Deity," the Divine Directive Principle or the Causeless Cause of creation anywhere in the universe. God then made him a teacher of men. The Truth that

www.makanologos.com

was given him was so precious that he swore to give it only to those who would value It in words and actions over their own lives. Thus unlike all lesser teachers who came after him, Enoch was not a public speaker; he taught but to truest seekers of the truth and light. Occasionally he would use his gift of persuasion to prompt the mass, but whenever persuasion was not successful, he would simply withdraw and move on.

After a fruitless effort to persuade the kings and high priests of his homeland, Ethiopia, to lead people virtuously in order for the most precious favors of God to be restored in the hearts of the people and the land, Enoch withdrew, gave up and left his native Ethiopia, and headed northward to Egypt, where he was affectionately welcomed by a small group of nomadic shepherds who were nevertheless attentive students of light and determined seekers of the truth. Enoch felt and thought he could illumine these shepherds by making them high priests of that land. Among these shepherds were the two most important figures of Egyptian civilization, Isis and Osiris, about whom one Masonic writer, John R. Bennett, said in his book, *The Origin of Freemasonry and Knight Templar*:

> *The two central figures of the Mysteries, as well as of Egyptian history, were Isis and Osiris. These, when stripped of their mystic garments and brought down to the level of humanity, appear to have been an early king (Osiris) and queen (Isis) of the country, who were at the same time brother and sister. These, by superior virtue and intelligence, won the admiration and confidence of these wild and untutored barbarians, led them to their degraded state, and guided their feet into the path of civilization and empire. Under their direction the land of savage darkness became the land of light and full of joy. Isis taught the people how to hold the plow and turn the furrow, and to make bread from ripened grain. While doing this she made laws for home society and restrained men from lawlessness and violence of their sanction. Osiris built Thebes with its hundred gates; erected temples and altars, "instituted the sacred rites," and appointed priests to have the oversight and care*

of the holy things. Having accomplished these things, and seeing their effect upon his own people, he resolved to raise a great army, and, leaving Isis as the ruler, to go through all the world, "for he hoped he could civilize men and take them off their rude and beast-like course of life." This he succeeded in doing, but shortly after his return he was slain by his brother Typhon, (page, 6).

To them, Enoch taught the Divine Principle, then revealed the Point of Contact with Inner Deity, what to do to retain that priceless favor, and how to pass it to wise kings and high priests of future generations. And with that, the Egyptian civilization, the mother of all civilizations, was born, or more precisely, the civilization of the lost continent Atlantis was effectively transferred to Egypt. As Dr. Paul Brunton, a great British philosopher and traveler, author of several books including *A Search in Secret India; A Search in Secret Egypt,* and *Discover Yourself,* would write this in his book *Discover Yourself Formerly,* published as *The Inner Reality* around the time of the Second World War:

The Republic of Rome and the kingdom of Chaldea have fluttered through history like vanished butterflies; the empire of Babylon and the civilization of Sumeria have become but desiccated dust. A century from now the world's greatest conflict will mean no more than the history book's description of the Napoleonic wars means today.

Egypt, its neighbor, had a far older culture than Palestine. The Jews had linked one land with the other. An entire chapter and a half of the Book of Proverbs in the Old Testament have been copied word for word from the text of the Egyptian sage, Amenamope.

Go into any Jewish synagogue today and you will find symbols, geometric and otherwise, which you could have seen in any Egyptian temple of the past. It is a striking thought, yet a true one, that the religion which Moses gave to the Jews was a side branch growing from the religion of Osiris, which in turn came to Africa from Atlantis. Attend, if you can, a Masonic lodge meeting and you will find the same spiritual heirlooms. The first Christian monastery was established in Egypt.

It was inevitable that Jesus had to face the Sphinx. He went to Egypt because in those days that nation still had the tradition of spiritual culture and secret learning on a vast scale and of great antiquity, and this he could not find in his own land...He studied and practiced the exercises, which he was taught. He travelled in various provinces...He left handwork at the age of eighteen and embarked upon purely intellectual study. The pathetic remnants of the Egyptian mystery schools and temples opened their doors to a young foreigner. On the Mediterranean coast, he found a group of mystics, philosophers, students, and teachers gathered in quest of Truth, (pages, 306-307).

Prosperity and harmony reigned in Egypt until rulers were outsmarted first by (the foreigners) Abraham, then Joseph and Moses, who caused kings and high priests to fear and doubt the knowledge that had served the country unfailingly for thousands of years. Because those snakes poisoned Egypt in its very heart, the downfall and death of Egyptian power came slowly but surely like the death of an incurably cancer-stricken person. The Light and the Truth withdrew from Egypt, kings and high priests lost the Point of Contact with Inner Deity, and ungrateful former foreign students of the African light dubbed Egypt the land of magicians and sorcery. Afterward, the shadow and all its miseries invaded the land of Egypt; its knowledge was taken as other civilizations sprouted roots from its ruins.

After teaching the pioneers of Egyptian civilization, Enoch proceeded to Babylonia, Persia, and later Phoenicia, where he married and started a family. There, too, Enoch taught the Divine Principles that generated and guided those civilizations for centuries, but he was later unhappy as the stubbornness caused by success hardened people's hearts; they could no longer listen to him, and he could not depend upon them, including his own children. Unlike in Egypt, students of Enoch

Exalted Secrets of Brilliant Minds   89

used their newfound knowledge and power to win the hearts of people through trade and made theirs the culture dominated by commerce, which to this day still reverberates throughout the lands that were inherited from the Phoenician civilization.

The use of Divine Knowledge for selfish gain and wickedness by the Babylonian and Phoenician people displeased God and frustrated Enoch as he was in his native land of Ethiopia. By the order of God, shortly before his transformation into angelhood, Enoch buried the Golden Plate on which the Divine Secret (the Point of Contact with Inner Deity) was inscribed at dozens of feet or meters below the surface of the Earth. The great flood that took place hundreds of years later almost sealed the desire Enoch had that the Golden Plate would never be unearthed by human hands and seen by the eye of an average man.

The secret, however, was mysteriously revealed to Melchizedek (remember the above quotation), Abraham, Isaac, Jacob, Joseph, Moses, Aaron, Joshua, Plato, and Sir Francis Bacon, but they were never permitted to sound or write of the Word — yes, the Lost Word, the ineffable Name. The Egyptian kings and high priests had known of the Holy Word for centuries from the mouth of the Teacher himself, Enoch, but between Joshua and King David, the word was completely withdrawn from the Earth until It (the Lost Word) mysteriously appeared again to the Prophet Samuel, who had authority to pass It from one generation to the next. Thus, he revealed It to King David but not until David passed the test of loyalty, courage, and humility, as the Psalms' poems express.

King David in turn passed It to his son, King Solomon, after Solomon passed the test of wisdom and promised to pass It wisely to future generations. The construction of the first Temple of Jerusalem by Solomon became a testing ground for worthiness of access to the holy knowledge by seekers. Thus, at the height of the reign of King Solomon, the Golden Plate with the Inscription of the Lost Word, or the TRUTH, on it, the same Golden Plate buried by Enoch, was found by two most

www.makanologos.com

virtuous, courageous, and trusted builders of King Solomon's Temple. Upon seeing the Lost Word (the TRUTH, or the name of the Point of Contact with Inner Deity), Solomon decided to establish a system through which the Secret would be handed down to worthy and wise leaders of the future generations — humble high priests, prudent judges, and a chosen few sincere seekers of the truth throughout the world.

To make a long story short, ever since the Secret or the Point of Contact with Inner Deity has been communicated to wise and loving kings, including the illumined high priests, fair judges of today's Judeo-Christian tradition primarily, and the chosen few around the world. It is absolutely normal for the reader to question why the Secret is kept out of reach of the masses. Christians, of course will remember that the Master adamantly recommended to never cast *"your pearls before the swine."* But I would refer my reader not only to the answer that Jesus gave his apostles when asked the very same question, but I would also ask him or her to ponder what the English writer H. Rider Haggard had in mind about the nature of the Secret in his book *She*, one of the best-selling books of all time, which reads:

So I lay and watched the stars come out by thousands, till all the immense arch of heaven was strewn with glittering points, and every point a world! Here was a glorious sight by which man might well measure his own insignificance! Soon I gave up thinking about it, for the mind wearies easily when it strives to grapple with the Infinity, and to trace the footsteps of the Almighty as He strides from sphere to sphere, or deduce His purpose from His works. Such things are not for us to know. Knowledge is to the strong, and we are weak. Too much wisdom perchance would blind our imperfect sight, and too much strength would make us drunk, and over-weight our feeble reason till it fell and we were drowned in the depths of our own vanity. For what is the first result of man's increased knowledge interpreted from Nature's book by the persistent effort of his purblind observation? Is it not but too often to make him question the existence of his Maker, or, indeed, of any

www.makanologos.com

intelligent purpose beyond his own? The Truth is veiled, because we could no more look upon her glory than we can upon the sun. It would destroy us. Full knowledge is not for man as man is here, for his capacities, which is apt to think so great, are indeed but small…The person who found it might no doubt rule the world. He could accumulate all the wealth in the world, and power, and all the wisdom that power is (pages 89-91).

So what do you think? Don't you believe greatness is forever linked to the truth? Are you still questioning divine (not religious) principles or association with God as the source of all true greatness? What say ye? Oh no! Pardon my inquisition! I will let you discover for yourself what the philosopher stone is. Keep your answers to yourself, but share them if you think they may light the hearts, heads, and hands of others.

Saying a few more words here about Enoch, Haggard — whose magnificent book *She* is entirely about the mysteries of the land of the kingdom of KOR that gave birth to the *seeds of light* of the Egyptian civilization — not only places this kingdom around modern Ethiopia, Kenya, Tanzania, Uganda, Somalia, and Sudan, but he goes on suggesting that, or at least reluctantly inquiring if, *"those people who sailed north may have been the fathers of the first Egyptians?"* (page, 137). He proceeds describing the Egyptian civilization basically as the carbon copy of the KOR tradition but still somehow inferior artistically as he writes, *"Yea. The children of KOR ever embalmed their dead, as the Egyptian, but their art was greater than the art of the Egyptians, for whereas the Egyptian disemboweled and drew the brain, the people of KOR injected fluid in the veins, and thus reached every part"* (page 138). Despite all the pains Haggard takes in his effort to disguise the truth from the eye of the ordinary uneducated in the mysteries of Egypt, he implies that Enoch is the high priest who built the great Temple of Truth before sailing northwards, the last priest, the "priest of the Great Temple, of Kor" who wrote:

Upon the rock of the burying-place in the year four thousand eight hundred and three from the founding of Kor. Kor is fallen!

www.makanologos.com

No more shall the mighty feast in her halls, no more shall she rule the world, and her navies go out to commerce with the world. Kor has fallen...Then, at last, a remnant of this great people, the light of the world, went down to the coast and took ship to the coast and sailed northwards; and now am I, the last Priest Junis, who write, the last man left alive of this great city of men, but whether there be any left in the cities I do not know, (page, 136).

Along the same lines, in *The Masks of God: Occidental Mythology*, thinking of the connections of the Christian church and the roots of Jesus himself and the mighty kings of both the Orient and Occident in the same geographical area of Africa, American writer and lecturer Joseph Campbell writes:

Who, for example, has written of the life and times of the forty-odd monolithic churches of Ethiopia Lalibela, and their relationship to the cave-temples of Ajanta? And what of the legendary serpent king of nearby Axum, from whose slayer the present Nahas or Negus (compare Sanskrit nagas, "serpent, serpent king"), Haile Selassie of Ethiopia, is descended? Or who has searched the background of the legends of Issa (Jesus) and of the king of Persia and Rome that Leo Frobenius traced through the Sudan as far west to the Niger? It is all, as far as the modern church is concerned, a lost world...But the loss of Africa was not the only calamity, (page, 413).

In *The Masks of God: Primitive Mythology* volume, Joseph Campbell goes on to write:

And the manner in which his skill increased in the not too easy task of chipping flints, from the days of his first crude pebble tools to those of his finest fist axes, reveals that, for all his rude and even ghoulish habits, he was no unmitigated lout. The higher center of human culture was still Africa. Here an incredible abundance of Paleolithic tools have been found. Indeed, some excavations (for examples, those of L.S.B. Leakey at Olduvai Gorge in the north Tanganyika) have revealed in perfect sequence every stage of evolution of the ax from the pebble tools of man's first beginnings to the finely finished, really elegant axes of the period of the

Exalted Secrets of Brilliant Minds　　93

Neanderthal. And if the view into the depth of the well of time that we obtained in the South of France was great, this of Olduvai is simply beyond speech...Already we have heard something of the early diffusion of this high culture complex to the Sudan. Far to the south, in the area marked by great stone temple ruins of Zimbabwe, in the south Rhodesian Matabeleland, ritual regicide appears to have been practiced until as late as 1810. The stars and the sacred oracle were consulted by the priests every four years and, without fail, the verdict would be death for the king...We can regard this Great Eritrean area as the first zone of diffusion of the mythology of our mythogenetic Fertile Crescent; for a basal Neolithic culture stratum has been identified as early as about 4500 B.C. in the Nile Valley; and a high Neolithic about 4000. Furthermore, there is now dependable C-14 evidence that something of the Neolithic had reached Northern Rhodesia as early as c. 4000 B.C. while the art of the Bronze and Iron Ages surely were established in Sudanese Napata by respectively, c. 750-744 and c. 397-362 B.C., (pages, 364, 420, and 422)

Those who have read the only surviving book of Enoch, translated only from the Ethiopian language, would very much agree that the Priest Junis is very likely the last student of the school built by Enoch in Ethiopia centuries ego as described by Haggard in his book, and the people of Kor are the true fathers of the Egyptian civilization, or human civilizations in general, as these writings are very similar to the writings in the book of Enoch found in Ethiopia in the nineteenth century. And of course, *She* was presented to the world as a mere "adventure" by a dreaming Haggard, a suspected amanuensis who by his own words denied the authorship of the book and by his own admission professed to have received the manuscript from two truth-seekers who left England for the Himalayan Mountains in Tibet. The masses, indeed, have sheepishly bought into the notion of adventure and so will it remain for them until the day they will face the light, while enlightened minds see the

www.makanologos.com

evidence as clearly as they see the sun in a cloudless sky at midday.

Nevertheless, just for the sake of argument—and assuming that Haggard is the true author of *She* and not an amanuensis or mere editor and the whole book is simply a product of his imagination—does it really alter the truth? In what language does God speak to us? Does He speak in the language of earthquake, thunderstorm, cyclone, flood, hurricane, any sort of natural disaster, or in the language of our imagination, the language of our feelings and thoughts, or the language of silence? In what language did God speak to Adam, Enoch, Noah, Abraham, Joseph, Socrates, Plato, and even Jesus, for that matter, and everyone else before and after ever since, including you and me? God speaks to us in the language of silence, a language that brings thoughts, feelings, pictures, and images constantly showing on the screen of our inner theater. A very small number of us get it perfectly, a few of us get it right, some of us get it almost right, many of us get it wrong, and a wide majority of us are confused and lost.

We are all entitled to our own opinions. My point is this: Haggard may not have gotten it perfectly right, but he must have come closer than few of us will ever come. In closing this section, let me say this: it may appear to some readers that I am advancing a particularly biased agenda, but I am not. I would like to confess to my readers that I thought it over and over. I am quite well forewarned that many readers may think of me as out of my mind, biased, and bent to promote an African correction of biblical history in stating that Enoch, a giant of the Bible, was Ethiopian or African. But that will be entirely missing the point if you take just one account of his life. The only book attributed to Enoch was not only discovered in Ethiopia, but it also was written in Ethiopian handwriting and language, *Ge'ez*, *"an ancient South Semitic language that originated in the northern region of Ethiopia and southern Eritrea in the Horn of Africa,"* as

Wikipedia.org defines it. Here is what Wikipedia writes about it:

The Book of Enoch (also 1 Enoch) is an ancient Jewish religious work, traditionally ascribed to Enoch, the great grandfather of Noah. It is not part of the biblical canon as used by Jews, apart from Beta Israel. It is regarded as canonical by the Ethiopian Orthodox Church and Eritrean Orthodox Church, but no other Christian group...It is wholly extant only in the Ge'ez language, with Aramaic fragments from the Dead Sea Scrolls and a few Greek and Latin fragments. For this and other reasons, the traditional Ethiopian view is that the original language of the work was Ge'ez, whereas non-Ethiopian scholars tend to assert that it was first written in either Aramaic or Hebrew; E. Isaac suggests that the Book of Enoch, like the Book of Daniel, was composed partially in Aramaic and partially in Hebrew. (http://en.wikipedia.org/wiki/Book_of_Enoch, accessed June 21, 2012)*

There are some who suggest that the book must have been translated from Amharic or Hebrew, but this argument does not stand the light of the day given that Enoch lived thousands of years before the birth of Abraham, the father of Hebrew people, walked the face of the Earth.

The Talmud, a central text of Rabbinic Judaism, explains how the Truth or the Supreme Secret came down from God to the children of Abraham in these terms:

36. "I am forever I am" (Exodus. 3:14). The Holy One said to Moses: Go tell Israel, I am He who is with you in this servitude, and I am also He who will be with you during servitude under other kingdoms. Moses replied: Master of the universe, sufficient unto the hour is its own affliction. [Why call to mind affliction yet to come?] The Holy One said: Very well, just tell them, "I-am hath sent me unto you." (Exodus 3:14)

37. "And thou shall take in thy hand this rod" (Exodus 4:17). The rod that was created at twilight [on creation's sixth day] was handed to Adam in the Garden of Eden. Adam handed it to Enoch, Enoch to Shem, Shem to Abraham, Abraham to Isaac, Isaac to

www.makanologos.com

Jacob, Jacob took it to Egypt and handed it to his son Joseph. When Joseph died, all his household effects were moved and deposited in Pharaoh's palace. Now, Jethro was one of Pharaoh's magicians. When he saw the rod and the signs on it, he coveted it in his heart and took it, brought it to his place, and planted it the garden by his house. No man could come near it until Moses arrived in the land of Midian, entered the garden of Jethro's house, saw the rod, made out the signs on it, stretched forth his hand, and took it. When Jethro saw this, he said: This man is destined to redeem Israel from Egypt. That is why he gave his daughter Zipporah to Moses as his wife. (The Book of Legends/Sefer Ha-Aggadah [Legends from the Talmud and Midrash], edited by H. N. Bialik and Y. H. Ravnitzky; translated by William G. Braude, pages, 63-64)

Not to put on trial the Talmud or the Hebrew explanation of how the Supreme Secret came to them, but the picture is not totally clear here because many prominent students of ancient religions and history have acknowledged that both Europeans, mostly Greeks, and Middle Easterners came to Egypt to learn the truth. It was here where Plato learned about the lost continent of Atlantis before illicitly proclaiming to the world the esoteric secret. Paul, a cornerstone of the founding of the Christian Church, was unequivocal about where the wisdom of Moses came from in Acts 7: 22: *"And Moses was learned in all the wisdom of the Egyptians, and was mighty in words and in deeds,"* according to the King James Version.

The Talmud claims that Abraham received the Supreme Secret from Shem, but it is a well-known fact that, unlike his descendants who came to Egypt in search of food, Abraham came in search of knowledge. To make it even murkier, elsewhere

www.makanologos.com

we learn that Abraham was instructed by Melchizedek. Yet it has always been suspected that while in Egypt, he got the knowledge directly from Pharaoh through Sarah, his beautiful wife, whom he deceitfully gave up to spy for him by offering her to the king for sexual pleasure. This point and many others concerning the lives of many biblical patriarchs, as well as the myths and origins of many books of the Old Testament, will be discussed in depth in the fourth book of these series, *Emancipated Intelligence.*

The handsome Joseph got his hand on the Secret through the Queen of Egypt, who had sworn to have an intimate relationship with the Hebrew boy even at the cost of her breath. Because Joseph's goal was to gain the trust and loyalty of the king, he deceived the queen nevertheless. Feeling betrayed, the queen swore to make Joseph pay for his deception with his life. The queen's rage was to no avail. Having acquired the secrets of the Gods and self-knowledge, Joseph had grown to become master of his destiny. He had learned to control the energy in and around him and thus was immune to the vicious feelings and thoughts of those around him. Moses, on another hand, was made to infiltrate the highest levels of the Egyptian government by vengeful and shrewd parents who by all means possible wanted to know what knowledge the Hebrews had lost with the death of their beloved patriarch Joseph. And thus were the Supreme Secret and its Light taken from Africans to the most secretive caves of the world, leaving Africa to battle self-destruction.

In Europe, despite centuries of worshiping Roman, Greek, Celtic, Scandinavian, and Germanic gods and many more centuries of Christianity, the Supreme Secret was practically unknown until It was personally deposited, centuries later, in certain European crowns and in the hands of luminaries by a mysterious person, a man who is both real and surreal, historical and mythical, literal and allegorical. The person is one of the few souls believed to have never incarnated on planet

www.makanologos.com

Earth in any other gender but a male, unlike the vast majority of us who are believed to have incarnated in one embodiment or the other as male or female over several incarnations. This person is believed to have been the major force behind the inception, illumination, and strength of Europe's most illuminating schools of wisdom and enlightenment, including Rosicrucianism and Freemasonry. He is a man very few people know how to describe accurately, even some of those who have had the fortune to meet him face to face or have been under his personal and direct tutelage; a man known to most people as the Wonder Man of Europe, or more precisely *Sanctus Germano* or the *Holy Brother*, aka the Comte de Saint Germain, the man Frederick the Great liked to refer to as "the man who does not die."

Not that Jesus has not blessed Europe, He has. Being the Cosmic Christ for this system of our worlds, He has blessed Europe in the same manner that He has blessed any other part of the planet Earth. But the task of illuminating Europe was left to His Cosmic Brother (who has always worked behind the scenes of every destiny-changing event on Earth) with Jesus's total, loving, and unconditional assistance and cooperation, we are told. Comte de Saint Germain, who throughout the centuries has always worked with the luminaries and brilliant minds of Europe and is well known in the highest and noblest classes of the continent, is believed to have been the guiding force behind the organization of the Catholic Church, the Knight Templars, Rosicrucianism, and Freemasonry, the four angles of the square of European illumination. The first is a sort of *public school* designed to seek the realm of a remote and an abstract far-off land, and simultaneously merciless judge and merciful father. Slightly skipping the search for the Kingdom within as the Master pointed out, the three last ones are sort of *private schools or brotherhood-based organizations* designed to pursue the dream of ancient Greeks, the Temple of Adelphi, to *KNOW THYSELF*, the search for the Kingdom of Heaven that

Exalted Secrets of Brilliant Minds　　99

is within, as the Christian Master pointed out. The Comte de Saint Germain, in one of his several incredible *metamorphoses,* is thought to have been the guiding power behind the first presiding officer of the Order of the Knights Templar and Grand Master of the Brotherhood of Jerusalem, who introduced many symbols and rituals from ancient Egypt and Atlantis. And as John Bennett writes in the above-mentioned book, the Grand Master of the Knight Templar Brotherhood was more influential and powerful than the Pope and all the kings of Europe. John Bennett writes:

The organization of the Templars embraced four classes of members — Knights, Squires, Servitors, and Priests. Each had their peculiar duties and obligations. The presiding officer of the Order was called the Master — afterward the Grand Master. England, Germany, France and Italy, in fact, nearly all states of Christendom, were divided into provinces, and over each was set a provincial Master. The Grand Master of Jerusalem was regarded as the head of the entire brotherhood, which soon grew in numbers, influence and wealth to be one of the most powerful organizations in the world. Counts, dukes, princes, and even kings, eagerly sought the honor which was everywhere conceded to the red cross and the white mantle of the Templar.

In course of time the Knight of the Temple became a sovereign body, owing no allegiance to any secular potentate. In spiritual matters the Pope was still regarded as supreme, but in all other affairs the Grand Master was as independent as the greatest sovereign of Europe. The houses of the Knights could not be invaded by any civil officer. Their churches and cemeteries were exempt from interdicts; their properties and revenues from taxation. So great were the immunities thus enjoyed that thousands of persons sought to be affiliated with the brotherhood in order to share its benefits, (page, 132).

The Rosicrucian school sought to reach the Inner Self by reconstructing the truth through the understanding of mostly ancient Egypt esoteric mythologies, understanding the thinking

www.makanologos.com

and workings of Osiris and his wife, Isis, the god and goddess of ancient Egyptian religion. About Rosicrucianism and its startling history, the *Britannica Online Encyclopedia* writes:

Rosicrucian, member of a worldwide brotherhood claiming to possess esoteric wisdom handed down from ancient times...The central feature of Rosicrucianism is the belief that its members possess secret wisdom that was handed down to them from ancient times. The origins and teachings of the Rosicrucians are described in three anonymously published books that have been attributed to Johann Valentin Andreae (1568-1654), a Lutheran theologian and teacher who wrote the utopian treatise *Christianopolis (1619). The Fama Fraternitas of the Meritorius Order of the Rosy Cross (1614), The Confession of the Rosicrucian Fraternity (1615), and The Chymical Marriage of Christian Rosenkreuz (1616) recount the travels of Christian Rosenkreuz, the putative founder of the group, who is now generally regarded as a fictional character rather than a real person. According to the books, Rosenkreuz was born in 1378 and lived for 106 years. After visiting the Middle East and North Africa in search of secret wisdom, he returned to Germany and organized the Rosicrucian order (1403). He erected a sanctuary (1409), where he was entombed after his death in 1484. The alleged discovery of the tomb 120 years later became the occasion for the public announcement of the order's existence. The secretive nature of the early brotherhood – if it actually existed – would have made contact with it difficult. The combination of alchemy and mysticism associated with it, however, became quite influential. Rosicrucianism was attractive to many thinkers throughout Europe, possibly including the English philosopher and scientist Francis Bacon. It declined dramatically in the 18th century, however, a victim of the skepticism and rationalism of the Enlightenment, though some Rosicrucian ideas survived in speculative Freemasonry.* (http://www.britannica.com/ [EBchecked/topic/510019/Rosicrucian](http://www.britannica.com/EBchecked/topic/510019/Rosicrucian), accessed July 15, 2012)

Freemasons, on the other hand, had the same goal at the center of their studies but more precisely through speculative emulation of operative craftsmen and master experts and builders of the unique and beautiful King Solomon's Temple in Jerusalem, as well as other creative and esoteric allegories. In the words of John R. Bennett, a Masonic writer:

Freemasonry not only presents the appearance of a speculative science, based on an operative art, but also very significantly exhibits itself as the "symbolic expression of a religious idea." In other and plainer words, we see in it the important lesson of eternal life, taught by legends which, whether true or false, is used in Masonry as a symbol and allegory, (pages, 2-3).

Further on in the same work, describing the design of Freemasonry, Bennett writes the following:

Freemasonry is not only a universal science, but a worldwide religion, and owes allegiance to no one creed, and can adopt no sectarian dogma, as such, without ceasing thereby to be Masonic. Drawn from Kabbalah, and taking the Jewish or Christian verbiage or symbols, it but discerns in the universal truths, which it recognizes in all other religions. Freemasonry is not Christianity, or a substitute for it. It is not intended to supersede it nor any other form of worship or system of faith. Its religion is that general one of nature and primitive revelations, handed down to us from some ancient and patriarchal priesthood, in which all men may agree and in which no men can differ. It inculcates virtue, but supplies no scheme of redemption for sin. It points its disciples to the path of righteousness, but it does not claim to the "the way, the truth, and the life." Neither persecution nor misrepresentation can ever destroy it. It may find no place in a generation of bigots; it may retire for a century, but again comes a Master Builder with the key to the "shut palace of the King," throws open the blinds, lets in the light, kindles anew the fire on the sacred alter, clears away the rubbish, when behold! The tessellated pavement is as bright as when it first came from the quarries of truth, the jewels are of pure gold and brightness at the touch, and the great lights are undimmed and undecayed. "When the candidate is ready the Master appears." And yet men are so foolish as to imagine that they can destroy this heirloom of the ages; this heritage from the Immortals! No age is so dark as to quench entirely the light of the Lodge; no persecution so bloody as to blot out its votaries; no edict so lasting as to count one second on its Dial of Time! These, one and all, serve only to keep the people in darkness, and retard the reign of universal brotherhood, (pages, 97-98).

He, the Comte de Saint Germain, is also believed to have been the guiding spirit behind the writing of the Magna Carta Libertatum, which brought the most direct challenges to the English monarch's authority in the thirteenth century; the US American colonies, then at war with Great Britain, regarded themselves as independent states and no longer a part of the British Empire; and the U.S. Constitution, the supreme law of the United States of America and a beacon of freedom and democracy to the world. Of the Magna Carta, the PearsonVUE social science examination preparation material writes, "*Magna Carta,* signed by King John of England in 1215…granted 'to all freemen of our kingdom' a collection of rights and liberties, such as due process. The United States Constitution, in particular the Bill of Rights, is based on the democratic philosophies and ideas first presented in the Magna Carta"

(http://wps.prenhall.com/chet_nes_socialscience96/12619855. cw/index.html (accessed January 6, 2013). These schools not only allowed Europe to conquer itself but also to conquer the world, at least in the thinking of European senses and minds.

The story of the Comte de Saint Germain is beyond the imagination, legends, myths, or any conceivable theory by any living human being. Described as living a life literally as above so below, the Comte de Saint Germain really transcends all human concepts, for no human language can really do justice in explaining him in an understandable way. Thus, little is really known about the Comte de Saint Germain. Even his own students, who have studied about him and with him in both esoteric and exoteric schools for decades if not centuries, barely know much about him. He, Saint Germain, we are told, is the God of Freedom, a Divine Twin Ray of a Majestic Cosmic Being known as the Goddess of Justice, who has lived in the Great, Great Silence for eons, holding in her hand the balance of justice. But unlike Lady Justice, the Greek mythological goddess, She (the Goddess of Justice) is not blindfolded. She is, we are told, a manifestation or embodiment of the Divine Balance of love, wisdom, and power. She purified Herself long before her Twin Ray (Saint Germain) did and withdrew into the Golden Flame of the threefold flame of pink (love), gold (wisdom), and blue (power) in the Great, Great Silence, where to this moment She abides in full glory. Unlike the justices of our world, the Goddess of Justice is not a judge of good and bad, an arbitrary dispenser of certain conditions (good or bad) in the universe, or anything of the sort. She is not involved in any legal activities or law enforcement, the endless pursuit of protection of the good guys from the bad ones or right from wrong in the human sense of these terms of judgment; She simply holds the activities of life in a divine balance of love, wisdom, and power so that the universe does not fall into chaos. In that capacity, She represents the Divine Balance of justice and life. We are told She is a Majestic Divine Being of Glory, indescribable in human words, a truly pure Freedom's Twin Ray.

In his last incarnation, because of his great love and desire to bring illumination to a certain group of mankind, Saint Germain kept his body young for more than 300 years in order to give services to mankind. Until he finished teaching, he traveled allover the world before he accepted his own Divine freedom. During that time he appeared to secret societies, kings, princes, politicians, wise judges, intellectuals, scientists, generals, and writers throughout Europe earning the name of the wonder man of Europe, as you can see in this YouTube video: https://www.youtube.com/watch?v=cVjSYWEUsXc.

Along with Jesus, Saint Germain is said to be a former pupil of the Great Divine Director. This Great Divine Being, from realms beyond the reach of the human intellect comprehension, is said to be a native of the planet Earth, a sinless High Priest who was born naturally, yet lived in a self-luminous body in the second Golden Age of our humanity and gained his complete freedom the original divine way without passing through the change called, – the Constrictive Way of Life-. The Great Divine Director, in His other life manifestation, is known as Lord Maha Chohan who is believed to be described in the Gospel as the Holy Ghost in John 14:16 and 26 and Acts 2:1-13. According to the Saint Germain Foundation website; *"Lord the Maha Chohan is Master of the Powers of Nature and Forces of the Elements. The orthodox world recognizes Him as the Holy Ghost, or Holy Spirit,"* refered to by Jesus as the Comfoter. In many schools, this Great Divine Being is described as one of the Trinity of the Godhead and is said to be the Authority over every life stream on the Earth and the power behind the four elements of nature. He is the One who releases the ultimate fiery radiation that burns the vestige of low vibrations of human feelings and miscreation from the emotional body of every human being who ever attained complete Divine Freedom from the planet Earth.

About Saint Germain this website write:

"He was called the Wonderman of Europe. Mystery surrounded him. He appeared here, he appeared there, he seemed to appear everywhere. One thing is certain – he was highly visible in the royal courts – AND invisible! This mysterious man visited kings and queens across Europe. He spoke at least twelve languages so fluently that everywhere he went he was accepted as a native. "Bonjour," he'd say visiting in France, "Hallo," while in Germany and "Buon giorno," in Italy. He also spoke English, Spanish, Portuguese, Russian and Eastern languages. He even traveled to Japan. There's no telling where else this Wonderman visited, for he would appear, disappear and reappear unpredictably all over Europe," Who was this mystery man? He was le Comte

www.makanologos.com

de Saint Germain...And who was the le Comte de Saint Germain? People living at that time, during the eighteenth and nineteenth centuries asked that question over and over. In the royal courts, you could hear people saying, "Who is that man?" as they pointed to the Comte. *http://tsl.org/family/2013/04/saint-germain-the-wonderman-of-europe/* (accessed 01/31/14).

In an effort to describe to the outer world who he Comte de Saint Germain really is, esoteric mythology has attempted to describe him in a way that would make a person uneducated in the craft get even more confused, leaving only the person's own faith to reveal the true identity of this wonderful friend of humanity. Here is some of what we are told about who the Comte de Saint Germain is. He is said to have been king/high priest on the continent of Atlantis, which submerged thirteen thousand years ago, for thousands of years, and all mythological scientific advancement of that continent was due to his ability to draw power from the very heart of God as long as the inhabitants of Atlantis were obedient to divine law. The sinking of Atlantis is said to have been a direct consequence of his withdrawal to the Golden City above the Desert Sahara (where he had earlier been ruler for fifty thousand years) after Atlantis's people chose to disobey God.

We are also told that Comte de Saint Germain was Ramses II, one of the greatest pharaohs of Egypt, and possibly Tutankhamen as well. In the Bible's Old Testament, he is believed to have been Aaron the priest, the older brother of Moses who represented the priestly functions of his tribe, becoming the first High Priest of the Israelites, the Prophet Samuel, the last of the Hebrew judges and the first of the major prophets who began to prophesy inside the Land of Israel.. He was hence at the cusp between two eras, and according to the text of the Books of Samuel, he also selected and anointed the first two kings of the Kingdom of Israel: Saul and David. Later, the prediction was made that the Messiah would come from the lineage of the House of David. This prediction was made over 700 years before Jesus was born.

In the New Testament, Comte de Saint Germain is believed to have been embodied as Joseph, the father of Jesus and His protector during Jesus's infancy and early years. Some also believe he was Lazarus, the Torah scribe in the synagogue and personal friend of Jesus whom Jesus brought back to life, much to the chagrin of the Jewish establishment. This account, however, may not be correct because Joseph and Lazarus were contemporaries; therefore, he could not have existed in two bodies at the same time. But *The Aquarian Gospel of Jesus*, a transcribed text of the book from the Akashic records by Levi (an amanuensis, of course) in 1908, indicates that Joseph passed away when Jesus was in his late teens or early twenties and away attending Invisible Colleges in Egypt, India, and Tibet. So if Joseph was also Lazarus working behind the scenes, he must have overtaken the body of the dead Lazarus to assist his former protégée and cosmic brother to fulfill a divine mission.

In the introduction to Rudolf Steiner's *Christian Rosenkreutz: The Mystery, Teaching and Mission of a Master*, describing how the Comte de Saint Germain is portrayed in the Book of Revelation, Andrew J. Welburn writes:

The sources indicate this further by associating him with the prophetic teachings of the Book of Revelation and its author John, and also the Gospel of John; it is said of him that he beholds heaven opening, with the angels descending (John 1:51 cf. Rev. 19:11), and the names written in the book of life (Rev. 3:5). The description of his tomb meanwhile is filled with further secret symbolism, his miraculous preservation when the tomb is opened above all suggestive of Egypt and Hermetic Mysteries (page 3).

Among his other lives, Comte de Saint Germain is said to have been Saint Alban, a Roman soldier in the third century A.C.;_Merlin, **the wizard friend of King Arthur (fourth century); Christian Rosenkreutz;** Roger Bacon, **scientist,**

www.makanologos.com

philosopher, etc.; and Christopher Columbus. As Columbus, he is thought to have reanimated the body of a deceased amateur Italian sailor and used it to completely change the course of the destiny of mankind forever. He is also believed to have been Francis Bacon, *the true writer of the Shakespearean plays.* And as the Comte de Saint Germain, he is believed to be the Wonder Man of Europe in the eighteenth century. Goethe's poem *The Mysteries* and Mozart's *The Magic Flute* are believed to have been dedicated to the Comte de Saint Germain.

Writing of the Comte de Saint Germain as Christian Rosenkreutz, Rudolf Steiner writes in *The Mystery, Teaching and Mission of Christian Rosenkreutz*:

Christian Rosenkreutz is an individual who is active both when he is in incarnation and when is not incarnated in a physical body; he works not only as a physical being and through physical bodies, but above all spiritual, through higher forces...

In a place in Europe that cannot be named...a lodge of a very spiritual nature was formed comprising a council of twelve men who had received into themselves the sum of the spiritual wisdom of olden times and of their own...The twelfth was a man who attained the intellectual wisdom of his time in the highest degree... The beginning of the new culture was only possible, however, because a thirteenth came to join the twelve. The thirteenth did not become a scholar in the acceptable sense of that time. He was an individuality who had been incarnated at the time of the Mysteries of Golgotha. In the incarnations that followed, he prepared himself for his mission through humility of soul and through a fervent life devoted to God. He was a great soul, a pious, deeply mystical human being, who had not just acquired these qualities but was born with them...He was kept apart from the rest of the world... The wisdom of the twelve was reflected in him. It reached the point where the thirteenth refused to eat and wasted away. The event happened that could only happen once in history...After a few days the body of the thirteenth became quite transparent, and for days he lay as though dead...His body, too, came to light in

www.makanologos.com

such a way that this revival of his absolutely transparent body was beyond compare. The youth now speak of quite new experiences. The twelve recognized that he had experienced a repetition of the vision of Paul (pages, 10, 13, 14, 15, 17).

Steiner goes on to say that in the course of a few weeks, the thirteenth reproduced all the wisdom he had received from the twelve in an absolutely innovative form. This new form, however, was as though given by Christ himself, and thus they called it true Christianity. Further connecting the link between the Comte de Saint Germain and Christian Rosenkreutz, Steiner writes in the same book:

When he was 28 years old he conceived a remarkable ideal. He had to leave Europe and travel. First he went to Damascus, and what Paul had experienced there happened again to him...It is the individuality of Christian Rosenkreutz. He was the thirteenth in the circle of twelve. He was named thus from that incarnation onwards...

The Count of Saint Germain was the exoteric name of Christian Rosenkreutz's incarnation in the eighteenth century. This name was given to other people, too, however; therefore not everything that is told about the Count of Saint Germain in the outside world applies to the real Christian Rosenkreutz, (pages, 18, 19, 22).

In her book *The Comte de Saint Germain: The Secret of the Kings*, Isabel Cooper-Oakley described him in these terms:

Among the strange mysterious beings, with which the eighteenth century was so richly dowered, no one commanded more universal comment than the mystic who was known by the name of the Comte de Saint Germain. A hero of romance; a charlatan; a swindler and an adventurer; rich and varied were the names that showered freely upon him. Hated by the many, loved and reverenced by the few, time has not yet lifted the veil, which screened his true mission from the vulgar speculators of the period. Then, as now, the occultist was dubbed charlatan by the ignorant; only some men and women here and there realized the power of which he stood possessed. The friend and councilor of the kings and princes, an enemy to ministers who were skilled in deception, he brought great knowledge to help the West, be stave off in some small measure the storm clouds that were gathering so thickly around some nations. Looking back from this distance of time it will be of interest to many students of mysticism to trace the life, so far as it may yet be told, of this great occultist. Sketches are to be found here and there from various writers, mostly antagonistic, but no coherent detailed account of his life has yet appeared. This is very largely owing to the fact that the most interesting and important work, done by M. de St. Germain, lies buried in the secret archives of many princely and noble families (page 9).

The significance of the point I am trying to express here is so important that I feel compelled to quote Isabel Cooper-Oakley even more in order to give the reader more meat to chew and digest as he or she will. Whether the reader chooses to just eat what is already presented on this dinner table or to pursue the truth to its deepest roots is not this author's decision, but at least the opportunity is presented. Again, here is Cooper-Oakley in the same breath detailing how the Supreme Secret, the Divine Secret, or Nature's Secret was carefully deposited in the European crowns by this enigmatic eighteenth-century man, known to many European kings, princes, and several members of the highest class and nobility by numerous names but mostly by the name of the Comte de Saint Germain, yet virtually unknown by the European masses except leading enlightened minds:

In France M. de St. Germain appears to have been under the personal care, and enjoying the affection of Louis XV, who repeatedly declared that he would not tolerate any mockery of the Count, who was of high birth...(page 10).

D'Affry paid me a visit, and while speaking of Linieres mentioned that he was connected with St. Germain...I repeated to M. d'Affry several particulars which I had heard about St. Germain concerning his manners, wealth and magnificence...M. d'Affry observed that he was decidedly a very remarkable man of whom all kinds of stories were told, each more absurd than the other; for instance that he possessed the Philosopher's Stone, that he was a hundred years old, although he did not look like fort, etc.!...Yorke spoke of him as being a very cheerful and very polite man, who had insinuated himself into the cabinet of Mme de Pompadour and to whom the King had given Chambord...(page, 97).

We have here a very singular man. It is the celebrated Count de St. Germain, known throughout Europe for his learning and his immense wealth. He is charged with an important commission in this country, and he talks much of saving France by different means from those formerly used by the famous Maid of Orleans. We must see how he will set about it. He has a store of precious stones of the greatest beauty. He claims to have snatched from Nature her highest secrets and to know her throughout. But the most curious thing is that he is said to be over 110 years of age; he looks, however, not more than 45, (page, 109).

In France, where Comte of Saint Germain's *"words of warning fell on deafened ears, and advice went all unheeded"* (as Cooper-Oakley put it), the Supreme Secret was forgotten or polluted to the very least by the ill-advised violence of the French Revolution and with it the respect and admiration that England and much of Europe had left for her (France). The second attempt of restoration or sanitization also utterly failed when the stubbornness and disobedience of Napoleon, a suspected student of Comte de Saint Germain, got into his head and made him think he could challenge the Master. And with Napoleon's stubbornness, the fate of France's glory was sealed in the cold, and the glorious destiny that could have been hers went elsewhere to her sister land in the north and from there west across the Atlantic Ocean.

As present-day creative and esoteric mythologies like to put it, in America (having no kings) is the Light's Cup and the Freedom Bell (not the Liberty Bell) of the Supreme Secret were put in the custody of three of the most trusted brothers who are believed to have been princes and the children of the Comte de

www.makanologos.com

Saint Germain in their former embodiments in Atlantis and a few other carefully chosen luminaries. It has since been guarded in the holiest of the holy caves of Yellowstone, Grand Canyon, and Grand Teton National Parks, surrounded by hallowed mountains and guarded by lethal weapons on the land, under the land, and in the skies and seas. It stays revealed only to a few of the wisest, low profile, and most illumined souls of each generation. Only misguided folks attempt to find this Light's Cup and the Freedom Bell unguided by the Master within, as it is a distraction to one's main goal of accomplishing greatness.

Thus the Divine Secret traveled from Africa to the rest of the world. While being distributed to the illumined few around the world, it is now apparently securely guarded in the hands of Anglo-Saxons until the next cosmic cycle. Unlike Hebrew "slaves" in Egypt who focused almost with a single eye on and eventually stole the Cup of Light from their masters in Egypt, African slaves in America were too sidetracked with physical freedom to focus like a laser beam on the Light's Cup and Freedom Bell of the Supreme Secret. Otherwise, they could have easily apprehended them (and taken them back to enlighten the motherland) with basic entrapments of sex, infiltrations, and stratagems, as Abraham, Joseph, and Moses did in Egypt.

Racial, religious, or mere ideological differences may cause many to fanatically reject the originality of the Divine or Supreme Secret from Africa despite the evidence to the contrary, but by taking a look at the words of the British philosopher and mystic Paul Brunton, one may be impelled to at least think twice. These words may not soften a rigid mind but could prompt it to seriously take another look instead of just sticking with a radical point of view. Here is what Brunton writes in *Discover Yourself*:

Why was it that this path of esoteric knowledge had to be taught to man from the beginning of time? Because, the ultimate truth about life is so subtle and transcends the imagination of man to such an extent that without divine revelation, he could never have

www.makanologos.com

discovered it. It was first given to man as a revelation from the highest embodied being then existent on this planet. It was taught originally to the adept-kings of early China, Egypt, and other primitive African, Asiatic, and American peoples. At the time this high knowledge was imparted several thousand years ago, as mentioned in the 'Bhagavad-Gita, the knowledge had long been lost and had to be brought back' (pages, 190-191).

I will let you, the reader, make up your own mind on this, but I want you to know that the reason for bringing this point up to this extent is not to argue for or against one civilization or the other. It is rather to try to impress on your mind quite strongly how timeless is the truthfulness of the idea that genuine greatness is always a by-product of a good understanding of divine secrets. Greatness has always been built on the understanding, consciousness, and application of knowledge of God, not necessarily religion but the flame of the Presence of God within, which makes you one with the heart-center of the universe. Great feats are achieved with determination and belief in the highest ideal, the highest ideal being God, not religion. Brilliant minds are sharp minds, and God (the highest good) is the sharpener of brilliant minds. Heed this counsel if you really want to acquire a brilliant mind, for it is the most important advice in this book. God is the philosopher stone.

Conscious acknowledgment and contact with inner divinity is what takes man to the highest height of greatness; anything less than that would be a temporary if not destructive power. Looking to that inner Presence of God is the "Supreme and most Divine Secret" of greatness. Unless one looks to his inner divine power, he cannot attain greatness. As Brunton phrases it:

To succeed in your quest you must turn your mind inwards, keeping it at rest in the heart-center, while with the surface mind you are living the active...Follow this path and you will find the undying life and the ever-satisfying reward. It is the one way, which ancient and modern teachers have pointed out to humanity throughout the centuries, (pages, 206, 216).

That is the cause of greatness—association with God, not religion, that is. No man or nation ever attained greatness without associating it, him, or herself with God. The Soviet Union and Hitler are two classic modern illustrations of this truth. Their greatness came as fast as the forces of evil could deceive their senses and went as fast as those same forces (of evil) could submit to the forces of good (God). Conscious, sincere, and persistent determination for a constructive desire opens all the doors in the heart of God. Constructive cause powered by persistent, sincere, and unwavering determination is truly a mighty bomb that can destroy and shatter all your problems as nothing else in the universe can.

"In God we trust" is printed on the American legal tender bills and coins. *"In God we trust"* is not a fanatical inscription. It simply means that with our faith in God and our consciousness of His Presence in all we feel, think, and do, we believe God will do for us what He can do through us, and because it is God doing things through us, we can climb any mountain of greatness that stands in our way.

Discouragement, like fear, doubt, and anger, is anti-God, anti-Christ, and of course, if you will, destructive. Discouraged, fearful, and doubtful people do not leave marks on the world when they are gone. "I will leave it to God," they like to say. But the truth is that no amount of theory means anything unless there is work or action per se. True, everything should be left to God, but leaving something to God does not mean abandoning and quitting your part—action. I make this point because I feel it is important to clarify it. Trusting in God or consciousness of the Divine Presence in all we do does not preclude the indispensability of actions or work, for it is through your work and actions that God will manifest His greatness for you and through you. The law of the universe requires, at the very least, our best conscious effort in order for greatness to be achieved.

www.makanologos.com

It is practically impossible for man to walk a thousand miles per day, but with the aid of an airplane or automobile, he can travel that distance in a few hours. We all know that it is a blessing to travel a thousand miles by plane or car safely, and this is done not only by turning the engine on, but more importantly by giving the machinery maximum attention; otherwise, a deadly crash may be certain. God also works the same way—not that God is blind like an airplane or makes automobile accidents happen, but because He requires our consciousness of His presence and our undivided attention in order for Him to manifest His greatness through us. Consciousness of the Divine Presence and the dedication of our full attention to his powers are the best defense against the discouragement, fear, doubt, and anger that keep greatness out of reach of most people.

I feel the need to emphasize the evil of discouragement and the meanness of its powers. The powers of discouragement are so cruel that they turn Gods against man. A seeker of greatness should fear discouragement as he would fear a viper, monster, beast, or poisonous gas. Nothing destroys the heart and soul of man like discouragement. The discouraged man does not just die once; he dies twice, physically and spiritually. A discouraged person is always feeling pity for himself; he feels like the world owes him everything, whereas a determined person feels pity for the world for not feeling the fire that energizes his heart. (I treated this issue in much more detail in my first book, *The Best Kept Secrets of Personal Magnetism*, in the self-pity section; thus I feel no need to return to it.) Rather than cursing life, a determined person understands that wisdom, strength, and harmony are acquired by pushing a little harder all the time. He is always thinking about the debt he owes the world and how to pay it back. He appreciates everything he gets freely, including the air he breathes; health, friends, and family; as well as disguised blessings that come to him in the form of obstacles that constantly arise in his way to give him opportunities to become a better and stronger person.

While determination instills better and more knowledge and wisdom every time one fails and tries again, discouragement teaches nothing at all; in fact, it kills the body, the mind, and the spirit. Determination gives twice the amount of energy needed to achieve a desire while discouragement drains even the very least needed to exhale the next breath. While discouragement leads to sadness and slow and painful death, determination leads to happiness and a glorious exit from physical life. Determination is that loyal friend who lifts you up when you are down, visits when you are in prison or in the hospital, clothes you when you are naked, feeds you when you are hungry, and fights your sorrow. It is at your side when crisis threatens your body, heart, and soul, and it celebrates your happiness. Most importantly, determination is that friend who brings light at the darkest moment of your life.

Determination is the price we pay to gain the trust of God and acquire a brilliant mind. Life is energy, and energy released forcefully but consciously is great power. Arrogantly or otherwise, man always thinks that he is the doer, but in reality man is the receiver. In everything we do, there is always an invisible doer or giver. That doer or giver of everything is called energy. Energy does not discriminate; it gives all according to the effort; it does everything through the actions and rewards accordingly. The channel through which energy comes to us is the attention we give to the thing we are trying to achieve and, of course, to the source of that energy.

This channel, like a waterway, can sometimes be interfered with by a lack of attention or self-confidence, or a lack of self-control over feelings, thoughts, and actions. Men with this channel widely open may have never been born and are literally called the anointed ones, the lucky few in the likeness of the Christian Master, Jesus the Christ, Buddha, Krishna, Pythagoras, Plato, and their fellow avatars. But you do not have to be an avatar to climb the mountain of greatness; all you need is to leave a constructive and lasting impact on the lives of your fellow men. Anyone can do this—maybe not necessarily by consciously having a wide-open channel of Divine Presence at birth, but by striving to open it bit by bit until it is open enough to sustain it while feeling, thinking, and determinedly acting positively in everything you do.

Because the channels for receiving creative energy are, for all of us, somehow congested, determination is the instrument used to unclog them. Of course, the channels are not all clogged to the same level. For some, the channel is so congested that it requires a very strong force to just make a crack to let energy out. For others, maximum effort releases some energy. Still for others, adequate effort opens the way with amazing results. There is no way one can tell how congested his or her channel is. However, the love you have for the desire you want to achieve is a good indication of how your channel might release the necessary energy for you to reach your goal. The more you love something, the more likely you will excel in that domain; the less you are inclined toward something, the more likely your channel is not quite open.

Nature provides a mechanism to open or improve your channel of creative energy no matter how congested or open it is. This mechanism is called determination. As said earlier, talent by itself does not match the power of determination, but the combination of both is almost alchemy. Talent is simply an indication that your channel of creative energy will flow smoothly if you make an effort to widen it. Many talented people who have neglected the importance of determination have gone on without leaving the mark they would have otherwise left. Nature is a fair giver; it does not give anyone a channel that cannot release sufficient energy to bring about accomplishment. Energy comes from above, determination comes from below, and they must meet in order for greatness to manifest. Remember, "Awakening below causes awakening above." Determination must come first before energy is to act. Energy is always present, waiting for you to release effort through determination. It may take time for the triangle below to meet the triangle from above, for the "Star of David" to form, but they eventually meet by the power of determination alone. Again, as said above, for some it takes considerable time, for others none at all, but whenever they meet, sooner or later, magic unstoppably happens. That is the power of determination; it brings the inspirations of God and the aspirations of men harmoniously together and empowers minds of men to brilliantly climb mountains of greatness. That is how awakening below causes awakening above. Awakening above is never caused with mere supplication or self-pity from below but rather by awakening below, which itself is caused by self-awakening, self-reliance, and self-determination that lead to the discovery of true God, the ideal and source of all brilliant minds.

While caring, the forces of nature have never expressed sympathy toward man. If they did, man would be just one animal among others. The forces of nature trust man to fend off any threat against his life. Whether that threat is from animals or man himself, nature trusts man to forcefully overcome fear and doubt in his ability to defend himself before invisible helpers can come to the rescue. Trust has never been built on sympathy — neither between men nor between men and God. It is built on the merit and ability of prospective partners. A man who thinks by screaming at the top of his lungs will have the trust of the forces of nature without sustained effort in certain constructive activities, will never know the beauty of greatness, and will never step into the gates of the kingdom of happiness. Anyone who thinks he can open the door of a locked house by merely holding the key and never inserting and turning it all the way will be outside for a very long time. If you want to open the door of your house, the key must be fully turned — not half, not almost, but fully. If the price you pay in order

www.makanologos.com

to step into your house is to turn the key all the way, guess what the price is for greatness? Determination! Determination! Determination!

Feelings, thoughts, and actions, the three points of achievement, must be determinedly connected to form a triangle if greatness or anything meaningful is to be accomplished. Nothing can be achieved without those three elements being brought into perfect harmony with each other. Many people think determination serves to improve knowledge and action, but there is more to it than that. Of course, better knowledge and better action are important for any great achievement, but they are just the tips of the iceberg. No matter how knowledgeable or good you are at doing something, you almost certainly cannot do anything great unless you also have good thoughts and feelings. No man of negative thoughts and feelings has ever achieved greatness. If you are always thinking or feeling negatively, nature will always find ways of keeping you from achieving greatness. Determination not only enables you to sharpen your skill, but it (unconsciously to most people) makes it possible for you to brighten your thoughts and feelings. There is not a determined person

who does not think or feel good about his desire and himself.

The reason the majority of people are not in jail is that most of us try to control our actions, at least to an acceptable degree or enough to keep us from getting in trouble with the law. The reason the majority of people are poor is that most of us do not control our thoughts. The reason very few people are truly happy is that most of us do not control our feelings; we are, on the contrary, controlled by our feelings. Controlling actions is hard; controlling thoughts is harder; controlling feelings is the hardest. A less confident, sad, angry, fearful, or hateful person never reaches greatness. It is that simple. Great people are not simply masters of their actions and thoughts, but most importantly they are masters of their feelings. Most people control their actions, and many people control their thoughts in one way or another, but clearly, extremely few people control their feelings effectively. Controlling feelings is very difficult, and those who can have the key to self-mastery and greatness at their disposal.

Those who have the ability to control feelings automatically have the ability to control thoughts and actions. Feelings are spiritual, thoughts are rational, and actions are mechanical. The spirit controls reason, reason controls actions, and actions produce manifestation. Actions obey thoughts; thoughts obey feelings; feelings open the doors of the universe and the secrets of the Gods. Once you control your feelings and your thoughts, actions will follow like water running down the valley, and no dam will ever stop it. While they do not leave thoughts and actions to chance, determined people strive to control their feelings. Practically speaking, this simply means that if you feel good about something, you will think well about it; if you think well about something, you will act well on it; and if you act well on something, you will achieve greatness. It is like this: If you feel beaten up and discouraged, your knowledge and actions, good or bad, do not matter. But if you feel upbeat despite the heavy blows that life has stricken upon you, in the end you will conquer the ignorance, doubt, and fear that may have caused you defeat in the first place. This is one of the most cherished secrets of brilliant minds, which they protect with their beings.

Not only does greatness depend on how we handle our feelings, but also the fate of each one of us here on God's green Earth depends on how we manage them. Unfortunately, most of us do not know that to be the case. There are millions of people suffering from depression and anxiety simply for a lack of feelings management skills. They suffer and torture themselves sometimes for something they do not have control over, or they have mismanaged feelings about what they do have control over. They are depressed perhaps because fellow voters have elected someone they do not like, or maybe they

www.makanologos.com

are driving a five-year-old car but wish they were driving a newer one. Management of these two feelings can make all the difference in the world. If one could simply understand that he or she has neither the power nor right to impose his or her will on fellow citizens and that there are literally billions of people around the world who would feel extremely blessed to drive a five-year-old car, all the depression and anxiety will be wiped away and conscious attention will be fully put where it should be—on the Divine Presence and the task at hand.

Having said that, let's also acknowledge that controlling feelings can be a complicated exercise. The subconscious of man is a strong magnet and very sensitive to the chaos that goes on in the world around us. Whenever we see, hear, or sense a negative condition going on in the world around us or in books or motion pictures, most of us start consciously or unconsciously judging, criticizing, and condemning the event. Unfortunately, when we criticize, judge, or condemn what was not our business to begin with, we invite that chaos to play and register in our emotional consciousness, not just to rest but to one day come to life as our own experiences in one form or another. While you may think it is cool, often there is a time bomb in your own life that will sooner or later explode. Very few people know this, but unfortunately, ignorance has never been an excuse for violation of the law, nor does it change reality.

This is not to say that you should not look at the manifestations of life around you, but it should rather prompt you to avoid making opinions on what is not clearly your business. Awareness of something is totally different from opinion about something. I know you want to tell me how hard this is, but did you know that we all look at the sun every day without letting it blind us? Just as we look at the sun without letting it blind us, so can we hear other people's business without making unnecessary opinions. The world has just started learning the impact of this magnificent power over our lives. There are volumes of books,

www.makanologos.com

written mainly in the last one hundred years, on the subject of how feelings literally destroy or improve our lives, how events that we have no control over shape our feelings and our lives. A good student of life would do himself a great favor by exploring more beyond this little hint dropped here.

Now, what does determination have to do with it, you may ask? The question is pertinent; the answer is staggering. Determination has everything to do with it, of course! Those who feel helpless do not achieve much in life; that is a fact. Hopeful people and dreamers are dubbed, and rightly so, the saviors of the world. Hope may not be thought of as a method, but strong hope builds strong faith, strong faith stimulates good feelings, good feelings cause rational thoughts, and rational thoughts engender right and effective actions. It takes time to overcome helplessness; it takes time to really build faith in one's own Inner Self. Most people would rather believe in a fatherly God they can blame everything for, a God who sits on the throne miles away or somewhere in the nothingness of the universe, rather than the God in themselves who beats in their hearts and who is closer to them than their own breaths or arms. Brilliant minds feel good and believe in God and in themselves. They can call for help and get answers at the speed of thought, and that is what keeps them determined — knowing that in their calls are their answers, and life is its own defense when one is truly determined.

The self-confidence and self-knowledge that control feelings and that lead to greatness require a sustained and sometimes persistent determination because their fruits may take years, decades, centuries, or sometimes millennia to appear. Consider how long it took from the time Archimedes shouted "eureka" to the time the world was finally able to build cargo ships or submarines; the time it took from the construction of the first calculating machine by Blaise Pascal to the time your desktop, laptop, smartphone, etc. were built; from the time man first invented the wheel to the time we built bicycles, cars, and

www.makanologos.com

locomotives. Many Nobel Prize winners started their research at a considerably young age but did not earn their recognition until they were beyond the prime of their lives.

This is not to discourage you in any sense but rather to remind you that the actualization of your greatness will be decided by the strength of your determination. The more energy you release, the sooner your accomplishment. Usually most of us perform miracles in times of emergency, anger, or great fear, when we face life or death decisions, but we do not give ourselves credit for it. Man basically flies like a bird in the face of a mountain lion. This is not to praise fear or anger but to advise you that if you release the same energy as you do in the case of great danger, your achievement may not take long after all. When we know it is now or never, we study and pass a test we would have never passed otherwise. When a loved one is facing great peril, we work hard to find money to bail him out or pay for his medical needs. Many times we look for a job and do not find it, but when we are facing eviction and the possibility of homelessness is looming, we exceed our expectations and find a job to solve our problems.

What do you think makes a crippled person stand and run in case of an emergency? It is determination and self-confidence released with great power. The human mind is like a turtle; it sometimes needs a little bit of fire to move forward faster. There is magic in doing things with a determined attitude, doing things as if your life depended on it, because it does; doing things as if today was your last day on Earth, because it may well be. This is what made Alexander the Great and Napoleon the greatest military strategists who ever lived at such a young age; it is what made Theodore Roosevelt at 42 and Ronald Reagan at 69 the youngest and oldest presidents of the United States of America respectively; it was what made Pascal a great mathematician and inventor at 13 years of age. Potentially great people know that there is a power within them that cannot possibly fail. They understand that money, work,

www.makanologos.com

or even knowledge alone cannot be the source of greatness. They understand that once they finally and perfectly connect or align with that power within them, anything they give attention to will be accomplished. They understand that once effective collaboration with that Inner Power is established, magic happens. Thus they keep trying, by monitoring their feelings, thoughts, and actions to the last breathe they exhale.

Nothing teaches the law of cause and effect better than experience. Nothing! Students of the secrets of greatness know this secret all too well. They know it to the point that nothing fuels them with energy more than failure. Nothing ignites their inner fire faster and stronger than failure. For them, failure is nothing but the revelation of cause and effect, and an opportunity to learn and improve their approaches, adjust strategies, and replenish their strength. They know deep in their hearts that it is always darker before the dawn, and they are never fooled by the darkness that precedes the sunrise.

All undertakings that have attained legendary success are not necessarily products of power or talent, but rather products of persistence and determination. Few successes were built upon success, but most of them were built upon failures as a foundation. If you are a good student of history, you will notice that no movement ever experienced setbacks like today's great religions, Christianity and Islam. Their founders were persecuted and for centuries their followers slaughtered, but today kings, queens, princes, and heads of states all bow before Christian and Islamic high priests.

We have learned that the first two or three hundred years of Christianity were a series of setbacks, starting with the violent death of its founder, Jesus, and most of his apostles. Add to this countless imprisonments, murders, and harassments of its members throughout the known world of the time, but because of its persistence and the experience gained over the years, Christianity demanded submission from kings and princes, statesmen and generals.

www.makanologos.com

The American Revolution almost surrendered to the "invincible" British military power. Washington and his generals, and Hancock and his fellow Continental Congress members could have faced death by hanging for treason against the British crown until the British became overconfident, relaxed, and let pride go to their heads. Afterwards, Washington struck back and never let up on the attack until victory was assured, giving politicians ample peace and security to plan the destiny of the nation.

J. C. Penney and Kentucky Fried Chicken are two examples of business empires built on the ashes of earlier failures. Failure is the best tool great persons use to ignite their determination; it allows them to remove the feeling that man outside has more power than the MAN within who has complete control over his mind, feelings, thoughts, and actions. Greatness is never a gift; it is a battle to be conquered and a prize to be won. That is how all great people of history won their greatness—by overcoming failures and obstacles with inflexible determination. Determination is one of the backbones of this book. We shall come back to it again in the last section.

www.makanologos.com

CHAPTER IV

The Highest Knowledge of Greatness

Mankind asks ever of the skies to vision out what lies behind them. It is terror for the end, and but a subtler form of selfishness — this it is that breeds religions. Mark, my Holly, each religion claims the future for its followers; or, at the least, the good thereof... Seeing the LIGHT which true believers worship, as the fishes see the stars, but dimly. The religions come and the religions pass, and civilizations come and pass, and naught endures but the world and the nature of man. Ah! If man would but see that hope is from within, and not without — that he himself must work out his salvation! He is there, and within him is the breath of life and a knowledge of good and evil, as good and evil are to him. Thereon let him build and erect, and not cast himself before the image of some unknown God, modeled like his poor self, but with a larger brain to think the evil thing, and a longer arm to do it (H. Rider Haggard, She, page 146).

Know thyself and you will know the Keys of the Universe and the Secrets of the Gods. (Ancient Greek temple)

I start this paragraph with, hopefully not a revelation to many but something that I truly wish my readers to remember and ponder seriously, not only as they enjoy analyzing and studying the rest of this work, but most importantly when the time comes to apply the lesson learned here in real life. I believe the most important lesson, I could impress on the minds and intellects of my readers, is this: Acquisition of self-knowledge is acquisition of self-mastery, and self-mastery is the skillful and total control of energy in and around oneself. When one acquires total control of the energy in and around him- or herself, that person is free not only from error and failure but also from pain and suffering, for he or she acquires mastery over everything in the outer world.

Whoever does this will never need a human teacher as a guide in achieving whatever his or her mind conceives, for he or she will hold a greater power, wisdom, and freedom as a human mind can possibly imagine. To come closer to this achievement is what distinguishes the chosen few from the rest of the masses. Having said that, now let's take up the hard task of suggesting how you can understand yourself, not necessarily physiologically but psychologically and hopefully spiritually. I anticipate the possibilities of falling short of some readers' expectations, but I promise that if you verify this information or if you keenly ask the Master who dwells deep in your heart, your Higher or Inner Self, you will be prompted toward what will satisfy your heart and needs. Now let's go.

Of all the truths that exist, I know of none truer than the truth that stood high on the ancient Greek temple dedicated to Apollo: "Know Thyself" and all the priceless rewards of life will be yours. Since "Know Thyself" stood on the Greek temple, many people have looked for it in the Holy Bible, but it is not there, at least not in the Greek version of it. It simply is not there. This of course does not diminish its value or even the fact that the idea is not expressed in different terms by authors of the Bible.

The closest Jesus came to paraphrasing the inscription on the temple of Apollo in Delphi is when He said, as quoted in Matthew 6:33 in the King James Version of the New Testament, *"But seek ye first the kingdom of God and His righteousness, and all these things shall be added unto you."* And in the Old Testament, it is rather a practical explanation than a fiat. I will let you ponder this allegory for yourself. In 2 Chronicles 1:7-12, it is put this way:

7 That night God appeared to Solomon and said to him, "Ask for whatever you want me to give you." 8 Solomon answered God, "You have shown great kindness to David my father and have

www.makanologos.com

Exalted Secrets of Brilliant Minds   127

made me king in his place. 9 Now, Lord God, let your promise to my father David be confirmed, for you have made me king over a people who are as numerous as the dust of the earth. 10 Give me wisdom and knowledge, that I may lead this people, for who is able to govern this great people of yours?"

11 God said to Solomon, "Since this is your heart's desire and you have not asked for wealth, possessions or honor, nor for the death of your enemies, and since you have not asked for a long life but for wisdom and knowledge to govern my people over whom I have made you king, 12 therefore wisdom and knowledge will be given you. And I will also give you wealth, possessions and honor, such as no king who was before you ever had and none after you will have." http://www.biblegateway.com/passage/?search=2+Chronicles+1 (accessed December 2013).

The whole purpose of this book is to show the reader how he or she can acquire greatness as few have done before. I cannot state this point clearly enough: there is no true greatness without a truly smart and wise (not fanatical or naïve) association with God. Greatness without God (the highest and perfect Ideal) has never been; it does not exist and never will. I do not mean religiousness but rather God, who is not a domain of religions but of self-knowledge.

This premise may not square well with the thinking of some of my readers, but that is the philosopher stone; that is the divine truth; that is the Supreme Secret; that is the holiest of the holy secrets that the wisest kings and princes, sages and seers, high priests and the audacious few have kept intimately for themselves for centuries. Unless you understand this truth first, everything else will be meaningless, because to this truth I shall neither add nor subtract but will simply assist you in clarifying how to utilize it practically. And of course, yes, it is a secret, but it is not so much a secret because you may have known this already. The only difference between your knowledge and that of great people may be how to get in touch with this divine

www.makanologos.com

truth and utilize it the old-fashioned way. That is what this book will strive to explain, for, as said earlier, I strongly concur with these words of Ella A. Fletcher:

It is for this reason that to sensitive souls, the souls awakened to the Presence of the Spirit, the immanence of the God-Presence becomes in all the secret haunts of nature an abiding fact ever present to their consciousness. Therefore, these enlightened ones see more, hear more, feel more, and receive more from intimate association with nature than those average folk whose chief characteristics are their gregariousness, their obtuseness to blatant noise, and their love of excitement – often indeed, their acute horror of being alone. They are afraid of the mystery of life which in silence knocks on the door of consciousness – afraid because it has been clothed in terror when it should be radiant with beauty ("The Law of the Rhythmic Breath," page, 250).

One of the biggest myths average people are fed every day is that someone is rich because he or she is a good businessperson. Someone is president, governor, or senator because he or she is a good politician. A musician or an athlete is a superstar because he or she is a good singer or agile, and so on. Of course, this is all nonsense. People succeed in what they do not because they are good at what they do but because they know and understand themselves better than others. Knowing oneself, knowing your Inner Self, has indescribable rewards. While the inscription "Know Thyself" was on the door of the temple of the Greek Apollo in Delphi for all the masses of ancient Greek to see, inside was hidden the reward of knowing oneself for the few true seekers to see: *"You shall know the keys of the universe and the secrets of the Gods."* The call to *know thyself* was loud and was exposed to the public, but the reward that *you shall know the keys of the universe and the secrets of the Gods* was reserved for the daring few who stepped in.

If we take Jesus at His own word, you will find that by looking inside yourself, you will discover the kingdom of heaven and, of course, God Himself. In his book *Man Know Thyself*, medical doctor Raphael Ornstein said, *"Know thyself. Knowledge of oneself is the only real know knowledge, for as one understands oneself, only then may one truly understand another. Hence, the Oracle of Delphi proclaimed to know thyself, for within each of us, all is contained."*

Self-knowledge is the most powerful knowledge in the universe. It is all that man needs to break the human shell that holds the courage, self-control, self-mastery, fearlessness, limitless joy, happiness, enthusiasm, and self-confidence that empowers him to excel in science, military affairs, politics, business, technology, religion, and all that preoccupies the interests of man. Mark my words in the letters of light in your heart: You will never be great in science, business, sports, politics, religion, literature, philosophy, and what have you if you choose to know them without knowing yourself. Greatness is nothing but a direct outcome of self-knowledge, and brilliant minds know this truth — first things first before moving to outer adventures.

Man makes contact with the greatest powers of nature and the universe within himself, making him or her bigger than what many of his fellow men can scarcely understand. Go deep within yourself. There is more than just the physical body, which, in fact, veils the true you, the overcoat that the true you frequently leaves every night and several times during the day whether you are aware of it or not. As long as you consider your body as your "self" and neglect to discover the real you, you will NEVER know what greatness is, and you will never acquire a brilliant mind. The physical you is simply an apparatus to be used by your consciousness to get in touch with the physical world as it steps back and forth between your mental and spiritual you, the sole point of contact with the Supreme Master of the universe.

The German novelist Thomas Mann once said, *"No man remains quite what he was when he recognizes himself."* Knowing yourself totally reforms and transforms you in a way that makes it hard for even those close to you to recognize you.

www.makanologos.com

David King hit the nail on the head when he said, *"An individual cannot successfully deal with life and its problems if he does not first understand himself."* The subject of life and its problems do not require outside knowledge as much as they require inside knowledge. Think about starting your own business. Well, maybe what you lack is capital to start with. Hell no! Right at birth, man was fully funded with all his needs to start his own business. We were all given all the virtues that the wisest and smartest man uses to excel in anything. All that is needed is for the man to go inside, know himself by discovering what virtues are buried in the depths of his heart, and apply them to any problem life presents.

When wise ones say that "impossibility simply does not exist," they are basically prompting us that there is no limit to what a man who knows himself can do, that limits do not exist, and if they do, it is only when we place them on ourselves. If you want to be great, if you really want to attain true greatness, and you do not want to learn too much mumbo jumbo, the only subject I urge you to study is yourself. Again, it is regrettable that this truth is not clearly stated in the Bible, and here is where many of us get lost as we try to find and learn more about this truth from the Bible. Let me say this very clearly: I do not claim to be wise enough to judge the wisdom of the Bible, but if I had to find any disservice that the Bible may have rendered mankind, not clearly stating and teaching the wisdom of the temple of Delphi would be the one. Imagine if for the last 2,000 years the Church had been teaching people to know themselves better. Well, let's not speculate too much. I do not know whether man would have acquired enough power to shorten his workday at least by half or to eradicate corporal pains, but what I do know is that we would have more self-confident, fearless, knowledgeable, understanding, loving, wise, strong, and happy people, and of course fewer wars and fewer conflicts between people, between labor and capital, and even between nations.

www.makanologos.com

Make no mistake—I have no illusion about the difficulty of self-knowledge! But what is easy in life? How easy was it to send a robot to Mars? How easy was it to send a man to the moon? How easy was it to build an airplane, a car, or even a wheel, for that matter? Did we just cross our arms because it was labeled by some as impossible? How easy is it to support life, to support family, or just to be a good person? Aren't we today enjoying the pleasures of the hard labor of those who gave their all trying to transform the impossible into the possible? Greatness is really the call of your life. Should you give up knowing yourself just because it is difficult? To quote David King again:

"The man is a fool who makes little effort to know himself. He may have fun for awhile, but life will become increasingly bitter for him. He stumbles blindly along, doing whatever sounds good at a moment, trying to dodge responsibility for his errors, even as he repeats them. Such a man is only deceiving himself."

Those who strive to know themselves as best as they possibly can discover the Point of Contact with Inner Divinity. They become masters of not only themselves but of their fellow men, as well. They become our kings, high priests, seers, prophets, presidents, governors, popular artists, athletes, movie stars, etc. They become those we look up to in order to fill the inner emptiness of our selves. No magic is more miraculous than self-knowledge. All the forces of the universe, the invisible helpers, or the Gods (literally) come together to empower a person who knows him- or herself very well as he or she becomes a great channel through which they can assist the rest of mankind. The Bible says angels visited many biblical figures. Believe it or not, these people were not visited because they were better than you and I, nor were they special beings to deserve the angelic visits. They were visited because they understood themselves sufficiently enough to attract heavenly visitors. Recall that awakening below causes awakening above! Ralph Waldo Emerson once said, *"If I lost confidence in myself, I*

www.makanologos.com

have the universe against me." Well, do you want the universe on your side? If you don't, heed Emerson's counsel and then start finding yourself if you haven't yet.

Those who fruitlessly sought the intervention of God in order to succeed in their ventures tried to find Him on the mountains, in the valleys, in the forest, in the rivers, or in the sun or the moon to no avail. Great ones do not find divine power further than their own breath. They find it right inside themselves, closer than their breath and nearer than their hands and feet, right in their mental and feeling worlds. To be more precise, they find divine power in their own inner consciousness and nowhere else. The phenomenal American singer Tina Turner put it in very excellent words: *"The real power behind whatever success I have now was something I found within myself...something that's in all of us; I think...a little piece of God just waiting to be discovered."* I am not talking about religion or church here, for I am not myself a religious fanatic. I am allergic to religious indoctrination, just as cats hate water. I love God, but when I say God, I do not mean the old man in the sky but the Master within me who is the Great Architect of the Universe as well. That is the God I am talking about, the God of the inexplicable power we all feel inside and around our beings, the power that from inside us generates courage, faith, confidence, and enthusiasm, the power that surges with fearlessness and determination but fades with doubt or fear.

I do not know about you, but for me, God and religion are two different affairs—separate, not opposing each other, but they do not necessarily complement each other. I am striving to show you the real secret of greatness. You do not have to be religious. You don't even have to go to church. But you can never find it unless you go to that sacred rendezvous and meet Him deep inside you, within your mental and feeling worlds, because there inside you, you replenish yourself with the energy, intelligence, wisdom, strength, life, and harmony you need to succeed in the outer world.

www.makanologos.com

There is no other way. Your doctor cannot do it for you. Your teacher cannot. Don't even think about your mother or father. You cannot meet God on the mountain, in the valley, in the forest, or anywhere else but deep inside yourself, where all the keys of the universe are not hidden but kept waiting for you to reach out to them and step into the kingdom of heaven, the kingdom of happiness. Describing this simple secret to a happy life, www.truegospelpeace.com/thyself.htm put it in these words:

The Seven Sages of Greece understood the simple secret to a happy, peaceful, satisfied, centered and meaningful life about 500 years BC...All summed up in two words: 'know thyself.' When we know ourselves we know the truth that sets us free...free from fear and deeply held false beliefs, and consequently, free to be healthy, happy, satisfied and contented.

We get in trouble not because we are betrayed by our inner self but because our intellects and emotions override the promptings that come from the part of us that knows the universe best; the part of us that knows the past and the present; the part of us that foresees the future and forewarns us of the danger that is about to take place or reveals to us the fortunes that are ahead of us; the part of us that travels to the edge of infinity and back to its point of station in the universe in no time; that part of us that knows neither space nor time; that gentle, inner man whose voice Gandhi described as *the only tyrant he listens to*; the knowledge of and cooperation with the man inside us whose gentle voice and kind words are for our own good, not necessarily to please us but definitely to instruct us. The man inside us, our higher or inner self, 24/7 as time is understood by our intellect, looks for ways to work through us. Total surrender to that man is true self-knowledge and the source of greatness. Acquisition of a brilliant mind and union with our Inner Self are what mastery in all its pure forms is all about.

www.makanologos.com

Of course, total surrender or union with the Inner Self is a very difficult task while in a physical body. It is almost impossible for a human being to achieve total union with the Higher Self while still clothed with a physical body. But the goal of this book is not to show the reader a way to achieve perfection. Rather, it is to show that the effort, the march to the ultimate goal of life is the way to perfection, not only because perfection is perpetual or endless improvement, but because greatness is about becoming a better person on a constant basis, not about an achievable goal.

With this in mind, I want to be candid with my readers here. I want you to understand that I do not pretend to know the exact answer to the upcoming question to your total satisfaction. Your heart knows that, and I have neither the intention nor stamina to argue with it. What I know and what I want to suggest to you is what I know to have been used by so many great people whose life stories fill our history books and libraries. Thus, I have no doubt that if you choose to follow in their footsteps, you will likely be one of them someday.

You may think that because you heard of a $64,000 question, you have heard it all. Well, here comes a much higher-priced question: How do you *"know thyself?"* I am not kidding—that is a multi-trillion-dollar question, if you will. If you know an easy answer to that question, you can literally own the Earth, you can live endlessly, you can walk on water, you can raise the dead, and you can bring to life the images of everything that has ever happened anytime in the past, and so on. In short, if you know the easy way to knowing yourself, you literally hold the holiest of holy grails. And of course, if knowing calculus or physics is not easy, why should the highest knowledge in the universe be any easier? It is the law of life and universe—what is easily learned is little appreciated; "easy come, easy go." Do you get the point? I invite you to think about the intricacy of self-knowledge through these words of Charles Haddock in his book *Power of Will: "The world is fooled with 'literature' every day, and most of its readers relax in its enervating tide. Evidence: few 'get on,' few discover themselves and the universe about them — infinite globe of dynamic influences for elevation of the human soul,"* (page, 240). Do educated people know themselves? Haddock proceeds:

"Nowhere, today, probably exists a college or university wherein the individual shall study and master himself to a degree, before engaging in the smaller conquest of the infinite worlds... The universe, as a field of endeavor, reacts upon the individual, to be sure. But the true goal is to get the man to react rightly upon the universe. This requires self-development, sought by direct methods, as well as by roundabout methods of objective analysis and attacks...a man who can stand alone or go alone, as his real interests may demand; he has achieved the Mood of the gods, confidence in his own throne and dominion," (pages, 393-396).

Seven ancient Greek sages decided to teach generations of seekers of Light that the noblest of all life goals should be to *"know thyself"* because it gives the grandest of all imaginable rewards man can seek: *"and you will know the Keys of the Universe and the Secrets of the Gods."* Yet little is known of the method of how that goal can be reached. And ever since, no seers or sages have come forward with a straightforward suggestion. Well, do not get me wrong here. My goal is not to frighten or discourage you but rather to caution you to never expect an easy method, because there may be none for you. Every suggestion I will make here will require a sustained effort on your part if you wish to achieve greatness, as all great people have done. Greatness has never been anything but a prize won through difficult and complicated undertakings, through pain and suffering, through failures and victories, through trials and setbacks, and so on.

Greatness is not for the weak, faithless, fearful, and timid or those disheartened spiritually, psychologically, morally, or physically. It is for the very, very CHOSEN or DARING FEW, if you will. I cannot emphasize that strongly enough, but this does not mean you cannot be among the CHOSEN or DARING FEW because I believe the chosen few choose themselves first before Providence favors them among all others. I hope you impress this last point into your heart and mind with all your power and strength.

There is no committee anywhere on the face of the Earth that chooses the chosen few. To be one of the chosen few, you must choose YOURSELF through courage, fearlessness, determination, and any other virtue as dictated by life's challenges. Remember, no one chose Socrates, Moses, Joseph, Plato, Alexander the Great, Jesus, Christopher Columbus, Shakespeare, Napoleon, Lincoln, Gandhi, Martin Luther King, etc. before they chose themselves. You have the same privilege they had because time or space cannot alter that great law of life; anyone who obeys it will reap the same reward.

It is important to note that all great people may not have outwardly been seekers of self-knowledge. In other words, all great people may not have been aware of their quest for self-knowledge, but the path they traveled before reaching their goal made them more aware of the greater power and strength of the weaponry that lay inside themselves than that of all the arms they could possibly find anywhere else. Note that nothing you can do physically will lead you to the discovery of your Inner or Higher Self — nothing, that is, because through virtuous feelings, thoughts, and actions, you will compel your Inner or Higher Self to reveal Itself to you, not necessarily in a prophetic or apocalyptic way but in the feelings of peace, harmony, self-confidence, strength, and beauty inside you regardless of seeming obstacles in life (as these are just opportunities thrown your way by life to enhance your excellence) and the transformation of your qualities. Here is that path or road less traveled to greatness.

www.makanologos.com

PART TWO

THE ROYAL SECRET

CHAPTER V

Harmonious Feelings

I am almost certain that before you chose to read this book, you must have had some interest in self-improvement, metaphysical, or religious literature. If not, that is okay, but I am going to assume that you have at least some sort of education in one of those subjects. You may have read or heard that controlling thoughts and actions is imperative if you want to succeed in life. Let me confess it upfront before going any further; I am a firm believer in the power of consciously controlled and directed feelings. But do not rush to a conclusion here. I value consciously controlled and directed thoughts and actions immensely as well. I also know they have an inestimable impact on greatness, and certainly I will have plenty to say about them in the subsequent chapters.

For now, let's agree that if you have the power to run twenty miles per hour, you certainly have the power to run nine, eight, or seven miles per hour. If you can lift 100 pounds above your head, you can lift 90 or 50 pounds with less effort. I do not know about you, but I believe that if you can do great things, you can do small things. I believe that if you can control your feelings, you should not have trouble controlling your thoughts, and if you can control your thoughts, you can certainly control your actions. That is the point I am trying to make here.

The supremacy of feelings over thoughts, actions, and the rest is so important that no matter what kind of pictorial or charming words this author or any other, for that matter, uses, they will always fall short of satisfying many readers' hungry minds. To their minds, I humbly confess my shortcomings and refer them to their Inner Masters who know the best way possible to clearly and unambiguously explain what I am trying to explain and may have come up short here.

"The Heart has its reasons of which reason knows nothing," said Blaise Pascal, a French mathematician, physicist, inventor, and writer, a practical child prodigy who was educated by his father, a tax collector. Blaise Pascal was one of the brightest minds ever in the history of mankind. And it shows clearly that Blaise understood the supremacy of feelings over thoughts and everything thereafter. He understood that feelings can go deep into the heart, time and space, or infinity as reason can only dream of. Reason can and will never know the reasons of the heart, but the heart does not only know, it also has great influence over reason and its motives. To be more practical here, think about it. Between a happy and relaxed person on the one hand and a sad or angry person on the other, who do you think is smarter or has the better ability to process ideas efficiently? Think about it and read on for more light.

I believe actions obey thoughts, thoughts obey feelings, and feelings compel your Inner Self or Higher Self to reveal Itself to you, stay away from you, come to your rescue, or let you perish, depending on the quality of your feelings. Great people are not simply people of great thoughts and actions; they are primarily people of great feelings that enable them to attract not only fellow men to their assistance but also higher forces (invisible helpers). Thoughts and actions are much easier to control than feelings. Most of us are relatively mindful of our actions; relatively few people are consciously in control of their thoughts and actions; still fewer are aware of what is going on in their feelings. This tiny minority who has the

www.makanologos.com

ability to consciously control their feelings is the class of the great ones of every generation. Thus let me say this—you must be master of your feelings and sovereign of your passion, neither intoxicated by your success nor disheartened by defeat. Mastery over feelings is the royal secret, the best kept secret of true greatness.

Ability or failure to consciously control feelings alone leads to wisdom and performance or to madness and destruction. The feelings of fear, discouragement, doubt, anger, selfishness, etc. can lead to suicide, murder, robbery, treason, rape, laziness, etc., whereas feeling of courage, faith, hope, love, confidence, enthusiasm, justice, etc. can lead to...well, I will let you finish the sentence here. We get the knowledge of our Higher Self, or better yet our Higher Self reveals Itself to us, when we cultivate a culture of high vibrations or constructive feelings. A person of low IQ who is constantly feeling fearless, confident, trusting, and determined, and who is constantly in action will certainly fare better in life than one with a higher IQ but who is constantly fearful, hesitant, and distrustful of fellow men and actions.

This is the cornerstone of greatness. If you miss this point, you miss the train of greatness. Let me repeat it again—*this is the cornerstone of greatness.* Controlling your actions is great. Controlling your thoughts is superior. Controlling your feelings is supreme for keeping your feelings harmonious and in high vibration; it is what brings you closer to God, literally, more than anything else can. Any aircraft flies high depending on the vibration of its engine. Any high-vibration feeling causes better thoughts and actions and ultimately better outcomes in life. Genuinely happy, courageous, self-confident, fearless, resolute, assiduous people do not lead lives of misery in any way, shape, or form. They may not have material wealth, but the universe always supplies their needs, and their happiness is immeasurable. Greatness is not primarily about working hard or working smart; it is first and foremost about feeling good about and harmonious with what you think and do. Mastery

www.makanologos.com

of life is not controlling thoughts and actions but controlling feelings, because the result of well-controlled feelings is clean thoughts and constructive actions. Everything man is or ever hopes to be has come but through one way, and that is feeling. If you are always feeling bad, life will give bad thoughts, bad actions, and bad things. If you are always feeling good, life will supply you with good thoughts, good actions, and good things. And if you are always feeling great, life will supply you with great thoughts and, of course, great things. Feelings are actually the vessel through which everything comes to us; therefore, the cleaner the vessel, the cleaner the supply.

Poverty and wealth are not necessarily products of intelligence or hard work but of good and bad feelings. Your talent may never get you anywhere if you are a pessimistic, fearful, or discouraged person. As much as you and I would like it to be the opposite, unfortunately the world is not ruled by the sharpest minds, and most businesses are not owned or run by the smartest people. The world is ruled and most businesses are owned or run by those who feel excellent about themselves, their thoughts, and their actions.

The downfall of a strongman or business tycoon does not come when he runs out of good ideas but when he stops feeling excellent about himself, his thoughts, and actions. Good ideas can always be obtained from assistants or bought from consultants, but feelings are literally priceless. They are neither sold nor bought. They cannot be faked and can never be purchased. They have to be authentic, genuinely felt inside. They have to stimulate thoughts and actions. And most of all, they have to bring inner peace and harmony with oneself; otherwise, they cannot be a foundation of greatness. Thoughts and actions, on the other hand, can be secondhand or borrowed and still work, but losing the compass of feeling is usually the beginning of a disastrous end to greatness.

It can be argued that if people of great feelings run the world and businesses, why is the world in turmoil? The situation may

www.makanologos.com

not be perfect, but despite appearances, every generation is better off than the previous one because of the better feelings of the contemporary generation. Do not be cynical; give credit where credit is due. We are better off than both our parents and grandparents, and our children will be better off than we are as long as the world and businesses are in the hands of courageous, optimistic, confident, and happy people. Feeling is really the powerhouse of greatness. God inspires not the angry, fearful, discouraged, or doubtful people but those who feel harmony, peace, confidence, and happiness.

Man is more of a spiritual or emotional than a mental or physical being. Our feelings own our bodies, thoughts, and actions. When you say, "I like or don't like that," or "I have an idea," you do not mean your body, do you? You certainly do not mean your body does not like that or your body has an idea or your body's body, do you? When you say that, what you mean is that your feelings like or do not like something, or that your feelings have an idea or your feelings' body." The I, Me, or My is not the body but the feelings, even though you can still say "I feel" or "my feelings." The I is always the element of feeling, the unknowable, the Higher Self. Bodies, much less thoughts, do not feel pain, suffering, or happiness; feelings do. When feelings are in trouble, so are the body and thoughts. Feelings dictate what body and thoughts must like or dislike and even pursue.

Unless feelings are taken care of and directed appropriately, controlling thoughts and correcting actions alone will never get you closer to greatness. Just as a snake rejuvenates itself by casting off its old skin, man changes the whole structure of his being by changing and directing his feelings in a new and more constructive direction. Nothing in the universe is more revitalizing than energy poured into us by good and constructive feelings. Good feelings replenish unceasingly while bad feelings drain even the smallest you may have left. Good feelings heal while bad ones kill both the body and the

www.makanologos.com

mind. Only feelings stand between man and the greatness he wants to achieve. Greatness is not a product of a high-power intellect; it is rather a by-product of controlled, directed, harmonious, and constructive feelings.

The universe does not trust people because of their intellect. While the intellect is important, the universe trusts those who have the ability to master their feelings as they would master little puppy dogs. There are millions of people who have super IQs in many parts of the world, but they have no idea what to do with their intelligence. (Caution: I am not disparaging the value of a good intellect; I am just comparing it to a successful control of feelings.) You can easily find very smart people in poverty, drug or alcohol addiction, prisons, prostitution—almost anywhere. Many of them are living in the depths of despair and hopelessness; still others are turning into their own enemies. But you will be hard pressed to see someone who is truly a master of his or her feelings living other than an honorable and happy life in all its dimensions—maybe not a life of material abundance, but certainly a life of boundless joy and health that is worry-free. The intellect does not control the feelings, but feelings do control the intellect. Of course, the intellect can and has the power and freedom to choose to refuse the guidance of feelings, but that is where the conflict begins, and that is where most of us get lost. That is where the outer reality is disconnected from Inner Guidance, and the march into trouble begins.

The world we live in is not as simple as most people think it is. It is by far more sophisticated than anything we know. A person I know, a member of a certain prominent brotherhood (let's call him Jack), once cried to me, *"When my time to pass away comes, I hope it is quick and painless. Adios! I will gladly say. I will neither look back nor be nostalgic of nothing. This planet is not an easy place to live in. When I move on, I will never want to come back here again."* This, of course, is only looking at the glass as half empty. Yes, it is still the same world that our forefathers

www.makanologos.com

lived in. But did you know that if visits from the graves were possible, those who passed away not 1,000 years ago, not 500 years ago, but just those who passed away 200 years ago would hardly believe this to be the same world they lived in? They would most certainly think we had invented a different world. And why shouldn't they think so? In their time, it took months of high risk to travel from Boston to London; today it is a short flight of less than five hours. In their time, it took months to deliver mail posted from London to South Africa; today it takes only one click of the mouse. Two hundred years ago, in many parts of the world, international trade was based on the exchange of goods against goods. National currency was an invention of outer space aliens. Today, with a valid credit or debit card and a computer, we buy and sell products to and from almost anywhere on the planet. Strangers buy and sell products and services online with total satisfaction.

Our progress today would be extremely overwhelming to generations past had it been possible for them to come back and see what we have achieved. Yet all the laws of nature that have transformed the world of today have existed since the beginning of time. We still don't know much about these laws of nature, and we will never know everything about them. They are laws of eternal study, and you can bet that this world we think to be so advanced is nowhere near how it will look like just two or three hundred years from now. Some say what we know today is like a drop of water in the ocean in comparison to what our descendants will achieve centuries from today. The world will be a totally different place as life reveals itself more and more to men of harmonious feelings.

Now let's go back to our original question after this short deviation. But let me say this: It is not by accident that I brought up this point. I brought it up to make a point that I believe to be of great value, and I also believe I would not do my readers a service if I spoke of it silently. The truth is that many people really have no idea or understand very little about the power or

www.makanologos.com

the magic of feelings for life in general. Our safety or security, joy or sadness, success or failure, health or illness, life or death are all more subject to invisible powers than the visible ones, and all invisible powers that affect our lives, one way or the other, influence us mostly through our feelings. It is practically impossible to overstate the magnitude of our feelings. There is no word in the human vocabulary that can overemphasize the value of feelings when you think that even the blessings of God or the curses of malefic forces come to us through our feelings. Your feelings can be your best friend and redeemer or your worst enemy and your haunting devil.

Speaking in religious terms, there is no question that your feelings can literally lead you to your eternal salvation or damnation, and in practical life, they can take you to the highest mountain of greatness or to the deepest valley of despair. It is said, "As you believe, so will it be done unto you," which is another way of saying that as you feel, so will it be done unto you. Let me expand a little bit on this very important idea. "As you believe, so will it be done unto you" — what does it really mean? In my view, it means the following:

Good feelings change your vision. When you feel good, you see possibilities many people cannot appreciate. While others stumble around in bad feelings, you know where you are heading, and you have clarity of purpose. It means good feelings change your focus. You basically change your focus in a new direction, and that focus expands. Instead of your narrow and short-range dreams, you have bigger and better dreams. Good feelings are free and inviting. Invisible Helpers do not intrude in the affairs of men; they wait until they are invited through constructive feelings. They enter your province in the universe by invitation only. You must feel good about yourself before they can come to your service. Only your feelings attract or repel invisible assistants. Good and harmonious feelings are a switch that turns the light of Invisible Helpers on you and starts you thinking about and doing good. The apathy of your

www.makanologos.com

old way of living dissipates as the power of Invisible Helpers rolls through your mind, heart, head, and hands. Good feelings make you harmonious because your mind, heart, head, and hands want the same thing and move in the same direction. When you have good feelings, you are in agreement with Invisible Helpers and become a part of their unstoppable plan. Good feelings give you courage when you place your trust in your Inner Self. Good feelings make you realize that your Inner Self is your protector, the commander of your ship, and the unconquerable Master within, your conductor who will show you where to go and what to do next. They (good feelings, when passionately felt) make you know your destiny and stick with you until it has been reached.

Those who win big lottery prizes, for instance, or live amazing exploits may appear miserable outwardly, but inwardly they are people of magnificent feelings. It is no accident that those who feel inwardly depressed or stressful get more stress and more depression, whereas those who feel joyous, healthy, and wealthy just get more of those feelings. Even when death comes, they face it with courage and accept it with joy and happiness in their hearts. Read again and think about this quotation from Ella A. Fletcher:

It is for this reason that to sensitive souls, the souls awakened to the Presence of the Spirit, the immanence of the God-Presence becomes in all the secret haunts of nature an abiding fact ever present to their consciousness. Therefore, these enlightened ones see more, hear more, feel more, and receive more from intimate association with nature than those average folk whose chief characteristics are their gregariousness, their obtuseness to blatant noise, and their love of excitement – often indeed, their acute horror of being alone. They are afraid of the mystery of life which in silence knocks on the door of consciousness – afraid because it has been clothed in terror when it should be radiant with beauty. ("The Law of the Rhythmic Breath," page 250)

www.makanologos.com

The much-spoken-about devils in most cultures and religions are not actual beings living or hiding somewhere in the universe around us or in a special place in space, but they are our own feelings, the qualification we allow our feelings to become. If you qualify your feelings with safety and security, that is your Guardian Angel. If you qualify your feelings with fear of death, that is your devil of death. If you qualify your feelings with love, that is your God or Goddess of love. If you qualify your feelings with wealth, that is your God or Goddess of fortune. Or at least that is how we connect with those Super Beings or Invisible Helpers who bless mankind with positive qualities, or how we disconnect from them through fear, doubt, anger, hate, irritation, resentment, etc. The more constructive one feels, the more visits by Invisible Helpers will he or she receive, and the more destructive one feels, the more visits by destructive entities will he receive.

The secret of life appears so simple that most people pay little attention to it. Brilliant minds climb the highest mountains of greatness by feeling strongly the constructive urge of their desires. Sometimes their actions do not have to be so great or so strong, but because of deep, sincere, and positive feelings, channels open effortlessly. A man of average intellect but with enthusiasm, courage, confidence, and actions deeply rooted in his own positive feelings will achieve more wonders than a man of exceptional intellect with his hope and faith strongly rooted in friends, government, church, or any other external bodies.

How many times have people rejected, given up, or sold great ideas because their faith in them was not a deeply rooted, positive feeling? How many times have simple ideas produced wonders just because initiators have felt incredibly good about them? How many times have people walked safely from accidents or horrible situations because they felt no imminent danger? How many people have had happy marriages with mates they chose solely based on their strong, deep feelings,

www.makanologos.com

not wealth or fame? How many people have been cured of incurable diseases because their feelings refused to accept pain and death?

It does not take a genius to create a hamburger, but it took the deep conviction of positive feelings for Ray Kroc's McDonald's, not the McDonald brothers, to sell it to more than 58 million customers daily around the world. It is probably not magic to create a drink, but it took, again, the deep and positive feelings of Asa Griggs Candler to transform a medical product, John Pemberton's Coca-Cola, into a carbonated soft drink and sell it in more than two hundred countries. Notice that both Coca-Cola and McDonald's were invented by certain folks, but bought and widely promoted by others of deep conviction.

Human minds and intellects certainly have many sources that feed them whatever they want to accumulate, but there is only one power that sharpens and guides them through the difficult and happy times. If you want to enjoy a constructive way of life, you must send good feelings to your mind. If you send vicious feelings to your mind, is there any question that you will end up being counted among criminals or miserable folks? You know that self-confidence and self-discipline are indispensable to all good achievements in life, but unless you send a feeling of trust and faith to your mind, you will never gain those qualities. Inventors, explorers, industrialists, great statesmen, famous artists, great writers, and so on do not start with an idea—everybody has ideas—but they start with good and positive feelings about themselves, their Inner Self, and their desires.

Now, I can almost hear you say, "Wait a minute! I always have good feelings! How come I haven't climbed the mountain of greatness?" I am with you here, but one thing I want you to know is this (and I will talk more about it later)—our senses oftentimes mislead us. What we sometimes think we know and what we pretend to know are sometimes the dreams of our senses, the grand illusion, the much-talked-about maya, the

www.makanologos.com

delusion. Just because I say I feel good does not always mean what I feel is really a good thing.

Our feelings do not have to pass just the test of positivity and constructiveness, but also that of sincerity and conviction—or to put it bluntly, just because you appear healthy does not mean you are healthy. People live with cancer, heart disease, diabetes, and many other physiological malfunctions without the slightest hint. Sudden, accidental, or violent death is a part of the fabric of life; so are destructive, low-quality feelings or negative energy. Many times we think we feel good, but actually we do not. Life is full of many causes that we barely have any idea of. The secret of brilliant minds is not simply self-examination but also persistence in fostering and maintaining good feelings regardless of the appearances.

Many times, people are victims of feelings they do not know they had and deny them when the truth is otherwise. Not many people will acknowledge feelings of fear or doubt when they really have them. Sometimes we really do not know, and other times we are just in denial. Many times, people feel resentful, and because it serves their short-term interests, they think they feel good, but the truth of the matter is, resentment is never a good feeling.

But this is not strange; it is a dilemma that has haunted man from the beginning of time. I will talk more about making a self-diagnosis of feelings, mostly about self-protection against low-vibration feelings later on, but for now what I want you to know is this: This book is about greatness, and as stated earlier, greatness is about association with God or the wise use of divine powers. As far as I know, or as the lives of all the truly great people in history bear witness, nothing in the universe brings man closer to God than high-vibrating, high-energy, positive, or harmonious feelings. The proof is that you truly know something not when you think about it but when you deeply feel its existence and its function.

www.makanologos.com

Exalted Secrets of Brilliant Minds   **149**

The knowledge that raises man to greatness is not knowledge from the intellect but from the mind, the feelings, or the heart. We are what we are not because of what we know but what we feel. The following story will best express what I intend to convey to you. The other day as I turned on television to watch a CNN Sunday program, Fareed Zakaria's *Global Public Square* or *GPS* program, the host was interviewing a former *Washington Post* Pentagon reporter and at the time of the interview a Senior Fellow at the Center for New American Security think tank, Thomas "Tom" Ricks, who apparently had lived in Afghanistan during the early years of his life. Here are the questions and answers I downloaded from http://transcripts.cnn.com/TRANSCRIPTS/0910/18/fzgps.01.html. I will let you read them, then my comment on the other side of the story. The interview is a long one, but we will cut it short and go directly to what serves our interests:

THOMAS E. RICKS:...The Afghans have survived by smart — by observing...

RICKS: I think we've consistently underestimated Afghans. I used to live there when I was a teenager. And one thing I learned there is...a lot of Afghans, though, are illiterate. Illiterate does not mean stupid. In fact, I'm not even sure it means uncultured. The average Afghan probably knows more poetry by heart than hardly anyone in America. You can run into Afghan tribesmen who know hundreds of poems and thousands of proverbs. And we would consider their conversation quite literate. Even when I lived there, it seemed to me that guerrilla warfare was the Afghan national sport. One of my favorite books on this region is by John Masters. It's called "Bugles and a Tiger." It's a memoir of being a British officer with a Gurkha regiment in Waziristan in the 1930s. At the end of that last war that the British had there, the Afghan cousins showed up rather angrily and confronted him. "Where are our medals?" they said. He said, "Well, you were the enemy." And they said, "No, no. You gave medals to the Pashtuns on your side. We want our medals, too. You couldn't have had a good war

www.makanologos.com

without us." This is very much the Afghan attitude. This is a kind of sporting event for them in many ways.

In that same interview, Ricks magnificently described how Afghans (Taliban) were smart fighters who survived by quick tactics, taking out the United States' heavy weapons first, then taking advantage of every window of opportunity. As these words were written the first time, the war in Afghanistan was at its height, and President Obama was deploying an additional 30,000 additional U.S. troops to Afghanistan as part of a strategy to reverse the Taliban's momentum and stabilize the country's government. Yet at the time of the edition of this book, one year later, the U.S. government is in the process of drawing down troops and eventually ending the war without a clear victory against the Taliban.

Did you notice that the U.S. government increased troops and started withdrawing them without a clear victory? It shows that when one has very good feelings about oneself and one's cause, the size of the obstacle many times really does not matter. With good feelings, even the most daunting obstacle may become an object of entertainment. The point here, of course, is not to show how Afghans know the poetry and proverbs by heart but how self-confidence, persistence, and fearlessness are inspired by the feelings of wisdom and love contained in that poetry and those proverbs. Poetry has always been a great source of strength to Arabs in particular and Middle Eastern people in general. In his book *She*, Haggard writes:

Among the ancient Arabians the power of poetic declaration, either in verse or prose, was held in the highest honor and esteem, and he who excelled in it was known as "Khateb" or Orator. Every year a general assembly was held, at which the rival poets repeated their compositions, and, so soon as the knowledge of the art of writing became general, those poems which were judged to be the best were inscribed on silk in letters of gold, and publicly exhibited, being known as "Al Modhahabat" or golden verses (page 174).

www.makanologos.com

With the feeling of that wisdom alone, the so-called "poor" and "uneducated" people of Afghanistan have successfully defended their country against every "superpower" that has invaded it, from the ancient powers to the British colonialists to the Soviet Union to, now, the Americans. It is, of course, too soon to draw a conclusion about the latest conflict because, as these words are being transcribed, the war is on and the United States political and military leaders, as well as the American public, are debating all options, including giving in and pulling out of Afghanistan altogether.

But these are the questions that can and should be asked at any time before, during, and after a deadly conflict, everything else being equal: Which power prevails in the end? Is it the power of guns, bombs, and the mighty dollar or the power of poetry? Is it the power of pride or the power of self-confidence? Is it the power of trial or the power of conviction? Is it the power of stubbornness or the power of humility? Is it the power of hesitation or the power of action? Is it the power of force or the power of faith? Is it the power of ambition or the power of self-control? Is it the power of outer wealth or the power of inner wealth? Is it the power of the excited mind or the power of the calm one? Is it the power of world outer knowledge or the power of inner knowledge? Is it the power of the wind or the power of the mountain? Is it the power of the sword or the power of water? Is it the power of the bullet or the power of the dust? Is it the power of construction or the power of time? Is it the power of noise or the power of silence?

Well, take it from here yourself—ask as many questions as you like in whatever form you choose and you will come to the same conclusion that deeply rooted harmonious feelings are a product of a calm and collected mind or silence, which is the highest power in the universe from which all sprang. That barely audible and calm voice that speaks only in your heart and in the language only you understand is the highest power, wisdom, love, and beauty throughout the infinite space.

www.makanologos.com

Sincerely harmonious, positive, fearless, and determined feelings have an incredible power; they can pull incredible forces of the universe and concentrate them at your point in the universe. They can transform a man into a magnetic force that human intellect can barely imagine. They can remove the veil between man and those who are higher than him. These kinds of feelings are truly the open door to the powerhouse of the universe. On the other hand, chaotic, insincere, fearful, doubtful, hateful, thankless, exasperating, resentful, or ruthless feelings darken the heart, the mind, and the intellect of man. These low-vibration feelings close the door of happiness and joy. They put man in a cave of darkness and a box of poverty and miseries untold.

Harmonious feelings give you the highest of all knowledge, the knowledge of yourself. They reveal to you the very seed of your own being, the essence of your life. They give you the power to move mountains from land into the sea. They reveal to you the Point of Contact with Inner Deity. Harmonious feelings maintained considerably for a good length of time will do for you what no human language can ever possibly describe.

www.makanologos.com

CHAPTER VI

Governing Feelings

"And the LORD said unto Moses, wherefore criest thou unto me? Speak unto the children that they go forward." (Exodus 14:15, KJV)

While "knowledge is power," as Francis Bacon once said, "imagination is more important than knowledge," said Einstein. I would like to complement these two thoughts by saying that both knowledge and imagination are worth only the impact of the action they instigate. The possession of both right knowledge and right imagination and their right application are among the most essential requirements of greatness. In other words, great knowledge and beautiful imagination are almost worthless unless they are applied to produce a good effect that can be perceived by the senses. While reading is a great and noble action, by itself it does not carry a person to the mountaintop of greatness unless knowledge and inspiration acquired thereafter are acted on correctly.

One may read all the best-selling books ever written by the best minds in the world, but unless the knowledge acquired is acted on, nothing will happen. Much will be said about action in the next section, but while I am still here, something important needs to be made plain and clear in order to encourage the reader to seriously focus his attention on the upcoming chapters if a rewarding harvest is to be obtained at the end of the study of this work.

In his book *God Does Not Create Miracles, You Do!*, Yehuda Berg makes a very interesting analogy to this point. *"Electricity is always there. It is always present, ready, able, and willing to fulfill all of your power needs – you just plug in!"* You see! You can live in the best-wired house in the world, but if you do not plug in or turn on the light, you will most certainly not benefit from the miracles of electricity. Just knowing or imagining alone will not make anything happen. Unless something is acted on, nothing will happen. As a Chinese adage goes, *"Talk does not cook rice."* Some people fool themselves sometimes thinking that just because they have a physical phone and a phone number, they can talk to anyone. While having a phone and a phone number is a great step, one must dial first—and not just dial, but dial correctly—in order to be able to speak to one's party.

As Yehuda Berg phrases it:

Appreciation, awareness, and faith aren't enough. If you are stranded in a dark room, appreciating and recognizing the existence of electricity would not turn on the lights. You must take physical action—such as walking over to the on-off switch and flipping it to the on position. Making miracles is about effort, not faith. It is about doing a bit of work; not investing a lot of acknowledgement in the unseen force. It is about taking action now, as opposed to waiting for some supernatural force to intervene on your behalf at some point in the future, (page, 27).

He who thinks that the Promised Land (greatness) is for those who wait for God to come and lift him up from Egypt (inaction) into Canaan without actually walking toward it will be in for a long haul.

Reading or thinking about the truth, while great, is not sufficient. While the truth must be discovered and analyzed, it must, most importantly, be personally tested through action alone to prove its viability. A teacher who asks his students to take his word for it may not be a wise teacher after all. Happiness is the motor of life, it is said, but no one can ever know true happiness unless he acts for himself on what he knows and thinks. Actions are so vital and powerful that they are the only thing that can rearrange or alter the natural order of things and the laws of nature. Thanks to actions, not only does man fly (with airplanes) like a bird in the twenty-first century, but he, in fact, flies faster than any bird can possibly do by walking on at least three continents in one twenty-four-hour period.

www.makanologos.com

Greatness is about revealing what is concealed, and only action strengthened by knowledge, thought, and imagination has the power to reveal the marvels hidden in the mystery called life.

Yes, it is good to know. Yes, you take a step closer to truly knowing or discovering yourself by knowing the importance of harmonious feelings. But it is great to know that actions help in harmonizing your feelings. It is incredibly valuable to know practical steps that may lead you, with sufficient investment of time and energy, to knowing your Inner or Higher Self. Knowing the importance of harmonious feelings is a tremendous step toward climbing the mountain of greatness, but there are actions that need to be taken in order to really reach the mountaintop.

In this chapter, I will still be centered on feelings, but this time, rather than showing only their importance, I will strive to explain how to govern your feelings practically. I say *strive* because I sincerely acknowledge the magnitude of the task. Great sages, philosophers, prophets, and scholars have tried to undertake this task only to end up with humble success. While I do not promise to surpass their work, I hope to shed some light on this subject that will enable my readers, with some effort, to intensify and project further and see clearly his or her way up to the mountaintop of greatness. My effort, of course, may still be humbler than that of the great ones who have tried before me, but that is less important. What is important is the indispensability of your application. This is so because the result of your application will be the right evaluative measure of not only how well you understood, but also how well the method has been useful to you and if the time and energy you invested were worth the sacrifice.

Yes, while it is true that a tree is always judged by its fruits, the failure of the student does not translate into the ineffectiveness of the teacher or even the value of the teaching itself. But a good teacher, like a loving mother, always wishes the very best for his or her students and does everything possible to facilitate

www.makanologos.com

their success. A good author is not different; he or she always wishes that readers get the best inspiration, the best ideas and guidance from his or her work to lead them to their life goals. But this is not a mere wish; it is a deep desire, for I know if you really give your best, this work will lead you toward your goals. Consciously or otherwise, you will know yourself much better than you did before. As for the speed with which your will reaches your goal, that is entirely up to you. It is totally in your hands. In the business of learning and teaching as in driving, after giving all the necessary theories and best practices, a good teacher takes the passenger seat while the student drives. The teacher may only assist with directional supervision, but the student must do the heavy lifting of assimilating the instruction and driving the machinery — be it a car, a bus, or a truck — safely.

When you finally reach the stage of maintaining harmonious feelings sufficiently and a conscious understanding of your Inner Self, not only will you lighten the heart (of this author), you will give the time I spent on Earth, the efforts I spent researching and writing this book, their truest meaning. Have you ever wondered why, for centuries, man has been fascinated by the sun, moon, and stars, orbs that are forever out of reach of our physical self, yet he totally ignores the pearls that are buried in his Inner Self, which are closer to him than the air he breathes? I will attempt to show you, my diligent readers, how you can discover for yourselves the invisible connection with God (the Highest Ideal sought by brilliant minds) that lies within us all, that leads to true greatness, yet unknown to a vast majority of us.

Self-knowledge is not child's play. It is not impossible, either, but of course, it is not what most people fear or think it is. If you can really know yourself very well, you can do almost anything that you can imagine. You can basically crack the ceiling and step on the snake of impossibility right on its head to destroy it forever. It is done not by strengthening your muscles or by merely controlling your thoughts but by governing your

www.makanologos.com

Exalted Secrets of Brilliant Minds 157

feelings. Governing feelings is not really a choice for someone who wants to acquire the secrets of brilliant minds, because either you subdue them to your will or they rule you and you create greater chaos in your life. With this in mind, now let us see how you can go about harmonizing your feelings.

Governing feelings???

Remember this! A student of life, not a prophet, wrote this book!!! The difference between the two is that the latter tells us how easy everything is if we would only have faith, while the former shows us the possible pitfalls, the mountains, the thorns, the roughness of the road, the supplies to carry along the way, as well as the possibility of failure or losing one's own life if one is not careful enough or does not invest ample time and energy in thinking and learning thoroughly. As a student of life, I am conveying to you the experience and findings of the teachers of the past and present whose voices can be heard in libraries, online, and in the atmosphere around us if the inner ears are opened.

I may have to repeat myself from time to time because, as a student, I have lifted the heavy load by flipping thousands of pages of books written by masters or teachers of times past so you do not have to. I have done that to make your job easier. Thus it is my responsibility to show you the price and the rewards so you can make your decision with awareness that will enable you to pursue your goals with all earnestness. Hence, when you reach your goals, you can feel good about yourself and find the joy in helping others lovingly and happily. As I sincerely believe deeply in my Inner Self, life is one, and you and I do not have anything which to do anything that affects simply ourselves but life everywhere; for the greatest happiness a person ever knows is when he/she lives for the happiness and freedom of someone else. The average man, of course, does not realize that.

I will now start repeating myself, but beware that it is for your own good and not for lack of words or expression. I am

www.makanologos.com

sure you have heard many times that it is important to control your thoughts if you want to master yourself. I say you must govern your feelings first, not only to master yourself but also and most importantly to KNOW THYSELF. I say govern your feelings rather than control your thoughts because it is easier to track down your thoughts and discipline them. That is not so with feelings. Feelings are not easy to govern, in all senses of the word, because many times we are not even conscious of them. They can be stubborn, hideous, elusive, and even hard to notice. Most notably, feelings are stronger than thoughts. A smart person governs his or her feelings first before attempting to control his or her thoughts. We go to school to learn how to control our thoughts so we can be masters of or responsible for our destinies, but in the final analysis, our destinies end up being shaped by those who learn how to control their feelings and the feelings of others more efficiently.

Thoughts are easier to bring to the surface and examine; not so with feelings. They can conceal themselves in us even for decades without our realizing it. Anger, hate, fear, jealousy, doubt, etc. can take root and grow precariously before finally exploding out. "You cannot teach an old dog new tricks," it is said, and that is true. On the other hand, study after study has shown that young people are more liberal than older ones. Young people are more open-minded than their parents or grandparents, and that is just the dichotomy of the society we live in. But, oh yes! I can hear you screaming loudly at the top of your lungs, "Old people were young once, too. How did the change happen?" We are talking about the concealment of feelings; remember that. From a young age to our later days, like spiders, we build around ourselves a web of sorts. Undetectable low-vibration or negative feelings and opinions from the five senses creep into our subconscious just to come out unexpectedly sometimes. And when they come out with force, they can, like a natural disaster, destroy the work of years, decades, or even centuries.

www.makanologos.com

We tend to ignore those feelings and opinions we think to be very negligible. But would you agree with me when I say that the oceans are not merely made up of mighty rivers and great lakes but rather of invisible H_2O molecules? When you ignore low-intensity feelings and opinions, those feelings and opinions do not ignore you. They pile up little by little. Like a colony of ants, they build huge termite (cathedral) mounds until they practically overshadow your better side.

These low-intensity feelings and opinions that cause all kinds of irritation, resentment, unhappiness, self-mistrust, anger, selfishness, and so on sometimes simply do not go away until death itself comes to the rescue. They become your masters, and you become their servants instead of the reverse. Every time you make contact with your fellow men or even nature itself in general, you make opinions, consciously or unconsciously, that will trail you for a long time. The good ones, of course, will produce good offspring, and the bad ones will bear their offspring as well.

The thing is that you do not always know what you have already stored in your inner-feeling closet. To avoid this unconscious or involuntary creation of opinions and feelings, monks have sought safe haven in monasteries, but it has not proved to be a safe haven at all, as the evidence of priests' misconduct keeps coming to light all over the world. I guarantee that I will not attempt to offer a formula of immortality in this work. I will, however, strive to show you how you can acquire the treasures of life, the flowers of joy, the master keys of self-confidence, courage, humility, determination, beauty, and splendor to enjoy here and now or to take with you at the supreme hour into the greater world, if you so please.

Moses tried to mold our lives by giving us the Ten Commandments. While the Ten Commandments are great tools for moral conduct, they are by themselves not effective tools to lead man to self-knowledge. It is more complex than that. While many people like to console themselves with the

www.makanologos.com

Ten Commandments as a tool of self-knowledge, the followers of Moses themselves or those of the Jewish faith have what they call 613 *Mitzvot*, or the principal laws, ethics, and spiritual practices contained in the Torah. The number 613 is not inspired by the number of dos and don'ts but is ascribed to the number of bones and significant organs of the human body.

And of course, if the Ten Commandments were the only requirement, we would have more living saints than the prison and jail population in the United States alone. The wisest men have told us "to love God with all your heart and your neighbor as you love yourself," but the problem is that we don't always know whether what we are doing is really what we need to do as far as loving God and our neighbors is concerned. It gets even murkier because there has almost never been a visible or sensible sign of approval from Mother Nature concerning our love. Mother Teresa is believed, at least in the Christian sphere of influence, to have loved God and her neighbor as she loved herself. Yet Mother Teresa herself, in her own words, confessed to have never received a hint at all of God's presence, and surprisingly enough, she even at one point doubted His existence.

The aim here is not to show you how to become a better person than Mother Teresa, much less a saint, but to tell you that popular standards are just what they are. The average and ordinary are always inadequate to take one to the top of the mountain of greatness. I am not suggesting here that Mother Teresa did not govern her feelings or did not know any of the things I am going to tell you on the subject. I am just using what I know about her personal life to inspire your growth, not to pass any judgment on anyone whatsoever, much less the admirable Mother Teresa. Neither am I suggesting in any way, shape, or form that Moses and Jesus gave insufficient teachings. I am rather trying to encourage you to see their coded teachings with your inner eye and not with your external eye. In doing

www.makanologos.com

so, you can take a step or two further toward standing with the chosen few who climbed the mountain of greatness before you.

If you have gotten hold of the idea I am trying to convey to you here, as I trust you have, you will notice that I said that ideas or thoughts are easier to control with an investment of sufficient effort and energy because it is relatively uncomplicated to follow the flow of thoughts, but not so with feelings. Feelings can be like breathing or blood circulation. Sometimes we are conscious of our blood circulation or breathing, but many times we are not. Many times we are conscious of all the feelings we receive through our five senses, but many times we are not.

While our senses may be reporting to the mind some kinds of feelings and opinions they get from contact with the outside world, our subconscious or sixth sense does not care to supply us, as we would like, with the opinions and feelings it is constantly making on our behalf unless we make a conscious request (I will get into this in detail momentarily.) And here is where the equation, the complexity of life, and its trouble begin. The good news is that some of the feelings and opinions made by our subconscious are very ugly, and if we know about them right away, they can keep us from doing what we are supposed to be doing now. The bad news is, a mountain of debt can make you look rich for a while, but sooner or later you will have to pay.

Any person can mask his or her ugliness with makeup, but sooner or later, the mask will have to come off. Looking healthy is not the evidence of heath. This is the choice you have to make if you want to climb the mountain of greatness. Do you want to know the possibilities of having heart failure or heart attacks and take care of it now, or do you want to ignore them and hope for the best? Do you want preventive medicine now or a major medical operation down the road? Answer these questions however you like, but know this: great people do not postpone their obligations—big or small, simple or complex,

www.makanologos.com

tangible or intangible—for the next time if they can do it here and now.

They take care of their feelings as they go. They constantly strive to harmonize their feelings minute by minute, hour by hour, day by day, and so on. This chapter started with an unmistakably strong call for the necessity of action if results are to be obtained in any enterprise, especially in the business of harmonizing feelings. I started with the call to action and ended up with the same call for one major reason, and that is that the rest of Part Two of this work will be dedicated to the things that will help bring your feelings into harmony. But as I said earlier, just merely reading about them will not command things as stubborn as feelings to quiet down and behave unless you take persistent kinds of actions willingly. Harmonizing feelings is one the most challenging tasks anyone can face, but with persistent right actions, it is quite within reach of all of us. Now let's see some of the things you need to take action on in order to harmonize your feelings.

www.makanologos.com

CHAPTER VII

Virtues

Think of this made possible by the little seed of faith planted in the consciousness of one man, then allowed to develop. What has happened? Can you realize it? Columbus, in his day, was thought to be an impractical dreamer. Are we not coming to the place where we believe and know that the dreams of yesterday are the realities of today? For who has accomplished anything who was not a so-called dreamer? In this way we may recount the many visions that have helped make the world a better place in which to live?...Just as the seed knows that within itself it has the power to express the greatest, so must we know that we have the power within ourselves to express the greatest? (Baird T. Spalding, *Life and Teaching of the Master of Far East*, Volume I, pages, 65, 68)

Harmonizing feelings is a great challenge, as we said earlier. I may have to repeat these words a few more times down the road, of course not for the lack of words but certainly to move your attention toward a more concentrated state of mind. I may do so as well to heighten your awareness that if you are looking for easy formulas in life, then you may have to forget about greatness altogether. Now, that said, know this. If there is one thing that can lighten the task of harmonizing your feelings and revealing your Inner or Higher Self, it is this one thing spelled V-I-R-T-U-E-S. I say *virtues* rather than *virtue* because the more of them you can master; the faster you will climb the mountain of greatness.

Virtues are phenomenal in the art of climbing the mountain of greatness. In fact, virtues are not simply the real seeds; they are the roots, trunk, and branches of greatness. If you cannot handle virtues, you probably cannot see or approach the tree of greatness. Virtues are never mastered by weak souls, but they elevate anyone to the highest admiration of his fellow men. All the people you know or will ever know who have left or will leave a lasting positive mark on the wall of history and still, to this day, are charming generations after their passing are people of virtues. Virtues are not just seeds, roots, trunks, or branches of greatness; they are its wings as well. Virtues are to greatness what the ether is to life.

It is practically impossible to imagine greatness without virtues. If in saying that virtues are the seed, roots, trunk, branches, and leaves of greatness we left something out, let's add this — if greatness were a plant, virtues would be everything that comprises it, including the soil from which it grows as well as the air it breathes. If greatness were a bird, virtues would be its wings, not only to fly but also to maintain balance in the air. Life can possibly survive for forty days without food, seven days without water, a few days or hours without heat, two to three minutes without air, but only one or two seconds without ether. You can have all the money, power, or prestige in the world, but without virtues, you will never stand among the self-chosen few. In *She*, Haggard writes of virtues:

Behold the substance from which all things draw their energy, the bright Spirit of this Globe, without which it cannot live, but must grow cold and dead as the dead moon. Draw near and wash you in the living flames, and take their virtues in your poor bodies in all its strength…It was the mere effluvium of the fire, the subtle ether that it cast off as it rolled, entering into us making us strong as giant and swift as eagles (pages, 216-217).

The first and most important lesson taught to seekers of greatness is how to saturate their hearts, heads, and minds with virtues. If you saturate your brain with virtues, you will have the purest thoughts man can seek; if you saturate your heart with virtues, you will have the purest feelings man can hope for; if you saturate your mind with virtues, the Cosmic Beings (Invisible Helpers) will fill your being with the purest desires and your Inner/Higher Self with the Almighty Presence of

God. The more your life is guided by virtues, the closer to God will you be, marching head up toward any endeavor life has thrown your way. Virtues, as Haggard puts it, make you:

Shake loose thy spirit's wings, muse upon thy mother's kiss, and turn thee toward the vision of the highest good that hath ever swept on silver wings across the silence of thy dreams. For from the seeds of what thou in that dread moment shall grow the fruit of what thou shalt be for all unreckoned time (page 218).

Nothing takes you faster into the gates of glory than virtues. God chooses and works through virtuous people to expand His work. A virtuous person is a soldier of God against the vices that have enslaved mankind. The shortest and easiest way to win anointment from God is to lead a virtuous life. A virtuous, principled life is a prize that those who want to climb the mountain of greatness must earn before the Most High engraves it in their hearts.

People all over the world crave virtuous leadership. In fact, a government of truly self-governed people cannot survive if its leaders pay no respect to virtues. This is not to say that politicians are virtuous—far from that—but those who dare to show public disrespect to virtues pay a very, very, very expensive price. For instance, former President of the United States Richard Nixon thought he could conduct himself as president as if no one was watching or cared; consequently, he was forced out of office by both public and political leaders' anger. The *Washington Post* reported the following on its website:

Richard Milhous Nixon announced last night that he will resign as the 37th President of the United States at noon today. Vice President Gerald R. Ford of Michigan will take the oath as the new President at noon to complete the remaining 2 1/2 years of Mr. Nixon's term. After two years of bitter public debate over the Watergate scandals, President Nixon bowed to pressures from the public and leaders of his party to become the first President in American history to resign. "By taking this action," he said in a subdued yet dramatic television address from the Oval Office, "I hope that I will have hastened the start of the process of healing which is so desperately needed in America." (www.washingtonpost.com/wpsrv/national/longterm/watergate/articles/080974-3.htm, accessed 06/26/12)

Former Arkansas Governor and United States President Bill Clinton, in his legal conflict with a former Arkansas state worker, Paula Jones, thought he could get away with lying under oath, disregarding law, ethics, and virtues. Consequently, Bill Clinton became the second president to be impeached in the history of the United States. Wikipedia reported the following on its website:

Bill Clinton, *President of the United States*, **was impeached** by the *House of Representatives* on December 19, 1998, and acquitted by the *Senate* on February 12, 1999. The charges, *perjury, obstruction of justice*, and *abuse of power*, arose from the *Monica Lewinsky scandal* and the *Paula Jones* lawsuit. (http://en.wikipedia.org/wiki/Impeachment_of_Bill_Clinton. Accessed 10/10/09)

Virtues—not guns, wealth, or knowledge—take countries, organizations, and people to the height of greatness. In regard to the United States, its greatness is not a product of the War for Independence, the Civil War, or any other war, for that matter. Its greatness is basically due to the virtuous vision its early patriots set for the country. From the inception of the American Republic, protecting the liberty and rights of its citizens, justice for all who reside within its borders, the relentless promotion of charity, and service to neighbors and country have always been the true gospel of the American way of life. In fact, the genius of the American founding fathers is more in setting virtues as the ideal of the nation than winning independence from England.

You will notice that big business does not prosper because of its capital or the genius of its managers. The fate of a big or small corporation is always entirely in the hands of the virtues it

www.makanologos.com

Exalted Secrets of Brilliant Minds **167**

puts forward and lives by. A company that behaves unethically without regard to professionalism and quality customer service is basically committing organizational suicide. When you go to a store like Wal-Mart, as you come and go, you unavoidably notice the display of some virtues by which the company strives to live: appreciation and gratitude. As you come into Wal-Mart, a courteous lady or gentleman greets you — "welcome to Wal-Mart" — and after your shopping is over, as you walk out, a polite employee is paid to just say, "Thank you for shopping at Wal-Mart."

Those are not just slogans but virtues that Wal-Mart strives to live by, and in fact they are the secrets of its success and the success of any other company you know. Many big banks and even Wal-Mart's competitors have adopted the same strategy, for their lives depend on it. A virtuous person is an instrument of greatness everywhere. Even in sports, talented but ethically unworthy athletes are fined and suspended all the time, and many are even cut from their lucrative professions in their prime despite their talents. This author is not so naïve to think of Wal-Mart as a perfect organization. It has its nasty imperfections. But the goal is to show you, the reader, positive lessons that the average person does not always see so you can learn from them for your own growth. Good organizations everywhere actively seek virtuous (not perfect) people to fill their most trusted positions. Even law enforcement, such as the FBI, NYPD, LADP, U.S. Army, Navy, and Marines, etc., will prefer a person with top security clearance (a trusted person) than someone with a top IQ who cannot obtain security clearance (cannot be trusted). Many fraternal organizations will not admit a person who is ethically challenged much less a former defendant in criminal court.

Virtues make the mammoth task of monitoring feelings doable. Virtues will not only take you to the gate of glory, but they will open the door for you to step in. Human desires can change the world but for a short time, whereas virtues change

www.makanologos.com

lives and the destiny of mankind forever. At some point in time, Napoleon, Hitler, Stalin, and other arrogant and despotic leaders were the masters of the universe, but the earth of their empires either collapsed under their feet as the sky fell upon their heads or collapsed shortly after their passing. Solomon, Washington, and Gandhi, on the other hand, not only changed the course of the destiny of the world, but the world is still benefiting from their time on Earth.

Virtues are the real powers that revolutionize society and the destiny of mankind forever. Virtuous individuals are always in the good care of the Most High, regardless of their apparent social status. A person who wants to climb the mountain of greatness must not only mirror virtues but also apply them in his or her life. Only morally ill people despise virtuous individuals. In other words, virtue, the monitor of feelings, is a moral attitude that is irreproachable by any sane person. A society that honors a dishonest over an honest person is a sick society in dire need of bitter medicine, for it is doomed to die.

Virtues may not make your life safe. History is full of virtuous people who experienced atrocious deaths — some on the cross, some by stones, some burned alive, some by death squads, some by hanging, some by hunger, some by hemlock — but the air they leave behind is always one of magnitude. An atrocious death or suffering is never an excuse not to live or not to strive to live virtuously, for death can only destroy your body (which sooner later will be food for worms anyway). It can never destroy your spirit, which will ultimately climb the mountain of greatness.

Man has no stronger enemies than his own passions, fears, discouragement, hopelessness, selfishness, arrogance, ignorance, or self-mistrust. As powerful as they seem to be, none of these enemies of man can stand in his way when he is saturated with virtues in his or her heart, head, and mind. As stepping on its head instantly smashes a snake, virtues bring feelings in harmony with each other to crush passion,

www.makanologos.com

fear, selfishness, self-pity, ignorance, and all their acolytes, mercilessly and triumphantly and in an extraordinary manner. A man who does not hold virtues in high esteem cannot ever reach the mountaintop of greatness regardless of the power and wealth he may possess.

Power and prestige can be bought, but greatness is neither sold nor bought; it is worn like a trophy with the sweat of wise actions. Virtues are the light that shines brightly within us and allows the radar of God to locate us despite what goes on in our world. It is by living a virtuous life that only a few men become magnetic like the sun, a powerful concentration of light; thus the chosen few become Great Masters of the Universe. Without virtues, man cannot attain self-mastery much less win the praise of his fellow men. A man who is guided by virtues will always guide himself, reach his Inner or Higher Self, attain self-mastery, and therefore guide others as well, for his are harmonized feelings.

Only virtues (the power to harmonize feelings) are capable of unlocking or revealing the reality of life from the inner standpoint and dissolving the illusions of the outer senses of man. Science and religion are guiding mankind today not because they hold any truth in themselves but because they try hard to inspire virtues. What do you think science would be for the world if "scientific integrity" was not held in the highest esteem? A South Korean scientist who thought he could fool the world by presenting counterfeit research outcomes learned this fate the hard way as reported by the *Los Angeles Times* in articles on its website:

A disgraced South Korean scientist who falsely claimed to have achieved major breakthroughs in stem cell research was convicted Monday of charges connected to his research and faced sentencing later in the day. Hwang Woo-suk, 56, was charged with accepting funds under false pretenses, embezzling and illegally buying human eggs for his research, which carry a total maximum penalty of life in prison. It was not immediately clear

www.makanologos.com

which charges he was convicted of. Prosecutors have demanded a four-year prison term for the man once hailed as a national hero for his purported scientific breakthroughs. (http://www.latimes.com/news/nationworld/world/la-fgw-skorea-cloning27-2009oct26,0,5787969.story, accessed Nov. 2009)

What do you think Christianity or any other religion would be today if humility was not the first law of priesthood? Asked by his bickering disciples, here is how Jesus shut down the misguided power of self-importance:

[1]At the same time came the disciples unto Jesus, saying, who is the greatest in the kingdom of heaven? [2]And Jesus called a little child unto him, and set him in the midst of them, [3]And said, Verily I say unto you, except ye be converted, and become as little children, ye shall not enter into the kingdom of heaven. [4]Whosoever therefore shall humble himself as this little child, the same is greatest in the kingdom of heaven. [5]And whoso shall receive one such little child in my name receiveth me. [6]But whoso shall offend one of these little ones which believe in me, it were better for him that a millstone were hanged about his neck, and that he were drowned in the depth of the sea. (http://www.biblegateway.com/passage/?search=Matthew+18%3A1-6&version=KJV, Matthew 18:1-6, King James Version)

Virtues are timeless. They never go out of style, and masters of life of all times know that. All great teachers in history have presented their teaching as explanation and common-sense living of virtues. Had Jesus, Confucius, Buddha, Socrates, Plato, and many more not based their teaching on virtues, not only would their names have been forgotten like billions of others who have lived on Earth, but also their teaching would have disappeared long ago.

"He who wants to be the greatest must serve others and be like a little child," said the Master. One day when I picked up my children from my ex-wife's house, on the way home, my son, Joseph, who was eight years old at the time, said this: *"Daddy, I will tell you what I know. I know that a strong man stands for*

himself, but a stronger man stands for others." Those few words told by a child entered my heart like a spear and have never ceased to come to my mind when an opportunity to help others offers itself. They were so strong to me that I decided to tell my trusted friends at work about it. When I told my coworker the story, he said, "Your son was right. And I would add to his thoughts that *"if you want to handle yourself, use your head; if you want to handle others, use your heart."* Wow! I was speechless.

Many days after those conversations, I sought asylum in the kingdom of silence, asking myself just one question—why? Why is a man who stands for others stronger than the one who stands himself? Why does handling others require a heart? When I came out of exile from silence and after a few exchanges with another good friend, I learned that one is stronger for standing for others, and it requires a heart to handle others because it involves the implication of several virtues.

The more virtues you bring together, the more energy and force you draw or focus in one point. The universe always propels a gentle wind in the back of a virtuous person. Even germs are frightened by the aura of a virtuous man. A man whose powers are driven by virtues not only conquers lands, but he also conquers the hearts of men. For centuries, the noblest souls from all over the world have always journeyed (or dreamed of journeying) to the apparently poor land of Tibet in the Himalayan Mountains. Why? Because people in that area of the world strive to worship virtues; therefore, there are more sincere disciples of light in that region than possibly anywhere else. Virtues have guided the wisest of children of man. Organizations, civilizations, and even the universe itself are guided by virtues.

Wise civilizations, nations, religious or fraternal organizations, businesses, and even individuals have always chosen for themselves special virtues to enlighten their lives, work, or missions. In his letter to Corinthians 13:13, Paul, one of the founding fathers of Christianity, set aside faith, hope,

www.makanologos.com

charity, and love as the theological virtues and the devotion of adherents of the Christian belief system. These virtues are believed to perfect one's love of God and man, and as a result, they harmonize feelings and enhance prudence. The Hindus have a range of virtues that followers regard with the highest esteem among others. They are *"altruism or a selfless service to all humanity; restraint and moderation: self-control in everything one does; honesty; truthfulness with all mankind; peace; cleanliness and non-violence etc."* The Buddhist tradition, on the other hand, has a kind of progressive list of virtues. The Noble Eightfold Path outlines the following as the virtues to be practiced by a devoted Buddhist believer:

Right View — *Realization of the Four Noble Truths*

Right Intention — *Commitment to mental and ethical growth in moderation*

Right Speech — *One speaks in a nonhurtful, not exaggerated, truthful way*

Right Action — *Wholesome action, avoiding action that would harm*

Right Livelihood — *One's job does not harm in any way oneself or others, directly or indirectly.*

Right Effort — *One makes an effort to improve*

Right Mindfulness — *Mental ability to see things for what they are with clear consciousness*

Right Concentration — *Wholesome one-pointedness of mind* (http://en.wikipedia.org/wiki/virtue, accessed Nov. 2011)

Greek philosophers, mainly Plato, defined four basic virtues — *Prudence, Justice, Temperance,* and *Fortitude* — which later became known as the four cardinal virtues and were adopted by the West as the Western virtues. From the four cardinal virtues, the Catholic Church, a central pillar of Western civilization and illumination, defined seven virtues. On top of the three theological virtues — faith, hope, and charity — it added the four cardinal virtues — prudence, justice, temperance, and fortitude — to form seven virtues.

www.makanologos.com

We can go on and on listing virtues as practiced in different cultures, religions, nations (a motto is a virtue regarded as an ideal for each nation), or even individuals. The goal here is not to tell the reader what virtues belong to which cultures, organizations, or individuals, for that matter, not only because virtues are universal properties but because they belong to no one. Only their users can claim them not as a culture or religion. An individual claim of any virtue does not make anyone great except through use.

Unused knowledge makes nobody smarter, wiser, or happier, and in fact, it passes out of the mind. To become great, acquired knowledge must be transmuted into actions. In presenting this wisdom to readers, I want to show them how this information can be used in order to attain greatness. For that reason, it would be a disservice to my readers to pass to the next segment without illustrating how one of the most admired great men in America, if not in the whole world, used virtues to harmonize his feelings and truly climb the mountain of greatness in everything he put his hands on, including philosophy, physics, politics, diplomacy, writing, printing, and business.

Few would disagree that this person's greatness did not impress generations long after he passed on. In the minds of many, his is a greatness whose star is still brightly shining high not only in the skies of America but of the world, or at least anywhere freedom, justice, and self-government of loving people are found. This man is Benjamin Franklin, and rather than trying to put words in his mouth, let him speak for himself. In his autobiography, Franklin writes:

It was about this time I conceived the bold and arduous project of arriving at moral perfection. I wished to live without committing any fault at any time; I would conquer all that either natural inclination, custom, or company might lead me into. As I knew, or thought I knew, what was right and wrong, I did not see why I might not always do the one and avoid the other. But I

www.makanologos.com

soon found I had undertaken a task of more difficulty than I had imagined. While my care was employed in guarding against one fault, I was often surprised by another; habit took the advantage of inattention; inclination was sometimes too strong for reason. I concluded, at length, that the mere speculative conviction that it was our interest to be completely virtuous was not sufficient to prevent our slipping; and that the contrary habits must be broken, and good ones acquired and established, before we can have any dependence on a steady, uniform rectitude of conduct. For this purpose I therefore contrived the following method.
(http://www.ftrain.com/franklin_improving_self.html, accessed June 26, 2012)

As Franklin tells it in the same publication, in 1726, at the age of 20 and when barely out of the folly of adolescence, while on a ship voyage on his way to Philadelphia from England, he was inspired by a New Testament verse from the letter of Paul to the Philippians 4:8, which reads, *"Finally, brothers, whatever is true, whatever is noble, whatever is right, whatever is pure, whatever is lovely, whatever is admirable – if anything is excellent or praiseworthy – think about such things"* (New International Version). Benjamin Franklin defined for himself thirteen virtues that he chose to be the compass of his life. Here are the thirteen virtues as Franklin defined them in his own words:

TEMPERANCE: *Eat not to dullness; drink not to elevation.*

SILENCE: *Speak not but what may benefit others or yourself; avoid trifling conversation.*

ORDER: *Let all your things have places; let each part of your business have its time.*

RESOLUTION: *Resolve to perform what you ought; perform without fail what you resolve.*

FRUGALITY: *Make no expense but to do good to others or yourself; i.e., waste nothing.*

INDUSTRY: *Lose no time; be always employed in something useful; cut off all unnecessary actions.*

www.makanologos.com

SINCERITY: Use no hurtful deceit; think innocently and justly, and, if you speak, speak accordingly.

JUSTICE: Wrong none by doing injuries, or omitting the benefits that are your duty.

MODERATION: Avoid extremes; forbear resenting injuries so much as you think they deserve.

CLEANLINESS: Tolerate no uncleanliness in body, clothes, or habitation.

CHASTITY: Rarely use venery but for health or offspring; never dullness, weakness, or the injury of your own or another's peace or reputation.

TRANQUILITY: Be not disturbed at trifles, or at accidents common or avoidable.

HUMILITY: Imitate Jesus and Socrates.

(http://www.flamebright.com/PTPages/Benjamin.asp, accessed Nov. 2009)

Franklin did not just write this moral prescription for himself and place it on the shelves of his library; instead, he placed it on the shelves of his life, his daily behavior. Whether he was always 100% obedient to his self-imposed rules is another story; nevertheless, he tracked his own performance on a daily basis. As to Franklin's obedience to his own rules, www.flamebright.com reported that:

He recorded his progress by using a little book of charts. At the top of each chart was one of the virtues. The charts had a column for each week and thirteen rows marked with the first letter of each of the thirteen virtues. Every evening he would review the day and put a mark (dot) next to each virtue for each fault committed with respect to that virtue for that day" (accessed Nov. 2009).

The same website also says that Franklin himself in his biography wrote:

I made a little Book in which I allotted a Page for each of the Virtues. I ruled each Page with red ink, so as to have seven columns, one for each day of the week, marking each column with a letter for the day. I crossed columns with red lines, marking the beginning

*of each line with the first letter of one of the virtues, on which line
and in proper column I might mark by a little black spot every fault
I found upon examination to have been committed respecting that
virtue upon that day,*
http://www.fordham.edu/halsal/mod/franklin-virtue.
html accessed Nov. 2009).

At the beginning of each day, Franklin would ask himself
this question: "What Good shall I do this Day?" And at the end
of the day: "What Good have I done today?" The questions for
you probably would be: Was Franklin always successful? Was
he perfect? Then why did he record his shortcomings and not
his achievements as far as the application of his chosen virtues
was concerned? To the first question, I may say yes, he was
successful to a great extent in observing the virtues he set for
himself. While staying true to his core values was not an easy
endeavor, eventually it served him well because it eventually
helped him to leave his foot- and fingerprints on the great wall
of history.

How many princes, lords, barons, presidents, or even
kings of the last two thousand years can match the impact of
Benjamin Franklin on modern history? For the last fifty years
of his life, observation of his virtues served him extremely well
to the point of earning him a place of high honor in the hearts
of his countrymen and countless people around the world. The
impact of Franklin is easily felt when you consider numerous
prestigious corporations that want to associate themselves
directly or indirectly with him by either adopting his name or
using his likeness to portray the integrity of their business. The
U.S. one hundred dollar bill generates pride and confidence in
the hearts of millions of people who carry it around the world,
not merely for its buying power but mostly for the moral
principles it mirrors through the image of Benjamin Franklin.

Now, was always Franklin perfect? Of course not! He never
came close to perfection. He was known to be a womanizer
despite his sworn observation of the virtue of chastity. He was

www.makanologos.com

known to dress impressively in order to attract the attention of his contemporaries despite his loyalty to the men he liberally chose as his role models, Jesus and Socrates, both for whom humility was one of the strongest pillars of their teachings. The question of whether Franklin was perfect in the observation of his virtues is both unfair and irrelevant. If you are looking for perfect men to be your role models, then Franklin is not one of them. The fair and relevant question is what was the overall impact of virtues on Franklin's life in general?

And the answer would be that while he was not perfect, as no man is or ever will be. Franklin was a distinguished and respected man not merely because of his social rank but mostly because of his personal conduct among his fellow men. His behavior was far above the average man's, and that is why he attained the greatness that he did. The average man rarely attains greatness, as he is many times shortsighted. Franklin's secret of greatness, on another hand, was his desire to shoot for the sun. He never got anywhere near there, of course, but he probably landed on Venus or maybe on the moon when a vast majority of us rarely shoot for the top of the tallest tree in our backyards.

Secondly, why did Franklin record his faults and not his achievements? For fifty years, he strived to measure himself against some of the hardest pillars of wisdom, the smartest and wisest men ever and he strived to stand against the strongest spiritual battle any mind could face. Did he conquer any one of them outright? Definitely not! By his own account, for more than fifty years he recorded failures on a daily basis, not that there were no successes, as these were incorporated in his actions, but to dedicate more effort to improving his weaknesses. In this regard, in his autobiography, he wrote:

I entered upon the execution of this plan for self-examination, and continued it with occasional intermissions for some time. I was surprised to find myself fuller of fault than I had imagined; but I had the satisfaction of seeing them diminished. To avoid the trouble of renewing now and then my little book, which, by scraping out marks on the paper of old faults to make room for the course, became full of holes…I never arrived at the perfection I had been so ambitious of obtaining, but fell far short of it, yet I was, by the endeavor, a better and happier man than I otherwise should have been if I had not attempted it. (http://www.ftrain.com/franklin_improving_self.html)

It is not known how many notebooks Franklin used and how much ink he poured onto papers to make a written account of his shortcomings. The final question now is, why didn't he record his achievements? While a good answer to this question has already been provided above, the better answer is that he left that for others to figure out, not just by making a long list of his successes but by following in his footsteps and walking a dignified life, which led him to climbing the mountain of greatness.

His contemporaries counted Franklin among the wisest of his time. Later generations have built monuments, buildings, streets, companies, and even cities in his name. Was it easy to live by virtues, and was it worth it? No and yes. No, it was not easy. But just because it is not easy does not mean that it should not be tried. Franklin revealed his practice of virtue to the world not as a mere public revelation of his secret life but to urge his own son, William, daughter, Sarah, and grandchildren to live by them. Did he win a bruising victory, and was it worth it? *"Yet I was, by the endeavor, a better and happier man than I otherwise should have been if I had not attempted it,"* he wrote.

Repeat over and again this confession of Franklin in your heart and mind, and see what other skies it will open for you. And should it open the mind of Franklin to you, you will notice that this great man credited all his success in physics, politics, business, or any other endeavor he undertook to his pursuit of virtues alone. I will have to confess that I was so carried away by Franklin's relentless love of virtues that I felt no urge to stop and move on to other topics. I will let the reader take it from here to find out more about the man who earned the title of the First American.

But before moving on to the next chapter, I want to close this one by reminding the reader of an old Roman adage: "All roads lead to Rome." From Los Angeles, California, you can get to London, England, by flying or navigating east, west, north, or south. Of course, there is a shorter and easier way of getting to London or any other point on the globe from anywhere on Earth. I strongly feel it would be a disservice to my readers if I did not mention the last point on the topic of virtues. That is why I want you to know that the most important thing to understand is that there are always several methods to choose from when achieving a goal as long as they are well defined. Just as you would go to London from Los Angeles by flying over Denver, Chicago, Boston, and Ireland, you can get there as well by flying west over Honolulu, India, Turkey, Greece, Italy, and France. It should not be distance or means to determine the direction you take to reach a destination but your safety first. Sometimes, what matters is not being smart, but acting like a very smart guy can pay lofty dividends.

The assumption for most people is that NASA or the U.S. government has unlimited funds. They do not, believe it or not, regardless of what popular wisdom thinks. I mean no offense to NASA here, but what serve them well are not their IQs but rather acting like theirs are the highest among men. If you have not noticed, NASA rarely postpones a mission due to budgetary concerns; however, it frequently suspends missions due to weather. That is not a budgetary matter but rather one of safety and comfort because, in the end, it all comes down to getting there safely and securely. Do you get the point I am trying express here? If not, worry not—keep on reading. I will not dig deeper but will just switch the light on for your mind to see better.

Just as greatness can be achieved by obeying or living by certain virtues, as with Franklin and many other great people, it

www.makanologos.com

can also be realized by avoiding vices. Vices are the opposite of virtues. Virtues and vices, or sins (as they are called in religious language), are as opposite to each other as fire is to water, light to darkness, death to life, and vice versa. They are opposite to one another like two sides of the same coin; they never see one another and will never cohabit. Unlike virtues, rather than following and obeying them, you must avoid vices in order to reach the mountaintop of greatness. www.deadlysins.com/sins/lists what are known as the Capital Vices, the Cardinal or Seven Deadly Sins that must be avoided in order to harmonize feelings and reach the height of greatness according to the Christian faith. They are defined as follows:

1. *Pride: is excessive belief in one's own abilities that interferes with individual's recognition of grace of God. It has been called the sin from which all others arise. Pride is also known as vanity.*

2. *Envy: is the desire for others' traits, status, abilities, or situation.*

3. *Gluttony: is an inordinate desire to consume more than that which one requires.*

4. *Lust: is an inordinate craving for pleasures of the body.*

5. *Anger: is manifested in the individual who spurns love and opts instead for fury. It is also known as wrath.*

6. *Greed: is the desire for material wealth or gain, ignoring the realm of spiritual. It is also called Avarice or Covetousness.*

7. *Sloth: is the avoidance of physical or spiritual work.*

These vices are based on Christian faith. You can either choose entirely new vices that you want to avoid — vices that you feel cause chaos in your feelings, obstruct your moral rectitude, weigh down your integrity, and deploy every effort and power of your being to avoid them at all costs — or you can combine them with the Seven Deadly Sins and come up with a considerable list of vices to avoid in order to lighten up your moral compass and your journey to the mountain of greatness.

www.makanologos.com

Mahatma Gandhi, one of the greatest personalities in the historic social and political changes of the twentieth century, used avoidance of vices to win a place of honor in the hearts of people in his country and around the world as well as the hearts of his supposed enemies. He designed a list of seven vices he considered to be the most spiritually dangerous to mankind and the roots of violence:

1. Wealth without Work.
2. Pleasure without Conscience.
3. Science without Humanity.
4. Knowledge without Character.
5. Politics without Principles.
6. Commerce without Morality.
7. Worship without Sacrifice.

Through the avoidance of these vices, Gandhi was able to carry on his message of nonviolence as he marched to the mountaintop of greatness. Avoidance of these vices was not a mere slogan to Gandhi. In practicing the avoidance of the second vice, it is believed that Gandhi and his wife severed their sexual relations while their physical needs were still very strong.

I can go on and on, and I still have a lot in store concerning how greatness has been achieved through virtues or avoidance of vices, but that is not the main objective here. The objective here is to choose and live a virtuous life while avoiding vices in order to harmonize your feelings and enable yourself to climb the mountain of greatness. Therefore, it is very important that attention be turned back to you, the reader, as the close of this chapter nears. It is and must be about you. I spoke of how Franklin and Gandhi climbed to the mountaintop of greatness by walking on the opposite sides of the same mountain not to fill the gaps in the book but as powerful illustrations so that you know that what I am talking about here is for real. It is this way that the great ones of old, whose influences are the compasses and enlightenment of our minds today, did it. They came by

www.makanologos.com

living and practicing virtues in ways an average man cannot even dream of, as well as avoiding vices through discipline and determination.

I brought up some of these light posts of our minds (Franklin and Gandhi) here as teachers from whom we can all and should learn if we want to climb the tall, slippery, rocky, and quite possibly deadly mountain of greatness. There is nothing more and nothing less. I am a strong believer in self-education. I believe the best way to learn is to learn from the Master within who patiently awaits your awakening below to releasing awakening above, to show you in enlightening letters and golden voice the secrets of the Gods and the keys of the universe. The hard way to learn is to learn from someone else, and the best way is to learn from the Inner Master, for He is the Master of Masters. It is my deep belief that there is no better or greater teacher in the whole universe than the Teacher that is within, the Inner/Higher or Better Self of our beings. A lesson learned from that Master of Masters, the Lord of Lords, the God of Gods, whose voice only you can hear, is never mistaken or forgotten and has the power to alter all the obstacles created by the dreams and illusions of our senses. Virtues and vices inspired by the Inner Master to be obeyed or avoided will give all the strength needed for you to climb any mountaintop man can envision.

One of the major reasons religions have not inspired mankind to the best of its abilities is that they simply keep sending people back to the prophets and seers of the past, when the prophets themselves said the vault of all knowledge and the secrets of God are within. In case the feather of doubt is scratching your conviction, let me ask you this question. Where did Jesus point out the Kingdom of Heaven to be? Is it in the sky; on the mountain; in the oceans; in the center of the Earth; in the galaxies; in the north, south, east, west; or WITHIN YOU? I would be glad to suggest the answer, but I prefer to let you check it out for yourself.

www.makanologos.com

The Good Lord knew all too well not to make the same mistake our priests keep making by asking us to open our eyes and look high up to God rather than telling us to look inside ourselves, which is the center of our universe where the Best Teacher awaits us to prepare ourselves for His appearance to your inner/higher senses. Virtues that worked for Franklin and avoidance of vices that worked for Gandhi may not work for you. No author can tell you what is suitable for you, for only your Inner Master knows best your strengths as well as your weaknesses. Thus, rather than suggesting what to do at this point in order to arm yourself with virtues that will carry you to the mountaintop of greatness or vices to sidestep as you climb that mountain, I will simply point out where to go to find virtues that will assist you on your way up to the prize that every human soul craves every day of his or her life—GREATNESS. Only your Inner Master or Higher Self can reveal to you the best virtues that you must observe with a balance of inspiration and reason, as well as your worst vices that you must check with a balance of judicious mercy and sound judgment on your way up to the mountain of greatness. This is one the best-guarded secrets of brilliant minds. Now you know, I hope.

www.makanologos.com

CHAPTER VIII

The Land Mine of Virtues

I feel the need to say a few words here before going deeper into the body of this chapter. First of all, I predict it will be one of the shortest chapters of this book. Second, in the upcoming chapter, the reader may have the impression of redundancy, thinking that I repeated myself somehow. Should this be the case, I will understand. But the reality is that this chapter is actually a sort of synthesis of both the previous chapters and the coming ones. For instance, you may notice that this chapter is about silence, while a bigger, deeper, and wider chapter on silence is coming up. Silence has such inestimable influence on virtues that I felt it was imperative to talk about it here more distinctively as related to virtues, particularly rather than greatness in general, hopefully to better impress it on your mind.

Now, let me say this—before I try to show how great civilizations and brilliant minds have been led by virtues, I want to say a word or two about the origin of all virtues so that you may decide to choose the virtues that you believe will lead your life to the best of your expectations. I trust you will have little problem, if any at all, doing so if you open your inner eyes wide enough to see the light I will strive to shed before you. I will, however, first invite you to read, as many times as you need, these words from Baird T. Spalding until you feel comfortable with your understanding of them. If you do not get it the first few times, continue reading the book, but be sure you come back until you are at ease with what you see in your mind.

This is called the Temple of Silence, the Place of Power. Silence is power, for when we reach the place of silence in mind, we have reached the place of power — the place where all is one, the one power – God. 'Be still and know that I am God.' Diffused power is noise. Concentrated power is silence. When through concentration (drawing to a center), we have brought all of our forces into one point of force, we have contacted God in silence, we are one with Him and hence one with all power. This is the heritage of man, 'I and the Father are one.' There is but one way to be with the power of God and that is consciously to contact God. This cannot be done in the without, for God manifests from within. 'The Lord is in His holy temple; let all the earth be silent before Him.' Only as we turn from the without to the silence of the within, can we hope to make conscious union with God. (*Life and Teaching of the Masters of the Far East*, Volume I, page 35)

Why did I suggest you ingrain the understanding of this teaching of Spalding before moving on? Because I want you to know that silence is the source of virtues and everything else you know or do not know. Silence is self-created and all-creating. It is the mighty voice of Infinity, the voice of God. It is from Silence that Light, Life, Truth, Wisdom, Strength, Love, and all other virtues and qualities find their essence. In the realms of Silence is where the teachings of Moses, Jesus, Buddha, Mohammed, or any other great religious teachers came. The science of Archimedes, Galileo, Newton, or Einstein; the philosophy of Socrates, Plato, Saint Augustine, or Descartes; and the legendary leadership of David, Alexander the Great, Joan of Arc, or Napoleon all came from the kingdom of silence.

If you have been observing carefully, you must have noticed that Moses, Socrates, Jesus, Buddha, and Mohammed were not enthusiastic scholars. Neither were many scientists and philosophers whose influences rule our minds today. Indeed, they were extremely well educated. They were scholars as no word can explain it. They got a good education that few men have ever gotten or will ever get, but not in the formal traditional schools you may have in mind like, but rather in the schools of silence. *"When asked how he came to discover the law of gravity,"* Frank C. Haddock wrote in his book *Power of Will,*

"Newton is reported to have answered, 'By always thinking about it'" — in silence, of course. And guess where Newton was when the power of silence revealed the answer to his longing to him. He was in isolation under an apple tree.

At the end of the last chapter, I purposely suggested inquiring of the Master within to show you your best virtues as well as your worst vices. I suggested you do so because I know deeply and feel the significance of the matter. Choosing virtues to live by and vices to avoid is not child's play. While this point is beyond the scope of this work, I want you to know that the whole Hebrew esoteric teaching better known as Kabbalah, alchemy, and white magic is mostly based on the understanding of the "tree of life," which is nothing but the knowledge of a wise and smart manipulation of virtues and avoidance of vices. That is what the correct manipulation of virtues and evasion of vices can do for you.

Now, if or when you want to choose virtues that you wish to light your life with, do not go far. Silently go to the center of the universe within your heart, and everything you need to know will be there waiting for you as long as your intentions are sincere, firm, and selfless. Let the voice of silence tell you what is best for you. You may want to settle for the average prize, but if you want the noblest virtues to enlighten your life, only the voice and torch of silence can reveal that to you.

The planets, the suns, the stars, the moons, even the galaxies and systems of worlds, angels, Gods, the four elements of nature, light, life, and other great powers of nature and even the universe itself get their initiations or secret education in silence. And their wonders are not only limitless, but they are impressive every time. Silence has been proven to be the most effective way of learning and teaching. Smart and wise governments, universities, corporations, and scientific research centers around the world spend billions of dollars just to provide their researchers with the calmest environment money can buy. While constant hurricanes, tsunamis, floods,

www.makanologos.com

volcanoes, and other natural and man-made disasters seem to make our Mother Earth look to be in chaos, the truth of the matter is that harmony has been maintained throughout the universe by the power of silence. The Earth is not broken, regardless of the folly and illusions of our senses. We are not here to fix nothing. Roads, bridges, airplanes, locomotives, computers, etc. are not made to fix anything in the structure of the Earth itself but rather to satisfy man's insatiable needs, not the needs of the Earth. The silence that reigns throughout the infinity has everything under control. If the schooling of silence is good enough for the celestial orbs and Beings, it is certainly good enough to pleasingly quench the thirst of your mind. Silence gives of itself and everything else unselfishly and abundantly with only one condition. In the fabulous words of Spalding in one of his several volumes:

The Great Principle stands forth as a Golden Light. It is not remote, it is within yourself. Hold yourself within the glow, and you will behold all things clearly. First, with all being, know one thing: that your own thought when you stand is one with thought that brought forth the world...Let pass through your mind, my son, only the image of your desire, which is Truth. Meditate only upon the true desire of your heart, knowing that it does not wrong any man and is most noble.

Silence can give anything it is asked for, as will be explained later on, but if you are asking for a greatness whose influence will inspire the minds of men long after your footprints have been wiped from the face of the Earth, you must do it as Spalding beautifully described. You can choose to rely on the Bible, Quran, or any book of your faith, but this you must know— they are words of God as far as their spirituality is concerned. Literally, they are indeed the words of men who walked on the ground we are walking on now; who breathed the same air; slept, worked, and ate like the rest of us; but who found their way to the source of timeless knowledge and courage to

www.makanologos.com

pass it to future generations by going in the silent centers of illumination within themselves.

The majesty of the power of silence is virtually indescribable by the tongue of man, much less the pen of this poor author. In striving to make the power of silence as clear as I can, I just wish I could whisper what my consciousness knows and feels about it, but hopefully you do not need the Inner Self of this author, or anyone else's for that matter, because your own Inner Self has the power to speak the very language of your own mind and heart that you can understand best.

Men who rarely seek the benefits of the power of silence have their souls and minds enslaved by the power of gravitation, whereas those who seek the benefits of the power of silence frequently levitate their minds and souls at will and explore the hearts of beings, matters, and affairs as only great souls and minds can. These blessed few who adore the power of silence with all their strength are present at the center of their universe and at their peripheries at the same time; they have the true understanding of what seems to be a mystery or myth and infinity to the mass.

Only in silence can man acquire and control the irresistible forces that move mountains standing in the way of mankind's progress and enlightenment. Only on the wings of silence can a man fly into the great cosmos of purest light. Only in silence can man conquer the greatest enemies of the human race: fear, doubt, anger, and self-faithlessness. Only in deepest silence can man hear the voice of infinity and learn the truest priesthood of God as only a handful of children of Earth has done. Only in silence is the Truth of the Beginning and End, above and below, within and without, Divinity and humanity revealed to man. Only in silence is the greatest command of creation—"Let there be Light"—still heard. Only in silence does man acquire the power of seeing the ends of great feats at their beginnings. Take a second to reflect on the eloquent description of the amazing power of silence by Brunton:

www.makanologos.com

The voice of Silence is better than the voice of the priest. "Noise is unpleasant to God. Men pray in silence," was the admonishment of one of the sacred books of Amen-Ra, the Sun God. Let go of your dearly-held dogmas, enter into the sublime Silence, and wait for the dawning of Light. It is useless to use verbal prayer, excepting under stress of great emergency; ordinarily your worship must be conducted in silence. This is true worship which will bind you to God and because it binds you to God it is real religion (Discover Yourself, pages 46-47).

A friend of mine once told me that everything Jewish is always wrapped in mysteries, and that is what makes Jews very thoughtful—their effort and willingness to find the deepest secret in everything visible and invisible. And nothing is more mysterious than the Jewish name of God. There are literally countless books written about the true name or names of God. For the last five thousand years or so of their history, Jewish people have been preoccupied by the search for the true name of God, to no avail so far. The futile search has led some Jewish people to some wild conclusions. Thus, in Judaism, the true name of God itself is believed to be the ineffable word, inaudible or inexpressible by the lips of man because it is written and pronounceable only in the language of God, the language of silence.

And as with everything Jewish, the end is seen in the beginning and vice versa. Therefore, the answer to latter-day Rabbis is nowhere else but at the beginning of all Jewish mythology. Consider this: The Talmud, a central text of mainstream Judaism—basically anthropology of some of the wildest legends the human mind has ever created and that have inspired and strengthened the Jewish people throughout the centuries—relates that Eve may not have been the first wife of the fabled patriarch Adam, the biblical father of the human race. His first wife, Lilith, says the Talmud was metamorphosed into a demon after overpowering Adam during an unsuccessful sexual intercourse attempt, causing her to dare pronounce the ineffable name of God in defiance. The myth of Lilith is, of course, beyond the scope of this work, and I will not go much further, but this I wish you to know as you ponder the power of silence: Many so-called secret societies, the ancient ones and their modern successors, were built on the idea that the path to salvation is the journey to discover the true name of God, a journey that many unfortunately never achieve by going into the mountains or to the man-made temples rather than seeking a path to the heart of the Temple of Silence, as Paul Brunton would write in the above-mentioned work:

There is no name we can give to God...in any language. What does it mean, then? In ancient Egypt the name of a person, or the name of a thing, was regarded as having major value, so much so that great care was taken in selecting a fit and proper name for anything or anyone. The name of God will never be found because it is a silent name – it cannot be uttered verbally – it is found in silence alone. It is therefore, a holy name. It must not be uttered; it must not even be whispered; it must be found, heard, and spoken only in silence. God's name is the only name which is holy. "Hallowed be Thy name," means "Too sacred for utterance is Thy name." We must not utter it. It must be found, heard, and spoken only in silence. We must silence our thoughts and feelings, if only for a few seconds, when we want to think of God, and in that complete silence we are hallowing the name of God. (Discover Yourself, pages 55-56)

In silence are all the treasures and powers of the universe maintained and in complete obedience of the law of harmony. In silence do suns, planets, stars, Gods, Goddesses, and other Cosmic Beings pay homage to the Great Principle of Life, the Directing Intelligence of existence or the Sacred Fire of existence that breathes all that is. In silence does man unite with the Absolute and Supreme Law and harness all the great powers of the universe. One (just one person, not two or more) with God is a majority, it is said, for in conscious silence does man really transform himself into true dynamite. Silence is such a force

www.makanologos.com

because it puts you in a spiritually receptive mood for some of the choicest divine powers.

Brilliant minds learn to seclude themselves from the noise of the outer world before, during, and after their journey to the mountaintop of greatness. Smart governments, corporations, and learning institutions spend millions of dollars to provide their best and brightest minds more secluded and calmer environments where they can concentrate without distraction. Immediately after His presentation to the public at His baptism by John the Baptist, Jesus secluded Himself for about forty days, and through His ministry, He frequently isolated Himself not only from the masses but also from His chosen twelve apostles.

All great achievers, leaders, philosophers, and seers utilized the law of silence to the best of their ability, for they knew that in silence man receives the power to control his feelings, thoughts, and actions. They knew that in silence, man feels the Presence of God and speaks to Him. They knew that in silence, man attains greatness by the training of thoughts to aim at the center of his own being, the source of creative principle and the ruling intelligence whence comes the light that guides man to greatness, greatness that, like a mountain, is never mistaken or forgotten.

If you are a true lover and seeker of greatness, if you really want to write your name in the sky with lightning letters for future generations, you must exploit the power of silence to the fullest extent of your abilities, because only through silence will you be able to see the flowers that are within the seeds, the oak that is enveloped in the acorn, the smells in perfume, the colors and music that are in the air, the wheels of the sun and the Earth. Only in silence will you be able to face the source of Light and see the Truth that has been so strange to man for so long.

Yes, I am talking about going into the silence to discover virtues that will lead you to the acquisition of a brilliant mind and the attainment of the mountaintop of greatness. Virtues

www.makanologos.com

are universal. They are good anywhere and anytime. However, they are decorations and treasures of the hearts of brilliant minds. You know this. Some people look good in green, blue, or yellow; others look fabulous in white, purple, or orange; and so on. Not that some virtues are bad, but our hearts and minds accept or work with some virtues (to achieve the same noble causes) better than others.

One thing I really want to strongly call your attention to is this: There are no virtues without TRUTH, for this is the imperial and divine, the infinite attribute of God; not just any truth but the truth that admonishes evasion, deception, and mental reservation; the truth that finds joy of expression in the open. I am, of course, not here to tell you what virtues are best for you or which one will smarten your mind and lighten your heart best. But this one you must know. Silence is the ever-open door that leads into the field in which you can plant the seeds, only to harvest the same seeds many times over after a short time of persistent good actions.

Consider this: when you enter into silence, you are not just a farmer; you are a wise one who knows how to plow the soil and plant what you want to reap at harvest time. Like a farmer, you cannot plant peanuts and expect corn. You cannot plant lemon trees and expect to harvest oranges. Depending on the energy you invested, the soil can give you more and better seeds than the ones you planted, but it will never give you a different kind of seeds. Silence is like a loving father. As the sages of the ancients tell us, there is no loving father who can give his child a snake when he asked for a fish.

Be true to yourself and the cause you're working for. You cannot fool your Self, and you cannot trick life. You can only destroy yourself if you choose to, that is for sure. You cannot go into the silence to ask your Higher Self with the intention to do good, then turn and harm life purposely. If you do, nature itself will make sure you never reach the apex of the mountain of greatness, and your feelings will never be at peace. This

www.makanologos.com

does not mean that you will not achieve whatever you have in mind. You may, as Adolf Hitler and others did. The fact is that you will certainly precipitate your own downfall in the most dramatic way.

Greatness is never a by-product of chance or hazard. One does not climb the mountain of greatness by being at the right place at the right time. Greatness is attained thanks to deeply and consciously felt and entertained right feelings and right thoughts, wherever and whenever you are. Simply put, greatness is a product of brilliant minds, and one thing that truly brilliant minds are by far more specialized in than average minds is thinking and feeling ahead of time. Speaking for itself, here is how one brilliant mind is written about in *The Scottish Rite Monitor*:

So I taught, and my influence lived after me and gave good fortune to my country. That is the noblest recompense of human virtue. Do so strive to live and act, obey and govern; and you too, may live in good opinion of men, after you are dead; and your influence may make you also a king over the minds of men (second edition, page, 463 down).

This is the outcome of peace in the feelings and the true greatness, this is the fruit of self-mastery, and this is the way to acquire the key of the universe and the secrets of the Gods. That is how brilliant minds acquire greatness. Going into silence to look for something to console yourself is one thing, but going into silence looking for something that will strengthen and enlighten you is the source of greatness. Silence, of course, cannot possibly give you something that strengthens and inspires you unless you go into it with a burning desire for truth, unless you are sincere to yourself and to your ideal.

The value of your journey into the silent world will be demonstrated by the quality of life you live through the virtues you choose as your directing principles. The harder you engrave your guiding principles in your heart, feelings, thoughts, and actions, the more likely your influence will rule the minds of men long after you have passed on. Going into silence for selfish reasons can prove to be a futile exercise. Of course, humans being human, you must of necessity sometimes err, and climbing a mountain of greatness is not an error-free process. Going into the silence with good thoughts, feelings, words, and deeds is the way of seeking the strength that aids you on the way up to the mountaintop of greatness and also harmonizes your feelings. When you go into the silence, make sure you uproot the weeds (falsehood, self-deception, mental reservation, truth evasion, or confusion) that may destroy the harvest.

As I prepare to move to a totally different topic but still in the line of harmonizing feelings, in closing this paragraph, I will say this from the same source as the quotation above: *"Virtue consists in having absolute empire, or control of one's self."* That said, if your preferred virtues are not leading you to a better control and harmonization of your feelings, it will be practically impossible for you to gain self-mastery and subsequently greatness itself. If this be the case, I am certain that the fault is not that of virtues, for they are light and cannot ever possibly lead in obscurity. Wisdom will always conquer folly; truth will always conquer deceit; knowledge will always conquer ignorance; light will always conquer darkness; courage will always conquer fear; faith will always conquer doubt; confidence will always conquer faithlessness; determination will always conquer discouragement; charity will always conquer greed; punctuality will always win over rashness or lethargy; forgiveness always wins over intolerance; order always wins over anarchy; and so on.

Should you face a dead-end type of crisis, just relax, go back to the drawing board, and review not your virtues but your application of them. Honest failure in climbing the mountain of greatness has nothing to do with your virtues but everything to do with your application. Like Franklin, keep checking and grading yourself, day in and day out, week in and week out, year in and year out, decade in and decade out. It does not matter whether it takes fifty years or a century — aim for perfection. You probably will never get there, but you will overcome the mountain of greatness that is in front of you as only a few chosen ones can.

How you appreciate virtues for victories or fault them for failure should be a good indication of whether you will make it to the top of the mountain of greatness or, like the multitude, you will spend the rest of your life looking for ways to circumvent it. Virtues are the foundation of understanding, and as it is written, *with all thy getting, get understanding*. With this will come wisdom, life, power, riches, and honor. Virtues are attributes of God, if not God Himself. Each one of them is perfect and invincible when used wisely. They are all planted in the heart of man, given to us by God free of charge like the air we breathe, to satisfy every individual's and mankind's needs, both materially and spiritually. Thus writes Spalding: *"If Humanity has lost the light, go within; there you will find recorded the concepts that will renew the light so that it may shine forth from you, the lost sheep that are wandering bereft of light"* (*Life and Teaching of the Masters of the Far East*, Vol. 3, page 173).

Virtues are attributes of God. They are also the fruits of the Tree of Life planted in the heart of man to nourish the soul, mind, and spirit of the seeker of greatness in the truest sense of the word. They are light bulbs made by the hands of God and placed in the heart of man to enlighten the minds and spirits of the noblest men on the path of a righteous life. Raise yourself to their rate of vibration and you cannot possibly do yourself a better favor. All that is required is simply to think honestly and feel their qualities, and consequently your hands will be directed to perform a noble or virtuous action.

Virtues are made to be acknowledged. Brilliant minds acknowledge the qualities they want, not only to have but also to become. That is why the words *I AM* are said to be the most powerful words in the vocabulary of man. They have been

www.makanologos.com

understood by many wise men of ancient times as the best expression of the name of God Himself *(Ehyeh asher ehyeh* in Hebrew; I AM THAT I AM in English). Their equivalents in other languages also have high vibrations, but the English (a major language of mankind) version is said to have the highest vibrations. Acknowledging or feeling the qualities of what it is one wants to become, have, know, or see has accomplished all great achievements. No genius ever discovered or invented something unless he or she raised his vibration to the same rate of that of the thing he or she wished to find. Vibrations are, of course, only raised or lowered by thinking and feeling the presence of the thing or the failure to do so. Great books, inventions, and discoveries come to man through feeling and thinking their presence. Even the resurrection and ascension of Jesus was accomplished thanks to His constant feeling and thinking of their realities. As Haddock said in the quotation, Newton discovered the law of gravitation by simply thinking about it. Wealthy people gain their wealth by feeling wealth and thinking all around them, and by feeling and thinking poverty do poor people live in poverty.

Repeated negative use of these two words *I AM* can have consequential outcomes. Those two words *I AM* have been thought to be *COSMIC WORDS, COSMIC MANTRA*, or the lost words that sages and seers of olden times spent lifetimes searching the world over for, and I cannot help but quote Ernest Holmes here a little bit more, as I did in *The Best Kept Secrets of Personal Magnetism*, my earlier book:

Can you imagine a power so great that it is both an infinite presence and a limitless law? If you can you are drawing close to a better idea of the way Life works. Most of the bibles of the world have said that all things are formed by Its word. This word has been called the Secret Word, the Lost Word. It is said that some of the ancients had a holy scroll upon which was inscribed the sacred and the secret name of Life. This scroll was supposed to have been

www.makanologos.com

put in an ark, in a chest, and laid away in a place which was called Holy of Holies, the innermost room of the temple.

What do you suppose was inscribed upon this scroll? Just this: the words "I AM." Here is a concept of the pure, simple and direct affirmation of Life making everything out of itself. This is why most of the scriptures have stated that all things are made by the Word of God.

Did you ever stop to think that everything that is visible is projected into form by some the invisible power? Now, what do you suppose could take One Substance, One Law, One Presence and One Power and make an infinite variation of things? It would be impossible to conceive of anything doing this other than Life speaking Itself into existence through many ideas.

This is what is meant by words "I AM." Life says "I am this" and "I am that," and immediately this and that appears, begins to make form according to law. Life always works in accord with law. It is intelligence plus law. It is law plus conscious volition. It is law plus will and choice.

Life works by direct affirmation, (The Art of Life, **pages,** 37-38).

And Spalding, on the same subject almost forty years later, wrote:

When man begins to assemble in his consciousness the activities of the principle, he begins to say "I am that." This is the centralizing of the authority of the principle in himself. "I am" renders mind dynamic instead of letting it rest in potentiality. It becomes dynamic the moment we focus thought upon "I AM." That focal point is the center always, and from it emanates the authoritative commands that control and determine the entire status of manifest man. The I AM must be used to indicate man's true estate, that which he is in fact, and not what he has seemed to himself to be manifest from. "I AM THAT I AM," which is the embodiment of the motivating authority of the universe. Besides "THAT I AM" there is no existence but delusion.

www.makanologos.com

This name "I AM" was God to Moses. It has come down through the ages as "I AM." To the Hindus it is AUM, which means the same. Likewise to the Aryans it is AUM. The Chinese use it as TAU...But the positive radiations of the Spiritual I AM, the declaration of that which man is in fact, penetrate through these static fields of his consciousness and it is as though they do not exist. The persistence of Spiritual facts regarding man's nature and his place in the Universe eventually will eliminate all these static fields in human consciousness as well as in his affairs, (Life and Teaching of the Masters of the Far East, Volume IV, pages, 25-27).

These words "I AM" are a magic or cosmic mantra inscribable in the language of our octave of life, that those above or the Angelic Host utilize to spread the harmonizing and lightening Music of the Sphere throughout the infinite space. Those in the world here below, who are conscious and knowledgeable constructive seekers, invoke these words "I AM" not just to hear the Music of the Spheres but also to see its Light that brightens the mind. These words ("I AM") are a mantra that summons the Guardian Angel, the ever-present Invisible Helper in time of trouble, for a powerful and immediate assistance or a much-needed inspiration. These two majestic words "I AM" are able to raise man to the highest elevation or sink him into the lowest hole. They have come to us in several concealed forms. For instance, in the Hebrew or Arabic name of the mother of Jesus, Mariam or Merry I AM, meaning Joyous I AM; and Jesus himself, Issa, or Joshua Ibn Mariam (Merry I AM), or Jesus the son of Joy (joy, of course, being the highest vibration there is).

Throughout his ministry, Jesus never said, "I know or I have the way," but rather "I AM the way; I AM the Light; I AM Life; I AM the salt of the world," and most of all "I AM the resurrection and the Life." And by so thinking, acknowledging, and feeling, it all came to pass. In closing this chapter, I want to remind you of something I know you must have heard, read, felt, thought,

www.makanologos.com

or dreamed, and that is this: "God is Truth; God is Wisdom; God is Love; God is Courage; and so on." Do not just have a list of virtues to practice. Be those virtues in practice, and there will be no mountain of greatness that you will not be able to climb, and your feelings will never be more harmonious.

"Let the dead bury their dead," said the Master. "Sacred things for the sanctified," or so may it have been heard by an attentive ear? Nonetheless, virtues are not simply attributes of God; they are Gods enthroned in the hearts of men of brilliant minds. Thus approach them with clean hands, pure heart, and sincere desire to serve your fellow men, and you will be a shining light not only to those around you, but also a bright light from the hill of greatness upon which all eyes of men will look up for enlightenment and salvation. Thus will you become a blessing to others, and your feelings will be harmonious like a fire of purification, an ocean of peace, and a garden of joy. That is greatness. That is what will transform you into a king and a ruler of the hearts and minds of men long after your earthly days have disappeared in the twilight of time.

What an average soul calls evil contains the germ of good, and when looked through an enlightened eye, it encloses good, the sense of evil disappears, and there remains only the sense that all things are working together for good. The apparent evil surrounding conditions of poverty and pain that are shunned by many of us would vanish if faced for the good within them. Jesus taught that blindness was neither an evil nor the result of evil but an opportunity to show forth the "glory of God." A problem is not foreign to the principle of mathematics, nor is it an obstacle to the one who wishes to become a mathematician. In other words, all the so-called evils are made to inspire or motivate the search for good. By choosing a right virtue, you can transform evil into good, but you need harmonious feeling to know which virtue is appropriate.

www.makanologos.com

CHAPTER IX

THE SOLAR PLEXUS

Life — what a complex thing. Looking at life simplistically, it seems easy to define, but in reality it is not. Every one of us has some sort of unconscious or conscious understanding of life, but in reality, many of us are not capable of defining it comprehensively. For the centuries that man has lived on this planet, he has been successful at defining and understanding many realities to the point of predicting almost accurately the outcome of their silent work. It is perfectly possible for a twenty-first-century person to avoid being caught off guard by weather or many other natural disasters simply by being connected to the World Wide Web on his computer or even a cell phone.

Imagine what horrible disaster, in terms of human lives, the recent tsunami in Japan would have been had it not been for an effective technological system warning the population of the oncoming danger. Imagine that! While great progress is being achieved on an almost daily basis, the complexity of life is basically getting more elusive and obscure with every discovery and understanding, while at the same time, every one of them looks like a tiny baby step in our ages-long march toward man's self-knowledge.

Such is life. It is so complex and fluid that, unfortunately, its minutest details that have the strongest impacts on our whole being are rarely noticed by the wide masses that are so busy trying to understand the effects and have little time, if any at all, to comprehend the cause. And because no genius, regardless of the greatness of his mind or intelligence, can understand the effects without first understanding the cause, generation in and generation out, we move in the world like blind people struggling to find the door in an absolutely lightened room or people with perfect vision trying to find their way out of a totally darkened roomed filled with hazardous sharp instruments.

Just as a man with perfect vision in a very dark room faces the same uncertainty as a blind man in a well-lighted room, so does a person with little or no knowledge of the impact of the solar plexus on life in general face the same peril as a ship in the middle of a furious sea. The role the solar plexus plays in the life of human being is ignored by 99.99 percent of the people, yet it is said to be the seat of life. Yes, the seat of life—there you can see the solar plexus. From the top down and from right to left, the solar plexus is at the very center of our bodies. It is not only the main but also the sole conduit through which we connect and receive life and its nutrients from our mothers. Not to mention, it is the most sensitive part of the physical system. A blow to the solar plexus brings the whole physical body to complete inertia almost immediately. Very few times in our public and private schools, if any at all, is the solar plexus even taught or mentioned for what it is in reality—the sun of the body.

The human body is usually said to be a universe of its own, and that is true. The solar plexus is believed to be the sun of the body. From early on in our formal education, we are taught the functions and the vitality of the brain, heart, lungs, blood, etc., but rarely much (at least not in my experience and that of many whom I have spoken with on this subject) about the solar plexus. All these functions and vitalities of the cerebral, respiratory, circulatory, and digestive systems are just effects of the functions of the solar plexus on our bodies, much as life itself here on our planet Earth and elsewhere in our solar system is the effect of the cause of life that comes from the physical sun.

Just as the energy that sustains life on Earth comes from the Sun, the energy that sustains our bodies comes to us through our solar plexus. The functions of the brain, the heart, the lungs, or any other part of our bodies are simply reactions to the function of the solar plexus. Man can somehow manage to live with an abnormal brain, heart, or lungs, but he cannot live with an abnormal solar plexus. Although man can live without food for up to forty days, without water for up to seven days, and without air for up to two to three minutes, he can live no measurable time without energy. When energy withdraws, life withdraws as well, and the body is lifeless. There is not one without the other, even in the minutest space of time.

The solar plexus is the center, the knot of our nerve system, if you will, from which all the nerves of our bodies go. It is the source from where energy spreads throughout our bodies. To give a slight idea of the impact of the solar plexus on all other components of the body, imagine if the sun were to cease supplying its light to the Earth. Would not everything die immediately? Such is the impact of the solar plexus on our physical bodies. Theron Q. Dumont, author of *The Solar Plexus or Abdominal Brain*, on the grimness of the sustainability of life with an injury to the solar plexus writes:

A man may survive a serious injury to any one of three brains; but a serious injury to the solar plexus, or abdominal brain, strikes right to his seat of life – and that life ceases to manifest itself further. If Man may properly say of any portion of his physical being, "Here is the seat of my life; here is where I live!" the solar plexus, or Abdominal Brain, surely is that particular part or portion of his physical being, (page, 7).

Elizabeth Towne in *Just How to Wake the Solar Plexus,* calling it *"the sun within,"* adds:

There is a real sun center in us, the Solar (or Sun) Plexus. This is a great nerve center situated in the back of the stomach. When this center Sun, from which all nerves of the body radiate, is in its normal condition, it steadily radiates a real energy, just as the sun does. This energy vibrates though the nerve highways and by-ways out toward the surface of the body in all directions (the mucous membranous surface, as well as the outer skin), and is thrown off in a real halo or atmosphere, which always envelops the body. If this radiation from the Solar Plexus is positive enough, the influence of the other person cannot disturb its steady, harmonious vibration in the least...

A continued contraction of the nerves results in a chronic state of nervous collapse. The nerves literally collapse, as does a soft tube from which fluid is withdrawn.

The nerves are tubes for the conveyance of life to all parts of the body. Contract the Solar Plexus and you withdraw life from the body. Solar Plexus is the point where life is born – where the Uncreated becomes Created; the unorganized becomes organized; the unconscious becomes conscious; the invisible becomes appears; that which is dimensionless becomes measurable, (The Wisdom of Elizabeth Towne: 3-in-1 Omnibus Edition, pages, 81-82).

On the spiritual side of life, the impact of the solar plexus is (use your own superlative here) beyond description. I am very hesitant to use a superlative in trying to describe the importance of the solar plexus, but I will say this just once: I will move on and leave it up to you to dig more into whatever avenue of truth suits you. Find the truthfulness of my statement, and that is this: angels get their illumination from the light in their foreheads and protect themselves by placing a powerful belt of light (stronger than any man-made steel or armor of protection) around their solar plexus, for without that protection, they will fall, become fallen angels, and become subject to error and death, just like men.

I leave that for you to ponder, and hopefully you will dare to seek a better understanding if I fail to satisfy your intellectual thirst. Only your own research in multiple sources and, most importantly, contact with your Inner/Higher Self can give you a better description of the solar plexus to satisfy your need. For the lack of better words, that is as far as I can go in describing the magnitude of the solar plexus in human life. Just think about it. While the analysis of the physical functions of the human body is beyond the scope of this work, I find it necessary to give my readers as many hints as possible about

www.makanologos.com

the incredible power of the solar plexus. My work is simply to show the reader the impact the solar plexus has on his or her feelings, the importance of bringing it under strict control, and to suggest some useful methods of awakening this dormant (to most of us) power and submit it to conscious control if self-knowledge is to be obtained.

In the first part of this work, we dealt with the philosopher stone. In the third part, we will deal with the elixir of intelligence. In this second part, we are dealing with the royal secret. If you have not yet deduced what the royal secret is so far, I am glad to give you a hint once more. I hope I was clear enough in the first part to define the philosopher stone as contact with the Grand Architect of the Universe, commonly known as God or the Inner/Higher Self. Contact with the Higher Self has been the deepest desire of all men, consciously or otherwise. The royal secret does not show the reader the freeway to the Higher Self. It does, however, give the reader the key secret to increase the chances of better self-knowledge that lead to the discovery of the Higher Self, and that key is harmonization of feelings. The solar plexus is that part of our bodies that has the exclusive power to calm or disturb human feelings. This knowledge is paramount to someone who wants to acquire a brilliant mind.

As said earlier, the solar plexus is located in the central part of the human body, not for the sake of convenience, of course, but for the power of life that it wields. The functions that are commonly known to be assumed by the heart are basically carried out by the solar plexus. To most people, fear, doubt, anger, etc. come to us through our hearts, but in fact, while we may feel the effects of fear, doubt, and anger through our hearts, their cause or origin is in the solar plexus. As Dumont wrote in the same publication quoted above:

The solar plexus is the seat of the emotional nature of man. In short, that part popularly held to be played by "the heart," is in reality performed by the Solar Plexus, or Abdominal Brain, the great center of sympathetic Nervous System...We know that

www.makanologos.com

fear, dread, and suspense are accompanied by a sinking or even a "sick" feeling at the pit of the stomach. We know that the heart beats rapidly when we are excited, angry, or in love...the position and teaching that the solar plexus, or the Abdominal Brain, is the great center and seat of the feeling and emotions; the source and origin from which all of all our strong and elementary feelings and emotions arise and from which they flow. This being seen, it is also perceived that if we wish to regulate, control and direct our emotional nature, we must begin at the seat and center thereof— the Solar Plexus," (Solar Plexus or Abdominal Brain, pages, 10, 17).

I understand that it may not be easy for some people to swallow, just as it was not easy for this author's mother to convince him when he was three or four years old that the rain was not God's urine, or his kindergarten teacher to convince him that the rain, in fact, originates from here on Earth rather than in the skies. Imagine what life would be if all illusions, lies, and phenomena were annihilated! Just because we think something is the way it appears does not make it so. Thank God that while reason and faith or science and religion do not always see things through the same lens, they do not always oppose one another. Thus, science plays a major role in the illumination of man both materially and spiritually. Many modern scientists have been proving this ancient teaching since the early twentieth century.

I will deliberately not cite scientific research on this subject, not for the lack of facts, but because it is beyond the scope of this work and for its relative easy availability online or at your local public library or bookstore. I say this because I know that by the end of this chapter, you will have enough understanding that, if you personally test it yourself, you will have more proof than any scientific research can possibly give you. No faith is required here; only your mind, vigilance, and willingness to strike the low-vibration feelings at the right time and the right place. Not that faith is less important, because it is not, but it

www.makanologos.com

does not require faith to know that if you open your eyes in a lighted room, you will see what is in it; or everything being equal, if you walk, drive, or fly in the right direction, you will reach your destination.

Control, direction, and submission of passions, emotions, and feelings are among the highest triumphs man can accomplish. It is the achievement of self-mastery and mastery over not only those around you but also the energy that fills your being and environment. In other words, it is the discovery of the royal secret. Unless you put to work the best knowledge possible or you are innately born with the highest gifts nature can bestow upon man, harmonizing feelings is one of the most spiritual imperatives that passes under the radar of most people unnoticed.

To give you an idea of what I am talking about, I wish I could let you read for yourself the discourse on the solar plexus and how we unconsciously attract to ourselves unwanted feelings and other potentially harmful forces thrown into space by vicious people, purposely or otherwise. It is from Saint Germain's (Spirit) lecture through Mrs. G. W. Ballard (aka Lotus) to a live audience of the I AM students in Chicago, Illinois. I asked for permission from the Saint Germain Foundation, owner of the copyright on this very important lecture, multiple times both in writing and by phone but to no avail. My requests were turned down. I concluded that it was the policy of the Saint Germain Foundation not to let any part of their work to be mixed with the work of others. And I respect that. But because the lecture holds an important explanation on this matter that I am compelled to paraphrase for my readers as best I can, I hope that the reader will get sufficient hints to get a better understanding of the impact of the solar plexus on our lives. If the reader wants to read for him- or herself the lecture I am going to paraphrase, it can be found in *Voice of the I AM*, March 5, 1944 edition, which can be obtained through the Saint Germain Press in Chicago, or contact your local "I

www.makanologos.com

AM" sanctuary. I strongly advise all devoted seekers that this paraphrase is by no means a substitute for the original text, because regardless of my efforts, I cannot possibly come close to the meaning of the Master. Thus, the seeker would do him/ herself a great service by reading the original. Here is the paraphrase:

The lecture describes what happens at the solar plexus. You go along somewhat harmoniously, so long as everyone in the outer world behaves in the way that makes you happy. This keeps the energy at the solar plexus calm. But because people are not supposed to run their lives according to your mind, very often they don't behave the way you would like them to, and here is where the trouble begins. Here is what happens to your digestion when something disturbs your nerves or when things do not go your way. This is possibly the most important thing that has been revealed to man so far. Feelings about people, places, circumstances, and things influence the health of the body, mainly the digestion and nervous systems, as well as the brain structure and the mind!

The solar plexus, which is at the back of the stomach, is a ganglionic mass of nerves and basically is like a sun to the body. These nerves depart from the back of the body and surge into the stomach. They act like an antenna on a radio or like feelers on a fly or other insect. They vibrate through the atmosphere, feel and detect things in the atmosphere about you, constantly sending waves out. The instant they come into contact with a vibratory action that opposes your desire or your self-control, hundreds of those nerves intensify the vibratory action of what is going on in your world.

Every time this activity occurs, a rate of vibration goes forth from your spine into whatever is in your atmosphere, which is a repellent force. Every time you dislike something, a wave of energy travels through those nerves into the world around you. This is what causes irritation, calumny, and a judgmental attitude because of the shock that is felt in the stomach. Because

www.makanologos.com

everyone's antenna is always up and ready to pick up what is around, when you send a critical feeling to someone or another part of life, the shock goes to that person's solar plexus. Thus hate, jealousy, criticism, fear, anger, selfishness, etc. are propagated throughout the world. This process has two different effects in the body. The first effect is that of changing the chemical secretions of the stomach right away, causing fear and anger to be created. The lecture has some very insightful information about the solar plexus's functions.

Unfortunately, I cannot go much further, but this I can quote lawfully. Speaking of how energy circulates in our bodies from the solar plexus, it says:

As it blazes out this way horizontally, it immediately goes vertically, too! It forms a cross! The shock of the energy goes this way, then it goes that way. The two other places you feel it, are in your head and your feet…Therefore, if your feeling reaches out to them and the condition happens to be vicious, your nerves go out through your feeling like an antenna; pick up that rate of vibration, bring it back into yourself and the next thing you know, you are all disturbed! ("Discourse by Beloved Saint Germain," Chicago, Illinois, March 5, 1944)

The Voice of the "I AM" #8, pages 7 through 12, published and copyrighted by Saint Germain Press, Inc., August 1950: This article is truly amazing, and interested readers who want to know more would do themselves a great service by requesting a copy of the *"I AM"* magazine from the Saint Germain Foundation in Chicago or local "I AM" Sanctuary for further reading.

A disturbed person accomplishes nothing of the above. Resentment, anger, irritation, fear, and doubt are some of the creepiest feelings that most of us fall to involuntarily. These feelings are the very seeds of hate, with hate being the opposite of love, the law that binds the universe in perfect unity. A hateful feeling compels us to work against our own best interests. Greatness is never attained by working against your

www.makanologos.com

own interests or by working against the interests of those who would make you a great person in the first place. A hateful man is always doomed to fail; his eyes never see the mountain of greatness, even at a close distance.

The strength of man is not measured by his mental powers, much less his physical ones; it is measured by the power of his will to subdue or control his feelings or passions. The most emotionally sensitive among us are also the weakest. It is a blessing to have both strong mental and emotional characters. While a balance of both is the ideal, if there is an absolute choice to make, the wisest option would be to select a strongly emotional or psychologically balanced character. The world of politics or commerce is not necessarily ruled by nerds or geniuses but by those who have the best control over their own feelings.

The reason modern urban cities around the world are almost chaotic while countless villages and small rural communities live in a sea of peace (unless invaded by exiles from big cities) is that in metropolitan areas, leaders are chosen mostly through propaganda, false impressions, or the so-called political campaign, while in villages, leaders are fairly well known by an overwhelming majority of members of their communities. They are chosen mostly on the basis of their ability to handle their own emotional feelings and how they treat others (or how they handle the feelings of others).

Suffice it here to describe the power of the solar plexus, its nature, and its functions. It is time to move on to the most important section of this second part. I suggest that the reader please pay strong attention here, because here will be laid out the most important information on this subject. If studied diligently, processed proficiently in your inner laboratory, and applied correctly in your outer activities, this information will give you all the evidence in the world of the possibilities of controlling your feelings by mastering the power of your solar plexus.

www.makanologos.com

CHAPTER X

AROUSING THE SOLAR PLEXUS

The solar plexus is one of the most useful parts of the human body, both spiritually and physiologically. I think it is the most important part of human body because it is the seat of life. Here at the solar plexus is where above and below, heaven and earth, life and death, and light and darkness meet. In the Orient, people spent years learning varied exercises on how to control the solar plexus. Only the heart and the brain, major physiological and spiritual centers, come close to the solar plexus in order of spiritual vitality.

This needs to be said first and foremost before diving deeper into the analysis of this vital organ. Despite its importance, just like the heart and the brain, the solar plexus is not a part of what man really is. Find me guilty if I raised your eyebrows. I know I must have done just that. Yes, your heart and everything else you have a relationship with is not a part of you. You know you have a relationship with something or somebody when you say "my" or "mine." You say "my solar plexus," "my heart," "my body," "my spirit," etc., just as you say "my spouse," "my parents," "my children," "my money," "my knowledge," etc., because they are not part of you. They are not who you are. They are, however, important and crucial to your existence, but they are not you. But briefly, who are you? Without going too deep and for the sake of what I just said, you are your consciousness because your consciousness is life and owns everything you are and have.

You are your spirit, but your spirit is the energy, the consciousness that is all you are, the fuel that keeps your soul going. You are not your food, but your food gives you the energy, the fuel that your body needs for its survival. You are not your heart or lungs, but unless these organs work perfectly, your presence here on Earth will likely be very painful and short. You are not your spouse, children, parents, friends, coworkers, etc., but unless you collaborate with them and they collaborate with you somehow, your life here on Earth will be miserable.

I will not go into detail about who you are because, like you, I still try to understand myself, who I really am. But note this: the mysterious, wonderful, and adorable "I" of the "I AM" is the greatest secret kept from man and revealed to us all only once we cross into the next world. That unknown "I" animated by the spirit of God is who we are, the immortal and eternal Son of God. This "I" is the mystery of all mysteries. Nobody really knows who the "I" is. The moment you think you know something about it, even more enigmatic questions arise on the horizon. I am still studying it and hope to have more to say in my next books.

The solar plexus is believed to be a dormant mind since it is also the center of unconsciousness or the subconscious. Most of us are unaware of the functioning of the solar plexus just as we are of our blood circulation or the working of our digestive systems. Our bodies, on the one hand, are like our spouses and friends—they are companions given to us by nature for a successful life. On the other hand, they are tools to be used appropriately for a successful earthly experience. In fact, it is a well-known factor among the students of life that while a good IQ is helpful, it does not guarantee your success in life. But surrounding yourself with capable and loving individuals and interacting with them efficiently will most likely make your success a *fait accompli*. This point is treated in my previous book, *The Best Kept Secret of Personal Magnetism*, so I feel no need to return to it. A good family, marriage, or friendship is not the one where hugs, kisses, and back patting are frequently given, but the one where honest and serious communication is kept open, smooth, and unobstructed.

www.makanologos.com

To awaken the dormant solar plexus, there must be regular and good communication within you. Just as you must communicate with your spouse, friends, parents, children, and fellow men for good and mutual understanding, service, and cohabitation, you must also communicate with your solar plexus if you want it to wake up and serve you well. This may sound outlandish to you, but being aware of this knowledge is one of the best-kept secrets of the greatness. Yogis disassociate themselves from their bodies and consider them as companions with whom they must cultivate an excellent communicative environment. On this point, Spalding writes:

How can you express youth, beauty, purity, divinity, perfection and abundance until you see it, feel, hear and know them and put them forth in thought, word, action and expression, yes by worshiping them? By so doing you impress them on or into your subconscious thought and this subconscious thought reflects these thoughts back to you from the picture you have presented to it, through vibration that you have established or set there... The more you impress the truth upon the subconscious by love and worship, the more it will send it back to you...You will find by talking to your body, the subconscious of you, and knowing that what you are saying is the absolute truth, it outpictures. (The Life and Teaching of the Masters of the Far East, Volume 5, pages, 164-165).

One of the most instinctive pieces of knowledge a human is born with is that he is not his body. Even a little child in early childhood understands the he is not his head, feet, or hands. He knows they are not part of him because he calls them "my head," "my feet," or "my hands," just as he calls his parents "my mother," "my father," and so on. No teacher ever taught us to disassociate ourselves from our bodies when we say "my body." We know almost instinctively that our bodies are not a part of who we really are. Yet we make a great mistake when we say "I am sick" or "I am that" instead of "my body is sick" or "my body does not feel well," because in reality the "I" or

www.makanologos.com

the subjective self is never sick or affected by any condition of the body.

Just because the body or the objective self is sick, it does not mean that the subjective self, the "I," is sick as well. Understanding the difference between these two entities is the first and most important step in acquiring the power of commanding the body for higher ends. Is there anyone who can get the most out of his vehicle if he confuses himself with it? Unless the driver understands that he and his automobile are two totally different entities, unless he understands that the automobile is a tool at his disposal, unless he understands that he is to make the vehicle perform his will, he can never get the most out of it. But like the automobile or any other tool, the body, your objective self, is at the disposal of your "I" or subjective self. We all know this truth inwardly, but we fail to live it outwardly.

When your automobile needs restoration, you take it to a repairman. Unlike the automobile, the best repairman for your body is not your doctor; it is, rather, you. The most the doctor can do for your body is to give you pills or advice, but only you can give your body commands and instructions to heal itself as no one else can. You can command the organs of your body to perform to their maximum, average, or minimum capacity or not at all. You can command your heart to pump and distribute blood efficiently, your lungs to breathe smoothly, your stomach to digest flawlessly, your brain to think brightly, your kidneys to impeccably remove waste from the blood and excrete urine, just as you can command your hands to feed you, your feet to transport you, your mouth to accept beverage and food, and so on. Once you understand that your solar plexus is a part of your objective self and therefore subject to submission to your subjective self, you can give it instructions, and it will gladly obey a faithfully and determined order from its master—you.

www.makanologos.com

On the power or ability we all have to command our solar plexus in particular or any other part of the body in general, the legendary Spalding again says this:

This subconscious is no portion of the brain itself, but it is a ganglia of true cells located just below the heart center...This group of cells, however, may be influenced to let go of all false statements or falsehoods and accept and register true and absolute statements simply by talking directly to them. Suggest that they let go all false and negative qualities, thoughts, and statements and you will soon be aware that only true and constructive statement are registered in your world, which in turn reflects to you and through you. (The Life and Teaching of the Masters of the Far East, Volume 5, pages 67-68).

Language or spoken words, as conventionally defined thus far, are a unique power that belongs only to man. While spoken words are used to facilitate communication among men, they are not meant to be used only between members of the human race. Just as man trains dogs, dolphins, monkeys, and many other kinds of companion animals to understand and obey spoken commands, so can he train his body to listen, understand, and obey his spoken commands.

Command of the body, of course, is not achieved by repeating selective words as one would do with a pet but by successfully applying a firm discipline to one's mind power. Our bodies really listen to us, but unfortunately most of us have only communication with our body's cheap talk; therefore, the output is a cheap response to us. If you want a serious response from your body, you must give it serious instruction, for cheap talk will result in cheap responses, and serious talk will result in serious responses. It is that simple. Just as your pet gets the clue when you are serious about something, so does your body. When Jesus healed the sick, He did not tell them to wait until they felt better before casting off the sheets from the beds; rather, He gave them the command to stand up and go according to their faith. According to the obedience of their bodies, they were healed.

Unlike any other part of the human body, the solar plexus is the seat of life, therefore the most sensitive part of our bodily apparatus. The energy that sustains the function of *circulatory, sympathetic, digestive, respiratory, reproductive, muscular, and skeletal systems,* or the fuel that supports life in general, is manufactured, transmuted, and stored right at the solar plexus. Many people are aware of this truth, but only seekers of true greatness consciously or otherwise know that in order to set themselves free from the bondage of the pettiness caused by anger, fear, doubt, and selfishness, they must bring their solar plexus under strict control by primarily talking to it or giving it some sort of nonnegotiable commands.

True seekers of greatness are their own commander-in-chief as well as their own sentinel; they literally give commands through the spoken word and make sure commands are complied with by imposing discipline on their mind. "Thy will be done" is the answer they get from the solar plexus. To bring the solar plexus to complete control is not a mere hope that some supernatural forces will impose themselves on us but a conscious command and demand that the solar plexus obey the will of the Inner or Higher Self, not the will of a rebellious mind.

Man is said to be partly animal and partly divine. The solar plexus is thought to be the dividing line between these two kingdoms. By letting the solar plexus remain dormant, man wanders more into the animal kingdom and is therefore subject to all kinds of emotional weaknesses. But by awakening it consciously, he wanders more in the divine kingdom and is therefore immune to the meanness of anger, fear, selfishness, doubt, greed, and even ignorance. Spoken words are not only unique to man, but they also have unique power. Just as spoken words have the power to make the call to the ghosts and the

www.makanologos.com

superhuman, they have the power to awaken a dormant solar plexus.

By the way, the use of the word *dormant* here should be taken literally. *Dormant* means unawake. The incredible power that our solar plexus holds is tremendous. If awakened, the unbelievable will happen. The solar plexus is dormant only to the masses that ignore its power, but the few true seekers of greatness are aware of it and work hard to awaken and activate it within a reasonable period of time. Do not take my word for it, for only your own experience will be your best teacher. Prove it to yourself now or next time you feel sadness, anger, fear, jealousy, or deceptiveness. Just tell your solar plexus to close the door to the unwanted baseness, but say it firmly and mean what you say. Before you know it, the opposite feeling of happiness, courage, love, selflessness, or any other type of higher sentiment will saturate your world.

If you're a teacher or if once you were a student, I am sure you have heard the excuse "the dog ate my homework." As students, we have all in one way or another given bogus excuses for not doing our assignment on time; especially when there is no pressure for us to really do what we are supposed to do. Well, the solar plexus is that sort of student who does not do his homework unless he is under serious surveillance. It knows very well that its primary duty is to protect us against low emotions, but it does not volunteer its services unless demanded. For most of us, the solar plexus is like a security guard sleeping right by our doorway.

Nothing against prayers—they have done wonders for mankind. They should never be looked down on despite what I am about to say here. The amazing thing about humans is that we spend countless hours praying for the invisible Holy Ghost and other Super Beings to protect us from our enemies when right in our own bodies lies the solar plexus, capable with a firm command to transform the energy of anger into that of tranquility, of sadness into that of joy, of fear into that

www.makanologos.com

of courage, of greed into that unselfishness, of doubt into that confidence, of hate into that of love, of ignorance into that of knowledge, of foolishness into that of wisdom, of confusion into that of discernment. What else can better protect you from enemies than your own love, tranquility, confidence, courage, knowledge, wisdom, or discernment? The solar plexus is the main gate that Cosmic Beings, Super Beings, the Holy Ghost, or Invisible Helpers close or open and secure when they want to protect us not just against our enemies but also against ourselves, meaning our fears, doubts, selfishness, anger, or any low vibration feelings.

God is not quite ready yet to make Himself available to the human eye and protect us against our own self-imposed limitations. Until He does, we MUST rely on the power He planted in and around us. The solar plexus is one of those powers; it must be harvested and used wisely. What would be the purpose of bringing the food from the store, then failing to cook and eat it for the nourishment of the body? The sages of old knew how indispensable the functions of the solar plexus were when they compared it to the most brilliant orb in the universe, the sun, because it really is the sun of our bodies.

Like the physical sun, the solar plexus alone allows either the cloud of sadness to overwhelm us or the rays of light to shine in and around our individual worlds. Like the physical sun, the solar plexus injects life into our bodies and withdraws it from them. The solar plexus listens to and obeys the slightest command by way of the spoken word or thought.

It is a willing servant of man. The solar plexus enthusiastically and gladly submits to the slightest command of its master as long as the command is firm, selfless, and determined. The relationship between the master and the servant is mostly defined as the influence of the master over the servant if it is to be a peaceful and productive one. When the master becomes incapacitated or fails to influence his servant, the latter usually either turns lethargic or takes advantage of the inability of the master and becomes vengeful. While I strongly doubt the solar plexus works against man in any circumstances, I certainly believe it does not work as positively for us as it should when we do not let it relax and open up for the rays of peace and joy to penetrate and let out those of hate, anger, fear, doubt, etc.

Since the dawn of time, harmony has been the strength and support of all those who successfully have climbed the mountain of greatness, the brilliant minds. No human institution, for that matter, can survive unless it has harmony as the vehicle to bear its weigh. If you are serious about climbing the mountain of greatness, you must be dead serious about harmonizing your feelings first, and consequently your thoughts, actions, and then greatness will follow course. While financial or political successes are gratifying, they are not the measure of true greatness. True greatness is the control of the energy in and around you, the ability to turn your energy in and around you from sadness to happiness, from hate to love, from fear to courage, from hesitation to confidence, from negative to positive, etc. with the speed of thought.

A man who has this kind of power also has the power to transform poverty into riches, sickness into health, the material into the spiritual, etc. Man is by nature inwardly harmonious, but corruption of the outside world makes him inharmonious. Nowhere else does the negative outside influence come into us as it does through the solar plexus. Awakening the solar plexus is an indescribable means of shutting off inharmonious feelings and their effects on our worlds. A person who has his solar plexus awakened is like a king working and sleeping in a palace well guarded by loving and vigilant guardsmen in the midst of unrest.

Ancient Hindus liked to say, "if God wanted to hide Himself, He would choose man to hide in." I like to add, if God chose man to hide in, He would set His throne at the solar plexus. This is not a joke. In the Far East, where inner harmony is the aim of religious practice, literally hundreds of thousands of monks

www.makanologos.com

throughout history have gone into asceticism just to learn to control their solar plexus. This is not to mean that only those who live in loneliness are able to awaken their solar plexus — not at all. It can be done just the same while walking the streets of New York, Chicago, or small town USA — even in your bedroom — as it can be done in the seclusion of the Himalayan Mountains. I prefer to say, let your goal of life, the mountain you want to climb, guide you.

There are several ways of awakening the solar plexus. In this work, I will deal only with the ones I believe to be most effective and practical. Of all the ways of awakening this extraordinary power, addressing it through spoken words or thoughts is the easiest one and the most practical. By talking or sending thoughts to your solar plexus, you also send warnings to your rebellious mind to behave, and by so doing, you get the undivided attention from the solar plexus that you need in order to better instruct it. I will soon discuss a topic somewhat different from this one as far as its practicality is concerned, but before I come to the close of this segment, I want the reader to understand that I cannot possibly overstate the importance of cultivating the habit of regularly talking, verbally or otherwise, to your solar plexus.

Yell to it if need be as you would do to an unruly dog, but remember to yell firmly and not angrily if you want it to shield you from the nastiness of fear, anger, greed, sadness, and all low-vibratory feelings and thoughts that keep many of us from climbing the mountain of greatness or mastering those exalted secrets of brilliant minds. The more you form the habit of talking to your solar plexus sincerely and vehemently, the faster it will comply with your demands. Remember that the solar plexus has antennas capable of foreseeing or forecasting the situation long before you are consciously aware of it. Like a security guard who answers to a tough boss, it will most likely act at the right time rather than being sorry by acting later or not at all. "Before you asked, I have answered" is the

www.makanologos.com

real promise by the Supreme Intelligence to man. If you train your solar plexus adequately, it will shield your harmonious feelings from being disturbed by nefarious or poisonous influences from the outside world. If you win this battle, be assured that you have won a key element of greatness. Count yourself truly among the GENUINELY CHOSEN FEW, for not only will your fellow men count and depend on you, but also you will be a worthy channel through which God, the Supreme Intelligence, will serve and manifest Himself before mankind. If there is only one price that is worth your life, this is it. To aim at and realize harmonious feelings is the highest wisdom; it is the ROYAL SECRET. Discover if for yourself and enjoy.

www.makanologos.com

CHAPTER XI

HARMONIOUS BREATHING

Nothing is more synonymous with life than breathing. In fact, breathing is not just synonymous with life; it is itself the symbol of life. And to many people, it is more than just a symbol of life; it is life. Even for highly trained physicians to still have a glimmer of hope of saving a patient's life, there must be an indication that the person is breathing, even if painfully. Once the breathing stops, life is gone. Breath is the most precious function of our physical bodies. As soon as the breath withdraws, the body of any living thing becomes lifeless and starts to decompose immediately.

We only own our bodies as long as we are breathing, and as soon as the breathing stops, our bodies do not belong to us anymore. So it is almost pointless to spend too much time and space trying to admire and praise the body's magnificent power. The objective of this segment, like the previous one, is to learn how to harmonize our feelings in order to acquire an empowering strength that brightens the mind as it seeks its way to the mountaintop of greatness. *"Man is by nature born nice, but it is the environment that corrupts him,"* said Swiss philosopher, writer, and composer Jean Jacques Rousseau. Inside all of us are harmonious feelings capable enough to keep man happy, healthy, and successful in whatever he undertakes. But man is a social animal; he is born among and lives with other people from the sunrise to the sundown of his life. In an article on its website, "Is there a genius in all of us?" the BBC says:

> *It would be folly to suggest that anyone can literally do or become anything. But the new science tells us that it's equally foolish to think that mediocrity is built into most of us. And there are no environmental factors that function independently of the genome. [A trait] emerges only from the interaction of*

*gene and environment. This means that everything about us —
our personalities, our intelligence, our abilities — are actually
determined by the lives we lead. The very notion of "innate"
no longer holds together.* (http://www.bbc.co.uk/news/
magazine-12140064, accessed June 27, 2012)

Therefore, where we live and what we do repeatedly have
great impact on what we become. The environment most of us
live in is basically a chaotic one as far as feelings and thoughts
are concerned. We constantly commit crimes such as murders,
rapes, thefts, adulteries, hate, etc. through our feelings and
thoughts every single day. The human law may not apprehend
us, but we are all guilty before the Supreme Intelligence. Those
chaotic and criminal feelings and thoughts do not just disappear
like sound waves. They circulate endlessly in the atmosphere
until they build up a momentum, amassing similar negative
forces, and on a return current, they push us off the cliff by
causing us to actually perpetrate the criminal act.

Our own feelings and thoughts do not just stay in
our environments; they go out and influence unguarded
individuals, as we also are influenced by outside thoughts and
feelings of the same vibration as the ones we sent out. These
feelings and thoughts from the outside world get in our inner
world through the solar plexus. In the last chapter, I laid out
how to awaken or gain the attention of the solar plexus by
simply addressing it in earnest and forceful terms. Here, I will
strive to show how practicing the art of balanced breath can
arouse the solar plexus.

All ancient, modern, and living spiritual teachers have
professed that man is the temple of God, meaning that
man does not need to go far in order to worship God, only
inside himself. That temple has many altars of slightly equal
significance on which sacrifices and offerings are offered to
the Supreme Power. But the two most important altars are the
heart and the forehead. The serenity and purity, the safety and
security of those altars depend only on the pillar that supports

them, and that is the solar plexus. Given that, you can safely say that the magic of man is not so much in his head or heart but in his solar plexus. I am not a yogi, and I am not by any means encouraging or discouraging anyone from learning and practicing yoga. But I would like to say this: yoga may or may not be a suitable sacred teaching of our time as it was in the centuries past, but it has singlehandedly produced more famed spiritual teachers than any other spiritual school known to man. A list of Spiritual Masters of the Far East can be literally endless. It has done so mostly by teaching its students how to awaken and gain the undivided attention of the solar plexus.

This may not be popular knowledge because for centuries, this knowledge has been kept secret and taught only in esoteric schools to a select few. Who said that this wasn't an exciting to time to live in? Well, it is indeed. What was once secret for our grandparents is no longer secret to us. What was previously kept esoteric to our forefathers is no longer esoteric to us. Whereas it took our ancestors hundreds or even thousands of miles of travel just to apply for admission with no guarantee of acceptance to the caves, today it is at our fingertips on smartphones or computers in the comfort of our cars and modern homes. Nevertheless, value this knowledge despite its relatively easy availability. Enjoy life and thank Mother Nature that brought you to Earth at this exciting time rather than four thousand or even some hundred years ago. Let's go back to the solar plexus.

Comparing gaining the attention of a deeply concentrating person to the awakening of the solar plexus, Professor Theron Q. Dumont asks and answers himself in his little book *The Solar Plexus or Abdominal Brain*:

How would you proceed in such a case, and such a person? Well, in the first place, you would probably endeavor to attract his attention by means of tapping his shoulder insistently, until he "woke up"; then after he had "come out of his trance" (again employing the popular, harmonious terminology), you would

www.makanologos.com

address him earnestly and forcefully. Well then, this is precisely the method followed in "awakening the solar plexus." But, you say, we cannot "tap the shoulder" of the Solar Plexus. But, we answer, we can do this figuratively – we can substitute a physical method which proceeds along the same lines, and which will produce a similar result (page 39).

It is easy for an average person to dismiss the power of the breath at once. Some of the most successful people may not know all about it, but they exploit the almost magical power of the breath like few of us can possibly understand. Everybody – well, maybe not everybody literally but many people – is familiar with meditational exercises of the yogis, so I will not put them forward as an example to illustrate this point to avoid repeating common knowledge. But did you know that Jesuits are some of the best, if not the best, educated people on Earth? How so? You might ask. And I say they incorporate breathing exercises in their culture just as the yogis of the Orient do. As the prodigious Paul Brunton wrote on this subject, *"Those who have not studied the subject cannot realize what striking changes can be brought in the body and the mind through the simple means of changing the breath rhythm"* (*The Secret Path*, page 71).

The breath is not only synonymous with life itself, but it also has more magical power than most people are aware of. It is one of the rare forces of nature that can both warm and cool down a body. When our hands are stricken by a cold body like ice, we instinctively use the breath to warm it up; when eating hot food or drinking a scorching beverage, we likewise use our breath to cool it down. Long before the marvels of technology changed the lives of people in many parts of the world forever, even today in many other parts of the world where technology has not made inroads, people made fire by gently breathing on a burning charcoal and by the same breath put out the flames. Breath does not just rekindle physical flames; it reawakens the flames of human intelligence as well. If you have taken a competitive test, I am sure you must have heard, "If you are

Exalted Secrets of Brilliant Minds   225

nervous, just TAKE A DEEP BREATH, then relax" before answering or even reading a scary quiz. And if you really followed that instruction, as soon as you took a good deep breath firmly and genuinely, all the fear left you in the way a burglar would run from the scene at the sound of a security alarm. *"The freer his breathing,"* writes Elizabeth Towne, *"the greater the degree of intelligent will be. He, who, breathes freely acts freely. He, who, breathes deeply thinks deeply."*

Breathing is synonymous with the presence of God in man as well. When a man or an animal stops breathing, people feel the absence or departure of the Supreme Intelligence in the fallen comrade or animal. Breath has unique and incredible powers that few of us really know or understand how to utilize effectively besides just keeping the physical apparatus functioning. A wide majority of us use it for mechanical reasons only, just to lubricate our body parts and allow them to function properly, while a very few of us use it for spiritual reasons as well. They use it to inhale the helpful spirits and attract divine powers that may be looking for a radiant channel through which to manifest wonders on Earth. These very few people use the breath not just to cleanse the body but to strengthen the mind for its physical and spiritual daily battles as well.

Among other uses of strategic breathing, none will be explored here other than just to say that there are many illnesses that we suffer that can be entirely removed quickly and safely from our bodies by nothing more than right and effective breathing methods. There is no stronger power against low vibrations or negative thoughts and feelings than right breathing.

Feelings of fear, hate, doubt, anger, jealousy, selfishness, depression, or anxiety, and thoughts of suicide or crimes are instantaneously dissolved and consumed by effective breathing exercises. If you are a lucky person who has never been in a depressing situation, ask a friend of yours who has and has consulted a competent psychologist or psychiatrist. He or she will tell you that the first and most effective treatment that was

www.makanologos.com

given to him or her by the practitioner was breathing exercises, and everything else was just added as the treatment proceeded. My wife and I once were victims of a rear-end car accident. For weeks we were practically incapable of trusting fellow drivers who came behind our car on the road. Every time we would start the car to go somewhere, the first and last thought in mind was of that fateful night. When driving downhill, we would have thoughts of someone hitting us in the rear and sending our car rolling like a rock to the bottom of the valley. At night, our sleep was frequently disrupted by nightmares caused by the accident.

In our quest to gain our peace of mind back, we decided to consult a psychologist. The good lady had only two prescriptions for us. First and foremost was breathing exercises, and second was saturating our auras with bright light (we will elaborate more on the use of light in the next chapter). After a disciplined application of the breathing exercises given us, not only were we declared healed in four weeks of treatment, but most importantly we truly felt healed. And ever since, whenever we sense the same feelings approaching, we strike them with the same weapon.

Now whenever we feel menaced by the malicious and vicious forces of life, we employ the same techniques, and almost effortlessly our peace of mind is left unharmed or restored completely. Right and conscious breathing not only replenishes our bodies with energy, but it refills us with the ether of the pure substance of life and fire. By right and conscious breathing, man can and does eliminate many of his physical, psychological, and even spiritual maladies, therefore extending his days on Earth, adding more joy to his time here, simplicity and more reward to his actions and occupation, and better inspiration to those around him.

Wherever and whenever you may be reading this book, regardless of my physical absence near you, I can hear some of my readers asking themselves, "What the heck? Man breathes

www.makanologos.com

from sunrise to sundown, from birth to death. Why are we talking about breathing?" If you asked yourself these questions or more, remember that man also thinks and feels from sunrise to sundown, from birth to death, but does he always think or feel right? Man thinks and feels uninterruptedly 24/7, and most of his thoughts and feelings are useless. Some of them are contradictory, and some of them are even sick, indeed. There is no exception to this rule; it affects all of us, whether you are Isaac Newton, the president of the United States, rich or poor.

Consider this: *"Isaac Newton once threatened to burn down the house of his mother and stepfather,"* wrote David Kidder and Noah D. Oppenheim in *The Intellectual Devotional.* President Clinton had a sexual relationship with an intern in the most powerful office on Earth, the Oval Office. President Nixon resigned for fear of a forcible removal through impeachment for crimes he committed in the office. Wall Street and Hollywood are full of examples of the rich and famous who have committed suicide or gone haywire.

While man does not think and feel good all day long, whether he is a genius or otherwise, it is the good thoughts and feelings that he thinks and feels consciously at strategic moments (sometimes short, sometimes relatively long) that change his life, community, and nation. And it is on those good thoughts and feelings received at special moments that civilizations have been built on. It is my belief that a person who aims to breathe consciously or strategically 24/7 would be the most foolish ever born on Earth. Breathing is a perpetual activity, for it ends with death only. Watching it consistently would exclude all other activities. Life has to be supported by man through work, nature has to be admired through exhilaration, and God has to be worshiped through silence. All these are important functions man must fulfill with the kind of care equal to what he gives to breathing. Breathing cannot be regularly attended to the exclusion of all other vital activities. It must many times be confidently left in the care of the Supreme

www.makanologos.com

Intelligence while other activities of lesser or equal value are given undivided attention. However, if the conscious practice of good breathing habits is effective, the subconscious will take care of the unconscious moments when effectual breathing has to be performed in order to brighten the mind as the journey to the mountaintop of greatness goes on.

Having said that, before I dive into the explanation of breathing methods, I would like to unambiguously put forward some warnings to my readers here in the clearest manner possible so that they can reap the best fruits possible from the art of breathing. Notice I said *art*, meaning man-made, not natural, thus the necessity of full mental alertness when practicing conscious breathing.

1. First of all, I completely and unequivocally discourage or even forbid it to anyone who may have health issues, especially those who may have heart or lung illnesses. A person who may have heart or lung disease should never practice breathing exercises regardless of human supervision unless it is done under the supervision of a wholly free, perfect, and spiritual Master, who of course will have to heal you first before administering this work on you. Cases like this are extremely rare because a Master's radiation will raise your vibrations, therefore taking away the pain or illness you may have, healing you before He even approaches you. I cannot emphasize this point strongly enough.

2. Second, I strongly discourage anyone from practicing breathing exercises when their minds are not fully awake, and I mean 100%, nothing less. By this I want to say that except when you are wholly capable of consciously monitoring the inhaling and the exhaling of the breath, breathing exercises should not be practiced. It should not be done when one is feeling dizziness or needs to sleep. To avoid losing charge of your total consciousness, a good position must be taken (this point will be discussed

www.makanologos.com

later). I once tried to perform breathing exercises in the middle of the night when I woke up from a deep sleep, and all of a sudden I felt I was going to leave my body altogether. I thought maybe a few deep breaths would help to get me back to sleep peacefully, but rather, I felt an invisible hand suffocating me. As sleep was returning, I lost count and time awareness. The next thing I knew, my heart almost stopped beating, and I was forced to exhale forcibly, a grave mistake in breathing exercises. On a few occasions, I have had serious chest discomfort. Thus, I encourage you to learn from this author's experience.

Breathing exercises are unlike common breathing. Natural breathing allows the organism to absorb the oxygen that our body needs and release the carbon dioxide that our body does not need. It allows us, as well as other living things, to attract forces of nature that support life while at the same time discarding transformed forces that may harm it. Breathing exercises are no different. However, their main objective is to free the mind from harmful qualities such as fear, hate, anger, jealousy, selfishness, doubt, self-distrust, and all other low or negatively vibrating qualities that impede the actualization of our God-given abilities, and toughen it (the mind) up with higher vibration qualities such as courage, hope, joy, fearlessness, confidence, persistence, determination, selflessness, and other qualities that allow us to express our inner powers. Thus to students of breathing exercises, I would issue the same warning Paul Brunton issued to practitioners of mental quieting, and it this is:

When moral weaknesses are conjoint with mystical practices, the result is not elevation of the mind into spirituality but degeneration of the mind into psychism. The practice of meditation without the cultivation of ethical safeguards can lead to self-deception, hallucination and

www.makanologos.com

even insanity. Therefore it is not a quick and easy passage into occult experiences that the aspirant should seek so much as a careful improvement of character (The Secret Path, page 55).

If you really want the oxygen you are drawing from the atmosphere to give you the nutrients of life, you must be willing to exhale the carbon dioxide that your body is producing. There is no other way around it if you must live. This same principle applies to placid or harmonious breathing. There is a reason why harmonious breathing is a secret of the chosen few. If natural breathing were the only valuable thing to life, or if harmonious breathing could not provide such a great benefit to its practitioners, then sages, seers, high priests, and the chosen few wouldn't waste their valuable time learning it. It bestows to anyone who takes the time to do it right inestimable advantage, and that is, it extends the hand of man to reach into the heart of infinity to bring pearls of immeasurable value that only masters among us possess. It restores fearlessness to the timid mind, confidence to the hesitant, hope to the desperate, courage to the disheartened, reason to the irrational, calm to the irritated, tranquility to the troubled, faith to the faithless, health to the ailing, happiness to the heartbroken, etc.

3. Thus my third warning: harmonious breathing should not be practiced for its own sake. It should be done for a purpose, and that is to improve one's character. You must be a person who is striving to live a constructive way of life to benefit from harmonious breathing. You must be aiming to rid yourself of your weaknesses and reinforce your strengths. Believe it or not, harmonious breathing has an amazing power. It has the power to dispel fear, hate, anger, doubt, discouragement, etc. almost instantly when done right. It has the power to give you courage and confidence to walk alone in the Amazon jungle,

www.makanologos.com

fearing no danger. It has the power to make you the master of your passions. It has the power to make you a master of yourself and a servant of your fellow men. It has the power to reveal to you the most inestimable knowledge there is in the universe, self-knowledge.

Of course, harmonious breathing is not for saints or angels. It is for sinners who want to improve their personhood, who strive to live constructively to rid themselves of their sins (ill behavior.) But if you are a sinner who is happy with your sins or a person who couldn't care less about improving your personhood, or if a constructive way of life means nothing to you, then I suggest that you do not practice placid breathing. As much as electricity is beneficial human life, it is foolish to stand in water unprotected and then insert a light bulb in the socket, hoping it will illuminate your room. No! It will not. Rather, electricity will kill you. Harmonious breathing works in similar ways. When done competently with a creditable cause in mind, harmonious breathing really reaches into the center of the highest power in the universe and brings forth powers that only few people know how to master. Its powers are real yet more dangerous than the powers of electricity or even the atomic or nuclear bomb, since electricity or any other man-made power can destroy only the body, but the powers of the Supreme Intelligence can destroy both body and…fill the blank.

You cannot deceive God, but you can deceive yourself, that is for sure. When practicing harmonious breathing, do it with a sincere intention of being not necessarily perfect, but a better person, of making a positive contribution to society. Thus, you must practice harmonious breathing with a sincere desire to climb the mountain of greatness and crack the cryptogram of the secrets of brilliant minds. The mountain of greatness is not overcome by

www.makanologos.com

self-service but rather by serving others. Brilliant minds did not gain and hold their positions by self-serving but rather by serving others. Practice harmonious breathing with determined craving for doing good to others and heaven will reward you in a way you cannot possibly imagine.

4. Lastly, I want to advise you, when practicing harmonious breathing, keep your thoughts from wandering from train to train, from subject to subject, from one distraction to another. I honestly do not know how harmful it is, if harmful at all. But I know it will do less good and will take time before you can really start to harvest the fruits of your breathing labor. Just as you would not trust your undisciplined child, student, coworker, or employee, the universe is very reluctant to trust an undisciplined mind. The more concentrated your thoughts, the faster the universe will open its doors and windows to you. Quoting Jesus, in his extraordinary travels in India and the Gobi Desert, Spaulding said — and quoting an Indian guru, Brunton also said — "One-pointedness is God." Concentration has an amazing power; in fact, there is no stronger power in the universe that pulls man faster to his desires or desires to man than concentration.

Highly skillful practitioners of placid breathing strive to stop thinking altogether while they are at labor. While halting the thought process as one is performing harmonious breathing is tremendously advantageous, I would never encourage or discourage my readers to do it for one simple reason: I have never experienced it. What I have learned from great teachers for whom I have the greatest love and admiration, and what I would like to share with my readers, is that light is its own defense, and sacred fire is its own revelation. Sometimes in life, all we need to do is try, to be prepared, but not to force. *"Chance favors only the prepared mind,"* said the French

Exalted Secrets of Brilliant Minds   233

chemist and microbiologist Louis Pasteur. At the right time and the right place, if we deserve it, things cannot help but to happen. When the student is ready, the master appears, and when you are facing the right direction, all you need to do is to walk, say Buddhists. While writing theories may be a great intellectual exercise, blending them with personal experiences makes theories more understandable and illuminating.

The practice of meditating while willingly shutting off all thinking has been attempted by all great mystics from every ancient times, but very few have succeeded. The attempts of the prophet Ezekiel resulted in the visions that are famously known as Ezekiel's chariot. According to the story, when t*he prophet Ezekiel successfully ceased thinking altogether while meditating, he was given a view into the heavenly kingdom that is unveiled in the first and tenth chapters of the book in the Bible bearing his name. His experience is similar to that found in the book of Revelation. Ezekiel's description of a "Holy Chariot" is considered to be the highest level of mystical philosophy in Judaism that instigated the practice of merkabah, which many Jewish rabbis strongly discourage due to the potential mental and spiritual dangers that may arise.*

To this day, students of mysticism continue to attempt to either replicate Ezekiel's experience or live a different one of their own. Here is how David Goddard puts it in *Tree of Sapphires:*

For the same reason, the eyes are closed in meditation and covered in prayer; for in deepest meditation or at the height of mystical prayer, we return to the void, to the No-thing of the Absolute. This profound state of consciousness is described in the text of the ageless wisdom as being with God. Like the angels we veil our faces and are alone with the Alone (who is the All-One). Jacob Boehme put it well when he wrote:

www.makanologos.com

"If thou canst, my son, for a while but cease from thinking and willing, thou shalt hear the unspeakable words of God...When thou art quiet and silent, then art thou as God was; thou art of which he made by nature and creature: Then thou hearst and seest even with that wherewith God himself saw and heard in thee, before even thine own willing or thine own seeing began," (pages, 54-55).

Thinking is for the most part an involuntary process. Like digestion, man can choose what to eat but cannot start or stop his digestion. Likewise, you can choose what to think about and how to think, but you can hardly stop thinking. Just because you choose to stop thinking about biology, philosophy, psychology, music, love, or money, it does not mean you stop thinking altogether.

Instead of fruitlessly trying to stop thinking or letting your brain run aimlessly from one subject to another like an unleashed little dog, train your inner eye to see LIGHT in and around you, and think and feel only that. Since the dawn of time, man in all parts of the world has always used light as a symbol of God. There is not a true religion that does not associate light with God. In the Bible, light is said to have been the first creation of God. Long before the ideas of modern religions conquered the world, man all over the world worshiped the sun as God or a representation of God because of its generous distribution of light. God is light; say all highly prized religious books. The absence of light strikes the heart of man with fear, desperation, uncertainty, anger, and all those feelings that make life truly miserable. Darkness is the single biggest threat to life, more than any illness, for it hits not merely our eyes but directly the center of life, the heart.

Hence, while practicing harmonious breathing, forget your desires for a while, for these will only make your thoughts uneasy and make them run uncontrollably. When you enter your room or temple of silence, leave your desires outside.

www.makanologos.com

Heaven knows our needs, for it is written, *"Before you have asked, I have answered."* As Migene Gonzalez-Wippler writes in her book *Kabbalah for the Modern World*:

There are no worldly ambitions in the heart of the mystic who follows this path, only the desire to unite with Higher Selves and to blend with the soul of nature. The rewards of this Path are, as we have said, illumination, and the perfect equilibrium of personality (page, 104).

Nothing unites man quicker with his Higher Self and illumines him faster than focusing his mind's eye on the light for the duration of spiritual exercise. Therefore, go in your temple of silence to charge yourself with the powers that ordinary man knows nothing about. Thus visualize light in you at your solar plexus, in your heart, at your forehead, and around your body, a brilliant aura of light of a thousand suns if need be. I hope to say more about the light later, but while I am here, let me say this: nothing brings mastery of life faster than frequent visualization of light in and around oneself. A simple act of visualizing flaming light in the forehead or in the brain regularly improves the quality of man's thinking process. Visualizing a bursting sun at the solar plexus shuts out all feelings of fear, anger, hate, jealousy, doubt, discouragement, etc., and visualizing brilliant light in the heart increases love and wisdom. There is magic in the light, for God is LIGHT.

Stick your thoughts and feelings on the light while performing your breathing exercises; you will charge yourself with the choicest powers of the universe, and your reward will be indescribable. A mind full of light kills the ego like an elephant stepping on a mouse. Sages and seers do not simply hide their bodies in the light; they hide their thoughts and feelings in it. Light is truly the cloak of invisibility and invincibility against all low-vibration emotions. The more you bathe your thoughts and feelings in the light while performing breathing exercises, the more you will grow in power, wisdom, and love. Rebellious thoughts, of course, will never let you

www.makanologos.com

discipline them quite so easily. They will always fight back to gain and disturb your attention. But if you remind yourself that the secrets of brilliant minds belong only to those who find no excuse to let their attention be distracted by an unwanted material or mental nuisance, if you remind yourself that the mountain of greatness can never possibly be climbed by the weak of heart and mind, you should have no problem bringing your thoughts back to light despite the multi-directional wind that may be blowing inside you.

Do the right thing—love yourself and the world you are trying to influence, heed these warnings, and your rewards will be tremendous. Harmonious breathings are just that—they bring mental and physical peace if performed correctly.

Now that I have sufficiently laid the ground for the introduction of harmonious breathing methods, it is time step in the water if you want to get wet.

1. <u>Conscious Breathing</u>

Most of us take breathing for granted. We think it is a right, but it is not. It is a privilege. Some people even go days, weeks, or months without listening to the beating of their hearts, breathing unconsciously, paying no attention to the essence of their very physical life. While going to a special place or taking some special position for conscious breathing is helpful, conscious breathing can be done almost anywhere and anytime.

As said earlier, breathing for the most part is an involuntary act. Many people go days, even weeks, without paying attention to how their bodies breathe, and still they live a good life. But brilliant minds do not always aim for good; they aim for the highest quality possible. The difference between unconscious and conscious breathing is that the former opens the door for us to go out and carry on with our daily lives while the latter not only allows us to go on with our daily lives, but it also opens higher doors that enable higher powers to work though us and allow us to live a life of higher purposes. The reason harmonious breathings transform man and enable him to live a great life is that they make man conscious of how the mystery of God animates a machine that is made completely of earthly substance. A few minutes of proficient conscious breathing do a great deal of good to our bodies as only a few medical substances can.

Yogis and monks spend hours on a daily basis performing breathing exercises. With our ever-increasing needs and ever-demanding modern life, most of us do not have enough time (most popular excuse, of course). But time we do have! Maybe not to exercise like a yogi or a monk, but even in the middle of a busy day, we can always find one or two minutes per hour to turn inward and listen to our heartbeats.

If for a day, for two to three minutes each hour of eight to ten work hours, you give attention to how your lungs function while breathing naturally but consciously, your body and mind will gain tremendously from it beyond your wildest imagination. If you are one of those who claim not to have time for thirty minutes of daily breathing exercises, conscious breathing will be a good fit for you. It can be done anywhere at any time, even in the battlefield or on a fishing boat in the high water of the seas. Do not take my word for it; try it yourself. Only conscious breathing should be done for this short time. The rest of the exercises that will follow are advised to take 15 to 20 minutes once or twice per day in special settings in order for them to be most useful.

Before I move on to explaining other kinds of breathing exercises, I want to make sure that I underline the importance of the position taken before performing breathing exercises, for position alone can make or break the leisure and benefit of this wonderful endeavor. When exercising breathing, it is important that it be done in a freely ventilated and sufficiently lighted area. There are two positions that can be employed. The first is to lie on a bed with the fingers barely touching at the solar plexus or the hands held along the body. The second

www.makanologos.com

position is to sit in a comfortable position in a chair with feet firmly on the floor and knees forming a perfect 90-degree angle, the back not necessarily leaning on the chair but entirely erect, while the hands are resting on the lap completely open and facing upward. A fresh shower prior to the exercise to clean and awaken both the body and the mind is strongly advised. Now you are ready; here are the exercises.

2. Rhythmic Breath

Rhythmic breathings are designed to give virtues that you breathe in sufficient and equal time to uproot unwanted passions that must be thrown out if the temple is to stand on the rock, to strengthen your stand, your discipline, or determination to seek the good and right despite all the chaos that shakes the feeble life around us. It is performed by slowly drawing in air deep enough, holding it there for 8 to 10 counts while pulling the stomach in, then reversing the process by exhaling the air slowly for the same period of time, 8 to 10 seconds. The process can be repeated several times, resting or breathing naturally between breaths. You can add to the time progressively as you master the body's caprices, but moderation should be the master key in the rhythmic breathing. Under no circumstances is it advisable to practice rhythmic breathing or any other breathing method described here under nervous tension, except the natural slow breathing to quickly quiet the mind and the whole body structure as you breathe effortlessly.

It is absolutely unnecessary or even harmful to hold the breath longer than the body is comfortable with. The goal is not to exhaust yourself but to stimulate the energy within you, to refocus your attention back to the source of life by awakening your solar plexus and all other spiritual centers in the body. That is all—not to wear yourself out. If after this exercise you feel tired rather than energized, that should be an indication to reexamine the way you are performing the exercise. For this and all other conscious breathings that you will learn here and

www.makanologos.com

elsewhere to succeed in reaching their objective, they must be systematic. While a sporadic rhythmic breath can release you from extreme pain in an emergency, a breathing that has been given a routine and systematic attention will surely awaken your solar plexus. As the Earth accepts and absorbs sunrays often and effortlessly, so does it bear the fruits that give life to its inhabitants. And as you form the habit of performing rhythmic breathing, so will your solar plexus awaken, guard, and protect you from the invading chaotic feelings of the outer world.

Rhythmic breathing, if performed systematically, serves to quiet, pacify, and magnetize the emotional body and mind. As you breathe out, it reaches the center of infinity, brings in peace, and attunes your radiations to higher vibrations, making you a magnet of higher ideals, including divine ideals that have transformed ordinary minds into brilliant minds throughout time and space. This is how one single individual can gain the power to affect and bless the lives of so many in a way that very few people can possibly understand. High ideals are obtained by physical, mental, and spiritual discipline. Rhythmic breathing exercises, as discussed, gradually affect all these three planes of life in just one single effective breath. Breathing exercise is not sports, but it shares some characteristics with sports. Unlike sports, breathing exercise should not tire the subject. You know something is wrong with your breathing exercises when you are tired after what should be an exciting 15 to 20 minutes of working out, just as sports are strongly inadvisable to an ailing person, especially those who may have heart complaints.

3. <u>Symmetric Breath</u>

Symmetric breathing aims to remedy the imbalances that naturally exist in some parts of the body—for instance, the lungs—by inhaling the invigorating substances of life and exhaling unnecessary ones. Naturally, for most people, the right hand is suppler than the left hand; for others, one hand or

www.makanologos.com

foot is heavier or suppler than the other. One side of the heart pumps blood more efficiently than the other, and one side of the lungs inhales oxygen and exhales carbon dioxide better than the other. For all of us, one side of our bodies functions better than the other at one time or another.

A good analogy of symmetric breathing is two spouses with an equal likelihood of earning the bread for the family, but only one of them is currently working at full potential. The problem is that one spouse is just short of only a few college credits in order to get his or her degree that will facilitate a good-paying job. Symmetric breathing works like a spouse who is helping the companion to go to school, get a degree, find a job, and then put his or her talent to work for the benefit of the whole household (the body). It is like a friend lifting up a friend, balancing out the differences.

The duality principle of the universe—the good and bad, right and left, life and death, light and darkness, in and out, up and down, etc.—works in our body system as it works anywhere throughout infinity. When balance is maintained between the two opposites, the direct outcome is peace, harmony, and consequently growth in every dimension of life. When one side overweighs the other in nature, we see the reactions in terms of chaotic natural disasters such as earthquakes, epidemics, tornadoes, hurricanes, destructive volcanic eruptions, and even the destruction of our crops by invading bugs. The spiritual body acts the same. When one side is more sensitive to higher feelings while the other is more sensitive to lower feelings, because it is always easier to come down than to go up, the lower feelings tend to pull down the higher feelings to balance out the physical, mental, and spiritual bodies.

This of course is not a big deal if you couldn't care less about greatness. But those who care about greatness strive to pull the vibrations of their feelings up rather than letting the higher feelings be pulled by the lower ones to the detriment of greatness. Here is where symmetric breathing, also commonly known as balanced breath, comes into play and renders a tremendous service to anyone who performs it symmetrically and correctly. Here again, I cannot describe this wonderful breathing technique before I strongly call the attention of the reader to its side effects when used inappropriately by quoting once again the fabulous Paul Brunton:

The ancient masters who knew the different effects of breathings tell us that through the breath we may make ourselves as powerful as gods equally as we may go down into insanity, incurable diseases and sudden death. You will then understand that where the rewards are much greater, the dangers are no less great. In our system there are exercises for different purposes and if some are almost harmless, others if wrongly done are potent for grave injury...But persons who suffer with heart diseases should never practice any form of breathing exercise whatever (The Secret Path, page, 72).

Of all breathing techniques, symmetric breath is the deepest and the fastest to reach into the heart of infinity. It transforms man, for better or worse (if misused), faster and deeper than any other breathing technique. Thus, those who desire to use this breathing technique cannot be called strongly enough to have selfless intentions when doing this exercise. It is the most unnatural and artificial breathing that only those who have deep feelings about selfless goals in their minds take pains to practice. It is not the duty of the author to tell you what goal to have in your mind, but it is his responsibility to forewarn you that, if you are going to practice symmetric breathing, have a constructive intention in mind because, rather than drawing from the universe positive forces that will facilitate your greatness, you may attract unwanted forces or negative psychic influences that may either precipitate your downfall or make it practically impossible for you to climb the mountain of greatness.

That said, here is how symmetric breathing is performed in very simple and easy terms. Start by holding down the

www.makanologos.com

left nostril. Then breathe in deeply and slowly through the right one while picturing the highest good or a brilliant light enveloping your body and the whole room or wherever you are. Gradually exhale through the right nostril after a period of 8 to 10 seconds. The whole process of inhaling, holding the breath, and exhaling it should take approximately 24 to 30 seconds—8 to 10 seconds to inhale, 8 to 10 seconds to hold the breath, and 8 to 10 seconds to slowly exhale it. After five to seven breaths holding down one side and breathing with the other, the nostrils should be alternated for equal numbers of breaths. A good 10 to 15 minutes symmetrically performed will transform you into a totally new and better human being.

4. Revitalizing Breath

Revitalizing breath, like other previously discussed breathing techniques, must be performed with the best intentions in mind and a thought to the source of light. There is a Higher Power in the universe that knows us and understands our needs far better than we do. *"But seek you first the kingdom of God, and his righteousness and all these things shall be added unto you,"* we are told. When we perform breathing exercises with selfless intentions in mind, the universe that knows us and understands our needs best will take care of us. The moment of exercising breathing is not a moment of supplication but of cleaning the house where precious gifts will be delivered and from where they will be distributed. This is the exalted secret of breathing exercises.

Revitalizing breath is one of the best techniques of renewing mental and physical energy. Your attention is again called here to avoid going to extremes and to avoid straining yourself unnecessarily. It is also important to note that even a modest practice of the revitalizing breaths may occasionally tire the human body, if only for a very short time; however, in the end, you will find it refreshing. It consists of taking a deep breath, filling the lungs either by mouth or through the nostrils at the

www.makanologos.com

same time, holding it for a while but comfortably, then slowly exhaling between the teeth with jaws tightening, blowing a gentle but slow whistle. Repeat this as many times as your body is in a comfort zone. A good 10 to 20 minutes of revitalizing breaths will charge you with new life.

The beauty of revitalizing breath is that it can be done anywhere and at any time. It can be done at work, on the street, in a room, in a stadium, anywhere and anytime you are in charge of your mind and body.

This concludes the best suggestions I know of when it comes to awakening the solar plexus. These suggestions, of course, are just what they are; suggestions, and they will remain so as long as you look down on them. But if you seriously use them, you will find them to be a set of such powerful knowledge that they will reveal to you the person you really are, your true Inner/Higher Self whose power knows no obstacle except the limits you impose on It, whose love hurts no fly, whose wisdom knows no impasse, and whose life is a spark of divine greatness. As Tony Burroughs put it:

You are truly a magnificent entity with powers lying dormant and feelings so sublime, ready to burst forth like a young flower that spreads its petals for the first time to greet the morning sun.

How long will you wait before you see yourself in your highest light and do what makes you truly happy? What will it take for you to open your heart and radiate outward the ocean of Love that lies within you? You have been bound up too long, shackled to your fear, imprisoned by ghosts who are not real unless you make them so. The world needs you to be happy, to shine your light on all that you see, to laugh without limit, to touch the hearts and minds of every man, woman, and child who comes your way. (The Code: 10 Intentions for a Better World, page 150).

In closing this part, rather than going into breathing exercises with your mind filled with your desires, which will do nothing but separate you from your best interests, take a break from them for just a little while and fill yourself with light inside out.

www.makanologos.com

Breathe in light and literally see it as tangible etheric substance; see it as sparks blazing flames throughout your body and the world around you. This will serve your best interests and will give you a tremendous advantage over those who have no knowledge of this incredible power. It will place you among the chosen few. No matter how deeply sleeping your solar plexus is, a sun of light brilliantly shining through the center of your abdomen at the time of your breathing exercises or at any time, especially at a time of emergency, will awaken the center of life in you and calm your feelings, bowing to and handing you complete mastery of your emotions. This is the secret of the greatest among us. You can, if you will, cultivate it and become one of them. It is entirely up to you.

There is an urge inside me, the urge to finish this segment on the solar plexus with some sort of poetic, prophetic, or magical words of my own. One side of me wants to bow to this urge, but the better side of me wants to resist and reject self-aggrandizement. I reject the former and follow the latter. Thus I refuse to close this segment on the solar plexus with my own words, for I want the reader to know that what I strived to present to your mind is not simply the product of my own imagination; it is how greatness has been achieved by brilliant minds. And I have struggled to dig it out of some of the most secret and illuminating sources. The title of this book is not a fantasy but an expression of reality of how greatness has been attained since the dawn of time. To obtain a brilliant mind, it is really a MOUNTAIN you have to climb if you want to attain GREATNESS. With these words, I choose to yield to my better side, and I now call one of my beloved *teachers*, the remarkable Professor Theron Q. Dumont, to close this segment with the words he wrote almost one hundred years ago. You are welcome to read his words over and over again if you want to benefit the most from them. Here they are:

You are the officer on the deck talking, as to an equal, to chief engineer below decks in the engine room, the boiler room, and the furnace room. Get this idea well fixed in your mind, and you will know how to proceed correctly in the matter.

Furthermore, you are to remember that you have promised to do your part in the work of establishing and maintaining the normal physical conditions — you have promised full co-operation in the matter, and must live up to this promise and agreement. If you expect the Solar Plexus to do its share of the work, you must be prepared to do yours. You cannot expect to "lie down" on your end of the job, and to have the Solar Plexus "keep busy" on its end. If it finds you falling short, it will be apt to do the same. You must "play fair" with your partner in your work of Health and Strength...You must see that the body gets sufficient exercise, sufficient rest, sufficient fresh air, sufficient water, sufficient food of the right kind, and it is kept sufficiently clean... — you must not be surprised if the Solar Plexus retaliates by first "firing back" to you; and then, if you persist, of "going on a protest strike" and rendering you inefficient service. You must "play fair" with the Solar Plexus. It is good-natured, but not a fool; and it has high sense of justice and co-operation, and resents any attempt to "put anything over" on it, as many have found to their sorrow and pain. Get on good terms with your Solar Plexus — and play fair with it, if you are wise, (The Solar Plexus or Abdominal Brain, **pages 50-51).**

ADDENDUM

Homework

The task of illumining both the human intellect and mind is a collective responsibility of all and each of us equally. No one has or should have less or more than the previous or next person, and that include all the teachers who came before us. Regardless of what you think of yourself or anyone else, each of us is more than tons of dynamite that can easily explode, blast, and break with the speed of light, the veil of ignorance, darkness, and the chains of spiritual, mental, and physical bondage that sadly still keep the human race in a deplorable situation even as we are navigating this truly first (twenty-first) century of electronics and the space age.

It is for this reason that I chose to close this part of the work with an assignment for the most earnest seekers among my readers to dig deeper and prepare materials on this subject that will contribute to the illumination of our human race. Those who really believe in the Divine or Higher Power in all of us; the power that lifts our fingers or eyebrows; the power that circulates in our blood; the power that feeds our minds and our intellects with ideas and feelings; the power that keeps us hopeful, confident, and fearless of going to sleep and trusting to wake us up unharmed; the power that moves the sun, stars, planets, systems of worlds and galaxies; the power that expresses itself in the willing and determined children of man.

Those who believe in this kind of power — for which I have no exact words to describe, since only one's mind can convey the exact picture — will do the world and themselves a great service by researching and compiling a work on how music can be useful in opening and keeping open the solar plexus and other important spiritual centers in man in their exceptional roles of harmonizing feelings. Here are a few words from

Migene Gonzalez-Wippler, in the publication cited above, to give a heads up:

The music must be vibrant and alive with sound and power. Interestingly enough, some rock music is ideal for building up energy because of its exhilarating beat...Any type of music that has a steady drum beat in the background is apt to create this state of nervous excitement with resulting flow of psychic energy (page, 140).

Go for it and enjoy the ride.

PART THREE

THE ELIXIR OF INTELLIGENCE

You may have noticed that the title of this work has four major words, and of the four, three key words make up the title of this third and last part of the book. That is not an accident. It does not mean, however, that the first two parts are less important, nor does it mean that this part is really what the work is all about. It simply means that the previous two were the cornerstones, the foundation, the walls and pillars of the building; this one is the capstone of the pyramid, or the roof. Probably the first two could exist without the third, but what is a pyramid without a capstone or a building without a roof? Nevertheless, a surveyor who wants to see clearly to the furthest ends of the landscape must climb to the highest point.

If you have read this book this far, it is my opinion that your goal in reading the content of this book is to acquire a brilliant mind, and I want you to know that it is exactly for that purpose that this author spent days, months, and years researching and writing this book in hope of compiling something that will help his fellow men in acquiring the indispensable elements of brilliant minds. Acquisition of a brilliant mind, which is itself a journey rather than a destination, of course cannot be accomplished with reading a single book, but here I hope to offer you, if not all elements of a brilliant mind, at least a frame and all central elements, making your journey readily less complicated. All you will have to do from here on out is to fill in the missing blanks, and before you know it, a brilliant mind will be standing within you like a sun in a cloudless sky at midday.

Exalted Secrets of Brilliant Minds   **249**

Before you embark and move on to your journey of acquiring a brilliant mind, here are some quotations that I hope, anticipatively, will give you a flash of what is to come, and I trust you will ponder them seriously as you go:

1. *Many people confuse "education" with "intelligence."* (Henry Ward Beecher)

2. *A mountaineer, who cannot read, may yet still have high mental horsepower or intelligence. You can thus have a brilliant mind, yet never have graduated from grammar school. Edison and Ford, Lincoln and Shakespeare and countless other geniuses held no college degree.* (Henry Ward Beecher, from The Kleinknetcht Germs of Thought Encyclopedia, Volume IX, page 199)

3. *Intelligence is not the same thing as intellect. The intellect means a well-stored and logical mind; the intelligence is a power...aims at developing faculty rather than amassing facts* (Clara Codd, *The Technique of Spiritual Life*, page 111).

In the introduction, I suggested that you read the article "Intelligence Is Overrated: What You Really Need to Succeed" from the online version of *Forbes* magazine at www.forbes.com/sites/keldjensen/2012/04/12/intelligence-is-overrated-what-you-really-need-to-succeed/ (accessed June 28, 2012). If you have not done so, I strongly urge you to read this very useful article to prepare your mind if you really want to benefit from what comes from the rest of this work. Even if you have read it already, please reread it to refresh your mind. Read or reread earnestly, as if your growth depends on it, because it does.

www.makanologos.com

CHAPTER XII

Intelligence and the Source of Intelligence
(Infinite Magnifying Field or Infinite Charging Battery)

Before I get deep into this third and last part of the book, I would like to make one honest confession. I hope this confession will not look to you like a sign of arrogance but rather a sincere expression of the deep feelings I have had throughout the time these ideas were being translated into a written language. The confession is this: as much as I would like this book to be a product of skill, I genuinely think and feel deeply in the very center of my being that it is in fact more a product of inspiration than of talent and of obedience to natural laws than of creativity. Nothing will prove this point better than this third part, especially this chapter here. Not all chapters of this part were written in chronological order. I did not anticipate it to be a product of systematic or crafty thinking but rather of intuition or a free and unobstructed flow of thoughts and feelings. It was not always as easy as it may sound. Like all mortals, I felt I knew better than that humble but clear and firm voice that speaks from the center of the beings of all of us. How foolish was I? For as I took my ego out of the way, the clearer was the vision of the work to me and the firmer I became in seeing my work through.

Nevertheless, somehow and on many occasions, I felt the compulsion to impose my intellect, to bow to my heart while standing on its own feet. With that inner obedience, I felt the wisdom and intuition of the heart and the strength and analysis of the intellect come together for a balanced achievement of my life. Rather than imposing the destination and much less the means, the heart gave me the freedom to go where I wished to go and the insight to adjust the sail while the wind behind my back gently blew. Thus I reach this milestone of accomplishment. The laws that will be discussed in this part of the book will attempt to show readers that intelligence is not a mere mechanism of accumulation and processing of information quickly and accurately, but rather obedience to the higher codes of nature for a constructive purpose. It is not a course of sequential thinking but the light that comes to us, sometimes in a split second; to make inexplicably clear a problem that has frustrated the quality of life we want to live in a lasting way.

It is easier to build a bridge than devise ways to walk on water. It is much easier and smarter to build a dam and harness electricity than to prevent a mighty river or even a small one from following its course to a lake or an ocean. The compulsion to write—not the easiness, because writing is not easy—as inspirations forced their way to my fingertips and into my laptop is the major reason most of the last part of this book was not written as chapters and why sometimes paragraphs do not appear in chronological order. Should the reader not find a logical bridging of ideas from one chapter to another, this would be the reason. The goal here was to obey intuition and inspiration rather than the technical rules, to obey natural impulses rather than artificial or crafty modus operandi.

By the way, how in the world would it be easy to effectively bridge chapters and paragraphs when the conclusion was sometime written long before the introduction, the third chapter written before the second was even fairly thought out? Writing was not meant to be done this way, but in a few instances, writers have no choice but to listen to the dictating inner voice. Please do not get me wrong—I made serious efforts to make sure hiatuses between chapters and paragraphs are practically invisible to most readers. I suspect, thus, that the average reader will most likely notice nothing, and only very skilled readers may be able to notice where my bridging skill came up

www.makanologos.com

short. However, the point I am trying to express here is that, of all the points that have been written in this book, none has been debated in my inner schoolroom longer and deeper than the subject of the last part of this work, and that is intelligence, the real definition of intelligence in the clearest way that will enable true seekers acquisition of a brilliant mind.

For the last seven years, maybe longer, I have been working hard to understand what intelligence really is. I have tried to force myself to accept its traditional definition but to no avail. Despite my efforts, I came to the conclusion that intelligence, as most of us know it, is a myth, or misconstrued at the very least. And every attempt I made utterly failed to basically prove otherwise. Involuntarily, I have come to believe that intelligence as we (most of us) know it is nothing but a myth or misconstrued at best. I repeat it to make sure not only that the reader gets the idea unambiguously, but I also hear it clearly and soundly inside myself. Intelligence as it is explained or at least implied really does not exist. The traditional understanding of intelligence makes it seem like something we become rather than something we already are. That is why I am urging my readers to read the *Forbes* magazine article. On the one hand, it is a consolation for me to know that I was not the only crazy person out there thinking differently about intelligence after all; on the other, it will lighten the task of the reader in absorbing what is presented in this work. I want the reader to know that this section of the book was written more than a year before the publication of the *Forbes* magazine article. I just inserted this portion while reviewing and editing the book.

This is the major reason why the conspiracy of arrested development seems very real to the masses. And believe it or not, arrested development is real, not because there are somewhere in the world some smart and busy folks working hard to keep some fellow men less intelligent, but because of the distraction that is keenly made to keep self-underestimating

www.makanologos.com

people to think otherwise. Intelligence is not a process; it is a state. Man does not become intelligence; man is intelligence. Thinking otherwise will be erroneous and a denial of the true nature of self. Those who believe they are intelligent are free and masters of the world, whereas those who believe they will become intelligent are the servants who will never taste the fruit of freedom here on God's Earth or elsewhere.

Believe you are intelligent—and I mean believe with all your feelings, thoughts, and actions; your heart, brain, and hands; your mind, soul, and being. Believe you are intelligent before every feeling, then feel or make an effort to feel intelligent. Believe you are intelligent before every thought, then think or make an effort to think intelligently. Believe you are intelligent before every action, then act or make an effort to act intelligently, and you will surprise the world. I wish my readers to understand that man does not make water; water is already there all around us. Water is in the sky, in the ground, even in us, and of course in rivers, lakes, and oceans. You may have noticed that in the same breath, I said man is intelligent. Don't worry, relax, and read on earnestly; you will get what I mean.

Like water, intelligence is really not dormant but active in nature and us. That which seems to be our best teacher is only the reflection of the intelligence that is in us. Just as it is harder for a person in the desert to find water, so it is more difficult for a person who wishes to become intelligent to really be intelligent or at least harness the fruits of his intelligence. And it is easier for a person who believes himself to be intelligent to really be intelligent and effectively harness the fruits of his mental powers, just as it is easier for a person walking in the forest to find water than a person in the desert.

Years after I had struggled with the debate inside myself about the nature of intelligence as I thought it to be, the compulsion to put my feelings and thoughts—at least for the

www.makanologos.com

sake of stimulating or contributing to (if there already is one) a public debate—was so strong that I felt an obligation to not waste time by getting to work promptly. When for the first time I tried to explain to friends and coworkers my thinking, their reaction made me think I was out of my mind. Even so, after they gave me a chance to explain further, their reaction did not change much. A few tolerant simply said or implied, *"You have got a point, but you cannot prove it scientifically."*

Maybe I cannot prove it scientifically, but that is what I deeply believe with all my heart, head, and soul and my being. I know I look foolish to many people, but science and faith may have the same roots and may work cohesively at the inner level, but they do not always coalesce to the naked eye. I would not blame you if you also think the same. But if you put your prejudice of my point of view aside and take an unbiased and closer look at it, you might scratch your head a little bit as some of my friends did. I refuse to pass on from this plane of life without putting this enigma of mine out there for others to think about or maybe even kick off a discussion that may be resolved as time goes on. Wherever I am, here or somewhere in the infinite cosmos, my happiness will be boundless that this puzzle of mine has reached you in a written form.

The study of intelligence is so confusing and confused that, despite serious study, it is less clear whether intelligence is an ability to accumulate and process one kind of thought or all kind of thoughts. If you say it is the ability to understand and process one kind of thought or idea, then even Albert Einstein, whose name is synonymous with ingenuity, was not intelligent after all, as he declined to be the first president of the state of Israel for lack of people skills. If you say that intelligence is the ability to understand and process all kinds of thoughts, you find yourself screaming from the rooftop that the world has more geniuses than people of average intelligence. But does it?

Intelligence is an extremely murky concept to define. It cannot be defined by some characteristics of all people or all

Exalted Secrets of Brilliant Minds   255

characteristics of some people. How can you say that Einstein was not intelligent because he confessed the mediocrity of his social skills? How can you say that a highly successful businessman who is but a highly miserable politician is not intelligent? How would you classify a Harvard University graduate and a PhD in mathematics from the University of Michigan, Theodore John "Ted" Kaczynski, also known as the Unabomber, who became a serial murderer to advance his opposition to industrialism and modern technology; an A+ student who ended up working for a dropout student; or a highly successful executive, politician, scientist, athlete, or businessman but a total failure in family, social life, and other occupations? Let me drop this question somewhere in your head before I move on: Who in your opinion is more intelligent between an excellent husband and wife, father and mother, neighbor and community activist, but who is academically and professionally challenged, or academically and professionally successful but socially miserable failure in all its dimensions? Think about it.

To avoid swimming in muddy waters, scientists have tried to convince the world that intelligence is measured by what they call the Intelligence Quotient, or IQ. This idea of IQ has been gladly bought by many of us, indeed. Unfortunately, nothing really serves the arrested development conspiracy better than the IQ theory. Fortunately, a few rational arguments and real-life experiences easily demonstrate that IQ has less or nothing at all to do with intelligence.

If you look properly, you will notice that most of our leaders in business, the military, politics, media, even science, mathematics, physics, or chemistry have or had average IQs, and many others had less-than-average IQs. A close look will show that many of them reached where they are for reasons that have less to do with their IQ and more with compliance with the laws of nature, among others perseverance, courage, fearlessness, and self-confidence, etc. And worst of all, you will

www.makanologos.com

find that more people with high IQs have their paychecks signed and orders given by, guess who, a person of possibly inferior IQ than their own. If you have been looking for work lately, I am sure you have not encountered any responsible human resources manager who prefers higher IQ over experience.

Moreover, if you happen to be lucky to visit NASA or any other high-level research center, you will notice that most of their "gods" or genuine geniuses are "gods" not necessarily because of their IQs but because of the time they have spent there turning the ancient wheel of trial and error. Few of them become truly "gods" in mid-career; many are so mostly toward the close of their careers as they become better students of the laws of nature, which are the subjects of upcoming chapters of this book. Unlike the GPA (grade point average), rather than encouraging self-confidence, resolve, and resiliency in exteriorizing what truly is inside, the IQ is used to stigmatize those it deems unworthy and to instill complacency, lethargy, or nonchalance in those it deems worthy.

Follow me closely, and hopefully you will judge me fairly. I deeply believe in what I am saying. I have never had a chance to discuss it with fair-minded people. I want to share it with my readers for the first time, not to indoctrinate anyone, but to sow a provocative thought that may be studied and hopefully better explained by someone out there for the benefit of our common human race's evolution. Of course, it is not about me, but I feel hurt when I try to explain what I believe to be a misguided conception of intelligence. I get ridiculed and insulted sometimes. However, the more I look into this idea, the more convinced I am that I am on the right side of the fence. I do not want or expect you to take my word blindly. I just want you to take a deeper look, dig deeper in your heart, and put these ideas to a tough test in your inner lab and field of action to prove for yourself whether the ability to score high on an IQ test or the ability to obey the laws of nature is the true measure of intelligence.

www.makanologos.com

Exalted Secrets of Brilliant Minds   257

People of high IQ are born, at least one, somewhere on Earth every century, every decade, every year, every month, maybe even every week, day, and hour, minute, or second. Ask yourself simple questions. High IQ folks are all over the world, it is true, but why did it take man millions of years to produce a small calculator, to build a car or telephone, to reject the flatness concept of the Earth, to learn such a simple notion as the rotation and revolution of the Earth, to come up with the wonders that have made twenty-first century medicine look like a miraculous moment compared to that of just the early part of twentieth century? Ask yourself many questions of why now and why not then? I will let you answer those questions for yourself, but I will answer for myself as well — because that is how long it took mankind to learn and master the laws of nature, whose understanding is prerequisite to all discoveries and inventions or so-called intelligence itself. Of course, the point is not just to deny or reject the definition of intelligence as we know it, but to lay out what I really think intelligence is and how anyone can truly, practically, and effectively cultivate it to the best of his or her abilities to create marvels for our common good.

It is a fact, free of argument, that 95% of the wealth of the world is basically owned and/or run by less than 5% of the world's population. Mensa is an organization that seeks to organize highly intelligent people. It issues memberships to applicants whose IQ test results have placed them in the top 2% of the population. On its website, http://www.mensa.org/about-us (accessed June 28, 2012), it states its three purposes: *"to identify and foster human intelligence for the benefit of humanity, to encourage…intelligence, and promote stimulating intellectual and social opportunities of its members."* Of course, every organization must have some membership criteria to join, but for the IQ test score to be the sole condition, it may be a self-defeating prophecy. Assuming a tree is judged by its fruits alone, and also assuming that financial and political successes are proofs

www.makanologos.com

of intelligence, how many Mensa members are parts of the less than 5% who own or run the means of economic production? How many Mensa members are parts of the elite class that governs the world?

The world, mostly the West and its copycats, has been toying with the notion of measuring intelligence using artificial elements. Rather than teaching and measuring the laws that lead to growth and the expansion of latent talents, our schools, from kindergarten to the universities and colleges, reward or punish us according to our aptitude to retain or reproduce what we have been told instead of our ability to transform and expand what we have been told. As result, most college students graduate without an idea of the power of intuitive comprehension, the magic of determination, self-confidence, or the pleasure of doing what one really loves. As a consequence, few get the job of their dreams. The majority get jobs they do without passion, and many join the unemployment line and stay on it long after graduation until they bow and take any job offer that comes their way.

Intelligence, a latent or potential ability to know and do something with varying degrees of health and wellness, is enhanced with adaptation and development of spiritual and moral qualities that practically hand you the key through the intuitive understanding and knowledge of the true nature of things and laws you want to comprehend. Unlike the West and its former colonies, Japan (and to some extent China and Korea), instead of focusing its formal education system on Western values has focused on its cultural education method, which is essentially based on the notion of understanding and application of spiritual and moral laws. Studies have shown that Japanese workers are among the hardest and happiest workers in the world.

As Ella A. Fletcher puts it, *"Through self-control that all great forces, working harmoniously to a given end, come out of the silence."*

www.makanologos.com

The Japanese cultural education system early on in childhood teaches self-control and the necessity of observing silence through martial arts and other traditional tools. The Japanese elixir of intelligence is basically a product of a now-defunct social class: the samurai. The samurai is an ancient class of Japanese warriors who lived by the Bushido philosophy. The Bushido philosophy basically taught its students to seek trustworthiness, honesty, honor and pride, and true valor; to have no interest in riches and material things; and to have no fear of death. Bushido, the way of the samurai, grew out of the synthesis of Buddhism, Shintoism, Confucianism, and the Zen, which teaches one to "know thyself" and not to limit oneself.

Through Bushido, also known as the Soul of Nippon, they *"teach the spirit of discipline and sacrifice, of gentleness and firmness, of honor and integrity, of heroic endurance and chivalry,"* according to Fletcher. *"It puts emphasis on loyalty, self-sacrifice, justice, sense of shame, refined manners, purity, modesty, frugality, martial spirit, honor and affection"* (Nippon Steel Human Resources Development Co., Ltd., page, 329). The samurai teach military nobility. There is no question that Japan, like many other parts of the world, has a lot to thank the West for. It has learned a great deal from the West. It may be an old empire and civilization, but its industrial revolution was mostly inspired by or copied from the West. While a humble student of life, Japan lifted up and transformed Western science and technology through Bushido and samurai spirits into something that now is giving migraines and dizziness to the West as the rest of the world gazes in amazement. Of the effectiveness and invincibility of the Japanese cultural education system, in the publication cited earlier, Fletcher writes:

> But the whole secret is that the Nipponese have never lost touch with nature. They have kept close to the soul of things, to the heart of the universe, with sense trained to consciousness of the nearness of the spiritual plane, which the Western people have blindly ignored,

www.makanologos.com

when not denied, in their head-long pursuit of things material. Japan's own peril is only from those of her people who imitate too closely Western commercial methods, forgetting the traditions of the past, or never themselves trained in them (page, 95).

Those words of Fletcher may seem baseless, a fantasy, or a dream from a passionate writer. I would probably agree with you as well had I not taken time to research and put them on the scale to see their weight before judging them objectively. I will let you weigh them yourself before judging them, objectively, I hope. But before you do so, read the samurai creed and seven principles from *The Zen Way to the Martial Arts*, which inspired the Bushido. If you think you cannot take and live by this vow, do not judge Fletcher hastily, but take your time to think about it meticulously, and maybe you can discover a way to infiltrate the mind of the Japanese and help America to reclaim the "land of technology" epithet it once was known for and that the descendants of the samurai now claim for themselves unchallenged.

The Samurai Creed

I have no parents; I make the Heavens and the Earth my parents.
I have no home; I make the Tan T'ien my home.
I have no divine power; I make honesty my Divine Power.
I have no means; I make Docility my means.
I have no magic power; I make personality my Magic Power.
I have neither life nor death; I make A Um my Life and Death.

I have no body; I make Stoicism my Body.
I have no eyes; I make the Flash of Lightning my eyes.
I have no ears; I make Sensibility my Ears.
I have no limbs; I make Promptitude my Limbs.
I have no laws; I make Self-Protection my Laws.

I have no strategy; I make the Right to Kill and the Right to Restore Life my Strategy.

www.makanologos.com

*I have no designs; I make Seizing the Opportunity by the Forelock
     my Designs.*
I have no miracles; I make Righteous Laws my Miracle.
*I have no principles; I make Adaptability to all circumstances my
     Principle.*
I have no tactics; I make Emptiness and Fullness my Tactics.

I have no talent; I make Ready Wit my Talent.
I have no friends; I make my Mind my Friend.
I have no enemy; I make Incautiousness my Enemy.
I have no armour; I make Benevolence my Armour.
I have no castle; I make Immovable Mind my Castle.
I have no sword; I make No Mind my Sword.
(http://beepbeep.tblog.com/post/1969745377,   accessed
July 11, 2012)

SEVEN PRINCIPLES
From *The Zen Way to the Martial Arts*
Bushido, the way of the samurai, grew out of the fusion of
Buddhism and Shintoism. This way can be summarized in
seven essential principles:
1. *Gi: the right decision, taken with equanimity, the right attitude,
   the truth. When we must die, we must die. Rectitude.*
2. *Yu: bravery tinged with heroism.*
3. *Jin: universal love, benevolence toward mankind; compassion.*
4. *Rei: right action – a most essential quality, courtesy.*
5. *Makoto: utter sincerity; truthfulness.*
6. *Melyo: honor and glory.*
7. *Chugo: devotion, loyalty.*

*These are the seven principles underlying the spirit of Bushido,
Bu – martial arts; shi – warrior; do – the way.*

*The way of the samurai is imperative and absolute. Practice,
in the body, through the unconscious, is fundamental to it, thus
the enormous importance attached to the learning of right action*

www.makanologos.com

or behavior. (http://www.shotokai.com/ingles/filosofia/principles.html, accessed July 11, 2012)

Of course, the samurai became obsolete during the Meiji Era in 1876 after more than ten centuries of inspiring Japanese people the value of laws of wisdom. However, just like the Knights Templar still ruling the West from the graves, the samurai are still ruling Japan from the hearts and souls of the Japanese people where not even the most audacious foreigner can reach. To this day, Japanese people are still looking to the spirit of the samurai to inspire their thoughts, feelings, and actions, which hearten them to make some of the boldest claims ever to the point of nicknaming Japan "the land of technology." The samurai spirit, a major piece of the modern Japanese character, is still flawlessly running in the young Japanese blood, and unless you share that blood or you are completely immersed in their culture, you may never get a clue.

But again, if you completely immerse yourself in their culture, you are very likely to catch flames of fire and be engulfed in the light of their greatness, finding neither the spring of analytical understanding nor the fountain of intuitive wisdom nor the source of the Japanese *kundalini* (tree of knowledge) to quench the thirst and hunger of the crybabies on the other side of the fence. Hence, you will wind up where you left the world, in total confusion as far as the Japanese experience is concerned. That is the dilemma; that is the quagmire that the rest of the world faces in trying to understand the Japanese stratagem of the mountain of greatness the Japanese have set for the rest of the world to climb. Again judging the tree by its fruits, who would say that the Japanese cultural system of shaping and measuring intelligence through spiritual and moral qualities is not effective? Yes! Japan started late compared to the Industrial Revolution in the West. Based on modern technological measurement, I think it would be reasonable to say that Japan mostly copied centuries of Western scientific research. At first,

www.makanologos.com

Japan was ignored and then ridiculed by the West, but who has the last laugh now? Is there a greater threat to American greatness in particular and Western greatness in general than the Japanese in particular and the upcoming powers of the East (China and the Koreas) in general today?

Given what is really happening now in the war of competition between Japan and its Occidental counterparts on all fronts, I believe it is fair to at least think that the spirit of the Samurai and Bushido imprinted something much stronger, more dynamic and inspiring on the minds of the Japanese people than what the minds of the Westerners felt from the spirits of the Knights Templar, as these words of Joseph Campbell in *Myths to Live By* (pages 50-51) unequivocally confirm:

I come to appreciate most vividly the life-amplifying service of ritual when, in Japan...I was invited to a tea ceremony of which the host was to be a distinguished master. Now if there is anything in this world more demanding of formal accuracy than the procedure of a Japanese tea ceremony, I should like to know what or where it might be. There are in Japan...people who have studied and practiced Tea all their lives without achieving perfection, so exquisite are its rules...The forms have not been bred into his bones; even his body is the wrong shape. And the tea ceremony...comes to its own formal culmination, after a number of ritualized preliminaries...Suffice to say that every gesture and even tilt of the head is controlled; and yet, when I later talked with the other guests, they spoke with praise of the "spontaneity" of this master. The only term of comparison I could think of at the time was the poetic art of the sonnet; for there too is a very demanding form; yet the poet requires within it a force and range of the expression that he could never have gained without it...I had the privilege of observing in Japan the styles of a number of tea masters and learned to see how each was actually relaxed and free in performance. The ritual of the civilization had become organic, as it were, in the master, and he could move in it spontaneously

www.makanologos.com

with expressive elaboration. The effect, in its own way, was like that of a beautiful Japanese garden, where nature and the art have been brought together in a common statement harmonizing and epitomizing both. **Do we have anything of the kind in our present North America civilization?**

While the Japanese model may be tough to duplicate, more and more countries and individuals are going into the inner silence to find moral as well as physical equilibrium, to learn the right course leading to more balanced rational feelings, emotional thinking, and spiritual living in order to engineer a more pleasant lifestyle. India, for instance, a country that has underestimated and mistrusted itself for centuries, subjecting itself to slavery and domination to foreign kings and powers, is just now strengthening its backbone to stand up for itself like its more daring neighbors of the East, Japan, China, and Korea.

For centuries, India has been a meek subject of foreign kings and powers, all this despite being the land of some of the holiest and oldest schools of wisdom on the planet, maybe second only to the pyramids of Egypt. An old civilization, India is a country that is believed by many around the world and over the centuries to have been *a spiritual breeding ground* of some of the best teachers mankind has ever known, including Jesus, Job, Confucius, Buddha, John the Baptist, Pythagoras, and Francis Bacon, who are thought to have either been born there or traveled to India for their fundamental lessons of spiritual education.

For centuries, India has attracted seekers of the Divine Truth from all over the world. In fact, one of the three wise men who were reported to have visited the Child Jesus is believed by many to have been from India. The construction of the pyramids in Egypt is believed to have been at least partially aided by commercial contact between the two countries. Illustrations of India's spiritual greatness are momentous. It is in fact the search for better ways of getting to India from Europe that led to the discovery of America, causing its native people to be wrongly

www.makanologos.com

Exalted Secrets of Brilliant Minds **265**

and probably forever named Indians. Yet India has never seemed to utilize the wisdom found in its hallowed mountains, caves, and monasteries to generate an effective governing philosophy that would eventually humanize the lives of its entire people. Now those days are slowly coming to an end. India is now looking inside itself for dynamic and efficient answers. While still hanging onto the Western education system, India today is learning to rotate on its inner axis and revolve around its own sun by adapting Western education to its fascinating spiritual values that made it a land that fascinated the world's greatest souls and luminaries for centuries.

Exalted secrets that have helped mold brilliant minds for centuries are now being taught publicly in many parts of the world with extraordinary results. They do not have to be selectively taught somewhere to the detriment of others. They are being given to us by those who are in charge of the destiny of the enlightenment of mankind, free as the air we breathe at this particular time as our mother planet, Earth, is going through its rigorous initiation of love. And of course, while it is free, every inch of it is one hundred percent deserved, for nature never rewards sluggishness, but it does lavishly reward any and all sincere and constructive efforts. Mankind, while it is maybe slowly moving forward, is certainly moving rightward. My hope is that more and more people will be bringing awareness of these laws of wisdom to the masses worldwide until they become part of world culture as people use them not as tools of last but of first resort. That is the goal of this part of the book, and it is incumbent on me to explain how for centuries, wise kings and princes, sages and seers, high priests and the audacious few have been harnessing these powers under the noses of the clueless masses. It is my hope that the explanation is free of the mystical and philosophical jargon that not only clouds the truth but also keeps average minds from attempting to search for what is otherwise their birthright.

www.makanologos.com

But before I lay the first stone down, let me caution my readers here. You will notice that this work is made up of three major parts: "The Philosopher Stone," "The Royal Secret," and "The Elixir of Intelligence." These three parts are independent only to some extent. Intrinsically, they are not only deeply related, but they are mutually dependent, and their interdependence is more bottom up than otherwise, in the same manner that the roof depends on the walls and the walls on the foundation, and of course the foundation depends on the roof and the walls to keep at bay, at least for a while, those persistent forces of nature such as wind and rain that destroy all man-made things with time. The third part depends on the second part, which depends on the first one, and vice versa.

In other words, before the third part can be well understood, the second must be well apprehended. The third part is simply the roof, if you want to make a construction analogy. The second is the equivalent of the walls, and the first is the foundation of the house, which can exist whether there are walls and roof or not, but without them, it will never be called a house. With that analogy in mind, consider this—if you missed the point of the first part of the book, go back, analyze, and discern it again, more critically this time around, to get the results from the lessons of the third part. This is how the most benefits can be extracted from this book.

Now, going back to the issue of intelligence, two major questions will be debated for the rest of this chapter. The first is, what is intelligence? And the second is, how does one acquire and sharpen intelligence? Most people believe that intelligence is a mental power in man that sets him apart from other creatures and allows him to improve or transform the conditions of his environment to fit his needs. If this is the way you have always viewed it, you have a point. Since this book is about the secrets of brilliant minds and how to climb the mountain of greatness as wise kings and princes, sages and

www.makanologos.com

seers, high priests, and the daring few have done throughout history, I will tell you how they view intelligence in a way that enabled them to benefit more from it than the rest of us. In other words, what takes brilliant minds above the average conception of intelligence and makes them rulers over not only our physical beings and material possessions, but also our thoughts, feelings, and actions?

While great people know that man is intelligent, they believe man is a channel through which Higher Forces of the universe are always attempting to act, and the most intelligent among us are those who position themselves appropriately to allow these mighty forces of the universe to flow unobstructed. Different people can define intelligence in different ways for different reasons; thus, working with definitions of different people can make work itself difficult if not impossible.

What is intelligence? Let me answer that question, but before I explain how you can acquire it, let's first consider these words of David Aaron from his book *Endless Light: The Ancient Path of the Kabbalah to Love, Spiritual Growth and Personal Power*:

> Great artists have confided to friends that they have looked at their own works and wondered, "Where did this come from?" Writers, composers, sculptors, singers all have said the same thing, testifying to an out-of-character experience. Bob Dylan was asked "How do you write your music?" And he said, "I just sit down to write and I know it is going to be all right."
>
> In other words, something else besides the self seems to be at work in the creative process, and the artist becomes a vehicle of greater creative spirit, a greater I. If you are self-conscious (which really means ego conscious) and try to impose your ego on the creative process, you can't create. In the Kabbalah, ego consciousness is a state called "klipah," literally meaning "hard shell." You become encased in a hard shell that separates you from the Divine I. For example, if you are a pianist who is ego conscious, and you have a feeling when you are onstage that "there is the audience, there

www.makanologos.com

is me, there is my piano, and there is my music," then it will never come together. You have to crack open that shell and let go. You have to become the music and let the Great Musician — Hashem — play through you, whether you admit it publicly or not. So the joy of a person in creative moment is really this strange kind of I-consciousness, rather than ego consciousness or self-consciousness. This experience resembles what the Kabbalah refers as becoming a "merkava," which really means "chariot." You feel like a vehicle for a higher spirit and you are humbled and grateful, not haughty or arrogant, (pages, 105-106).

And in *The Power of Myth,* a robustly mind-stirring conversation between Joseph Campbell and Bill Moyers, this is recorded:

Moyers: *You say that elites create myths, that shamans and artists and others who take the journey into the unknown come back to create myths. But what about ordinary folks? Don't they create the stories of Paul Bunyan, for example?*

Campbell: *Yes, but chat is not a myth. That doesn't hit the level of myth. The prophets and what in India are called the "rishis" are said to have heard the scripture. Now anybody might open his ears, but not everyone has the capacity actually to hear the scriptures.*

Moyers: *"He who has ears to hear, let him hear."*

Campbell: *There has to be a training to help you open your ears so that you begin to hear metaphorically instead of concretely. Freud and Jung felt that myth is grounded in the unconscious.* (Author's note: Now pay attention to what is coming.) *Anyone writing a creative work knows that you open, you yield yourself, and the book talks to you and builds itself. To a certain extent, you become the carrier of something that is given to you from what have been called the Muses — or, in biblical language, "God." This is no fancy, it is a fact. Since the inspiration comes from the unconscious, and since the unconscious minds of the people of any single small society have much in common, what the shaman or seer brings forth is something that is waiting to be*

www.makanologos.com

Exalted Secrets of Brilliant Minds   **269**

brought forth in everyone. So when one hears the seer's story, one responds, "Aha! This is my story. This is something that I had always wanted to say," (pages, 70-71).

Intelligence is the inner light that illumines the mind of man through the never-ending course of capturing and processing feelings and thoughts that are sent our way by the forces of the universe for the purpose of achieving a constructive end. This, of course, is the object of the rest of this work; thus it will be explained and understood as the reading progresses.

If you have driven on a major U.S. highway for a long-distance trip, I am sure you must have taken some time off the wheel to appreciate and enjoy fresh air or to recharge yourself with new energy and strength at one of several rest areas along the way. I will do the same here. I will get outside the box and try to walk through what a reputable source of knowledge says intelligence is. The Merriam-Webster online dictionary (May 23, 2010 entry) defines intelligence as follows:

Main Entry: in-tel-li-gence:...1 a (1): the ability to learn or understand or to deal with new or trying situations: REASON; also: the skilled use of reason (2): the ability to apply knowledge to manipulate one's environment or to think abstractly as measured by objective criteria (as tests) b Christian Science: the basic eternal quality of divine Mind c: mental acuteness: SHREWDNESS 2 a: an intelligent entity; especially: ANGEL (http://www.merriam-webster.com/dictionary/intelligence, (accessed Nov. 2010).

Analyzing that description of intelligence in depth, as I would like could take precious space unnecessarily; thus I will just point out the most important points that are crucial to our purpose. In its first definition of intelligence, Merriam-Webster simply states that intelligence is the ability to learn...skilled use of...ability to apply. Quoting Christian Science in its b entry, it basically describes intelligence as the *"basic eternal quality of divine Mind,"* and further down it gives "angel" as an example of an intelligent entity. Now, looking at it from one prospective,

www.makanologos.com

it may be deducted from Merriam-Webster's point of view that you either have intelligence or you do not; you either have the ability to learn, to understand, to apply knowledge, or you do not. It does not seem to suggestion that the ability to learn, the skill to use reason, or the ability to apply knowledge can be acquired and how. Christian Science, on the other hand, in its definition seems to show the source of intelligence but does not show how the Divine Mind streams down it into the human mind.

This is not an easy task. It is not impossible, either. But should I succeed in translating correctly all the ideas that are flowing in my mind and head on this subject, I will pat myself on the back, if not on my forehead. Not to undermine the work of Merriam-Webster — not at all — but the truth is that if there were an easy way of defining and acquiring intelligence, the world would be full of geniuses. But to be honest, the way to acquire intelligence really does exist, except most of us either look in the wrong place or simply do not bother to look at all because of the misconception that it does not exist.

The knowledge that there is a source of intelligence and a way to acquire it is what makes the biggest difference between wise kings, princes, sages, seers, high priests, the daring few on one hand and the rest of us on the other. Intelligence alone makes man more divine than all other terrestrial creatures. Let me repeat the definition of intelligence I gave earlier: Intelligence is the inner light that illumines the mind of man through the never-ending course of capturing, analyzing, and transforming feelings and thoughts that are sent our way by the forces of the universe for the purpose of achieving a constructive end. Did you hear that? I just said "capturing, analyzing, and transforming thoughts, ideas, and feelings."

Why attracting, analyzing, and transforming and not manufacturing? Attracting, analyzing, and transforming because ideas, thoughts, and feelings are not man-made. Ideas,

www.makanologos.com

thoughts, and feelings are timeless. They know neither time nor space. They know neither beginning nor ending. They fill and travel throughout the universe seeking for an outlet to transform themselves into visible things. Man cannot manufacture ideas, thoughts, and feelings any more than he can manufacture sunrays. He, if he puts himself in the right position and at the right time and space, can attract sunrays and transform them into food, health, or any other desired good thing when the law is applied correctly or even a bad thing when the law is misapplied.

The most important question I can expect the reader to ask and I feel is imperative on my part to answer, anticipatively of course, is, if man does not manufacture ideas, thoughts, or feelings, what in heaven's name is the purpose of man's intellect? A relevant question, of course, but now let me elaborate as much as I can. I will answer that question, but let me say these few things first. In the universe, there exists a spring of good ideas, thoughts, and feelings, but they are made bad or negative by man through the violation of the laws that govern their nature and function. This spring or fountain of ideas, thoughts, and feelings is what I would call the Infinite Magnetizing Field, or the IMF for short. While a human being is incapable of manufacturing ideas, thoughts, or feelings, his role is to attract and transform them into visible things. I will make a brief description of this all-powerful body in the remainder of this chapter and then spend most of the effort describing the principles that stimulate it and how to go about it in subsequent chapters.

The IMF is a body that has been talked about down through the ages. It is described in the dazzling golden letters in most sacred books of men as well as in the Book of Nature. Many of us have heard about it but have never understood it; we have seen its codes but have never accurately deciphered them. Ella A. Fletcher called it *"the Great Central Dynamo of life itself"*;

www.makanologos.com

Ralph Waldo Emerson called it *"Universal Soul"*; Jesus called it the *"Kingdom of Heaven"*; the Hindus call it *Akasha*; scientists call it *energy or ether*; and many thinkers have given it names that have suited their thinking and needs; but I have chosen to call it the Infinite Magnetizing Field, or IMF for short.

This IMF is both the generator of ideas and thoughts that make everything that exists anywhere in the universe and the material from which everything is made. While man appears to be the doer, in reality he is only a channel used by an Higher Power to extend Its creation, the only way it found satisfaction. Thinking of the IMF, Emerson wrote:

> *Man is a stream whose source is hidden. Always our being is descending into us from we know not where. The most exact calculator has no prescience that something incalculable may not balk the very moment. I am constrained every moment to acknowledge a higher origin for events than the evil I call mine* ("Self-Reliance," page 58).

He goes on further in the same essay, to say:

> *We lie in the lap of immense intelligence, which makes us receivers of its truth and organs of its activity. When we discern justice, when discern truth, we do nothing of ourselves but allow a passage to its beans. If we ask whence this comes, if we seek to pry into the soul that causes, all philosophy is at fault. Its presence or absence is all we can affirm* (page, 78).

About the IMF in his book *Harmonic Wealth*, James Arthur Ray writes, *"All great minds, from modern science to spiritual traditions, agree that everything physical and tangible comes from the nonphysical, intangible spiritual domain."*

To the question, what in heaven's name is the purpose of man's intellect? While the IMF generates and transports ideas, thoughts, and feelings to all parts of the universe when they are rightfully attracted, the intellect, which I would prefer to call the Temporal Magnified Field, or TMF, performs two roles. The first role is that of a mirror when steadily and accurately

www.makanologos.com

exposed to the sun. Just as the mirror does not produce any sunrays, man does not manufacture ideas, thoughts, or feelings. The second role is that of the Earth. While the Earth does not produce sunrays, it does transform sunrays into energy and things that sustain life. The four elements of nature and the food we eat, are all sunrays transformed in different kinds of bodies.

Man can choose ideas, thoughts, and feelings, but he cannot make them. You can choose to be happy, but you cannot manufacture happiness. You can choose to gather ideas of geography, history, music, or any subject of your choice, but you cannot manufacture those ideas. As the sun produces and sends sunrays throughout the solar system, the mirror—as long it is not covered or shaken—reproduces and retransmits the very sunrays with the same effects in a chosen direction. Like the mirror, the intellect is endowed with the power to reflect and blaze itself in any direction instantaneously. Our intellect, the TMF, has even more power to attract and retransmit ideas and thoughts from the IMF according to our capacity to keep our inner feelings harmonized and constructive (just as the mirror has to be kept firm if the sunlight is to be reflected accurately).

The major differences between the so-called geniuses and the rest of us are that they work in a peaceful environment (they hold their mirror firmly), they harmonize their feelings, and more than anything else, they make themselves very receptive, and with that they open the channel between IMF and their TMFs as they sharpen their power of intuition without delay or obstruction. They know, whenever necessary, a constructive thing to do and how to do it. Just as a shaking mirror would never accurately project sunrays in a desired direction, a fearful, doubtful, hateful, or faithless TMF can never correctly reproduce the feelings, ideas, and thoughts of the IMF.

It has been proved that the only things that prevent the TMF from reproducing what the IMF desires to convey to the TMF are chaotic and undisciplined feelings that most of us, consciously or otherwise, fix our attention to. How to harmonize and discipline the feelings in order to open the channel between the IMF and the TMF is the subject of the rest of this book. It may seem nonsense or small knowledge to small minds, but great minds know that in the calmness of the mind comes the clarity of comprehension, the illumination of things visible and invisible, and the power of mind to control anything under the sun, ideally to bring happiness to the world around as well as to life everywhere.

Intelligence works according to the state of the mind. If your mind is chaotic, so will be the fruit of your intelligence. If your mind is harmonious, disciplined, and attentive or as focused as a laser beam, it will absorb feelings, ideas, and thoughts (or consciousness of an Higher Power) from the IMF like a sponge sucking water to enable you to climb the mountain of greatness as only a few can. So long as calmness reigns in the mind, the IMF will at any moment flash pictures and ideas that will make it possible to fulfill your desires. The Master told us that with faith, we can displace a mountain. While that is perfectly true, a lesson from Ella A. Fletcher must be recalled as well and reflected upon seriously to get an idea of what faith really is and how you can make a breakthrough between your TMF and the IMF:

Always, the purer the thoughts, the finer, the more rapid the vibrations of mind-stuff whose reflection is mirrored upon the physical plan. Know, too, that spiritual consciousness cannot be taken by assault. It can be won only by perseverance, patient devotion to the lofty purpose of union with the highest. It requires effort and continuous effort, and especially the self-discipline of restraining all irritation or depression. Boundless faith, cheerfulness and happiness create those harmonious vibrations that prepare the lower sheaths to reflect the higher, and release subtle forces to pass freely from one medium to another. No other investment of time or labor returns so soul-satisfying, enduring rewards...By concentration, the diffused, latent soul-power is made manifest and definite – comprehension. Meditation is the crown of concentration. It is only in meditation that we reach the heart of anything...The first successful stage is to be able to hold the mind to a single point; the next to sweep the surface clean of any object, literally to fix the attention upon nothing, (The Law of Rhythmic Breathing, page, 225).

I just could not praise all the wonders of the IMF that are ours for the asking and free as the air we breathe without stretching the importance of faith in all this. The upcoming chapter will basically be talking about faith in one way or another, but let me close this chapter with a few words on how some parts of the body play crucial roles in the whole mechanism.

While all parts of the human body interact with the IMF, the nervous system, more specifically the brain, is the opening of the channel through which we receive the sparks of light that inflame our desire and determination to extract the good we seek. The brain being the engine, by itself it doesn't do much unless it is started for it to create an effective Temporal Magnetic Field (TMF) to receive information and process instructions to fulfill physical needs. The positive feelings, thoughts, and actions of man create a powerful TMF to flawlessly interact with the IMF and produce happiness, but if those feelings are negative, they create an impotent TMF, and as a result, man experiences unhappiness in everything he does.

To this extent, you can confidently reject or at least question the notion of IQ, which paints intelligence as mostly a genetic rather than a cultural and social by-product. A society that values and practices justice, work, equity, integrity, self-confidence, bravery, peace, wisdom, love, and other precious principles will have more intelligent people because individual intelligence is sharpened with cultural and social attitudes. A nation that does not value virtues cannot possibly create an

www.makanologos.com

environment that allows its people to cultivate intelligence. A man who does not value or practice virtues cannot obtain the constructive intelligence that will take him to the height of greatness.

No man can possibly define the nature of the IMF with 100% certainty, but its functions are felt and noticeable in our daily lives, knowingly or otherwise. As we send feelings, thoughts, and actions into the world around us, sometimes the IMF responds to our inquiries by intuition and rational means. And sometime when our TMF seems to be unresponsive to the prompts of the IMF, we are simply attracted more by fate than choice to fellow men, things, or circumstances that will either inspire us or merely hand to us the answer we have been seeking. Thus, the more principled or virtuous thoughts and feelings you send out, the more likely the IMF will likewise send thoughts and feelings back to you, not necessarily when you want them but when it sees suitable, thus the need to be ready to receive. Many times it comes without warning, as all intuitions always do.

There are two ways you can think of the IMF. One way is to think of it as a mirror. As a mirror, it only reflects back what it is presented to it. If you send negative thoughts and feelings, so will it reflect the same objects back to you. Is there any person who can look in the mirror and possibly see anybody else? The second way is to think of the IMF as the physical sun. Just as the sun gives light indiscriminately, the IMF uses or desires to use all men as its channels, but only those who seek under the guidance of certain principles transform their TMF into a magnetic force. The IMF is a highly vibrating substance and interacts best with the highly vibrating feelings, thoughts, and actions of the TMF.

There is no power in the whole universe that raises the vibratory power of feelings, thoughts, and actions like a principled life does. Principles of life are more or less the same as virtues, and I know I talked substantially about virtues

www.makanologos.com

in earlier chapters of this book. Earlier I spoke of virtues as instruments of harmonizing feelings. This time I will talk about them as principles or pillars that stimulate the nervous system to work in accordance with the IMF or to situate man correctly in an excellent position to send good vibrations to and receive appropriate radiations from the IMF.

In the following chapters, rather than talk about principles or virtues in general terms, I will be more specific, choosing those virtues I know to possess the power to transform or to cause an elixir of intelligence. *"Those who are capable of humility, of justice, of love, of aspiration,"* wrote Emerson, *"are already on a platform that commands the sciences and arts, speech and poetry, action and grace. For whoso dwells in this moral beatitude does already anticipate those special powers which men prize so highly; just as love does justice to all the gift of the object beloved"* (page 61). A man who is seeking intelligence for the ultimate goal of climbing the mountain of greatness for that matter can only ignore virtues at his own peril.

Intelligence and greatness are not for cowards, and only principles and virtues can free or shield you from the merciless destruction of cowardice. I know you want to tell me that you know people who are intelligent who are not principled or virtuous. So do I. I know people who were or are intelligent, yet they were or are not principled or virtuous. But you can bet that a person who is "intelligent" but does not value principles will never use his intelligence constructively; therefore, he or she will never climb the mountain of greatness. The fate of being at the right place at the right time does not make man great; it is constructively and consciously sought feelings, thoughts, and actions that make man as great as greatness itself.

The first requirement for admittance in most highly effective academic, scientific, athletic, governmental, military, and religious profit or nonprofit organizations is never education or experience but the potential for strict adherence to a code of ethics. In the whole Old Testament, nothing is more important

www.makanologos.com

than the Ten Commandments, as is the New Commandment in the New Testament. In the management of human affairs, the constitution is always the most important document in every nation because it lays out the principles and virtues or the code of conduct for every person who lives under its jurisdiction. Banks—institutions that affect the lives of one hundred percent of the people—are called TRUSTS. Unless you are fully trustworthy, you can never possibly work for a bank, regardless of your IQ or experience. In all well-functioning countries, from the lowest- to the highest-skilled potential bank employee, no application is processed unless the criminal background record is satisfactory. A criminal record alone is basically capable of making one's life a living hell in almost every area of life in America. Still wonder why the Ten Commandments and the New Commandment are the most important scriptures in the Bible, and the constitution the most important document in every nation?

Principles or virtues are like colors and numbers; with just a few major ones, you can create a web of them. Thus I will describe those that I know can raise the vibratory rate of the human nervous system or the TMF high enough to effectively and positively interact with the IMF. Feel free to substitute these principles with the name of God, for in many books of man as well as nature, they are so written in black and white; or give them the same reverence you would give the "Guy upstairs" if you want to benefit from them greatly. I hope it is not a curse to you when I say God is Truth, God is Love, God is Silence, God is Attentiveness, God is Fearlessness, etc. because He is, and that is the elixir of intelligence. Now buck up, and let's go to the exploration of these mighty principles that transform man's intelligence into God's creative power. Because these principles assume multiple roles of stimulating, elevating, and sustaining the TMF, I will call them PILLARS.

Wisdom Joseph Ombe Ya Makano, the author.

www.makanologos.com

With the best friend any truly inspired dreamer can ever possibly dream to have in life, my companion of this earthly journey, Mwajuma Yvette Makano.

www.makanologos.com

Exalted Secrets of Brilliant Minds

My mother: Laliya Oropa Abala Makano "Namkyoku," Thank you Mom for the unconditional love that inspired me to be the man "I AM" and ever hope to be.

www.makanologos.com

My best friend and companion for life, Mwajuma Yevette Makano with our son Malaika Lusambya Makano. Thank you my friend, without you this work would have been unthinkable.

www.makanologos.com

With those I tightly hold near and dear, my son Joseph Jr., my wife Mwajuma, my son Malaika, my son Wisdom Persistence, and my daughter Laliya Nada.

Those whose unconditional love and support are the cause of this work. From left to right: Joseph Makano Jr., daughter Laliya Nada Makano, baby Malaika Lusambya Makano on the laps of his sister, and Wisdom Persistence Makano.

www.makanologos.com

With those I hold near and dear, whose unconditional love and support are the cause of this work. From left to right, my sons Alimasi, Joseph Jr and my daughter Laliya N. Makano.

www.makanologos.com

Wisdom Joseph Ombe Ya Makano, the author.

www.makanologos.com

Wisdom Joseph Ombe Ya Makano, the author

www.makanologos.com

IN LOVE WE TRUST!

www.makanologos.com

CHAPTER XIII

The Courage Pillar

"Fortune favors the bold." Latin proverb

Integrity — what a magical word. "In-te-gri-ty" — that four-syllable word is truly miraculous. Here on Earth, upon integrity rests trust, and upon trust rests, or must rest, the cornerstone of social organization's evolution, i.e., governments, churches, education systems, commerce, and so on, entities of a well-functioning and more coherent nation. Without integrity, I strongly believe, the world would yet be perhaps not in the Stone Age but very likely in the Dark Ages. Integrity is truly the SUN of a man who wants to gain the privileges the good Lord bestows on only the few who have successfully passed every test the Supreme Intelligence has placed in their paths.

This work is not what many of you would term as scientific, and I understand that; however, it is an alternative to what science would never dare tell us, either for fear of criticism or for lack of evidence to support its claims. Whatever I overtly say here may or may not be for or against any scientific argument, but by no means is it an endorsement or rejection of any scientific point of view. While science likes to, as a general rule, tap its empirical knowledge from the head, this work comes from both the heart and the head, but more so from the heart than the head, and only those who challenge both their hearts and heads will benefit most from it. Those readers who are looking for any scientific evidence in what you read here, I am afraid I will fall short and may be unable to satisfy their quest. This is philosophy. Here I am striving to define intelligence as I defined leadership in the first book of this series, *The Best Kept Secrets of Personal Magnetism*, in a psycho-mythological perspective.

Nonetheless, I encourage you to read the book through, maybe just so you can enrich yourself with how other people see, perceive, and get the most from life and the world we live in. However, if you are interested in discovering the mysterious (I say mysterious, but it is not really mysterious, but rather the laws that the average man neglects either for their simplicity or for lack of the necessary discipline required) but also acquiring intelligence; if you are interested in understanding why very smart people, some of the brightest people among us, work for and/or get manipulated by intellectually normal ones; if you want to understand why a far bigger majority of A-grade students are happy servants of C-grade ones or even school dropout bosses; then it is my hope that you will find answers that will, at the very least, lead you to the source of answers so you can sort out for yourself which one will satisfy your quest.

I cannot say that your search will be over after you reach the last page of this book, but I know for sure you will be energized to use simple and common sense laws explained here. I know that because your eyes will be opened widely enough to see the star that will lead you to Bethlehem where your Master is waiting for you to arrive with the gift of your heart, mind, and soul for him to anoint, bless, and equip you against the forces of ignorance and darkness, with light that illumines the paths of the boldest minds, greatest souls, and toughest hearts among men.

Creative intelligence is not a special gift for the geniuses, sages, or seers. It is not for geniuses, sages, or seers, but only for the daring few. In fact, while you and most people think of the geniuses, sages, seers, kings, princes, and high priests as the chosen few, they think of themselves as the DARING FEW. They see no difference between you and them except in courage and the relentless pursuit of constructive inner qualities. In the subtitle of this book, I reluctantly used the word *chosen*, since in reality, regardless of the popular view, no man is ever chosen because he is special. People simply distinguish themselves from

www.makanologos.com

the masses due to their externalization of inner constructive qualities, which cannot help but almost involuntarily attract visible and invisible forces that make them seem to be what we call the chosen few. Regardless of the misinterpretation or misreading of the Bible and other spiritual writings on the concept of the chosen few, no one is ever chosen; all men are chosen, and all are special.

Be it Jesus, Moses, Mohammed, Einstein, Alexander the Great, Sir Isaac Newton, Napoleon, Washington, Saint Paul, you name it, they were not chosen. If they were, they were self-chosen through their courage, self-confidence, determination, and so on; therefore, they were the daring few. Each of them had to go through a perilous quest in order to be what we know them as today. That is the law of nature that even the highest master of the universe cannot break. God never works with cowards or fearful and self-mistrusting people. For centuries, the expression "chosen few" has been purposely used or misused to keep "weak" minds fearful and submissive to the authority that willfully and misleadingly claims to have come from God, which of course is true—yet not just for the so-called chosen few, but anyone who dares to dare. If there is one thing that the reader will get from this chapter, it is that there are no chosen few anywhere on this Earth, but there are only DARING FEW.

I say again loudly, DARING FEW. If you look carefully, you will notice that the common thread among all who have left their indelible footprints forever here on Earth is that they were all VERY COURAGEOUS, extremely self-confident people, and fearlessly determined to do the right thing. They overcame some of the most difficult obstacles man can possibly come across. The kings of Egypt left their marks for building the everlasting pyramids of about 146 meters in height and 232 meters each side with incredibly heavy stones lifted not with cranes but by hands; Moses for standing up to the mighty kings of Egypt and taking his people to an unknown homeland; Alexander the

www.makanologos.com

Great for conquering the world of his time; Jesus for refusing to give in to a powerful Jewish establishment for what He felt to be the truth; Saint Paul for spreading Christianity in the most perilous conditions possible; George Washington for defying the mighty king of the British empire; Nelson Mandela for standing up to a powerful racist regime; Mahatma Gandhi for employing nonviolent civil disobedience in demanding independence from a mighty British government; Martin Luther King for advancing civil rights using nonviolent civil disobedience; Einstein, *"whose slow development caused his teachers to think 'he would never be successful at anything,'"* according to http://gardenofpraise.com/ibdeinst.htm (accessed March 14, 2010), for defying slim odds erroneously given him and ultimately changing the course of civilization with his Law of Relativity; the fourteen-year-old girl Joan of Arc for almost magically leading the French army to numerous key victories during the Hundred Years' War by claiming divine guidance and ultimately being responsible for the coronation of King Charles VII. She refused to obey the careful strategies that had characterized French military command.

"Galileo's greatest accomplishment was the stand he took against the Roman Catholic Church [mightiest political and religious authority of the day] *of the Renaissance. At the time it was considered an act of rebellion to teach that the sun was the center of the solar system, a theory that had originated from Copernicus...In his treatise Dialogue Concerning the Two Chief World systems, Galileo used the observations he made with his new telescope to defend Copernicus"* (The Intellectual Devotional, page, 95).

The list could go on and on. Anyone who thinks courage has little or nothing to do with acquisition or development of mental power is in for the long haul and probably will never get it.

God, the Mighty God, has power incompatible with cowardice. God does not hate, but He does not work with cowards. He is no friend of the fearful or the timid. "I am" and "I will" followed by a positive verb are His favored expressions, not "I am not," "I will not," or "I cannot." He would rather pacify and work with a "criminal" and "slaughterer" but a courageous Soul (Saint Paul) than attempt to collaborate with any timid and fearful person. I say this because I want you to know that the first thing you need to do if you want to ignite your creative intelligence is to burn to ashes and rid yourself of all feelings of fear and timidity in you. Here, of course, you just use your power of mental alchemy, which is nothing but switching your thinking from negative to positive. That's all it takes. There is no magic pill for creative intelligence. Neither is it a gift for the so-called chosen few. It is in all of us, mostly dormant and waiting to be aroused by the fire of courage that only you can IGNITE and blaze like a forest fire on a sunny summer day.

I will say this again: creative intelligence is not a special gift for a special chosen few. It is a part of the comprehensive package we all came with. The race or nation that has developed a culture of courage and work has the most citizens with the most brilliantly blazing creative intelligence. As a part the comprehensive package, Providence has endowed us all with creative intelligence, given to us all just as we are given legs, eyes, noses, heads, fingers, mouths, ears, or any other part of our bodies. Great singers, wonderful public speakers, or charismatic leaders have voices no more special than the rest of us; they chose to develop their voices by fighting the fear of facing the countless eyes of the public. Athletes, artists, craftsmen, pianists, typists, or anyone who uses his or her legs, hands, or fingers extremely well have no special fingers, hands, or legs different from the rest of us; they just choose to ignite the power of their membranes courageously despite the difficulty encountered along the way. This simple truth alone makes all the difference among kings, princes, sages, seers, high priests, or the daring few and burdened masses of the world. Creative intelligence is here in all of us, given to us free like the air we breathe and closer than our hands and feet, but it must be stirred by a stroke of courage.

No sage or seer, Jesus included, has ever claimed special access to God or special powers. The acknowledgment of our weakness and unwillingness to climb the mountain of greatness serves as an excuse to treat Jesus, Mohammed, Buddha, Washington, etc. as special beings. *"Even greater things than these shall you do,"* declared the Master Himself. Why would Jesus recognize the ability of any man to perform better and greater manifestations than His own if we did not have the same creative intelligence as He did? There is no science, art, philosophy, or religion that teaches its students something that they cannot perform to the best of their abilities. And there is no teacher who can teach his or her students if he or she were unsure of the lesson. There is no teacher who can teach his or her students something that they cannot do at least like him- or herself. A kindergarten teacher who is caught seriously teaching her students algebra will lose her job almost instantly. Thus, whatever was taught us by the great ones, we can do as they did or better if we only have the courage to overcome the obstacles that stood before them, that still stand before us, and that will ever stand in the way of anyone who wants to climb the mountain of greatness or anyone who wants to crack the codes of the kings, princes, sages, seers, and the daring few.

Kings, princes (despite their inheritance of power), sages, seers, and the daring few did not gain or maintain their position as a matter of right or chance but by fending off incredible and persistent challenges. In England, Canada, Australia, and elsewhere where the queen or king of England holds head-of-state status, there are seriously organized forces that want any rightful citizen to have a shot at occupying the position through democratic elections. By the way, more recently, the nationally ambitious politicians who also wanted to have a chance to someday become the head of their country, not just

www.makanologos.com

king, ousted the king of the former mountainous kingdom of Nepal. More than three decades ago, his cousin, plunging the country into a long and violent civil war, ousted the king of Afghanistan while on a foreign trip.

Many times, if not all the time, the only thing that is required is self-confidence, not money, much less physical strength, as these purely civilized but deadly serious sports and political competitions illustrate the point. According to http:// en.wikipedia.org/wiki/Upset (accessed March 18th, 2010), here are some of the most shocking upsets of all time in politics and sports where winners won despite all the advantages of their opponents simply because of their willingness to feel, believe, think, and act confidently and courageously, nothing more, nothing less.

- *1945 – Winston Churchill called a snap election at the end of World War II to take advantage of his heroic status as a war leader and 83% approval rating in the polls. Labour had never had a majority in the House of Commons, but they took 239 seats, the Tories lost 190 and Clement Attlee became prime minister with an overall majority of 145. It was one of the biggest landslides in British politics and the most unexpected.*
- *1948 – Unpopular Democratic United States President Harry Truman defeated the highly favored Republican candidate Thomas Dewey, which was featured in a famous newspaper headline: "Dewey Defeats Truman." It is considered by most historians to be the greatest election upset in American history.*
- *1950 – In the World Cup, the United States shocked England in a match considered one of the biggest surprises in World Cup history.*
- *2002 – In the World Cup opening match, Senegal defeated defending champions France 1-0. The French subsequently left the competition in the first round, winless and goalless.*

All the heroes of history have always been, Jesus included — and I underscore the word—underdogs who had been mistakenly or otherwise not called the "chosen few" until after

www.makanologos.com

they had won their battles in the lion's den. God fights our battles only after we have fought for him against the evil of fear in us and better trusted the power and His presence in us. From the very first few days of His life, Jesus had to flee to Egypt to escape the malicious forces of Herod Antipas, who wished Him no chance at all to even start his mission, and He never had anything easy thereafter. He suffered humiliation at the hands of the high priests who belittled Him for saying the truth — "Before Abraham was, I AM" — at the age of twelve. He angered the powerful interests of the moneychangers and merchants (who never forgave Him and were suspected to have been the invisible hand behind His arrest and ultimate crucifixion) by whipping and chasing them from the temple. He faced a monkey trial by the chief priests and Jewish elders who condemned Him to death, only to be proclaimed the King of the Jews on the cross (INRI) by a foreigner, the Roman governor in Judea, Pontius Pilate. Every time He faced turmoil, Jesus had to win the battle not with help from God, apparently, but with trust in Him. In the end, Jesus is the Messiah Christians love to praise and worship. That is the power of courage; that is how courage stirs the intelligence that takes us to the highest level of our potential achievement.

The spirit of the underdog did not disappear with the giants of the past. It is very well alive with us today. In the National Basketball Association and many other sporting events, or even in democratic elections, we usually hear the words *upset* and *underdog* used frequently — not that it is a good thing to be an underdog, but simply to imply the endurance of the human spirit when faced with seemingly insurmountable odds. The so-called underdogs realize that size and strength are advantageous, but by no means do they make one twice as big as the opponent in a duel. Your stature does not give you any advantage or disadvantage if your opponent is more courageous and determined. Despite your underdog status, you can overcome any limit set for you by the outside world if

www.makanologos.com

you can first discard it from your mind. That is why courage is such an extremely sensitive fuel of creative intelligence. Unless you understand and know how to use it, you will always carry the raw material of intelligence inside you, which will one day be wasted when you pass away, much to the chagrin of the world, which could have greatly benefited from it.

The understanding of this one point alone is the key to the understanding of the rest of this portion of the book. Unless you understand the inimitable role of courage in the ignition of creative intelligence, nothing else will matter. How can you hope to know how to read and count if you cannot understand the alphabet and such basic numbers as 0, 1, 2, 3, 4, 5, 6, 7, 8, and 9? It is unfortunate that our education system almost never expresses the role of courage in developing creative intelligence at the very beginning of life. We are like newborn babies whose mental development has been suppressed by inadequate nourishment at the hands of our parents. And the proper creative intelligence we strive to develop in adulthood, while suitable, seems to be too little too late to enable a late development of an effective nervous system capable of getting us to the finish line of greatness.

You will recall that I started this chapter by glorifying integrity. I talked about it at the very beginning and never did again throughout the body of the chapter until now. Why? What does integrity have to do with courage, you might ask? The answer is "a lot!" The chapter has covered most of what I wanted to communicate to the reader. I think it deserves to come to an end, but this I want you to know: the courage that I am talking about here, the courage that stirs or ignites the flame of creative intelligence, is the courage that is inspired by the inner sincerity, poise, and honesty of a constructive course; thus it is integrity but not fear, anger, or deceit. While integrity illumines your outer and inner eyes, deceit literally blinds both your inner and outer eyes. Do you wonder why integrity is such a magical word? If courage is a flame, integrity is coal that

www.makanologos.com

produces it. To have the right courage for a right cause, you must have integrity to dare try for the highest good.

Courage is indispensable to intelligence and life in general. A discouraged man, a man without courage, is like a dead man walking, for he lacks hope and faith in himself and life. Courage gives hope, faith, and power of action, the ultimate measure of intelligence. Courage reveals the truth that is the ultimate pursuit of intelligence. With courage, man has his battle half won in the search for intelligence, for courage is the revealing activity of life. Life is a battle. Things are not always given on a golden plate. We must fight and fight aggressively, and unless we have courage, we cannot resist, much less attract, Invisible Helpers to our assistance. *"The hotter the battle, the sweeter the victory,"* said the singer Bob Marley, and the former British Prime Minister Margaret Thatcher added, *"You may have to fight a battle more than once to win it."* But how on God's Earth is it possible to win a hotter battle or fight a battle more than once to win it without courage?

Courage not only illumines the human intellect, but it also illumines the trinity of feelings, thoughts, and actions. It illumines the trinity of the heart, head, and hands. Truly intelligent people are never weaklings or discouraged. Truly intelligent people are courageous in the fiber of the beings; they are winners in most of their endeavors because they are primarily, more than anything, fortified with courage. Without courage, there is no victory in anything worthy of dignity.

Invisible Helpers are constantly seeking for courageous people to work for the advancement of the affairs of mankind. They inspire more strength to anybody who self-selects him- or herself in order to work with them through a demonstration of courage. Their task of illumination is made easier if the person they have chosen is obedient and self-disciplined enough to avoid all temptation of self-glorification and self-service. The courage to stand against discouragement, fear, faithlessness, selfishness, ignorance, anger, self-pity, etc. is what intelligence

www.makanologos.com

is all about. Man does not create laws either of nature or of man. Laws are revealed to man on the sole condition that man be a worthy channel so the Great Ones may serve mankind. Isaac Newton did not create the Law of Gravity; Albert Einstein did not create the Law of Relativity; Archimedes did not create what is now known as Archimedes' Principle; Marie Curie did not create the laws of radioactivity; Benjamin Franklin did not create electricity; and man did not create science, physics, chemistry, or mathematics. I could go on and on. These laws existed at the very beginning of the universe. They were simply revealed to man. But they were not revealed just to any man, but to men of courage to go to the bitter end of their quests despite daunting or sometimes even deadly obstacles.

Courage is the power that earns you the trust of the Invisible Helpers to illumine or reflect to your mental screen or mental mirror the light of their knowledge and wisdom and the know-how of all things you want to understand and act upon for the highest good, the selfless or constructive way of life. Fear begets weakness, and courage begets strength. The man of courage is a man of power. The human intellect is a mere mental screen on which the cosmic screen constantly reflects and reveals the secrets of life and the universe. The human screen is kept firm by the pillars that are being discussed in this last part of the book, among them courage.

Here again I cannot help but call the attention of the reader to use integrity to temper courage because the power that is not balanced with love and wisdom could be very destructive. It is good to have courage, the essence of power, but in the end, what is the benefit of having a power that may be destructive? Therefore, the need to call the attention of the reader to integrity or truth (a balance of wisdom and love) cannot be emphasized strongly enough. Courage, the mother of power, can be unruly sometimes. Courage is nothing less than fire. It cooks our food, warms our dwellings, and lights our cities. It is like electricity that can destroy everything, yet when watched cautiously,

www.makanologos.com

it lights our cities and facilitates the manufacturing of many wonders of the modern world. Unrestricted electricity can burn down forests and cities as well as destroy life completely. Unrestricted courage can do no less. Restricted electricity can, as well, produce the almost unthinkable. Like electricity, courage must be wrapped in the insulation of wisdom to choose the good over the bad, the selfless over the selfish, the lasting over the temporal, and the love of fellow men first above all.

Let me give one more metaphor before moving on. Courage is the basis of power just as gas or fuel is the basis of fire, or to say it more directly, courage is the fuel of power. Governments around the world for obvious reasons tightly regulate the use and transportation of gas and fuel. It is transported only in securely controlled containers and handed only to responsible people. Unlike gas or fuel, a stronger hand than government such as wisdom and love must rigorously control courage. I cannot possibly make myself clear enough on the need to balance courage and its by-product power with wisdom and love, because the power of courage in the hands of mad men such as Hitler, Joseph Stalin, Pol Pot, or Saddam Hussein is the only thing capable of rendering the planet Earth to dust in a matter of seconds. Therefore, there is a need for stronger hands than any government or any human authority such as wisdom and love in order to keep courage unconditionally compliant and loyal to a constructive way of life.

For this reason alone, I decided to end this chapter with a poem, not because of its beauty but to strongly underline that if you dare to acquire courage, you must seek it for the highest good and not for selfish or destructive interests. You must seek it not for your own satisfaction but for the satisfaction of the common good because that is how courage inspires true intelligence, the power that brings the Invisible Helpers and the powers of nature to the service of mankind. This is one the best-kept secrets of brilliant minds, this is how **intelligence is**

www.makanologos.com

aroused, and this is the ELIXIR OF INTELLIGENCE, because light is its own defense and inspiration is its own revelation. This is how you watch and look within the light. Seeing all within it, you make joy live in you and others, for there is nothing hidden that is not revealed a constructive seeker needs to know, so long honor to life is the motive for which you do everything. This is the end of the road, for this is how the great ones gained their immortality and a place of honor in the hearts of all generations to come, and so can you, so long as you stand for the Highest Ideal in the universe and as long as honor to life is the motive for everything you do.

For the Highest Good, Dare to Dare

For the highest good dare to dare,
And heaven will favor you
A special agent of itself shall you become
As others learn its message through you
Its choicest gifts on you shall be bestowed
To dispense to thy brothers and sisters.

For the highest good, dare to dare,
And all the challenges of knowledge
Your intelligence shall stimulate
To seek wisdom thru understanding
And understanding thru wisdom
Action thru reaction and reaction thru action
Cause thru effect and effect thru cause

For the highest good, dare to dare,
In you creative intelligence shall blossom
Your intelligence problems shall stimulate
As fire boils water, and water cools fire

www.makanologos.com

For the highest good, dare to dare,
And lower feelings transmute to the better
Fear shall become courage
Doubt into confidence
Discouragement into persistence

For the highest good, dare to dare,
As the alchemy of wisdom does its magic
Knowledge will reveal itself to you
At the right moment, for the right cause
As the last grain of fear catches
The flaming sword of all-knowing mind

For the highest good, dare to dare,
And the secrets of brilliant minds will be shown you
As eyes of fellow men seek you
You will be the torch held high
Like the sun in the sky
Giving light to all

For the highest good, dare to dare,
Your life shall be the hope of the world
The hungry will look to you
For food of their spirit, mind, and body

For the highest good, dare to dare,
And your fellowmen will look up to you
For guidance and salvation
You will be a friend of the wise,
A teacher of the bright,
And master of the true seekers

For the highest good, dare to dare,
Like a midday sun your creativity shall shine
The most vicious beast shall bow before you
The stars of heave at daylight shall you see clearly

www.makanologos.com

For the highest good, dare to dare,
And birds of heaven shall bring messages
From masters of the sky to you
Flowers of the garden shall sing and dance
The song of joy upon feeling your presence
As from you only joy to all flows

For the highest good, dare to dare,
And sun will come out at midnight
To illumine the darkest hour of the night
As your feet find safety and eyes see all

For the highest good, dare to dare,
And you will be a child of old of days,
A friend of Angels but a master of mortals
All limits and obstacles shall melt at your approach
As you become salt of life for those around you,
The lamp of illumining their way in the world

For the highest good, dare to dare,
And fear will fear you
Love will love you
Virtues shall teach your mind
Wisdom and understanding shall encircle you
The voice of silence shall talk to your heart
And humility will raise you up

For the highest good, dare to dare,
And your mind will see the whole truth
Patience will strengthen you
Yours will be the heart of a lion
As heaven makes you a jewel of its heart

www.makanologos.com

For the highest good, dare to dare,
And your life will be a blessing to future generations
All that breathes and lives
Shall remember and admire you
As your name will survive the damage of time

For the highest good, dare to dare,
Because men worship only daring men
At your passing if not proclaimed a god
Be assured you shall be declared a saint
Or at least a legend as your name
Is inscribed above time and space.

For the highest good, dare to dare,
And the sound of your name will be so melodious
To all that all live in time and space
As it inspires joy and peace

For the highest good, dare to dare,
And to you miracles shall happen naturally
Nothing shall ever be the same
Your story shall inspire generations
As in their hearts it fills hope and joy

For the highest good, dare to dare,
And your imagination will be unleashed
Like a pristine-life-giving-spring-of-purest-crystal-water
As you are led, shielded, and inspired
By the LIGHT of God that never fails forever

For the highest good, dare to dare,
In the words of Norman B. Rice,
The former mayor of Seattle, Washington,
Dare to *"dare to reach out your hand into darkness,*
To pull another hand into the light," and we shall transmute
Our mother planet Earth
From a shadowy into the brightest star in the sky

www.makanologos.com

Exalted Secrets of Brilliant Minds **305**

For the highest good, dare to feel, think, believe and act
Confidently, faithfully, correctly, and humbly now
And the secrets of the wise kings, princes, sages, seers,
High priests, and chosen few shall be revealed
And trusted to you by the Supreme Intelligence

For the highest good, dare to dare,
To you Royal Secrets shall be revealed
From your being the Elixir of Intelligence shall flow
You the Philosopher Stone shall be given
To pass into the hearts and minds of brave
Generations of the audacious few to come

For the highest good, dare to dare
And life will honor you
With the trust of raising other
In the realm of selflessness
And brotherly love

By Wisdom Joseph Ombe Ya Makano, the author

CHAPTER XIV

The Love Pillar

"ANYTHING will give up its secrets if you love it enough."
George W. Carver, American polymath

"When you can sincerely love everything and everybody you will be astonished at the result, for love is the magnet that attracts the best of everything."
Venice Bloodworth, author of *Key to Yourself*

"Of all the qualities, love is the most important, for if it is strong enough in us, it forces us to acquire all the rest, and all the rest without it would never be sufficient."
Jiddu Krishnamurti, author of *At the Feet of the Master.*

To most people, apparently, it seems easy to write about love, but is it really? I will not dare to answer the question. Love—what a multi-semantic word. Very few words in the vocabulary of man have been used, abused, and misused like the word *love*. Let this author confess right here and now—from adolescence up, until I met my first wife, I was never really romantically or truly in love with someone. I enjoyed friendship with very few girlfriends, most of whom I never even kissed. Many, of course, longed for my kiss, but I just did not know then how to read female body language. I know now, but I am already locked up in an indefinite social contract that I cannot break without severe consequences.

Why am I telling the reader this? Well, because I want you to know that I have almost zero qualifications to write about love in the romantic sense of the term. I have very little knowledge from my life experience to inspire me in that domain. When you read the title of this chapter in the table of contents, you might have expected to read more, deep inside the book, about romance. I am afraid I may disappoint you. Nevertheless, if you give me a chance and follow and think about what I will give you here, you may get something of equal value at the very least, but if you really put what you are about to discover here in your feelings, thoughts, and actions, you will get, with great probability, both your time and money's worth for buying and reading this book. There is no greater secret of greatness than love, as you will see in just a moment. If you value what you will learn from this book and take one or two steps further, you will gain for yourself the golden key of greatness that even some kings and princes still dream of, and there will be no mountain of greatness on Earth that you cannot climb.

"We are shaped and fashioned by what we love," said the great German writer and polymath Johann Wolfgang von Goethe. What you love will shape you. If you love sex, you may be a sex addict; if you love illegal drugs, you may be a drug addict; if you love math, you will be a mathematician; if you love physics, you will be a physicist; if you love politics, you will be a politician, etc. It is that simple, so be careful what you wish for, we are told. It is almost impossible for you to become a mathematician, philosopher, statesman, etc. if you honestly do not love the subject that shapes people in those professions. Love alone is the first and most important prerequisite of success in any field of labor. Unless you love what you do, you will never climb the mountain of greatness set by that line of work. It is practically impossible to win the soccer World Cup, for instance, if the players do not love the game from the bottom of their hearts.

The kings, princes, seers, sages, and high priests know all too well that understanding a subject alone is not the secret of greatness, but loving and understanding something is the secret of geniuses. What do you think enabled geniuses such as Plato, Moses, and Paul to write hundreds and hundreds of pages at a time when paper and pen were so rudimentary that

www.makanologos.com

it probably took them a day or a week to just write a page that still sends countless future generations the wisdom that many geniuses of today can only dream of? Do you think it was Santa Maria or love of adventure that allowed Christopher Columbus to find his way to "India," the Bahamas? Love of work, not love of money or benefit, causes success. Love of your vocation is the umbilical cord of your success; it is the secret of the greatest among us. John Ruskin once said, *"When love and skill come together expect a masterpiece."* A masterpiece is never a product of casual work. Muhammad Ali could never have possibly been "the greatest," the champion, unless he loved boxing with all the strength of his being. Abraham Lincoln could never have been a beloved American president unless he had loved politics despite all the setbacks.

If ancient wisdom is to be yielded the right of the way, never try to start anything that you want to take you to the mountaintop of greatness unless you build its foundation with love, love, and more love. *"Nothing can endure which has not its foundation upon love,"* says an act of Horodlo in the year 1413 AD. And to that Edwin Markham adds, *"Being able to love is one of the greatest talents one can possess."*

You can be the most talented man in the world, but if you do not love your work, you will probably earn a living, but you will never be great at it. How many talented cooks do you know in the world? Let's make it simple. According to www.en.wikipedia.org/wiki/world.population, "As of 30 May 2010 [this paragraph was written on that date], the human population of the world is estimated by the United States Census Bureau to be 6,824,000,000. The United Nations estimated the Earth's human population to be 6,800,000,000 in 2009." Let's just assume for the sake of argument that only 1% of the population estimated by the United Nations are talented cooks, which would be 68,000,000. The last time I googled famous and great chefs in the world, I saw only a few dozen names, and I do not know how many of them are as wealthy as Rachael Ray.

www.makanologos.com

Exalted Secrets of Brilliant Minds   309

There is no single sane human being on God's Earth who would never like to achieve greatness. All seven billion people currently living on Earth would like to someday reach the mountaintop of greatness. The question, of course, is how many of us are capable or willing to love our work at hand with all our strength, body, mind, soul, and heart? It is probably believed and universally agreed among all orthodox religions that God is love, and all other principles of life or nature, including light, harmony, and oneness of the universe, are its direct radiation. So if you love something strongly enough, you will put in motion all other laws and subsequently not only demand it to make its way to you but also to surrender its intimate secrets to you as well. This four-letter word spelled l-o-v-e is truly and innately magical.

A person who speaks the genuine language of love needs neither passport nor visa to enter into anyone or anything's heart. When you genuinely love lilies, they will irresistibly show you their heart's secrets right before your eyes. It is a well-known fact that those who truly — underline truly — love animals have been shown on television and other media outlets playing and living harmlessly with some of the most dangerous animals, including lions, tigers, vipers, or scorpions, having gained their complete and unconditional trust and obedience through love. Love-speaking people, as opposed to English-, Chinese-, Arabic-, Swahili-speaking, or any other human language speakers, need no interpreters anywhere they go worldwide; therefore, they have no trouble finding a partner to share their lives with despite the apparent obstacle of verbal communication.

All the money in the world cannot genuinely turn real enmity into friendship. Only love, we are told, has the power to transform old enemies into new friends, distrust into trust. Speaking of trust, the only thing that prevents people from knowing more about something is that there is not enough trust between people and whatever people want to know.

www.makanologos.com

You will find people who truly feel love for their jobs, who know and perform excellently their daily work. When you love your job, your job will reveal to you its secrets. As I said earlier, thoughts or ideas are not man-made any more than breath is man-made. They are products of the handiwork of the IMF, God. Isaac Newton never created thoughts of the Law of Gravity any more than Einstein created the thoughts of the Law of Relativity or Franklin created thoughts of electricity or Christopher Columbus created thoughts of sailing westward. Thoughts were there already for billions of years, waiting for someone to give them enough love to reveal themselves.

The fact that we take electricity or electronics for granted today is no reason to think we have more electricity or electronics now than in olden times. We neither have more nor less; we just happened to live at the time our generation has sent more love to them, and consequently they reveal themselves to us now more than at any other time in the known history of man. So if you wonder why your coworker performs better at work than you do, seek the reason no further—he or she loves his or her job more than you probably do. You will be hard pressed to find a single person who enthusiastically does his daily activity and does not perform well.

Genius ideas and thoughts do not come to us by way of rational thinking. Rational thinking has never led man to a major breakthrough. Love arouses intelligence as very few virtues can. Innovative ideas always come to man intuitively, and intuition is activated by love alone. It is after intuition has delivered the goods that geniuses seek ways (rational thinking) to explain them to the rest of mankind. But love must shine on intuition first before the bell of knowledge can ring and the train can deliver. Hate or even mild love cannot stimulate intuition constructively. Thus, the more you love your work, the more you will silently concentrate on it, the more it will reveal its precious secrets to you, the more your intelligence will be

www.makanologos.com

aroused, and the more you will be enabled to read between the lines and comprehend what is being revealed to you.

Average people sometimes think it is magic to know something that is very innovative, and behold, so it is, but that magic is the manifestation of love that alone raises intelligence to higher dimensions of comprehension. Smart people work hard to understand something, but wise folks just love it more and more to enable the work to open itself up and cast in the light of the day as it reveals its secrets. These words of Venice Bloodworth can be taken lightly only by a fool: *"When you can sincerely love everything and everybody near you will be astonished at the result, for love is the magnet that attracts the best of everything."* Henry Drummond, a Scottish evangelist, writer, and lecturer once wrote in *The Greatest Thing in the World*, *"A schoolboy today knows more than Sir Isaac Newton knew; his knowledge has vanished away"* (page 45). Forget about the schoolboy of today. How many PhDs or university professors of today love the Law of Gravity enough to go a slight step ahead of what Newton discovered toward what is still to be known? Newton, Goethe, Einstein, Galileo, Leonardo DaVinci, Shakespeare, George W. Carver, etc. only slightly dug into their fields of knowledge. With more love, the world can and will learn immeasurably more.

It is basically useless or unwise to spend time trying to understand something you do not love, for frustration will only increase as you waste more of your effort and time. One of the persons who basically founded the Christian faith, second only to Jesus, was Paul. Speaking of faith, hope, and love, he wrote in 1 Corinthians 13:1-3, *"If I speak in the tongues of men and of angels, but have not love, I am a noisy gong or a clanging cymbal. 2 And if I have prophetic powers, and understand all mysteries and all knowledge, and if I have all faith, so as to remove mountains, but have not love, I am nothing. 3 If I give away all I have, and if I deliver up my body to be burned,[a] but have not love, I gain nothing. If I speak with the tongues of men and of angels, but have not love, I am become*

www.makanologos.com

sounding brass, or a clanging cymbal." And in 1 Corinthians 13:13, he wrote, *"And now these three remain: faith, hope and love (charity). But the greatest of these is love."* And if I may say it otherwise, if I work with all the best tools modern technology can provide and have no love of my work, frustration will wear me out like an old garment to be thrown to the Dumpster. Successful doctors, lawyers, engineers, laborers, parents, politicians, accountants, cooks, trainers, players, farmers, businessmen, teachers, students, etc. are those who fearlessly love their work.

Can you imagine a gardener who does not love his or her garden producing better flowers than the one who loves his or her garden? *"Love is success. Love is happiness. Love is life... Where Love is, God is. He that dwelleth in Love dwelleth in God. God is Love,"* wrote Drummond in *The Greatest Thing in the World* on page 21. This, of course, may appear as a myth to some people, or better yet to at least 95% of the people, but to the 5% who compose the class of kings, princes, seers, sages, high priests, and the chosen few, love is the heart of the secrets that take men to the mountaintop of greatness. Of love, Drummond continues:

Love *"thinketh no evil," imputes no motive, sees the bright side, put the best construction on every action...Rejoice in the truth... for he who loves will love the truth...He will accept only what is real; he will strive to get at fact; he will search for Truth with humble and unbiased mind, and cherish whatever he finds at any sacrifice,* (page, 33-34).

When you love something, you give it your all. You give it your most intensive desire, your most patient determination, your most focused energy, your most silent meditation, and only thereafter does talent or intelligence rise to the point of making you a king, prince, seer, sage, high priest, or one of the chosen few. Come, for then you can see the unseen or hear the voice of silence, the Law of Gravity or Law of Relativity and other laws of nature. Love is intrinsically built with the power to arouse the intelligence or the ability to hear and see

www.makanologos.com

the unseen and the voice of silence. The mountain of greatness is not a product of blind effort but of conscious love of our feelings, thoughts, and actions, and as Drummond concludes in his masterwork, *"You will find as you look back upon your life that the moments that stands out, the moments when you have really lived, are the moments when you have done things in the spirit of love,"* (page, 53).

Whether you know it or not, bear in mind that the greatest achievement in heaven or on earth, the greatest achievement of God or man, has been a pure product of love and love alone. What do you think does wonders? Do you think the pyramids of Egypt, the Great Wall of China, the Statue of Liberty, the Golden Gate Bridge of San Francisco, or any other masterpiece of man were products of the hands of men or products of love? Do you really think the Eiffel Tower, the Hoover Dam, and the Space Shuttle are products of hands or of love? Think about it. There is no greater gift than the gift of love. Go to an art museum anywhere and you will see how love vibrates in and around the building. Look around you and you will notice that anything that does not project an image of love is literally disgusting, gross, and ugly. Aren't we told that beauty is as important as food or the air we breathe? Beauty reflects the love of the maker of the object, the builder of the road or the building, and with it the inspiration and the joy of life.

The work of hands cannot possibly satisfy the heart of man unless there is a substantial dose of love poured into it; otherwise, it will utterly fail to inspire or to arouse the intuition and intelligence of the people. Our outer senses — vision, hearing, touch, smell, and taste — serve us through observation of facts; our Inner Self serves us through inspiration and intuition. You can never get inspiration or intuition from something unless you have given it extensive love. Love is a feeling of the inner. Just as our intellect uses physical senses to process information, the Inner Self uses love to do the same. Love feels and detects only constructive qualities and rejects negative ones. Love

www.makanologos.com

does not feel hate, criticism, selfishness, condemnation, fear, or doubt. The easiest way to destroy man's vision is to destroy his eyes. The easiest way to confuse your Inner Self is to hate something. Science and art are better understood when given sufficient love. I bet you will agree with me when I say that you do not need formal education to be a good scientist, lawyer, writer, or journalist, for with true love, you can self-teach and become any of the above.

The principal prerequisite of any profession is not training or education but the l-o-v-e feeling. *"Follow your bliss"* is the wisest career advice one can ever get. And here is the major reason why many A-students end up working for a C-, D-, or even an F-student. There is no teacher or textbook that can teach you writing if you do not love writing. Your bliss or happiness is a direct result of love; therefore, it arouses your intelligence to the point of comprehending exactly what you need to succeed. There is no genius professor or MBA School that can teach you business if you do not genuinely love business. Those who truly love business own businesses, and those who understand business work for business owners. It is that simple. Those who understand politics are called strategists, consultants, or experts, but those who love it are called leaders or politicians. The art of business reveals its hearty secrets not to those who understand it but to those who love it, just as politics, business, mathematics, physics, etc. reveal their precious secrets to those who love them. Love alone has the power to open both visible and invisible doors anytime, anywhere. To get into any realm, you must love that realm enough for it to feel harmonious with you, because harmony is the ONLY feeling that love understands. You must send that realm thoughts and feelings of kindness; in return, it will surrender like a girl or boy madly in love for the first time. Love is the crown of the intelligence; it opens channels of wisdom, understanding, and beauty that no other quality can possibly dare to. Love is the most wonderful power in the whole universe. It is not merely a power to

www.makanologos.com

neutralize or destroy but to reveal the secrets of nature, the secrets that for many centuries man has longed for to no avail.

Because of the need to keep love really vibrating, many research centers and workplaces are regulated by a strong work ethic to promote teamwork, tolerance, diversity, mutual respect, etc. Love, the mother of happiness, is also the basis of understanding and wisdom. If you want to leap ahead in your line of work, you must consciously send feelings of love and harmony to your daily work. Like an arrow, the thoughts and feelings of love will fly directly into the heart of the problem you may be facing at work. And because nothing or no one can stop those thoughts or feelings, they will reach their destination, and they bring back to you, on a return current, more love in the form of intimate secrets of that which you love.

Less wise people can underestimate the value of this advice, but this is the secret of kings, princes, seers, sages, high priests, and the chosen few.

This is one of the best-kept secrets of brilliant minds, this is how intelligence is aroused, and this is the ELIXIR OF INTELLIGENCE, because light is its own defense and inspiration is its own revelation. This is how you watch and look within the light. Seeing all within it, you make joy live in you and others, for there is nothing hidden that is not revealed to a constructive seeker who needs to know it so long as he/she stands for the Highest Ideal in the universe and honor to life is the motive for which you do everything.

This is the end of the road, for this is how the great ones gained their immortality and a place of honor in the hearts of all generations to come, and so can you, so long as you stand for the Highest Ideal in the universe and honor to life is the motive for which you do everything.

True kings do not stay in power because of swords and arrows at their disposal but because of the love they send publicly and privately to their subjects. You cannot become Warren Buffett because of capital or trade power. It is by the

www.makanologos.com

love of trading honestly and wisely that you become a famed investor. God is love; aren't we reminded of that time and again? Projecting love for a constructive purpose is the best technique of seeking knowledge. By so doing, you utilize God and Invisible Helpers to work for you, and because no secret is hidden to God or Invisible Helpers, everything you need to know will be revealed to you on time, ahead of time, the right time, and all the time.

Of course, there are always two sides to everything under the sun. You can increase or sharpen your intelligence the hard way or the easy way. If you want to do it the easy way, love whatever you are doing with all your strength, and Invisible Helpers will arouse your intelligence or inspire your intellect and intuition as no teacher or book can.

Love is called the first principle of life; therefore, only through love does one become a well of knowledge and wisdom. Socrates and Plato became celebrated philosophers because of their love of philosophy. Shakespeare became the greatest English writer of all time because no other English writer has loved the art of writing more than he. Pelé, Muhammad Ali, and Michael Jordan became the greatest athletes of their sports and their times not because of their talents but because of the amount of love they had for their sports. When the talk about ending the *Oprah* show in the late 1990s or early 2000s was heated, an audience member begged Oprah Winfrey to please not end the popular show. Ms. Winfrey had a three-word answer: "I love television." And with that, the show's popularity and prestige became almost mythical.

Love is the axis of the universe around which everything rotates, including thoughts, ideas, feelings, and actions. Without love, there cannot be faith, courage, self-confidence, etc. Unless you love something or someone, you cannot have faith in it, him, or her. Unless you love something, you cannot have the courage to do to the best to your knowledge. Unless you love yourself, you cannot trust yourself. If you love destruction, love will destroy you because you will be revolving in the opposite direction. But if you love constructiveness, love will reveal to you the mysteries or secrets of any field of knowledge of your choice. Love begets love. You send love to a plant; the plant will send love back, ultimately disclosing itself to you. It is through the love of plants that Gregor J. Mendel discovered the theory of heredity, the breakthrough in the science of genetics.

The beauty of love is that it never ceases to vibrate, unless of course you turn it into hate. Then it does not cease to vibrate, but it vibrates negatively. Love is the shortest wave of vibration there is. It vibrates endlessly in the universe and comes back with stronger positive impacts, mostly at an unexpected but the right time. When you truly love something, you are stimulating that thing to vibrate at the same wavelength as you so that both of you can rise from the confusion of the mass to higher vibrations in order to see, hear, and understand each other more harmoniously. Thus, as long as you truly love something, it will come back to you in one way or another, including in the form of intuition or sudden discovery. When you are working with love, you are working with the power that sustains the whole universe at your disposal. Mediocre people work with their strength, smart people work with their intellect, but wise people work with love. Thus mediocre people struggle to get by, and smart people work for wise guys who own the means of production.

Love is the power of harmony that unifies the universe by bringing all parts together. It is the power that makes the forces above and within to inspire those below and without. The forces below and without, when wrapped in the shroud of love, joyfully mirror the forces from above and within. Thus the hermetic axiom, *"As above, so below; as below, so above; as within, so without; and as without, so within."* Love is that mysterious force we can hardly describe, but we know that it somehow brings thesis and antithesis together, reconciles the infinitely big with the infinitesimally small, and counterbalances the two

www.makanologos.com

extremes to maintain the equilibrium that has maintained law and order in the universe for times past, present, and all that is yet to come.

The best engineer, doctor, or lawyer is not the one who has read the best books or studied under the guidance of the most reputable human teachers. The best performer in every avenue of knowledge is the one who loves what he does with more strength and determination than anyone else. Two people who love music differently cannot possibly perform it with the same mastery, at least not in the ears of an objective audience. When you love something with great and sincere intensity, your love of that thing will teach you the secrets or the nature of that thing far better than any human being possibly can. It will reveal to you, if need be, the invisible characteristics of the subject of your love; it will make audible and understandable, if necessary, the voice and language of what it is you so deeply love. Love alone lets man penetrate the deepest knowledge, understanding, and use of power that only few men have ever known.

Love itself is a magic word. When it is shouted publicly, it draws the attention of everyone and injects some sense of peace in the heart of everybody. Its magic is not limited to human beings. When in the form of feelings, it is sent to mineral, plant, animal life or even to the laws and elements of nature. Everything surrenders and avails itself to total self-revelation. Be it a mineral, a plant, or an animal, when loved enough, it reveals its qualities in a way no book or teacher can. When loved greatly enough, things send back love to us, directly to our subconscious, which in return sends it to us, to our intellect, by way of intuition. When the attention of man is powered by love — and I mean the love that ignites the desire of knowledge — it becomes a very powerful magnet that attracts all the help possible from the four winds of heaven to your localized position in the universe to reveal all that you long to know. Even human beings have no protection against genuine

www.makanologos.com

love. When a man or woman feels enough love, he or she surrenders not only his or her body but also, most importantly, his or her very intimate secrets. That is the power of love.

There is no greater secret in the business of arousing intelligence to climb the mountain of greatness than loving whatever mountain you are determined to climb with all the fiber of your being. America was not discovered with the ships of Christopher Columbus. The gun of George Washington did not win America's independence. The brains of Newton, Darwin, and Einstein did not reveal the theories of gravity, evolution, and relativity. By the love they intensely sent out to the laws of nature, through their love of their work, America was discovered; the American War of Independence was won; the theories of gravity, evolution, and relativity were discovered; and any other great achievement was accomplished. There is no stronger decipherer of solutions to human problems than love. Love is the greatest decipherer of any and all problems man can ever face, and whoever trusts his instincts as well as intellect to love unwaveringly will sooner or later find a solution to all his or her problems. When the love of something is so intense, like a flash of lightning in the sky, in no uncertain terms, the truth is revealed in just one breath with complete satisfaction of the heart and head when it could have taken much longer using a more traditional human method of trial and error.

Unlike trial and error, love reveals knowledge at the same time it shows how to wisely and intelligently materialize the outcome. Intelligence has no better enhancer than love. Those who perform extremely well in their lines of work are those who love best what they are doing. Whenever they have a chance, they send a feeling of joy, enthusiasm, and harmony to their work, and because everything in the universe has a rate of vibration, their work vibrates back to them with fewer disclaimers and more disclosures of themselves, including how to get along with their energy.

www.makanologos.com

This part of the book contains some of the very treasured and highly prized secrets of rousing intelligence as only the wise kings, princes, seers, sages, high priests, and chosen few who have climbed the mountain of greatness know. I can assure you right now that there will be no substitute for the *Love Principle*. And if you can study and apply this principle, you will be a blessed being indeed. If you learn to apply the Love Principle in your daily undertakings, knowing that there is no substitute for it anywhere, there will be no boundaries to what you can know and perform regarding anything you send your deep and sincerely love to.

If you let sincere love be the feeling and motive that drives you in anything you do, there will never be a mountain in human affairs or in the hearts of men that you cannot climb. Just as salt and sugar dissolve when they come in contact with water, so does the heart of things, or natural laws, capitulate to the law of love. Some people have been blessed to start a career in the line of work of their love and have lived a happy life. But not all of us have been so lucky. Many have spent their lives working in the line of work they have very little love for. Some have spent theirs trying to love what life has imposed upon them, or so they feel, whereas others got into something they did not have much love for but learned quickly to love it. Love snuffs out suffering just as a good dose of water extinguishes fire.

Sounds crazy, doesn't it? Not at all. Those who consider their work a product of love do not mind or care where on the chain of command they start their careers. Many of them in fact start exactly at the beginning, at entry level, and easily wind up at the top of the company or organization. An almost perfect illustration would be American politicians. With only few exceptions, most of those who end up as presidents, U.S. senators, governors, congressmen and -women, secretaries in the administrations, and other high-level officials in various

Exalted Secrets of Brilliant Minds 321

governmental agencies start their political careers at the very bottom of the food chain, at the local levels.

I understand that politicians, being frequent subjects of skepticism, may not be the best example to cite as an illustration for this law. Thus let me bring just two remarkable illustrations of professions in which it is most difficult to rise to the very top unless the intensity of one's love of occupation is extremely high. Those are the former New York Stock Exchange chairman and chief executive Richard Grasso and the Portuguese writer and 1998 literary Nobel Prize winner José de Sousa Saramago. While I would like to tell you in my own words about these two remarkable individuals and why I chose them to illustrate this section of the work, I prefer to let the words of others speak on my behalf. Let's start with what I read about Richard Grasso:

> *Richard A. Grasso (born July 26, 1946(1946-07-26) in Jackson Heights, Queens, New York City) usually known by the nickname 'Dick,' was chairman and chief executive of the New York Stock Exchange from 1995 to 2003, the culmination of a career that began in 1968 when Grasso was hired by the Exchange as a floor clerk. After the September 11, 2001 terrorist attacks, Grasso became the reassuring public face of the Exchange, and was praised for his role in helping re-start operations...Grasso was raised by his mother and two aunts in Jackson Heights in New York City since his father left the family when Richard was an infant. He graduated from Newtown High School, and attended Pace University for two years before enlisting in the Army. Just two weeks after leaving the Army in 1968, Grasso became a clerk at the New York Stock Exchange...Grasso moved up rapidly in the ranks, becoming president of the exchange and then CEO in the early 1990s. As CEO, he was widely credited with cementing the NYSE's position as the preeminent U.S. stock market. Grasso also served as an advisory board member for the Yale School of Management.* (www.http://en.wikipedia.org/wiki/Richard_Grasso, accessed June 19, 2010).

www.makanologos.com

"King of the Club" documents Mr. Grasso's early years as a working-class youth from Queens who originally aspired to become a New York City police officer, only to fail the eye exam. Although he had almost no college education, Mr. Grasso managed to get a job in 1968 as an entry-level listings clerk at the New York Stock Exchange...Mr. Grasso was also a master salesman and promoter...He competed tirelessly. (http://www.nytimes.com/2007/11/18/business/18shelf.html?_r=1&ref=richard_a_grasso, accessed June 19, 2010)

Regarding Nobel Prize winner José de Sousa Saramago, Portuguese writer, this is written:

Portuguese writer, who combined in his work myths, history of his own country, and surrealistic imagination. Saramago was awarded the Nobel Prize in 1998...José Saramago was born in Azinhaga, in the province of Ribatejo. He was forced to abandon school in order to earn his living. Saramago was educated as a technician, and before becoming a journalist, translator, and writer, he did a number of manual jobs. (http://www.kirjasto.sci.fi/saramago.htm, accessed June 19, 2010)

José Saramago was born in 1922 in a family of landless peasants, in Azinhaga, a small village in the province of Ribatejo, on the right bank of the Almonda River, around a hundred kilometres north-east of Lisbon...He was a good pupil at primary school: in the second class he was writing with no spelling mistakes and the third and fourth classes were done in a single year. Then he was moved up to the grammar school where he stayed two years. For financial reasons he abandoned his high-school studies and trained as a mechanic. (http://www.booksfactory.com/writers/saramago.htm, accessed June 19, 2010)

If the works of Richard Grasso and José Saramago were not creations of love, I do not know what would be. Love, of course, did not lift a stone to build a pyramid, hold a pen to write a masterpiece, or do any physical thing to materialize the action. What love does is to remove mental and spiritual obstacles such as fear, doubt, discouragement, frailty, and pessimism that make realization of any great achievement practically impossible. Love makes you believe in yourself and others. It makes you forgive shortcomings of others as well as your own. It makes you grateful for the good health, ideas, and opportunity to serve others as well as yourself, and so on. Love is an incredible power. We are told that love is so powerful that even the planet Earth is said to be going through an initiation of love. And if it is a quality that even a planet is better off learning, don't you see it is a quality you are better off learning and practicing as well? Love is a power that draws all good things together.

Love begets love. When you send love out, it comes back to you on a return current with similar qualities, this time with stronger power than before. Love brings not only the supply of our physical needs but of our mental and spiritual needs as well. Like the sunlight or the air we breathe, the power of love is free and ready to be used constructively to the amazement of your wildest imagination. It may seem strange to some of you to read for the first time such praise for the Love Principle. But this you should know: many people know this law, yet it has been seldom used by only a few who not only understand its power but also understand that love does not work as well and as fast as we would like it to unless it is intense yet patient. When love is really intense, it lifts us to higher levels of knowledge. An intense love illumines the brain, the heart, the action, and even the atmosphere around an individual. It shows not only the causes of things but the effects that result from them as well.

When love is intensely poured on a thing to be achieved or a subject to be learned, it harmonizes or heightens our level of comprehension and performance to that of knowledge to be understood or work to be performed. Love by itself is capable of injecting courage, persistence, confidence, and even knowledge and strength necessary to achieve or climb any mountain that stands in the way of greatness. Jesus, Moses,

www.makanologos.com

Newton, Darwin, Joan of Arc, Lincoln, Washington, Gandhi, M. L. King, Mandela, Mother Teresa, and any other great man or woman did not do it otherwise. If you have difficulty acquiring courage, persistence, self-confidence, or any other constructive quality, the shortcut to acquiring all of them with less uncertainty and pain is to intensely and genuinely love what you want to do, for love contains within itself all the constructive qualities you will ever need to arouse your intelligence and climb the mountain of greatness.

Just as it is practically impossible for light and darkness, death and life, left and right, or negative and positive to cohabit, so is it impossible for love and discouragement, doubt, fear, or selfishness to find common ground. Greatness is never achieved by some sort of half-baked love of constructive qualities. It is whole love or none. If you take a second look at the above quotations on Richard Grasso, you will notice, *"master salesman and promoter…competed tirelessly"* is how he is described. Love inspires mastery of occupation and wholeness of effort. Love in itself is not an idea but a feeling that inspires ideas. If ideas come from the mind, love is the flame that ignites the fire that takes man to the height of greatness. A man who does not love his occupation cannot possibly attain greatness in that line of work, for the power that sharpens the ability of man to perform resides in the love he gives to the work at hand. Without love, there is no element of creative fire in man.

While few man-made achievements are destined to last forever, those that are love-made rather than handmade last the longest. Take these two simple cases, for instance—the United States of America and the Soviet Union. The former was built on and with the love of freedom, while the latter was built with the hands of communists. In the first entity, people and their states were brought together voluntarily and lovingly, while in the second, people and their states were conquered and forced into the union. Consequently, the United States of America, as these lines are being written, is expecting to celebrate its 234th

www.makanologos.com

anniversary of its independence, while the Soviet Union lasted only roughly 68 years. Question! What do you think of the European Union? Is it a work of love or hands? How long do you think it will last? Ponder that for yourself.

Love alone connects man to the source of knowledge and wisdom. The more intensely you love something, the closer you get to its heart or the more willing it is to open its heart to you. The opposite of love, of course, does nothing but disconnect man from that source. If you believe in the magnetic power of ideas, and if you want to strengthen that power, your best bet is to love whatever you are doing with the greatest strength your heart can exert, and at any time or anywhere, the waves of priceless ideas you need will pop up at the most convenient time and location you could possibly wish for.

There is no realm of knowledge of achievement that a loving man cannot penetrate, for there is no door anywhere in the universe that the key of love cannot unlock. If you think the brain of Isaac Newton was sharp enough to open the door of the Law of Gravity; that of Copernicus to see the Earth circulate around the sun; that of Henry Ford to revolutionize transportation; or that of Joan of Arc to liberate the French from English humiliation; then think again. Greatness cannot possibly be achieved with the hands and the brains of men alone. The world is full of geniuses and hard-working people who not only live miserable lives but also go to their graves barely known by their next-door neighbors. Most of all, great heroes in history were not really "geniuses" as our modern dictionaries define the word.

Now let me ask you a few simple questions. Did Columbus discover America because of the greatness of his intelligence or because of his love of exploration? Did Albert Einstein discover the Law of Relativity because of the superiority of his intelligence or his love of the function of the universe? Did Nelson Mandela end apartheid because of his political ingenuity or his love of all South Africans? Did Gandhi free

www.makanologos.com

India from the British peacefully because of his knowledge of the law or because of his love of nonviolence? Go ahead — ask yourself a few more, and answer them yourself as well.

Everything else being equal, if your passport can open the door of any country you want to visit, love is the passport to the highest achievement of greatness. Paul greatly loved preaching so much that he was a great preacher! Michael Jackson greatly loved music so much that he was a great musician! Pelé greatly loved soccer so much that he was a great soccer player! Plato sincerely loved philosophy so much that he was a great philosopher! Napoleon greatly loved the military so much that he was a great general! Warren Buffett intensely loves investing so much that he is a great investor! Shakespeare sincerely loved poems so much that he was a great poet! Go ahead — name a few for your own inspiration but not before you answer the following questions.

Compared to their enemies' power, why do you think the American Colonies won the War of Independence from the world's mightiest military power of the time? Do you think the British Empire with its military superiority really loved victory as much as the Americans loved freedom? Answer those questions and know this: the love that arouses intelligence and helps achieve greatness is not a rational thing; it is not a conceptual thing, but rather a deep feeling of oneness with what you want to know or achieve to the best of your ability. That feeling is the vessel that took Newton into the heart of the Law of Gravity, Einstein into the heart of the Law of Relativity, Bill Gates into the heart of software, Warren Buffett into the heart of investing, Henry Ford into the heart of the automobile, M. L. King into the heart of the dream of freedom for all, Muhammad Ali into the heart of boxing, Mark Twain into the heart of writing, Dan Brown and J. K. Rowling into the heart of fiction, and so on.

Love is truly magic, and the absence of it spells c-h-a-o-s and m-i-s-e-r-i-e-s. A person who is seeking greatness should

www.makanologos.com

never do anything that is not worth his full and unconditional love. All governments of the world that have laws that express anything less than love of the people either collapse or plunge into deep darkness and untold miseries. There are both spiritual and psychological reasons why no dictatorship or tyranny ever prospered in the history of civilization. Without the best efforts of government erecting laws that unequivocally express love in the form of justice and fairness, no science or commerce can possibly flourish in that country. No nation or government survives without implicitly expressing love for its people. Unless love governs the daily activities of a person or a government, life will be torturous. A great leader of any government or organization is the one who leads not with fear or bribery but with love.

As cynical as it may seem, people will follow a loving leader to their death rather than follow a tyrannical one to salvation. In the age of widespread terrorism, it should not be hard to understand why some people choose suicide bombing rather than the millions offered them to betray their leaders. When people are led by love alone, they can resist and defeat any enemy regardless of the odds. For centuries, Europe tried to impose peace on itself through sword and spear until it almost annihilated itself. Then the loving treaty that engendered the European Union came to the rescue. Wise men turn to love for greatness, but the unwise turn to force, unfortunately for more frustration. Love is the incredible lubricant of the (human) machine that manufactures greatness.

No man can possibly achieve greatness without lovingly concentrating or focusing his or her energy on the object of the work at hand. In case you need a reminder, concentration is an action of love. Unless you love something, you cannot possibly concentrate on it. Concentration—attention, that is— is an obedient servant of love. I will deal with attention more intensely in a later chapter, but while I am here, let me just throw some sparks of light in the sky of a moonless night.

www.makanologos.com

Without attention, no great realization is possible. Great achievers are those who give undivided attention to what they are doing. And unless you love something, there is no way you can give it your full attention. Can you possibly believe that Warren Buffett reached the mastery of investment by giving 50%, 65%, 75%, or 85% of his attention? Do you really believe Plato, Shakespeare, Jean-Jacques Rousseau, or Goethe became great philosophers and writers by giving their occupations divided attention? Now, if you asked the greatest of them all, Plato himself, he would tell you this from the grave through the inestimable gift he left to mankind, *The Republic*:

I don't know anything that gives me greater pleasure, or profit either, than talking or listening to philosophy. But when it comes to ordinary conversation, such as the stuff you talk about financiers and the money market, well, I find it pretty tiresome personally, and I feel sorry that my friends should think they're being very busy when they're really doing absolutely nothing. Of course, I know your idea of me: you think I'm just a poor unfortunate, and I shouldn't wonder if you're right. But then I don't THINK that you're unfortunate – I know you are (from *Being and Learning: A Poetic Phenomenology of Education* by Eduardo M. Duarte, page 38).

I will leave it to you for further investigation if you like, but this I wish you to know: attention unsupported by love will either make you dumb or a low performer. When we love something dearly, all our faculties, like an antenna, stand mobilized and ready to receive and translate the waves of radiation. And like a reliable servant, they stand ready to serve us with unprecedented loyalty.

There is almost no situation that can be handled with true love that will fail. Greatness is achieved by self-conquest first and foremost, and only love enables man to self-conquer. The reason most of us fail to achieve our life's dreams is not that our dreams are somewhat difficult, impossible, or otherwise. It is simply because most of us cannot bring our faculties under

Exalted Secrets of Brilliant Minds   329

control and pointedly bring them together to love what we want to achieve. When man is able to harmonize his feelings, control his thoughts wisely, persistently act constructively, feel good about himself or have self-confidence, focus attention on the task at hand, and trust himself as a tool of a Higher Power, there is nothing he cannot do, including walking on water or even moving a giant mountain to any distance.

How do you think all those faculties or qualities of man come into focus? Well, through the power of love. When one loves dearly or hates deeply something constructive or destructive, he or she becomes a tool of the Gods or diabolical forces, depending on what he or she loves or hates. If it is something constructive that you love, you will become a force of good, an instrument of the Gods, and a custodian of mental or physical wealth of the world. If it is a destructive thing that intrigues your heart and mind, you will be an instrument of the diabolical or negative forces of the world. This, of course, I will talk about more deeply in the chapter dedicated to truth. Greatness is always a result of several qualities. But if there is one quality that you would like me to point out as the most likely to include all other qualities as far as the achievement of greatness is concerned, I will tell you that it is definitely love. No one can be victorious without love. Love is all we need to climb any mountain of greatness. Attention, silence, truth, self-confidence, faith, hope, charity, hard work, and any other quality are useless unless they are impregnated with the seed of love. Just having the longing of love before thoughts and actions is a battle half won. Of course, *"no man can become a saint in his sleep,"* wrote Henry Drummond in the same publication on page 53. Action is still needed in order to achieve greatness, but if you already have genuine love for your goal, not a mere wish or fantasy but true love, you already have God on your side, as it is said that God is love, and *"one plus God is majority."* And by the way, didn't Paul write, "Now abideth faith, hope and love, but the greatest of these is LOVE"?

www.makanologos.com

I do not want to sound like I am preaching or promoting Christianity or any religion. Love is not exclusive to religion. In fact, I am promoting no religion at all but rather the Principle of Love that works regardless of whether you are a religious person or even an atheist. While believing in a Supreme Being is magnificent, the power of love is almost blind. It works whether or not one consciously believes in God because most of us believe in God one way or the other in our subconscious. History is full of many self-proclaimed "atheists" who achieved some level of greatness—among others, Karl Marx, Friedrich Engels, Mao Tse Tung, etc. You and I can argue about the justification of their greatness, but their works inspired millions around the world, affected the lives of people in both the Western and Eastern Hemispheres. Progressive and liberal political organizations as well as labor unions of the West may not be communistic entities, but they got a lot of their ideas from the works of these great writers and theorists, and even conservative organizations do not ignore them completely.

However, I need to make it clear here before proceeding— an atheist in the strictest meaning of the word does not exist. As stated in the first part of this work, God is the philosopher stone, and there is no greatness without deep belief in Him. The self-proclaimed atheists are not really atheists at all. They may not believe in the almighty old man in the sky, but they believe in the power in them that enables them to perform whatever it is they want to achieve. That power is their God and the God of all of us, because that power is not man-made. It is nothing but God within us acting through us. Now let's move on.

Yes, it matters what you love (more on this point in the chapter on truth), but this you must know: when you genuinely love something, you have the greatest power of manifestation at your command. Men do their work by their hands (or so they think), and that is why it is always a product of trial and error subject to perpetual improvements. But Spirits (or Nature) do all their work with LOVE, and they do it perfectly once and for

www.makanologos.com

all. Mother Nature created air, earth, water, and fire once and never improved anything afterward. Just as oil melts before fire, knowledge and the secrets of nature melt before love and reveal themselves unconditionally. In fact, anything that is wrapped with love cannot help but melt itself and reveal its real secrets. The intellect of man itself vibrates the fastest and most accurately when it is stimulated by love. So when you truly love something, not only the thing itself will melt before your love, but your own intellect will also vibrate fast enough to comprehend what you want to know and do.

While it melts things, love also magnetizes things. When you love something, love attracts other things you need in order to accomplish what you want to accomplish. Let me illustrate this point with my own life experience, a fact drawn from the experience lived while writing this book. Like most great readers who have never written a book, I used to admire writers (I still do, but not as naïvely as back then) and almost worshiped them as I sometimes considered them as extraordinary people for the extraordinary work they do. I still admire and respect them, but now I consider them fellow human beings after I discovered how the Love Principle works for them and went through the same experience myself. Most people think that when an author is writing a book, he or she has planned everything meticulously, and everything is worked out before starting the project. In fact, that is far from the truth. While a rough plan is always at hand, the actual plan and juiciest ideas are revealed as the love of writing unfolds.

The truth is that all an author has before writing a book is simply the love of the work ahead. And that love alone takes him to places where he or she finds the materials he or she may not have planned for or dreamed of to be essential for the project. Love of a writer's work brings him in contact with knowledgeable and helpful people to the project, sometimes intentionally but many time coincidentally. Invisible Helpers who know and feel your love of the project at hand and who

www.makanologos.com

want to operate through you bring in visible helpers and helpful materials in a way that no human being can possibly anticipate. Before I started writing this book and my previous one as well, little did I know which reference materials I would need to successfully enrich my work with inspiring substance. But as I gave my work the most genuine love my heart could give, materials would come to me or me to them almost mysteriously. I would find stuff on TV, online, in conversation with friends and coworkers, etc. I would find books to read in places and times I little expected and so on. More than 90% of the works cited in the bibliographical section were obtained unexpectedly. That is the power of love. It will break down knowledge for you as well as gather it from all four corners of the Earth.

I have done my best here to go the greatest lengths I can to reveal this great secret to you, my readers. Actually, I did not reveal but rather reminded you because your Inner Self already knew about it and knew it a gazillion times better than me. I can only hope you give love a special place in your heart and life, and as you do that, it will give you a special place in the hearts and minds of your fellow men. It will place you on the highest mountaintop that men's eyes have never seen, human feet have never stepped upon, and hands have never touched. There is no higher creative power anywhere above and below than love. Yes, you can fail if you use it wrongly, but you can never fail if you use it correctly. When you understand the energy generated by your love for whatever you want to accomplish, when you intend to use that energy constructively, all the powers of the universe will come to and concentrate at your point in the universe to aid you, stand up for you, and open the door that no man can shut for you to step into the realms of knowledge and power of action untold. Love, my friend, is the utmost hand of greatness. It is the highest power that takes brilliant minds of great kings, wise princes, seers, sages, high priests, and the chosen few to the top of mountain

www.makanologos.com

of greatness. Love arouses intelligence as few other qualities can.

It would be unfair to the reader to bring this very important chapter to a close without giving him the opportunity to reflect on these words of Jiddu Krishnamurti as found in his work *Education and the Significance of Life* (pages 66-68) on how intelligence is not separate from love, and how it cannot possibly be if the eye of man is to see and his hand is to bring out into the visible from the invisible world the wonders that await for the awakening of our consciousness:

Modern education, in developing the intellect, offers more and more theories and facts, without bringing about the understanding of the total process of human existence. We are highly intellectual; we have developed cunning minds, and are caught up in explanations. The intellect is satisfied with theories and explanations, but intelligence is not; and for the understanding of the total process of existence, there must be an integration of the mind and heart in action. Intelligence is not separate from love...

Information, the knowledge of facts, though ever increasing, is by its very nature limited. Wisdom is infinite, it includes knowledge and the way of action; but we take hold of a branch and think it is the whole tree. Through the knowledge of the part, we can never realize the joy of the whole. Intellect can never lead to the whole, for it is only a segment, a part.

We have separated intellect from feeling, and have developed intellect at the expanse of feeling. We are like a three-legged object with one leg much longer than the others, and we have no balance. We are trained to be intellectual; our education cultivates the intellect to be sharp, cunning, acquisitive, and so it plays the most important role in our life. Intelligence is much greater than intellect, for it is the integration of reason and love; but there can be intelligence only when there is self-knowledge, the deep understanding of the total process of oneself...Only love and right thinking will bring about true revolution, the revolution within ourselves. But how are we to have love? (A quick look

www.makanologos.com

at this website will unearth this portion of the book for fast reference: http://www.katinkahesselink.net/kr/emotion.html, accessed July 5, 2010.)

"But how are we to have love?" Good question. Answer it correctly and apply your answer strictly, and your mind will be brighter than you could possibly dream.

There cannot possibly be a final word on such an important topic as love. It is utterly impossible. But living in the world of limited time and space, I must move on to fulfill other obligations. But if you have to retain one thing from the Love Principle, this is it: *Men (the mass of mankind) create with their hands and heads. They create through trial and error. Several times they miss the target; thus they painfully and rarely reach the mountaintop of greatness. Gods and Invisible Helpers create with love alone; hence their works transcend greatness, transcend the understanding of man's mind.* If you want to climb the mountain of greatness, don't do it like the masses; rather, do it like the Gods. Create with love and you will be astonished how great your greatness will be, how high your intelligence will rise. To create with love, there is a simple but powerful formula: *Love what it is you are doing now as if your life depends on it because it does. Love those you are working with because your love will melt their resistance, bring them to cooperate with you, and stimulate their intellect and intuition. Love where you are because here and now is the only place and time from which you can control all the forces within and without to achieve anything.* If you do this, no mountain of greatness will ever seem difficult for you to climb. Remember, man does disappoint and betray love, but love does not betray or disappoint man. You will always be better off in whatever you are doing with true love.

The time invested to put this chapter on paper alone, excluding research, took me a good number of days. In the final days, as the train of thoughts of love was slowing down to a stop in order to allow me to transfer to the train of TRUTH (next chapter,) something happened in the news, something

www.makanologos.com

that I considered to be a godsend kind of illustration for my readers to pick up more light in regard to the indispensable role of love in the excellence of intelligence. The illustration in question is the story of a 98-year-old lady named Verna Oller. Without comment, I will let the reader discern for himself the light and nourishment that are enclosed in these words as reported by Huffingtonpost.com and abcnews.go.com

Secret Millionaire

The sturdy old lady with no formal education amassed a not-so-small fortune: $4.5 million. It was up over $5 million before the recession. Before she died, she directed Guy Glenn to spend every cent of it, but not on her, on her home town. The town of Long Beach, Washington, will receive its very first swimming pool. Money will also be set aside for scholarships for students and grants for teachers. (http://www.huffingtonpost.com/2010/06/10/verna-oller-leaves-45-mil_n_608155.html, accessed July 5, 2010)

Keeping A Secret

Oller never made much money, earning an hourly wage filleting fish until she was in her 70s. She cut her own firewood until she was in her 90s. But Oller was carrying a secret, a big one, and she entrusted the Glenns to keep it. It turned out she was a master investor. "She went to the library and read Barrons," *Guy Glenn said. "She read the* Wall Street Journal." *She called Glenn "the paperboy" because he would give her his already read copy of the paper. She never wanted to spend money on it herself. Oller was so savvy; she gave the Glenns' son stock investing tips, telling him about how she made a 50-percent return on AT&T when it was at a low point.*

(http://abcnews.go.com/WN/american-heart-secret-millionaire-helps-hometown-grave/story?id=10870876, accessed July 5, 2010)

When things are done with love, even Invisible Helpers, Invisible Friends of mighty powers, come not just to the rescue but to illumine and do what they can only do through men who

www.makanologos.com

radiate love of the task at hand. In their conversation in *The Power of Myth*, on page 150, Bill Moyers and Joseph Campbell respectively called these Invisible Helpers and "hidden hands." And as this chapter on love is winding down, let's ask Campbell and Moyers to refresh the reader on the importance of doing everything with love. It goes like this:

Moyers: *Do you ever have this sense when you are following your bliss, as I have at moments, of being helped by hidden hands?*

Campbell: *All the time. It is miraculous. I even have a superstition that has grown on me as the result of invisible hands coming all the time – namely, that if you do follow your bliss you put yourself on a kind of track that has been there all the while, waiting for you, and the life that you ought to be living is the one you are living. When you can see that, you begin to meet people who are in the field of your bliss, and they open the doors to you. I say, follow your bliss and don't be afraid, and doors will open where you didn't know they were going to be.*

Moyers: *Have you ever had sympathy for the man who has no invisible means of support?*

Campbell: *Who has no invisible means? Yes, he is the one that evokes compassion, the poor chap. To see him stumbling around when all the waters of life are right there really evokes one's pity.*

Moyers: *The waters of eternal life are there? Where?*

Campbell: *Wherever you are – if you are following your bliss, you are enjoying that refreshment, that life within you, all the time.*

Let me now close this chapter with few words from Master K. H. as quoted by Clara M. Codd in *The Way of the Disciple*:

"Of all the qualifications love is the most important, for if it is strong enough in a man, it forces him to acquire all the rest, and all the rest without it would never be sufficient...It is indeed the will to become one with God in order that because of your deep love for Him you may act with Him and as He does," (page, 252).

www.makanologos.com

Love

Love, what art thou?
Long have we waited to know what thou really art,
Hoping all the mysteries around thee to melt like ice on fire,
All the secrets to evaporate like fog on a morning sun
But in vain have we waited, indeed.

Then to far-off listeners we did send our quest
A distant star in our ears speaks
An ineffable idiom a bit like this whispered:
"I am a radiation of the Sacred Fire
From the heart of existence
I am an ocean of life and light."
Then of thee my heart thought like this:
In thee, Gods and Goddesses create and rule all in the universe.
In thee, all big and small celestial orbs live and breathe

In thee, existence finds strength and support to carry life on
    forever
In thee, elements of nature sing and glorify life
In thee, air and fire elements renew and recycle life
In thee, water and mineral elements feed life
In thee, all creation finds peace and joy
In thee, harmony, prosperity and happiness find roots
In thee, brilliant minds find poise and wonders

In thee, piercing intellect find creative power
In thee, far-sighted souls find nourishment
In thee, fittest bodies find strength and support
In thee, above radiates below as below reflects above
In thee, the Causeless Cause reigns above all
In thee, Justice finds its balance,
In thee, Victory finds its resolve,
In thee, Courage finds its sword

www.makanologos.com

In thee, faith and hope find charity
In thee, the sun provides life to distant stars
In thee, the Supreme One rules infinity
In thee, wisdom, harmony and strength find trinity

Oh love, thou art Sun of suns
"*Gupta Vidya*" of holiest and wisest men
Breath of heavenly Beings
Supreme truth is thy name

About thee sons of men should comprehend
When all the rulers of the world in love alone act
And in love all the people pull strength together
Their sword of courage shall defeat fear
Their spear of selflessness shall kill the monster of greed
Knowledge shall vanquish ignorance
And the destiny of man of peace and joy
Shall be here, now forever and ever

By Wisdom J.O.Y. Makano, the author

www.makanologos.com

CHAPTER XV

The Truth Pillar (Integrity)

Sages and historians often tell us that all wars are products of heinous vices, among which are greed, exploitation, self-aggrandizement, and just human folly — and they are heinous vices. But if there is one virtue that can be blamed for some of the longest and pitiless wars, that virtue is spelled T-R-U-T-H. Almost all religious wars have been justified by one and one only virtue: "the truth," the desire to impose the truth on the other parties. That is it. Not that the truth causes war, but some of the ugliest wars have been waged in its name — the Muslim or Islamic Conquest from present-day Pakistan to North Africa, the Middle East, the Iberia Peninsula, and the Pyrenees; the French Wars of Religion between the French Catholics and Protestants (Huguenots); the series of religiously sanctioned military campaigns waged by much of Latin Christian Europe called the Crusades; the "Reconquista," the purging of Muslims by the Christian Kingdoms of the Iberian Peninsula; the Muslim Jihad of the seventh century; as well ongoing modern terrorism. The consequences for and against it have been justified by one side or the other as the fight for the truth. Saints Augustine and Thomas Aquinas even went so far as to theorize and elaborate on a "just war" within the Christianity used by the Roman Catholic Church to control the actions of the European countries.

It is truly incredible how the fight for such a virtue as truth has spilled human blood possibly more than any evil has caused or even all of them combined. The truth, the mother of all virtues, is said to be the fuzziest, the least understood, and the most misunderstood of all concepts there is in human language. One author went as far as saying that all truths are only half-truths, implying that the truth is simply a myth and thus doesn't exist. All philosophers have claimed to shed light on the truth or bring us closer to it, yet the more light they pour on it, the more confused we get and the farther away from it we seem to be. Laws that are supposedly meant to shield us from the untruth seem to smash us against one another every day. I am not by any means saying that philosophers have purposely misled us—not at all. I am simply lamenting how dicey the concept called truth is or can be. In fact, thinking of the vagueness of truth, in his masterpiece, *The Republic*, Plato wrote:

When the mind's eye rests on the object illuminated by truth and reality, it understands and comprehends them, and functions intelligently; but when it turns to the twilight world of change and decay, it can only form opinions, its vision is confused and its beliefs shifting, and it seems to lack intelligence.

"*The philosopher is in love with the truth,*" said Plato, but just as prophets did not invent God, philosophers did not invent the truth. If Jews have Moses and Aaron, Christians have Jesus and Paul, Muslims have Mohammed, Buddhists have Siddhartha Gautama (Buddha), I think—and it is a highly defensible case to suggest—that Western philosophers have Socrates and Plato. The definition of the truth by Plato, while seemingly simple, is even more divisive or dangerous. I am sure this poor genius Plato exhausted his human brainpower when he defined truth as what really is, the reality, what exists. "*I assume that by knowing the truth you mean knowing the things as they really are,*" he wrote. The question is, what really is? The answer to that question alone has been responsible for some of the worst conflicts the world has ever experienced. Do you still wonder why Plato, scratching his head, asks, "*And isn't it a bad thing to be deceived about the truth, and a good thing to know what the truth is?*" While the world conventionally agrees on some visible realities, we barely agree, if we agree at all, on many unseen or hidden realities, and here is where the swords of man collide with each other.

www.makanologos.com

Exalted Secrets of Brilliant Minds **341**

I will not dare to walk in the shoes of the great philosophers of old, but I honestly sympathize with their pain. They took a difficult subject as the object of their study. Therefore, I will not give a philosophical definition of truth. In fact, I will strive to get the mumbo jumbo of philosophy out of it as much as I can. I will attempt to give a definition that will be relatively specific to the mountain of greatness that you want to climb but subject to the scrutiny of the greatest examiner of all, time. The great ones who successfully climbed the mountain of greatness understood the truth as a seed of an imperishable cause, a cause that does not die or go with you at that majestic moment you step into the next world, a cause that may be controversial in your lifetime but will definitely thrive after you have passed on. This seed may or may not decay in your lifetime but will eventually germinate even if you are no longer around. Thus, in your quest for greatness, consider the truth as something that is a selfless, noble, and great cause you can possibly give your life for or something that you believe your descendants will be proud of—something that could transform your detractors' descendants into sympathizers, at the very least, if not outright friends and genuine admirers. This is the truth that is aimed at by brilliant minds; this is the truth that arouses the intelligence of men.

Jews crucified Jesus, but how many of the descendants of his crucifiers would render the same judgment today, or how many of them think that he did not deserve the treatment he was subjected to? George Washington probably could have been hanged had he fallen into the hands of the British army, but how many British today think he was not a great and noble man? Both Gandhi and Martin Luther King Jr. from their graves have successfully transformed many of their former detractors into proud admirers. That is the power of truth. That is the seed that rots in the lifetime of its cultivator only to germinate amazingly and forcefully even after its planter has passed on. That is the truth that enables one to climb the mountain

www.makanologos.com

of greatness. That is the truth that will be debated in the rest of this chapter. Now the question is, how does truth sharpen brilliant minds?

As I was reading *The Kleinknecht Germs of Thoughts Encyclopedia, Volume IX* the other day, I came across a quotation credited to *Alberta Grand Lodge Bulletin* that captivated my mind. The quotation in question is this: *"Integrity goes hand in hand with high moral purpose, straight thinking, lofty idealism and a love of humanity"* (page 198). Whether your mind is captivated by the quotation as mine was amazed by everything in it matters not. I ask you to pay attention to just three words, if you will, and those three words are *integrity* and *straight thinking*. People with brilliant minds are not necessarily highly educated, but they are still very good thinkers. Good thinking is never a product of chance or coincidence; it is a planned and sustained process. Unless there is a specifically targeted objective, good thinking is absolutely difficult, to say the least.

Brilliant minds are good feelers and great thinkers, and that is one of the things that set them apart from the rest of the crowd. Unfortunately, there is no school for good feeling and good thinking. Logic may be said to be the science of reasoning, but very few people can credit their reasoning ability to that science; otherwise, it would be taught to schoolchildren from the very early years of life. As great as logic is as a science, it is not the finest tool for thinking, at least the kind of thinking that allows certain minds to climb the mountain of greatness, effortlessly or otherwise. To be a great thinker, one must always aim for the truth. The truth never behaved capriciously or unjustly. Only those who deserve it, those who have complied with its requirements, find it. When you seek to climb the mountain of greatness through the acquisition of the truth, your thinking will consequently straighten, heighten, and deepen at the same time while causing the mind to brighten and find the ways and means to where very few have reached.

www.makanologos.com

There is no intelligence or mind that cannot be trained and perfected by a serious search for truth. When one sincerely seeks the truth, his intelligence works like a mighty river that goes deep, almost effortlessly wiping all resistance against it along the way. This, of course, does not happen because of your desire but because of Invisible Helpers who are 24/7 seeking daring souls in human bodies to work through for the purpose of mankind's evolution.

While the search for truth does not by any means guarantee a trouble-free journey, it strengthens both the mind and body in the face of intimidating obstacles. A truth-seeking individual is never fooled by appearances or brief success. He does not pat himself in the back and is not satisfied with minor and temporary success. He understands the dangers that he faces; thus he develops the most important prerequisite quality of success that most people, at their own expense, couldn't care less to cultivate — persistence. He knows when to act and when to react. He is immune to rashness, has passion for punctuality, for when found at the right time and right place, the truth conquers all.

Brilliant minds are always leaders of society in their lines of work. To lead people, one must always be in possession of the truth or at least seeking the truth. Of course, the truth by itself is rarely a religion, but you are more likely able to start a new religion with 1% truth than with 100% untruth. When you know the truth and use it correctly, people will follow you to their deaths. Brilliant minds understand that. That is why they make the search for truth their fundamental goal for their own enlightenment and the attraction of the masses. A person who knows the truth and shares it selflessly may physically die but is immediately reborn or resurrected and lives forever in the hearts of countless generations. The ignorant and liars are forgotten or washed from the memory of man as soon as they pass away, but a truth-bearer is basically immortal, transcending time and space as well as culture because *"truth is common stock,"* as Charles C. Colton once said, and *"the breath of life to human society"* in the words of Oliver W. Holmes.

Brilliant minds understand that, to remain in public life, one must always either possess the truth or perpetually look for it, or else their other talents are worthless. As you seek the truth, however, you must be very (I cannot stretch this long enough) careful. Yes, by all means always seek the truth, but never allow yourself to be obsessed with it lest you become a fanatic and foolishly try to impose it on others. Like a compass, the truth must be the guiding light for the pilot or the captain, not the passenger, because it is never easily found, much less understood. The truth is sometimes extremely difficult to attain in just one lifetime. It may take generations or centuries to reach the heart of the truth. The law of nature never intended the truth to be the goal of life in our journey to the heart of infinity, but rather a Christmas star to guide the wise men to the source of light, because otherwise there would be no infinity. The perpetual search for the truth is what infinity is all about. Once the truth is found, infinity instantaneously ceases to be. Not to say that the truth is elusive, but it is gradual, and it comes to us by way of inspiration, which requires patience, and by way of the senses, which may just be dreaming or foolish sometimes.

In your search for the truth, if you find yourself as a magi looking for the child Jesus by the aid of the lightening star, the truth will always reveal itself progressively to you. Of course, you may never find the child Jesus, but you will be heading in the right direction, and the right direction is what you need to set the feet of the next generation on. For, as said above, you and your generation may not be the ones who will eventually find the truth, but your obligation is to start movement forward in the right direction. Nature, purposely or otherwise, does not show the whole truth to one individual but rather to the race. And because of nature's progressive self-revelation of the truth to the human race through generations rather than individuals, the evolution of man is practically unending, unlike that of

www.makanologos.com

Exalted Secrets of Brilliant Minds   345

other creatures. The endless nature of the truth must not to be seen as an obstacle or reason for discouragement, but rather a good excuse to spring the mind and imagination further into the inner space and bring clarification to enlighten our science and philosophy, our reason and faith, or our civilization in general. It would be catastrophic if the truth revealed itself to one man and then disappeared. If that had been the case, horses, donkeys, and camels would still be the most luxurious modes of transportation today. The Ford Motor Company would still be selling its Model T vehicles, not the Ford F-Series, Ford Fusion, or Ford Escape. Microsoft would still be producing its MS DOS application, not its Windows series. Apple would still be manufacturing Macintosh computers, not the iPad, iPhone, and iPod, and maybe AT&T would still be busy commercializing Alexander Graham Bell's telephone and not Apple's popular touch-screen cellular iPhones.

Can you imagine a world like that? Without doubt, life would be stagnant, without progress, and ultimately uninspiring. I bring up this point because I want you to understand that greatness is most of the time not defined by finding the truth but by setting the course toward it. Did Henry Ford find the whole truth about cars? Did Alexander Graham Bell find the whole truth about the phone? Compare Ford's Model T to the Ford Edge, Escape, Explorer, Flex, Focus, Fusion, etc. or the touch-screen cellular phones of today to Alexander Graham Bell's telephone. If you think about it, you will notice that these giants of the twentieth century barely scratched the surface of their line of work, but most importantly, they set the feet of future generations in the right direction. They pointed the way to the Christmas star, leaving future generations (of Fords and Bells) the task of carrying on the unending task of finding the truth.

The truth is such an intoxicating substance that it should never be sought by either hearts or heads alone but by the equal combination or balance of both. When sought by heart alone,

www.makanologos.com

it causes obsession, and when sought by the head alone, it provokes arrogance, both of which are blinding and intolerant forces that keep the truth virtually imperceptible. While the conflict between your head and your heart can stand in the way of finding the truth, people, misguided public policies, or traditions also may discourage a seeker from keeping the course toward the truth; however, many times it is self-distrust and doubt that are the biggest obstacles to the truth. Thus, in your search for the truth, you must guard yourself against external negative and destructive forces as well as internal ones. It can only help to remember these words of Arthur Schopenhauer: *"Every truth passes through three stages before it is recognized. In the first, it is ridiculed, in the second it is opposed, in the third it is regarded as self-evident."*

As you prepare to climb the mountain of greatness, remind yourself that finding the truth alone does not enable you to reach the summit. The peak is reached only when you share with others what nature has trusted you with. Can you imagine the world worshiping a Jesus who kept his spiritual knowledge to himself, or admiring a Bill Gates who could not find ways of sharing his knowledge and love of software with the rest of the world? I understand that there are seemingly rational arguments against spreading the truth, but brilliant minds are brilliant not because they have the truth but because they found ways to share it. Even secret agencies of good governments understand that unless they find ways of sharing their secrets with the public, they are totally irrelevant and inefficient. What would the FBI or CIA be without public assistance? It is this love of truth and creative ways of sharing it with others that arouses the intelligence of men. Good writers are those who strive to find the truth and creatively share it with the public.

When it first started in the early 1960s, the Internet, then known as ARPANET, was a top secret United States government project. It was so top secret that the U.S. Department of Defense's Defense Advanced Research Projects Agency

www.makanologos.com

Exalted Secrets of Brilliant Minds   347

(DARPA) managed it. Thus, the U.S. government, for high treason reasons, would have probably hanged anyone who could have tipped it off to an antagonistic government or even to an unauthorized friendly foreign government. But to make it relevant and useful, the U.S. government had to find ways to disseminate that information to the general public worldwide. Today, not only is it freely used in the former Soviet Union republics, it is also used in North Korea and Iran, two sworn mortal enemies of the American government. *"The one who buries the truth in the ground for safekeeping will lose it, while the one who does something with the truth will receive more Truth. This is why some grow spiritually and some do not,"* wrote Christian writer Chip Brogden. The deeper you bury the truth in the ground, the harder will it be for you to climb the mountain of greatness; the more wisely you reveal it to others, the higher will you climb it. To arouse your intelligence, the task is not just going after it but also sharing it with others, sometimes even with your sworn enemies. If discovered today in the United States, the cure for cancer will be dispatched to treat leaders of both Iran and North Korea should they need it. That is not a moral obligation on the part of the United States but the law of nature if the intelligence of the human race is to be aroused to reach the higher stars.

I promised to take all the philosophical mumbo jumbo out of this discussion about the truth, and I hope I have succeeded. If not, I leave that task and honor to you, to immerse yourself in the cleansing flames of your mind and hopefully get where I have not been successful to reach. Before I can come to the final station as far as this train of truth is concerned, I want to make sure these words of Leo Tolstoy ring in your head as they have rung in mine: *"Truth, like gold, is to be obtained not by its growth, but by washing away from it all that is not gold."* The truth does not grow any more than the stone does; it is only polished in order for it to shine and attract men. You cannot possibly invent the truth, but you can make it sparkle with more thinking about

www.makanologos.com

it. Ford Motor Company did not go from the Model T to its current line of products by changing or expanding the truth but rather by improving and deepening its original idea of the automobile in all its dimensions.

Finally, you probably do not need me to tell you this, as I am sure you must have heard it by now, but "like attracts like." What you send out determines what comes back to you is the supreme "law of cause and effect," as it is called by many. When you desire, seek, think, act, and feel the truth, the truth will find you, reveal itself to you more clearly, and slowly but surely arouse your intelligence as it takes you up the mountain of greatness one step at a time. The ancient law of cause and effect is for real and works favorably for you if you are mindful of it and act accordingly, but it nonetheless works one way or another whether you are conscious or not. It has led scientific research to the discovery of wonders from the dawn of time, and it has the power to brighten your mind many times over if your thoughts and feelings take the form of an image, belief, expectation, or action of truth.

This chapter on the truth is included here for a much-intended purpose. I intentionally did not want to define the truth, and I still do not want to. The reason is that this author believes that the truth is incomprehensible and unattainable. All we know and feel are basically the dreams of our senses, our illusions. Let me be less cruel and try to be sensible, if you will. All we have known and felt up to this point in our journey toward the star of the truth may not be entirely illusion; it is certainly not the whole truth but rather stepping stones toward the truth. Intelligence is aroused by one stepping stone at a time. Thus, the more you love and seek the truth, the more your intelligence will experience progressive arousal until you climb that mountain of greatness as only the chosen few (who, by the way, know this law) can. Love and seek the truth, and your intelligence will never know boundaries. Your body and mental abilities will practically defy the viciousness of age. Love and

www.makanologos.com

seek the truth assiduously one stepping-stone at a time, and your greatness will never know either time or space. This is one the best-kept secrets of brilliant minds, this is how intelligence is aroused, and this is the ELIXIR OF INTELLIGENCE, because light is its own defense and inspiration is its own revelation. This is how you watch and look within the light. Seeing all within it, you make joy live in you and others, for there is nothing hidden that is not revealed a constructive seeker needs to know, so long honor to life is the motive for which he/she does everything. This is the end of the road, for this is how the great ones gained their immortality and a place of honor in the hearts of all generations to come, and so can you, so long as you stand for the Highest Ideal in the universe and honor to life is the motive for which you do everything. I will leave you with a Buddhist question and poem by this author for your own reflection: *"Everyone knows orange trees grow from orange seeds, apple trees from apple seeds. Why do you think good things can grow from evil seeds?"* What is the seed of greatness? Is it truth or otherwise? Enjoy your meditation.

Truth

The jewel above all thou art
The seed of sacred fire of the Nameless Creator of all
The Magnetic and harmonizing power of creation
The Grail that surpasses the understanding of the mind
In wisest Cosmic Beings care thou dwells
In blistering light art thou clothed

Man's eye seeth thee not
Man's ear hears thy voice not
Man's mouth thy name dares not pronounce
Only truly inspired man's mind sees thy majestic light
Wise man's heart longs to feel thee
Truth,

Thy art neither seen nor unseen
Neither heard nor unheard
Neither present nor absent
Never half, always all or none

Thru senses and radiation comes thee to man
Wisdom and understanding thy radiation art
Windows thru which man's eye perceives thee
Nose through which man's nose smells thee
Hands with which man dares touch thee
Wings with which man flies to thee

Ever flying
Ever touching
Ever smelling
Ever feeling
Ever perceiving
Never comprehending what thou art

At last, at peace my heart rests
Knowing one day in thy soft hands
Shall my soul sleep, play, and live
In fullness of love and joy
Point I to thy star
My brothers and sisters
For thee we shall yearn forever

Wisdom Joseph Ombe Ya Makano

CHAPTER XVI

The Silence Pillar

"This is called the Temple of Silence, the Place of Power. Silence is Power, for when we reach the place of silence in mind, we have reached the place of power – the place where all is one, the one power – God. 'Be still and know I am God.'" B. T. Spalding, Vol. 1, page 35

I have dealt with silence before in this work; I am back at it again. But as you know, what goes around comes around. So goes the saying, not in the sense of paying any retribution in this case but so as to highlight the importance of silence in the business of brightening the mind and arousing intelligence. It is no accident that I have come back again to this subject, which, in fact, attentive readers will recall I promised to do. I have come back to discuss more about silence. I can assure you that it is an intentional plan to talk about silence in both the second and the third part of this book. Earlier I demonstrated how silence helps to quiet or harmonize feelings; here, I will try to show readers how they can use this incredible power to arouse their intelligence and consequently sharpen their minds as they seek to climb the mountain of greatness.

But before I start scratching the surface of this minefield, let me say something I honestly feel deeply from the bottom of my heart. Long ago, when I was simply dreaming about writing books, I imagined writing as an expression of my fantasies. As I read numerous books that were written more than one hundred years before I saw the light of the sun, my heart started to view writing with more light than I had ever thought before. Rather than an expression of my fantasies, I started to see writing as a responsible expression of my thoughts and feelings for educating mankind, not just my contemporaries but also generations yet to be born. Thus, I came to believe writing to be not just a privilege but also a responsibility of proportional dimensions.

My viewpoint was so transformed that I realized that beside God's, writers' words, thoughts, and feelings are the only human bells whose rings are thunderous enough to crack the walls of time and space and echo into men's ears, hearts, and minds thousands of years and thousands of miles away. Thousands of years later, the writings of Moses are still the precepts of justice of major religions of today. *The Republic* of Plato is still dictating the management of public affairs and politics in the twenty-first century. The *I Ching* or the *Yi Jing* is still running the philosophical and political minds of millions in the Orient. With that newfound vision of life, I started to weigh very carefully every thought I translate into words before I put it down in writing. I judged myself to the highest standards I know of to avoid, to the best of my ability, any possible crucifixion by readers. I beg your mercy here in case I fall short of the bar I set for myself, for I hope you will believe me when I say that every effort necessary was undertaken seriously to keep my promise to you and to myself as well.

The reason I wanted you to know this is very simple. Unlike truth, which is hard to define, silence, on the other hand, can be easily misunderstood, and its misconstruing can be catastrophic. Thus, I want to make sure I contribute to the enlightenment and right use of this incredible yet sophisticated power rather than carelessly sow the seeds of confusion in the minds of people and the suffering that may be caused by it. Of course, I cannot help a reader who uses his reading magnifier to find human flaws or who is bent on finding ambiguous expressions in order to justify his point of view, but open-minded readers capable of reading lines as well as between the lines will readily notice the earnest effort that was deployed in that regard.

That being said, I will start by removing the veil of what I believe may cause confusion in the minds of some honest but

www.makanologos.com

less attentive readers. Like many great qualities that are the basis of a constructive lifestyle, when viewed through human lenses, silence can easily become a double-edged sword, usable for protection against negative forces as well as self-destruction. It is my deepest desire that these writings inspire readers to use silence constructively rather than destructively. I believe that Mother Nature gave us the power of speech for a good reason (whether we know it or not). Therefore, it is incumbent on us to use it fully and constructively, or abuse and misuse it at our own peril. I do not know if a writer can disclaim his work, but I did just that in the introduction of this work and feel compelled to do it again here to disclaim all responsibility of possible negative influence this work may cause to inattentive readers and those intentionally bent on misusing the work anyway.

Because silence is such a valuable power, there is no reason why the power of speech should not be exercised appropriately to the fullest extent. While it is my hope that one day (in the distant future) our Mother Earth will become a sun and life on it perfect, at this moment the two ancient pairs of opposites, good and evil, that govern the affairs of man are still going to be with us a little longer than any one of us would hope for. Thus, while it is here, the evil element of the pair that takes life to the most worrisome side of the pendulum must be fought against by all means at our disposal. Nothing gives unwise governments and misguided men a free hand to misuse and abuse their fellow men as an ill-advised silence. Francis Bacon, who is considered one of the wisest and smartest men of the last two thousand years, gave two very contradictory thoughts about silence. In praise of silence, he said, *"Silence is the sleep that nourishes wisdom,"* and in its damnation he said, *"Silence is the virtue of the fools."* And two great French thinkers also offered two diametrically opposed thoughts about silence. While Charles de Gaulle praised silence as the ultimate weapon of power, Anatole France said it was a wit of fools. I could not agree or disagree with all the above three thinkers more.

www.makanologos.com

While it is said that dreamers are the saviors of the world, realists will always be its builders. Dreamers may save us against some of the deadliest forces within ourselves (and that is a good thing); builders, on another hand, erect the walls that protect us against the equally fatal forces from the outside world. In the relentless search for good, a wise person is always mindful that malignant forces of destruction are alive and are tirelessly seeking victims, day in and day out. Therefore, they must be met with equal vigor and resolve; anything less is abuse and misuse of the power of silence. When silence is maintained in the face of devious oppression and aggression, it gives consent to the assailant to carry on with their unacceptable belligerence. *"In some causes silence is dangerous,"* says Saint Ambrose, and when quiet is maintained in the face of assault, Plato says, *"I shall assume that your silence gives consent,"* and of course the assaulter will happily keep up its preoccupation of abusing you.

Not all truths are good to say publicly, it is said, but the truth that must be acknowledged is that mistreatment of the weak by the stronger is a reality. Unchecked governments treat their citizens like objects. Domestic violence is still a hazard to many women. Countless children are daily victims of child abuse. I can go on and on counting all kinds of human animosities against fellow men, including abuse of consumers, prisoners, workers, and taxpayers, but the point I am hoping you get can be summarized in these few words of the ingenious Jean-Jacques Rousseau: *"Absolute silence leads to sadness. It is the image of death."*

It is one thing to be naturally weak and avoid any confrontation that might destroy you, but it is another to be effectively competent in self-defense and the defense of others but act cowardly. When you are able to defend yourself and others by the power of speech—or any legitimate power, for that matter—that power must be used to the fullest extent of the law. Hoping that a violent situation will suddenly change

www.makanologos.com

itself just because you want to experiment with your power of silence, not only is it wrong, it is self-destructive, cowardly, and very dangerous against the best interests of mankind. At the height of the Balkan War in the last decade of the twentieth century, which caused untold miseries to many people in those countries, Holocaust survivor Elie Wiesel, confronting the "non-interference in internal affairs" policy of the United States, the European Union, and much of the world, said the following: *"I swore never to be silent whenever and wherever human beings endure suffering and humiliation. We must always take sides. Neutrality helps the oppressor, never the victim. Silence encourages the tormentor, never the tormented."*

That is exactly what I want you to understand. The silence that I will soon start discussing is not the silence that strengthens evil or bad behavior but the good in oneself and community. Humility is strength, not weakness; it should never be confused with cowardliness. Serving others includes defending and protecting them against human predators or any other predator, for that matter. It is legal, it is moral, it is the right thing to do, it is the most magnificent use of the power of speech, and it is a call to all the forces and powers of nature to come to your aid as you render that service to mankind even as you inspire the living and those yet to be born. *"Oppression can only survive through silence,"* wrote one author. Let this not happen on your watch or mine, for that is against the law of our own being and the Supreme Law that sustains life itself. Now that I have made the possible erroneous use of silence as clear as I possibly could—and I hope you understand that silence is not synonymous with lethargy, and by no means am I suggesting or condoning in any way, shape, or form anything of the sort—I think it is time to start the analysis and synthesis of this very special natural power.

The silence that arouses intelligence and brightens the minds of some of our fellow men is the silence that very few of us are capable of adhering to. It is the silence whose principles

www.makanologos.com

demand of us to consciously take a moment and go into isolation, not simply to free ourselves from the mundane but to charge ourselves with the power of thought and desire. It has been said a deep river is almost noiseless, and it is rather a river that is full of stones and debris that makes much noise. As much as the power of speech is inestimable, it must sometimes be used sparingly. One of the most important secrets of life that has never been communicated to the masses of people of the world is what we call infinity, space, sky, or the universe. Call it what you will, it is but a reservoir of intelligent energy that communicates with us silently. In that energy, one finds power, wisdom, love, truth, wealth, safety, courage, determination, or a supply of anything in any good quantity, as well as the opposite of these qualities, depending on how you relate to it.

Because that energy is intelligent, it flows in all of us the same way, maybe even in the same quantity, but it is never transformed in all of us similarly because not all of us understand or ever strive to understand it. Those who have increased their power of understanding to the point of arousing their intelligence and being worthy to be called brilliant minds have done so by consciously or unconsciously observing this natural phenomenon. They oftentimes cast aside their power of speech, thought, and imagination and consciously go into isolation for a few minutes (10, 15, or 20 minutes at the very least) at specific moments and places two to three times per day and silently offer themselves to the higher powers of the universe. When I say they cast aside their power of speech, thought, or imagination, I mean just that. When they go into the silence to recharge themselves, they leave their human problems and desires behind, regardless of how pressing they may be.

The impracticality of blocking thoughts from passing through our mental filtering screen completely has already been addressed; I will not return to it here. However, this I want you to know: while the likelihood of absolutely staving off thoughts

www.makanologos.com

is very much close to zero, the effort to restrict and control thoughts pays tremendous dividends. Allowing your mental filtering screen while in silent mode to let pass only desired positive, selfless thoughts and images as it blocks negative and selfish ones is what the moments of silence are actually all for. If anything, the moment of silence should never be confused with moments of prayer or pleading, but rather the moments of self-strengthening and cleansing for the purpose of receiving divine favors by not necessarily imagining how and when they will come. This is the moment you let the Invisible Helpers or Friends of mighty power use your being as a Temple of Cosmic Sacred Fire for them to worship the Master of the universe as only they know how — not that your thoughts, imaginations, or desires are less important, but because most of us do not know what is best for us in the first place and because higher powers are less concerned with human desires and more with divine desires.

So, when they go into the silence, brilliant minds go with one and one intent only, and that is unification with the highest power of the universe, which knows better about divine desires. Since it is very helpful to have in mind the image of the highest power and because no one knows for sure what the highest power looks like, all sages and seers throughout history have suggested the mental vision of PURE DAZZLING LIGHT to be the closest thing to the Highest Power. Thus brilliant minds go into silence to visualize themselves in a light as intense as the light of thousands of suns, if possible.

When you go into the silence but you take your thoughts, imagination, and desires with you, it is not really much different from sitting in a noisy environment and keeping your mouth shut. The way to see it is like recharging your phone battery. Let's say it takes 15 to 30 minutes to fully recharge the battery. If you keep plugging and unplugging your charger from the electrical outlet every few seconds, even if you do it for an hour, plugging and unplugging 60 times, you probably will not have

www.makanologos.com

enough power to last the normal duration. But if you plug in your battery until it is fully charged and unplug it just once, then you can rest assured that you will have enough power in your device to use for the intended purpose. Life is always lived on the verge of silence. It takes man very little time to slip into the kingdom of silence. In fact, the whole universe is filled with silence. But silence is consciously transformed into power when one feels the invisible flame of life that animates our being.

It has been the experience of a few pensive people, when in total silence, to have felt that someone other than themselves was in charge of their worldly affairs as positive solutions unfolded before their eyes with little effort on their part. Winston Churchill was once quoted as saying that he sometimes felt the intervention of an invisible hand that he could not explain but unmistakably felt. When you go into silence for what many people would say is for meditation or contemplation, and then you keep interrupting the flow of light with your negative thoughts and desires, you are like the person who plugs the battery in and out of the charger. The powers of nature have a language they use to communicate with life throughout the infinite universe, and that language is called silence. In silence, they command waters of the seas to keep waves uninterrupted, winds to blow, fire to warm, sun to light the universe, and earth to not dissolve under our feet.

The human intellect neither speaks nor understands the silent language. It can, of course, speculate, but it does not know with certainty its message. Thus the eternal wheel of trial and error moves endlessly. However, the flame of life, the mysterious "I," the Inner Self that lives in each of us is the only power that speaks and understands the language of silence. Unless effort is made to get in touch silently with the Inner Self, the arousal of our intelligence by Invisible Helpers is very unlikely. But for it (the "I" or Inner Self) to perform its task effectively, it demands total silence from us in order to recharge

www.makanologos.com

us with the power to understand what usually comes to us in the form of intuition. There is no better teacher anywhere in the universe than silence. Like a good teacher, silence has a voice, but in order to understand the voice of the silence, it is imperative for us to take a few moments, two to three times a day, to surrender our thoughts and desires for just a little while in isolation, to give the Directing Intelligence of the universe an opportunity to instruct and strengthen our beings.

A moment taken consciously for silence provides great relaxation to the physical and emotional bodies. In most cases, a well-relaxed individual is always stronger than a fatigued one. Why? Because when you are rightly relaxed, you will come to a point where your breathing is balanced, and because breath is life and life is power, you will sharpen your mind as very few people can. A person who is always fatigued or tense all the time is in a fight against him- or herself, and we all know that it is said that a house divided against itself cannot stand. If you are fighting yourself, you are doomed, for you are choking yourself, your ideas and desires, that is. If you want your thoughts and desires to flourish and take you to the mountain of greatness, you must sometimes, like seeds of plants, abandon them, put them down to rest in the soil, and allow them to decompose while the rain or water falls upon them in order for them to give you an abundant supply.

In the silence, there is music that loosens up the mind.
In the silence, there is wisdom that brightens the intellect.
In the silence, there is knowledge that lightens understanding.
In the silence, there is a breeze that cools the heart.
In the silence, there is health that strengthens the body.
In the silence, there is wealth that softens life's challenges.
In silence, there is beauty that kindles love and strength.
In silence, there is strength that empowers action.
In silence, there is all.
In silence, there are jewels.
In silence, there is fire that illumines life.

www.makanologos.com

In silence, there is air that supplies life.
In silence, there is water that cleanses the mind.
In silence, there are fire, air, liquid, and gems.
In silence, there is all we need and seek.

No human being can tap these treasures of life unless he gains the habit of maintaining moments of poise sometime each day, until the feeling of easiness saturates the environment and one understands his life as well that of others. We all crave to hear from God. But God (inner voice in us all) speaks to us every moment, yet very few of us hear and understand Him because He speaks in the language of silence. There is no louder voice that will deliver God's message to you than the voice of silence, and that is why the few among us who have climbed the mountain of greatness set it as their top priority to listen to that voice in the silent private chamber of their lives. For here, in the silent chamber of your being, is your intelligence aroused by the Invisible Helpers.

The truth is never revealed to those who seek for it in the mountains or in the valley, not in the cities or in the countryside, not in the churches or the schools, not in the waters or on the lands, not in the skies or underground. It is revealed only to those who seek for it in the silence because that is the only place where it is found. If you are looking for money, the best place to find it would be at the bank. If you want to seek monks, the best place to see them would be at the monastery. If you want groceries, the likeliest place to find them would be at the grocery store, and so on. Thus, if you are looking for the truth that will arouse your intelligence and take you to the mountain of greatness, you have got to surrender all your thoughts and desires (at least for a little while) and acquire the habit of going into the silence, because that is the only place it can be found.

Yes, for the good part of the day, we are silent, because we do not speak 24/7. Many times of the day, we are alone and, of course, silent. But that is not the kind of silence I am talking about here. Silent moments during which you keep thinking

www.makanologos.com

about your life challenges, dealing with fantasies, or giving your imaginary movie stars the freedom to play any act on your mental screen while you laugh, cry, or stare emotionless — those moments do not count. It has to be a conscious silent moment taken for the purpose of surrendering all you have or are to the higher powers and letting them project the truth onto a blank screen in your mind. Those are the moments you absorb the wisdom and knowledge that will arouse your intelligence and enable you to climb the mountain of greatness. The silence that is consciously commanded is a very powerful moment indeed. When deeply felt during the moment of conscious silence, light, by its nature, reveals itself, and along with it the truth. In most instances, it reveals the truth right then and there, but later on, the truth unmistakably comes to you in a way you never imagined before, be it through intuition, a fellow man, a book, or another unpredictable means. Right then, the difficulty will be easy to understand, the invisible will be visible, the complex will be simple, and the mysterious will be natural after all.

Silence is said to be God's greatest power, and all great souls who have affected the destiny of human race have used it to the fullest. And no one used it more fully than Jesus the Christ. If you are an attentive reader of the Bible, you will notice that at many instances, He would just leave the masses as well as His own apostles and go into seclusion, not to submit His grievances or wishes but to completely surrender His human self to "Thy will be done above as below." The ancient sages also said that silence is the greatest power of God, for in silence all the most dominant powers of the universe work at their best. When attention and concentration are sanctioned by the power of silence, they become magnetic forces capable of burning any wall of ignorance, and they become a sword of knowledge strong enough to eliminate even the most frightening monster of ignorance.

www.makanologos.com

Of course, it is one thing to keep the mouth shut, but it is another thing to silence the thought. I am not talking about shutting off thoughts but controlling them effectively while cutting off any desire from the mind, at least momentarily. Thought control is a 24/7/365 commitment. Every time a wrong, negative, or evil thought comes to mind—and it can come anytime, anywhere—it must be avoided and immediately replaced by a more enlightening, positive, and constructive one. That has to be done as life goes on, but during the special few moments of silence, negative thoughts and desires must be momentarily abandoned for the purpose of allowing the human mind to absorb illumination like a sponge or to feed itself from the Divine desires that strengthen what one cannot get otherwise.

Thus, brilliant minds become brilliant. They consider themselves as mirrors, moons, or satellites of the source of all light, the master orb of the universe, the sun. And the better they position themselves, the more light they will absorb and project in the direction of their choice. This is one of the best-kept secrets of brilliant minds, this is how intelligence is aroused, and this is the ELIXIR OF INTELLIGENCE, because light is its own defense and inspiration is its own revelation. This is how you watch and look within the light; seeing all within it, you make joy live in you and others, for there is nothing hidden that is not revealed that a constructive seeker needs to know for the service of the highest good. This is the end of the road, for this is how the great ones gained their immortality and a place of honor in the hearts of all generations to come, and so can you, so long as you stand for the Highest Ideal in the universe and honor to life is the motive for which you do everything. The silence that produces these kinds of outcomes is conscious and sustained by silence, not involuntarily. In his book *The Power of Myth*, in a question from Bill Moyers on calling a power from within, Joseph Campbell describes the process of controlling thought and inhibiting desires in these terms:

There is a form of meditation you are taught in Roman Catholicism where you recite the rosary, the same prayer, over and over and over again. That pulls the mind in. In Sanskrit, this practice is called japa "repetition of the holy name." It blocks other interests out and allows you to concentrate on the thing and then, depending on your own powers of imagination, to experience the profundity of the mysteries, (page, 261).

Silence is one of the most mysterious phenomena in the world; it rarely speaks to the head but usually to the heart. Only the most enlightened people understand its voice and language clearly. Engineers and architects, for instance, when their heads come to an impasse, usually abruptly go into recess or call off the work and "sleep on" the problem. Suddenly the solution will come almost inexplicably, and behold, the work is complete. So the quieter the thoughts and desires, the deeper the silence; and the more strength you gain inside, the sooner the truth reveals itself to you and the more power you gain to arouse your intelligence and climb the mountain of greatness. All it requires is a sustained willingness to train oneself. The ability to get into the heart of silence is the real power to bring down the very veil that exists between man and the truth (Invisible Helpers who use the All-seeing Eye of God for they are the all-knowing mind of God, since they stand for the Highest Ideal in the universe).

At no moment do the eyes of the mind see the light more than when man enters into deep silence. And the more one's mind sees the light, the nearer one is to touching the keys of the universe and seeing the Gods, because the light does not show anything but the unmistakable truth. If the light of a light bulb can show you everything in your home, imagine what the light of the Inner Self can show your mind. In case you want me to give you a hint, only the light of the Inner Self is capable of showing your mind the path that leads to the most precious treasure of all, the truth. When the relaxation and the control of attention that come from deep silence are sustained

www.makanologos.com

considerably, the intellectual eye is stimulated as its vision is sanitized, and consequently intelligence is aroused.

We can keep going almost infinitely, but what is important to know is that the benefits gained by a good few moments of conscious and sustained silence in a special setting are abundant. As a writer, my job is to point the way, but it is up to you, the reader, to discover those ways that square with your needs and goals in life. I can only give illustrations and advice, but you must do the real study and application. While reading is great and strongly encouraged, only application, the practice of these ideas can prove the reality of what you are reading. Experience is the best teacher, and no God or adept man will prove it to you better than you can prove it to yourself, for God can do for you only what He can do through you. Silence illumines, silence teaches, silence strengthens the body, mind, and the intellect. Silence speaks—no word or thought has power equal to that of silence. It is all I can say, but you have to prove it to yourself by application, not by merely reading.

I am not by any means discouraging you from reading— not at all—since I believe that great doers are equally great readers. I am simply repeating what ancient sages have said: knowledge is power, but knowledge unused passes from the mind, possibly never to be recovered again. The law of nature does not permit unlimited promptings to a person who simply does not want to act on what has already been given. What they call experience is simply a cluster of used knowledge, and because it has been used, it has been retained; because it has been retained, it has become wealth; because it has become wealth, it is precious; because it is precious, it is sought. That is why in a sane world, all things being equal, an experienced person will always be trusted with duties before one with unused knowledge freshly from college.

As I said before, Mother Nature gave us the power of speech for a good reason; therefore, it must be used fully but wisely at all times. While I believe the power of silence to be stronger than

www.makanologos.com

Exalted Secrets of Brilliant Minds   365

that of speech, I also believe the power of speech must be used whenever a good opportunity presents itself. Going back to the example of the phone battery, sometimes it only takes less than an hour to charge a battery with the power that will enable you to talk all day long. However, there are moments when speech is unnecessary or even detrimental. At those moments, silence, even in the middle of the masses, must be observed in order to recharge yourself with more power. This way, you deny your foes strategic ammunition to take you down with. You collect all your faculties together more rapidly, and the outcome of your march to the mountaintop of greatness will be easier than you could have possibly anticipated.

While most people always find the causes of their troubles to be the fault of actions and circumstances caused by others rather than themselves, if they could just take a moment and see it at a different angle, they could easily see how rashness, impatience, and lack of daily dedication are rooted in the lack of precious daily moments of silence. Some short but precious time (maybe 15 to 25 minutes) to ourselves — in a private corner of life, quiet and undisturbed by words from our tongues or thoughts from our minds but in deep contemplation of our Higher and Inner Self — can make one powerful dynamite in whatever line of work one is in. Silence, without doubt, enables people to absorb great powers that can arouse our intelligence and carry us to almost any height of greatness.

The ability to shut off our mouths and minds frequently for short periods of time daily, to turn our sight from outside to inside, allows the flame of life in the royal rooms of our hearts to grow and join that of the universe to become one in wisdom, strength, and beauty, qualities without which no man can possibly climb the mountain of greatness or gain the choicest place in the hearts of generations to come. Much can be written and has been written in praise of silence. I am quite sure you would agree that no book or writer can say everything about this incredible power. In it you will find illumination, wisdom,

www.makanologos.com

power, light, life, creativity, accomplishments, miracles, protective armor, concentration, victory, and dominion over every obstacle life will throw in your path. All other powers you can possibly imagine and those human languages you are not yet able to name, those that our minds are still unable to picture and our intellect still inept to think of, are here and now concentrated in the mysterious hand of silence. While there are millions of people around the world who are silent most of the time, either by nature or by being forced by the circumstances of life, such as prison or any involuntary isolation, that is not the kind of silence that empowers the flames of life and the greatness that is in the heart of every man. Empowering silence must be a pure product of free will and consciousness.

What good do you think living in the long silence of a prison cell—where your mouth can be shut but not the thought of defiance and resistance, not only to your mind but also to your own body—will do to you? How much tranquility, if any, can be gained by a free but geographically isolated fellow who occupies his mind most of the time with his own desires for self-satisfaction and self-pity? Answer these questions and you will find that it is not just silence I am talking about here, but it is the kind or quality of silence. And by that I mean a special and precious portion of life, CONSCIOUSLY, VOLUNTARILY, and PURPOSELY set apart to go into the stillness, to attract illumination from the Inner Self as a sponge absorbs the water from the mighty river or as the moon absorbs and reflects the light of the sun to the Earth. When man acquires the habit of calming his mouth and thoughts while showering his mind and heart in the great rain of wisdom, enlightenment, beauty, and truth from his Higher or Inner Self, that man is on the verge of acquiring such power as few men have ever known in the history of the human race.

Therefore, in closing this magnificent topic, as I must, if there is only one thing that an attentive reader should extract from this chapter, it is that power—and I mean constructive

www.makanologos.com

power that has guided the evolution of the man—has never been acquired any other way. I wouldn't say that acquisition of constructive power any other way is a fraud, but it is temporary and ephemeral, if not simply unrealistic. The power that takes man to the mountaintop of greatness, the power that arouses the intelligence of man, can never possibly be gained by the aid of education, reading, sword, or heritage, for it is knowledge learned not the traditional way; therefore, it can never be written, spoken, seen, touched, or felt by the outer senses but by the Inner or Higher Self alone. Hence, only the hand of silence can deposit it in the throne room of the heart of a consciously quiet man as he learns to become a worthy tool or a channel of invisible forces that rule the universe to bring more demonstrations in the affairs and lives of men.

If you have heard of the Door no man can shut, the Narrow and Straight Way to the kingdom of greatness, the Golden Stairs, the Divine Password, and all those good things, silence is it. Dare to open it and no man will shut it again. Dare to walk through it and you will reach the height of greatness. Dare to climb through it and you will discover the seat of wisdom, love, and power. Decode it and you will enter and be received into any brotherhood of light anywhere in the universe. This is one of the best-kept secrets of brilliant minds. This is how **intelligence is aroused**, and this is the ELIXIR OF INTELLIGENCE, because light is its own defense, and inspiration is its own revelation. This is how you watch and look within the light. Seeing all within it, you make joy live in you and others, for there is nothing hidden that is not revealed to a constructive seeker who needs to know it for the service of the highest good, so long as you stand for the Highest Ideal in the universe and honor to life is the motive for which you do everything. This is the end of the road, for this is how the great ones of old gained their immortality and a place of honor in the hearts of all generations to come, and so can you. Here I pause from this sermon on silence, hoping you will dig deeper and

www.makanologos.com

wider in your feelings, thoughts, and actions as you go on your way to the discovery of many wonders for the benefit of the world, as you enjoy this poem of silence.

Silence

Silence,
The narrow and straight path to greatness
Unknown to the masses of the living
The cave in the hearts of the enlightened
By no man's hands thy kingdom is built

Silence,
The golden stairs to the middle chamber
In the highest temple thou art
In thee the light of the soul, thou shine like a sun
From thee courage undaunted by the peril of live sprouts
Refreshing lives highest joy thy find
Opening minds love's gift you bestow upon true seekers
Sane intellect bonus in your temple worshipers get

Silence,
Great teacher thou art
Loyalty and obedience to the truth
Brave declaration of virtues
Fearless defense of victim man's folly
Courageous survival of personal injustice
Constant eye to the ideal of life
Art thy credo

Silence,
In thee Divine Password is held
Secure in thy hand, head, and heart
In thy eternity the word transformed into flesh
From thy immortality the word all creation sprouted
In thee is the pollen path to the center of the boundless realm
Encircled by beauty before, behind, right, left, above, and below
www.makanologos.com

Silence,
You fill every space there is in existence
In thy soft arms rest worry-free solar systems and galaxies
The godmother of the world of radiance thou art
With truth and wisdom, strength and peace
Thou uplift the heart of wise
In thee the sun displays its grandeur
In thee the Gods dispense power
The calm minds absorb it like a sponge
In thy Temple everything confidently grows

Silence,
The dome of the sky wide house of virtues
In thee the trinity of faith, hope, and charity ever expands
Yet in thy shadow the foolish get crazier
Receptive hearts of the sages come closer to the Master within
Thoughtful minds get schooled on the Law of laws
They get into the door that no man can shut
To receive humbling glory
As to them the beauty and secrets of life self-reveal
Self-reveal, reveal, and reveal
As man's mind absorbs, absorbs, and absorbs
The light and counsel like a sponge. Silence,
The spoken language of the Gods and Cosmic Beings

By Wisdom Joseph Ombe Ya Makano, the author

www.makanologos.com

CHAPTER XVII

The Attention Pillar

What is work worth without end? What is a journey without a destination? What is a life without a purpose? It is pretty obvious that work without an end is meaningless; a journey without a destination is wandering; and life without a purpose is as uninspiring as sleepwalking. Because most of us work with an end in mind, travel to a specific destination, and have a certain purpose to achieve in life, so the question here is not to have or work with an objective in mind, travel to a targeted destination, or have some sort of purpose to achieve in life. The fact of having a goal or a destination to achieve does not necessarily enable one to climb the mountain of greatness or set one apart from the masses who almost blindly travel to an unclearly defined destination.

What allows one to walk through that straight and narrow path of greatness, what enables one to reach the mountaintop of magnitude, what makes one eligible for the club of the chosen few, what makes it possible for the "camel to go through the eye of the needle" is not just having a goal but rather concentrating on that goal almost with a single eye and intensely enough to become one with it, for as the Master said, "I and the Father are One." The likeness of the Father being the goal of Jesus, He concentrated on it to the point of identifying Himself with it; thus His goal was achieved.

In this chapter on the attention principle, I will endeavor to present some of the very important features of this power that I basically consider to be one of the most invaluable powers Mother Nature has endowed upon man, and how the forces of nature, the Invisible Helpers, come to the assistance and arouse the intelligence of the one who has done his homework correctly. *"Luck comes to the prepared mind"* said Louis Pasteur.

Man is never entirely the architect of his success; otherwise, we all would be happy. They are forces of nature, invisible or otherwise and that none of us can clearly explain, that come to the assistance of the one keenly seeking or knocking on the door of the temple of happiness that no man can shut once opened. These forces may be invisible to us, but they themselves are not blind; they know unmistakably who deserves their assistance and who does not. When they decide to assist, they come at the right time and to the right place. Earlier, I paraphrased what the former British Prime Minister Winston Churchill said about these Invisible Helpers. They are true, they exist, and they come not only to the Winston Churchills of the world but to all of us who seek their help rightfully.

To deserve their favors, one must focus undivided attention on the feelings, thoughts, and actions pointedly directed at the goal to be achieved. The importance and description of this power, attention or concentration, is the subject of this chapter. It is my sincere hope that the attentive reader will gain invaluable information that will not necessarily make him great (as unused knowledge passes from the mind and becomes worthless) but will certainly inspire his feelings and thoughts if **acted** upon properly with a deep desire for the manifestation of the intended objective.

Before getting deep into the heart of the subject, let me just remind my readers that I consider myself to be mostly a student of philosophy, metaphysics, and esoteric mythology rather than a student of psychology and physiology. That said, most of my analysis of this subject will be done through the lenses of philosophy, metaphysics, and esoteric mythology, and less so those of psychology and physiology. The question of attention as explained in this work, in my opinion, is more one of philosophy and esoteric mythology than psychology — not to undermine the importance of the latter but to show another perspective that has not yet been explained to the general public more thoroughly. You will notice this when you

www.makanologos.com

realize that there are very few people who would disagree with the fact that attention is one of the most decisive faculties in the fulfillment of any goal that man sets for himself. The question now is why the vast majority of us are just not putting it to work for our own sake. The answer to this question alone can fill volumes, describing causes that point in similar or opposite directions, all right or wrong at the same time. To make it simple for the sake of the task at hand, let me say that the most likely reason is the fact that it is explained to us in sophisticated and confusing technical terms of psychology and other disciplines that scientists choose as vehicles of clarification.

What would you do if you were at an intersection and suddenly all the arrows pointing east and west, north and south, above and below suggested that it did not matter, that any direction you chose would get you to your destination as surely as your nose, eyes, and mouth are on your face? "All roads lead to Rome," said the Romans. Yes! While different paths can take one to the same goal, a wise doer always does it with two strategies in mind, and that is to save as much time and energy as possible. The time and energy saver is always the most efficient and smartest achiever. Just because any road can take you to Rome does not mean you choose blindly; a good understanding of detours and other obstacles will determine your safe arrival or not. I will not pretend to suggest the fastest and safest way to reach your goal, because that is entirely up to you. A reckless car driver may go faster than a wise biker to the same destination, but the biker may reach the finish line first and safely if the reckless driver driving mindlessly causes trouble along the way. I will thus strive to give you some clear and useful substance that I hope will illumine your way as long as you give it your best sustained effort.

A pertinent question may be asked—what is it about attention that makes it so crucial in the arousal of intelligence and the business of greatness? Attention is the ability to fix one's thoughts on a desired object until the object surrenders its powers to you and reveals itself or its nature and functions to you, thus making your utilization of it easier. Because attention is concentration of thoughts on a specific object, thoughts must be chosen and controlled in order for the attention to yield the intended and productive outcome. The mysterious thing about thoughts is that they are not man-made, as many people erroneously believe. I have said this before. No man can possibly fabricate a thought or an idea. Just as a moviegoer does not create anything he sees on the screen in the theatre or on the television screen, for that matter, no man, regardless of the power of his ingenuity, can create thoughts that pass on his mind or mental screen.

Thoughts are just like actors or the events on the screens of our minds produced or stimulated by either outer or inner agents totally independent of our will except for the desire to fulfill our needs. Just like television or a movie, you can choose the channel to watch with your remote control; you can choose the movie to watch, but you cannot tell the actors on the television or theatre screen how to act or what and how to say or do something. Thoughts are freelance actors that play on any mind screen that will welcome them. Ideas that you are reading here are not ideas that this author created but ones that he simply chose to write. And you, the reader, can choose to read what you will in this book, but you cannot change anything here. This is how ideas work—we can choose what to entertain in our minds and mental screens, but we cannot create them.

While we have the power to choose what thoughts are welcome in our inner home theatre, thoughts, especially malicious ones, can easily overpower an individual for better or worse. If left unchecked, thoughts can run fast and freely on the mental screens of our minds, and if left unrestrained, they can run our lives like rising water in an overflowing river or a disturbed sea. Then we lose control like banks of the river that are overrun by flooding water, and consequently, we become

www.makanologos.com

powerless. At the very least, we become their servants, and lo and behold! Here is where most of us get lost and doomed forever.

The strategy is, thus, to control, discipline, and focus ideas rather than let them run amok and control you. Just as in the movie theatre, the operator chooses the film to display to you on the screen and not otherwise. You have to choose the thoughts to be displayed on your mental screen and never let thoughts choose your mental screen. Yes, in instances of intuition, ideas sometimes will come uninvited, and they should be welcome if useful, but like any guest, they must behave well and remain in the perimeter allowed by the host. Here is where the difference between a fool and a wise person is on full display. Both wise and foolish persons have streams of thought flowing unceasingly, but while the wise person works hard to keep his thoughts within the banks of his mental river, a foolish person lets his overflow uncontrollably.

A movie theatre that chooses to play attractive pictures will certainly attract many good customers. The same is true for attention — the person who chooses and controls the thoughts that will enrich his mind will attract like-minded results as well. Nowhere does the much-talked-about law of attraction work better and more accurately than in the thought process. Remember, we cannot create thoughts, but we can choose them. Like attracts like, and thoughts attract thoughts of the same quality. People do not suddenly become criminals or saints. Criminals become what they are by first letting criminal thoughts freely play on their mental screens; they allow multiple scenarios of criminal acts to play uncontrollably in their minds until they overpower and push them to commit a criminal act. And so does one become a saint, simply by letting saintly thoughts play on the mental screen until one acts saintly in the eyes of his fellow men.

No one can possibly think criminally most of the time, and then become a saint or act virtuously instead of becoming a

www.makanologos.com

criminal. That is just impossible, for it is against the law of nature. No one can descend while ascending, and no one can ascend while descending. It is that simple. *"And if you gaze for long into an abyss, the abyss gazes also into you,"* said German philosopher Friedrich Nietzsche. If you keep thinking negative thoughts, they will consume you as you become their agent in the outer world. Having a mind-set focused on anger, fear, doubt, selfishness, jealousy, emptiness, and contempt only perpetuates those feelings and thoughts deeper and deeper within us until they have nowhere to go but to the external world, where they will almost certainly cause destruction.

If you choose to let only constructive thoughts play on your mind screen, most likely your actions will be constructive. "As a man thinketh, so is he," says the Bible. James Allen wrote a magnificent book on this very subject that I would enthusiastically recommend to my readers. Thoughts are independent of man; they do not belong to man. The mind, on the other hand, belongs to man, hence man's ability to control the mind, to choose what is to be shown on his mind or mental screen. The choice one makes as to what will cross his or her mind is the key to the achievement of greatness; the arousal of his or her intelligence and attention is that power of mind control. Actions are the external expressions of thoughts, and when a thought is well chosen and strongly forced to external expression, its actions are usually well performed and result in the achievement of greatness. People who perform daily tasks with half a mind engaged or allow all sorts of thoughts to pass through their minds not only rarely achieve their tasks effectively, but they never reach the mountaintop of greatness because their intelligence rarely rises to its potential.

Attention is the wholeheartedness of the thought, feeling, and action. A house divided eventually falls. When a man is able to think about something undeviatingly for a considerable period of time, allowing only like-minded thoughts and pictures about whatever it is he wants to understand better, he strengthens his power of attention. When this power of attention completely develops, man becomes capable of what Clara M. Codd calls *"looking at that which is invisible, listening to that which is soundless."* *"The secret of success can be expressed in the simple words: Pay attention,"* wrote Alice A. Bailey in her book *From Intellect to Intuition.* I assume that Bailey's point will make sense to any reader, but in case I am so naïve as to assume *common sense* to be what it is, *common sense*, then someone out there may think I am out of my mind and rush to accusing, judging, and convicting me in absentia. In anticipation to that scenario, I present my arguments in defense of Bailey's fiat.

Of all the differences between man and other creatures, the most striking ones are that man possesses spiritual and intellectual powers. We may all be animals, but only man is able to worship God (according to his personal definition of God) and is capable of thinking progressively as the environment presents new challenges and opportunities. Now, the most striking difference between brilliant minds and the rest of humankind is that brilliant minds consciously control their reactions to every action of nature or otherwise to the minutest detail. Rather than being a tool of his emotions, he uses them to not only avoid or inhibit impulsive actions and reactions, but also and mostly to prepare for deliberate actions. A truly attentive person is never a member of the majority of the human race; he is rather one of those rare stones at the peak of the pyramid of society where he is able to stand upon the shoulders of others and see what is hidden to the majority beneath his feet.

Where the majority sees the apple falling from the tree, an attentive man sees the law of gravity. Where the majority sees the cliff at the horizon of the ocean, he sees the New World. Where the majority sees death, he sees resurrection and glory thereafter. Where the majority sees victory through violence, he sees it through nonviolence, and so forth. Do you know a man who made history by just using the old, conventional

www.makanologos.com

ways and means? To be successful, one must see what many do not see. The fact of the matter is that only attention allows man to penetrate the deep reality of any idea or substance and not just the surface of things. *"Optimism is one of the greatest treasures of humanity,"* wrote Hans-Ulrich Rieker, *"but it becomes a source of scourge if we use it to lie facts out of the way, instead of paying attention."* We can argue endlessly about the need for attention, but one thing is indisputable — there is no substitute for it anywhere in the universe.

"Another word of concentration is attention, that is, one-pointed attention," and an attentive reader will recall Baird T. Spalding quoting Hindus saying, *"One-pointedness is God."* More on the divinity and attention later, but this must be clearly understood — a *"monkey or a nomad mind"* will achieve very little in life, if anything at all. Unless one is capable of staying on the same path long enough, he will never reach the destination. A mind that jumps to every thought that comes its way, that is uneasy at handling the same idea like a barefooted man walking on burning charcoals, not only will his intelligence not be aroused, but he will never climb the mountain of greatness and will certainly never even see it to begin with. Greatness is an exclusive privilege of those who are willing to do what it takes to understand *"the deeply hidden laws of nature"* and are willing to *"arrange their lives according to them, using reason and common sense,"* as Krishnamurti Alcyone put it in his small but priceless book *At the Feet of the Master* (page 34).

Attention is not so much disciplining the thought process, as it is the ability to discipline the mind. There is always a fight between thoughts and the mind. The mind is basically a mental screen through which thoughts make themselves known. The mind can easily be run by thoughts if it acts like an operator who sleeps at the switch and lets thoughts run unrestricted. When the mind becomes the subject of thoughts that is where the danger lies; unfortunately, that is the case for the vast majority of people. But when the mind chooses which thoughts

www.makanologos.com

it will allow to be displayed on its screen and lets them run on its own terms, that is not only the power of attention, but it is where greatness rests.

When your mind is able to capture one thought at a time and display it long enough for your inner eye to meticulously monitor it, you have discovered the golden elevator that will not only safely but easily carry you to the mountaintop of greatness, because when the mind lights the heart, the heart lights the intellect; and when the heart lights the intellect, the intellect lights actions; and when the intellect lights actions, greatness is assured. Thus, when the mind is controlled, it illumines the intellect, and when intellect is illumined, actions are brilliant, and greatness becomes a by-product. This is one the best-kept secrets of brilliant minds. This is how intelligence is aroused, and this is the ELIXIR OF INTELLIGENCE, because light is its own defense, and inspiration is its own revelation. This is how you watch and look within the light. Seeing all within it, you make joy live in you and others, for there is nothing hidden that is not revealed to a constructive seeker who needs to know it for the service of the highest good, so long as you stand for the Highest Ideal in the universe and honor to life is the motive for which you do everything. This is the end of the road, for this is how the great ones of old gained their immortality and a place of honor in the hearts of all generations to come, and so can you, so long as you stand for the Highest Ideal in the universe and honor to life is the motive for which you do everything.

A man who pays little attention to his feelings, thoughts, and actions is by no means a lesser man, but he will never—underscore never—climb the mountain of greatness. His intelligence will always be dormant and never will he be a host of Invisible Helpers. Therefore, a person who wants to reach where few have reached must start by schooling his attention. Just like a doctor, a PhD, or an engineer must start by learning the alphabet, addition, and subtraction in kindergarten, brilliant minds start by schooling and disciplining their

www.makanologos.com

attention. No one can possibly obtain the highest education in any field unless he is the master of the lower education. No college or university will ever grant a bachelor's or master's degree, let alone a PhD, to a person who can barely spell his name or count from one to ten. Attention is the alphabet and basic mathematical operations of greatness. It is literally the "door that no man can shut" when it comes to the arousal of intelligence, because once your attention is schooled well enough, the sky is the limit insofar as the height of greatness you want to climb is concerned.

It is practically impossible for a man or even an angel, if you will, to realize what his attention is not on. Failure and success are always determined by the quality of attention given to a thing or situation. You can bet on this—"better attention results in better action, and mediocre attention results in mediocre action." Attention allows you to concentrate your energy, and concentrated energy is a bomb of mental power, whereas distraction or a "swinging mind" is scattering the very energy you need to achieve something. If you disagree that concentrated energy is not a mental bomb, what would you rather have, concentrated or scattered energy? Which one do you think has more power? Man discovers nothing unless he gives his attention first to whatever his mind wants to understand. When man gave attention to the laws of physics and science, airplanes, trains, computers, atomic bombs, etc. were discovered.

What do you think, more than anything else, is the mother of science, philosophy, or even religion, for that matter? I do not know about you, but let me tell you that I more than believe it is a-t-t-e-n-t-i-o-n. Very few know that attention is one of the most powerful powers in the universe. When it is wisely applied, it brings knowledge, wisdom, determination, courage, silence, love, truth, and passion together. Only intuition and illumination are higher than attention, but they also do not come to man but through the quality attention that was given

www.makanologos.com

first. Attention is basically what the Master said in John 16:6: *"I am the way, the truth and the life. No one comes to the Father but through me."* Unless you school and discipline your attention, your chances of getting into the kingdom of the great ones are zilch, zero.

When you give your attention to something, it is like a flashlight in the middle of a dark night focused on something that, by the law of nature, must be compelled to self-reveal and surrender its precious secrets to the beholder. Knowledge does not come to man because he seeks it, or better yet, if you will, man does not seek knowledge; knowledge carefully seeks men to reveal itself to, and it seeks only attentive people. Knowledge is no friend of daydreamers or absentminded people. Throughout the centuries, many people have sought knowledge the world over, travelling hundreds, sometimes thousands of miles and not finding it, while attentive people never need to lift a foot in its search, for it finds them right where they are, in the comfort of their dwellings.

The power of attention is a concentration of life energy in general and mental energy in particular upon a given objective. Through it, man can travel to the center of the Earth just as he can easily crisscross the planets and stars in the sky and enter the center of the cosmos. As my "teacher" Joseph Campbell masterfully put it in *The Hero with a Thousand Faces* (page 21):

The dreamer is a distinguished operatic artist, and, like all who have elected to follow, not the safely marked general highways of the day, but the adventure of the special, dimly audible call that comes to those whose ears are open within as well as without, she has had to make her way alone, through difficulties not commonly encountered, "through slummy, muddy streets"; she has known the dark night of the soul, Dante's "dark wood, midway in the journey of life" and sorrows of the pits of hell:

Through me is the way into the woeful city,
Through me is the way into eternal woe,
Through me is the way among the Lost People.

www.makanologos.com

Precious ideas come to us in exactly what Joseph Campbell skillfully calls a *"dimly audible call that comes to those whose ears are open within as well as without."* And just as mail is delivered to us by the postal service and e-mail by an electronic service, great knowledge is delivered to us by the forces of the universe through the power of attention. Attention connects man with anything and everything he puts his mind on. Just as the veins carry blood from the heart to the extremities of the body, attention carries knowledge and wisdom from the heart of the universe to the individual world of each one of us. Anyone with clogged veins is almost assured to die, and if he is lucky enough to live, he will certainly have a very poor life. So too will an inattentive person, by fostering an undisciplined mind that jumps from one thought to the other without examination, jam or dry his mental channels and never be able to decode any knowledge from the cosmic source of all wisdom.

All it takes is attention — not a book, computer, PhD, or any man-made instrument — to acquire supreme knowledge that leads to greatness. The pyramids of Egypt, the Great Wall of China, Stonehenge, and other marvels of antiquity were products of precision thinking aided not by computers, books, or PhDs, but by strict attention. To this day, our modern space science still utilizes knowledge of the planets that was discovered by the naked yet attentive eyes of ancient men. If they used any tool at all to discover far-off special orbs, by today's standards, that tool would be called primitive and possibly barbarian. All it takes to acquire cutting-edge knowledge about any planet, star, galaxy, angel, or even spirit is to start thinking slowly about it. Give it your sincere attention, and it will reveal itself to you, and the more you give it your attention, the better knowledge it will convey to you. Gradually your knowledge of it will grow with the quality and intensity of the attention you give. There is no magic about it. That is all it takes. *"When the student is ready, the master appears"* is a great Buddhist teaching, and it is also a great law of nature. When your attention is strong enough, the universe cannot help but supply your mind with its choicest knowledge and wisdom. This is one of the best-kept secrets of brilliant minds. This is how intelligence is aroused, and this is the ELIXIR OF INTELLIGENCE, because light is its own defense, and inspiration is its own revelation. This is how you watch and look within the light. Seeing all within it, you make joy live in you and others, for there is nothing hidden that is not revealed to a constructive seeker who needs to know it for the service of the highest good, so long as you stand for the Highest Ideal in the universe and honor to life is the motive for which you do everything. This is the end of the road, for this is how the great ones of old gained their immortality and a place of honor in the hearts of all generations to come, and so can you. *Nota bene:* I am not trying to undermine PhDs or education in general, for they are all products of attention at various levels.

It is a fact that, here on Earth, any man-made object can be bought with money, including money itself. Well, as above, so below. If Mother Nature is to be seen as a merchant, she trades her knowledge and wisdom against attention. The more attention you give to anything, the more stepping stones to the knowledge of itself it will set on your path. It is that simple. Everything in the universe is revealed by the power of attention. Attention is the currency with which man buys knowledge and wisdom from the supermarket of the universe. Have you ever wonder why you are told to pay attention? Well, it is because the more attention you pay to whatever you want, the more about it you will know.

By the power of attention alone does man rise to the highest greatness or sink to the lowest class. Intelligence rises to the highest wisdom and understanding or falls to stupidity and folly. And according to attention does man's mental power find its place on the spectrum of intelligence. Through his ability to consciously control his attention does man choose the types of events that will make up his life experience. The key words here are *conscious control*. Why conscious? Because consciousness is awareness and awareness is LIFE. The most meaningful way to live life is to be aware of it. When you are conscious, you are aware, and when you are aware, life literally vibrates. The higher your awareness, the higher the vibration of life, and when life really vibrates to higher levels, all the pieces of the riddle of life fall in place amazingly well. And can you tell me a better master of life than the person who not only has all the pieces of the puzzle of life but also knows how to place each of them in the right place in a reasonable length of time? The more conscious you are of your attention, the more consciously you keenly choose and examine every thought your mind permits to display on your mental screen, and the more likely you will rise to the highest ladder of wisdom and greatness, or the more likely your intelligence rises to the appropriate level. Through the power of consciously and positively controlled attention, truly brilliant minds find themselves literally walking with God and Invisible Helpers face to face.

This is one of the boldest, indeed the boldest, statement in the whole book that can be made by a humble student of life such as this author. Thus I feel the obligation to elaborate a little bit more in order to shed more light in the mind of the reader before letting his own experience teach the whole truthfulness of this declaration. An avid student of comparative philosophy and religion will recall that all major religions and philosophies teach that God and his kingdom do not exist anywhere but inside man. *"Know thyself and thou shall know the secrets of the Gods"* is a well-known inscription on the Temple of Delphi in ancient Greece. *"The Kingdom of God is within,"* declared the Master. In the preface of his farsighted book *The Hero with a Thousand Faces*, Joseph Campbell writes:

It is the purpose of this present book to uncover some of the truths disguised for us under the figures of religion and mythology by bringing together a multitude of not-too-difficult examples and letting the ancient meaning become apparent of itself. The

www.makanologos.com

old teachers knew what they were saying...As we are told in the Vedas: "Truth is one, the sages speak of it in many names (pages vii-viii).

Not in heaven or on Earth, not above or below can there be found a way that leads man inside for better knowledge of himself or the Kingdom of God but through the power of attention. Attention is the journey to the very center of existence of everything.

All great teachers of major religions and philosophies have received their teachings not on the mountains or in the jungles as the orthodox world would like us to believe, but through meditation or concentration, which is the highest point of attention. Meditating people wrote all the books of the Bible including the Ten Commandments. And the books of Ezekiel, Job, Jacob, and the Torah itself in the Old Testament and the Apocalypse in the New Testament are the best illustrations of this truth. Kabbalah, the mystical philosophy of rabbinic Judaism, teaches that all the wars and difficulties, including the mountains, the return to the promised land, and even the victory of the boy David over the mythical Goliath are not factual or historical events but the conquests of Israel's religious leaders in struggles over their egos, ego being the only veil between man and God. (No need to go deeper here, as I said enough about the ego in my previous book, *The Best Kept Secrets of Personal Magnetism*.) In fact, the whole Bible is the story of struggles between prophets and their egos, including the temptation of Jesus in the wilderness. *"Verily, verily, I say unto you, He that believeth in me, the works that I do shall he do also; and greater works than these shall he do,"* (John: 14:12) said the Master, recognizing that they, like Him, all great prophets and philosophers, all have this power of attention that can take us to the edges of the universe as well to its very center, and most importantly inside ourselves where all the most precious treasures of the universe are found.

www.makanologos.com

Exalted Secrets of Brilliant Minds   385

It is believed by many in the orthodox religious world, naively of course, that a land in the Middle East is at the root of a deadly conflict between Jews and Arabs (Palestinians), a land that has known anything but peace; that land, they believe, is the Promised Land. If what they mean by "Promised Land" is a sacred land, then they are right because every land is a sacred land to its people. And this conversation between Bill Moyers and Joseph Campbell in that wonderful book *The Power of Myth* gives a very obvious clue in this regard:

Campbell:...And then comes an interesting thing, just as in the Old Testament — all we have heard is the story of this particular group, the Navaho, let's say. But when they come out, the Pueblo people are already there. It's like the problem of where did Adam's sons get their wives? There is creation of these people, and the rest of the world is somehow there by another accident.

Moyers: This is the idea of the Chosen People.

Campbell: Sure it is. Every people is a chosen one in its own mind. And it is rather amusing that their name for themselves usually means mankind. They have odd names for the other people — like Funny Face, or Twisted Nose (page 130).

Moyers: China used to call itself the Kingdom of the Center and the Aztecs had a similar saying about their culture. I suppose every culture using the circle as cosmological order put itself at the center (page 270).

It is particularly impossible to convince any people that their land is not a sacred land and they are not the chosen people. I have been lucky to travel in a number of countries around the world, and in most countries I have visited, foreigners are always considered outsiders and are given somewhat despicable names, as Joseph Campbell just said in the above quotation. Even in countries of immigrants, newcomers are always looked down upon and considered invaders. Throughout history, people have always chosen death over the abandonment of what they consider sacred land, their land, that is. Countless

www.makanologos.com

wars have been fought and immeasurable blood has been shed in the defense of the fatherland all over the globe.

However, if what they mean by Promised Land is the Land of Ecstasy and Bliss, then that Land is the borderless Land that exists within each one of us and can only be attained by the submission of the ego by the power of attention. This is the Land that Moses failed to enter because his hatred of the Egyptians, his superiority complex over the king of Egypt, and his failure to give credit to his Egyptian HIGH PRIESTS, HIS TEACHERS, from whom he learned the doctrine of monotheism and the wisdom of the Egyptians, mighty in words and deeds (Acts: 7:22), whose esoteric works he transcribed almost word for word to make up what is known today as Torah (recall the earlier quotation from Paul Brunton). This Land was revealed to Jesus after His conquest over the tempter, and thus He came out alive, stronger and wiser, whereas Moses simply got lost in the same wilderness.

Jesus ultimately cracked the shell of human ego and entered into the Land of Bliss through the dazzling door of unwavering attention, despite the agony His physical body was enduring while still on the cross when He, unlike Moses, sincerely and humbly forgave his assailants, notwithstanding their maliciousness. Jesus overcame His ego; Moses did not. The rest of us enter this Land of Bliss briefly before we enter our mothers' wombs and at an undetermined moment beyond the tomb after graduation from schools in the higher octaves of life.

The claim made here about Moses may sound preposterous to some readers, even though it is well documented in both the Old and New Testaments of the Bible. Nevertheless, I wish to say something about it before moving on. Let me hope that the overwhelming majority of readers will digest it objectively, but to those who may not be inclined to do so comfortably, I wish to bring more light from a modern scholar whose academic credentials speak tremendously well for themselves. On page 267 of *The Hero with a Thousand Faces*, Joseph Campbell writes:

www.makanologos.com

The Zohar "light, splendor" is a collection of esoteric Hebrew writing, given to the world about 1305 by a learned Spanish Jew, Moses de Leon. It was claimed that the material had been drawn from secret originals, going back to the teaching of Simeon ben Yohai, a rabbi of Galilee in the second century A.D. Threatened with death by Romans, Simeon had hidden for twelve years in a cave; ten centuries later his writings had been found there, and these were the source of the book of Zohar.

Simeon's teaching were supposed to have been drawn from the "hokmah nistarah" or hidden wisdom of Moses, i.e. a body of esoteric lore first studied by Moses in Egypt, the land of his birth, then pondered by him during his forty years in wilderness (where he received special instruction from an angel) and finally incorporated cryptically in the first four books of the Pentateuch, from which in can be extracted by proper understanding and manipulation of mystical number-values of the Hebrew alphabet. This lore and the techniques for rediscovering and utilizing it constitute the cabala…[He adds the following in the footnotes of the same book on the same page.] *Moses first studied it with the priest of Egypt, but the tradition was refreshed in him by the special instruction of his angels.*

Ponder the whole content of the quotation, but open your mind and inner eyes widely, especially on this point, and much will come to you as you sharpen your power of attention. Now let's move on to the matter of the subject.

Attention is a twofold action power—it is illumining as well as self-illumining; it harmonizes both the home and the environment. Because of the peace and harmony that a positively attentive person brings within him- or herself and to the atmosphere around him- or herself, it empowers him or her to earn the trust of Great Cosmic Beings, the Invisible Helpers, including God Himself.

Positive attention is awareness

Positive awareness is consciousness

Positive consciousness is illumination

www.makanologos.com

Positive illumination is light
Light is God and God is light
Thus he who walks in light
Not only does he walk in God
He walks face to face with God
And because light is the greatest revealer there is
All the secrets of the Gods are revealed to him

Do you still wonder that through the power of conscious control of attention does man walk and talk with God face to face?

The power of attention is so indispensable that it is practically impossible to know anything unless that thing is given some kind of attention, and the degree of attention alone determines the degree of knowledge as well. If you give ten percent, then your knowledge of it will be ten percent. If you give it one hundred percent, so will be your knowledge. A good schoolchild is not he who thinks he knows the rules of his schoolwork but he who gives the most attention to his schoolwork. A good businessperson is not he/she who thinks he knows more rules of business but he who gives his business the most attention, and so it is in every profession. The one who gives the most attention to his duties is by far better off than the one who may know all about them but does not give sufficient attention to embody perfection through actions.

Here is where education and performance come into collision with performance always holding the upper hand. A well-run company does not promote based on education but based on performance. You will remember the former NYSE chairman Richard Grasso, a college dropout, who started at the lowest level possible at the NYSE to rise to the highest level of the organization. *"By their fruits you shall know them,"* says Matthew 7:20. You may have heard that American students lag far behind in math and science compared to Malaysian or Singaporean students, etc. But where do you find the best practical mathematicians and scientists in the world? Where

www.makanologos.com

are all the research and development laboratories (creative work undertaken on a systematic basis in order to increase the stock of knowledge, including knowledge of man, culture, and society, and the use of this stock of knowledge to devise new applications; as defined by en.wikipedia.org) located? They are not in Malaysia or Singapore but in America. Why? Because American employers not only insist on it, but they have better training environments and programs since their survival demands the quality of work that cannot possibly be obtained any other way but by close attention to detail.

Without holding attention on a certain thing, it is practically impossible to know much about it. Everything that has ever come to man—including religious, philosophical, artistic, and scientific knowledge—has come by way of attention. Even the intellect, which is somewhat dormant intelligence, automatically rejects anything as unreal if attention is not focused on it first. Early in the evolution of human transportation, when our attention was focused on our feet, we walked hundreds and thousands of miles migrating from one land to another until we focused our attention on the camels, asses, horses, and other animals for transportation, and so we moved. Animals prompted our attention to the wheels, and so we moved it there, and from there came carts and wagons and so on. Now we have trains, cars, planes, spacecraft, etc. Every invention directs attention beyond the image of its own reality to bring improvement. That is why civilization is always progressive and never-ending, since everything that is uncovered causes attention to go deeper, wider, and beyond to bring new information to the surface.

Greatness is never attained by chance. Yes, a lucky man can find gold or any earthly wealth of his dreams. A lucky person can find the companion of his or her dreams. When it comes to greatness, though, there is no such thing as luck. You can win a Powerball lottery and become rich beyond your dreams over night, but you cannot obtain greatness unless you pay consciously controlled attention to whatever you are doing. The power of attention alone can bring greatness to any human being in no time as long as it is held where it belongs instead of letting it swing like a monkey hanging on its tail from one tree to other. Thus it is said, *"Where your attention is, there you are! What you attention is upon, you become!"*

Of course, if your mind is on good and right things, the control of attention should be sustained, for if you really care about greatness, it is almost imperative to know that greatness is a by-product of good and right things. Attention is, above and below, the sole power that enables man to do things the best way possible, as he constantly sees room for improvements at every corner. It is a great challenge to describe the power of a controlled attention.

With it come many great privileges God can bestow upon man, but it has to be sent out first, then on a return current, it brings all like itself or better. Through attention, man can obtain freedom, happiness, and lasting and genuine wealth of any kind. A controlled attention does not only propel man to greatness more quickly, but it also empowers him to subdue unbecoming emotions that may sink him to the lowest level, such as anger, jealousy, resentment, irritation, hate, and slandering. This is truly a gigantic and far-reaching power when masterfully controlled. No great man in Heaven or on Earth ever obtains his greatness without mastering the power of attention. From Enoch, Archimedes, Pythagoras, Moses, Confucius, the Pharaohs, Alexander, Columbus, Shakespeare, etc., greatness has always been obtained through the same ancient formula of controlled attention.

Yes, it sounds simple, and so it is. That is why the greatest power available to men is appreciated and proved only by those who pay attention to the details. What you choose to hold your attention on will determine not only the outcome of what you are seeking but also the destiny of your whole life.

www.makanologos.com

Pay attention to the common things and you will be a commoner;

Pay attention to great things and you will be a great person;

Pay attention to noble things and you will be a noble person;

Pay attention to crimes and you will be either a victim or a criminal yourself;

Pay attention to spirituality and you will be a spiritual man;

Pay attention to politics and you will be a good politician;

And the list goes on.

As long as man keeps his attention on common thoughts and things, he will be a commoner and will never know or see in his life the mountain of greatness. To climb the mountain of greatness, to be a truly brilliant mind, to arouse one's intelligence, one must keep his attention on great and noble ideas and things. *Great and noble* simply mean constructive, in other words, something that may change the lives of others for the better. It does not have to be sophisticated or complicated; it can be as simple as cooking a truly satisfying and healthy meal, creating an inspiring home decoration, practicing effective parenting techniques — anything positive in your line of work will do it. If you are a rocket scientist, your greatness will come by paying attention to something that will make the work of your generation and generations of rocket scientists after you easier. If you are a cook, paying attention to healthy and delicious meals will bring you greatness. If you are a teacher, paying attention to creative and inspiring teaching methods will do it. If you are a computer scientist, attention to better and cheaper machines will facilitate your ascension to the peak of the mountain of greatness.

Duality is the most basic law of the nature. We can only go above or below, right or left, and we can either be pulled by or pull the forces of nature. If you do not mind being a subject of the pull by those stronger than you, then you need not to be concerned. But if you want to pull and direct the forces of nature, then the control of your attention is a must. Man is weakened by the forces of nature by dispelling his energy through unstable attention, but when he controls his attention skillfully enough, he becomes a dynamo and magnetic; he acquires the magnetic power that attracts what he wants while releasing what he does not want. When man acquires the power to tell his attention to go from one point to another, to look into this and not look into that, as long as is needed, that man becomes a vault of magnetic power that few men have ever known.

This is the reason why the vast majority of us are not masters of the worlds around us. There is only one way man can control the world around him, and that is through the one and only channel called attention. You can have as much love as you want, have as much knowledge as possible, be silent as a stone, or have as many virtues as possible, but if you do not have the ability to control your attention, you will never have the magnetic power to penetrate the heart of the truth that enables brilliant minds to climb the mountain of greatness and to control the world around you by the power of arisen intelligence. Do not get me wrong; while I may not be suggesting the supremacy of attention over all others virtues, I may as well be doing just that by simply questioning the relevance of all other virtues without attention. For if you look closely, what good are these extremely luxurious vehicles without roads? *"Bugatti Veyron: $1,700,000. This is by far the most expensive street legal car available on the market today or Lamborghini Reventon: $1,600,000. The most powerful and the most expensive Lamborghini ever built a McLaren F1: $970,000. In 1994, the McLaren F1 was the fastest and most expensive car"* (http://www.thesupercars.org/top-cars/most-expensive-cars-in-the-world-top-10-list-2007-2008/, accessed August 29, 2010). What good is a high-speed train or a luxurious private airplane without a railroad or airport? Only through attention can all other virtues be put to use in as meaningful way as possible.

www.makanologos.com

Exalted Secrets of Brilliant Minds 393

What good is an infinite first-class gold mine in a country that does not know peace? What good is a first-class education that is not put to use? What good is knowledge that is not practiced? You see, it is not always what you have but rather the means to acquire and deliver. The ways and means of acquisition and deliverance count the most. In observation of this point, Alice A. Bailey writes in *From Intellect to Intuition* the following:

Through meditation [the highest level of attention — this book's author's words] *we contact a part of the Plan; we see the blue prints of the Great Architect of the Universe, and are given opportunity to participate in their emergency into objective being through our contact with and right interpretation of, the ideas we succeed in contacting...It may be true that "God" works out, in many cases, His plans through the agency of human beings...He needs men and women who are intelligent agents...God looks for those who have trained and highly developed minds and fine brains (to act as sensitive recorders of the higher impressions), so that the work may be carried forward rightly* (page 239).

Do you get what I am talking about? A little bit further in the same book, Bailey goes on to quote a Master to his students who have been successful in developing meditative abilities: *"Be of good cheers. You are making good progress. You are a chosen worker and to you the truth shall be revealed,"* (page, 243).

Even love will not lighten up someone whose power of attention is very weak, and so it is with the truth. It never reveals itself to someone who is careless with its extremely sharp double edges. Attention is, as we said earlier, the open door that only you can open or shut for yourself. This is a part of the book that I really want strongly anchored in your mind, and I wish I had magical words to transmit it to you in a clearer way. It is really paramount to the understanding and practice of many of the principles laid down in this book. Indeed, there are many of principles in this work, and I make no apology for giving my readers all I know about these great secrets of brilliant minds.

www.makanologos.com

In my quest to find the best expressions to communicate with you, the reader, on this subject, my mind suddenly hit a snag as I reached this section of the book. I saw my mind mentally display to me as a blank screen. Rather than panicking, I felt an inner calm, and slowly a feeling of joy to be alive and the privilege of speaking to the future readers spread into my consciousness. I could see my thoughts and mental images displaying on a blank screen inside me. The faster the thoughts and images, the more confused I seemed to be, and the slower the thoughts and images, the more comfortable I was with the greater understanding of what was going on inside me.

All of a sudden, everything became clear to me, and like Archimedes, I inwardly shouted, *Eureka! Eureka! Eureka!* But rather than running naked outside, with the same inner strength and happiness, I celebrated inside. I felt and knew I had grasped something of more extreme value than I had planned to pass on to our readers. I sensed empowered by something I knew would allow readers' mental eyes, ears, mouths, hands, or noses to see, hear, taste, touch, or smell what I had to say, and that is the most accurate description of the human mind. The human mind—I would say a little bit more than I said of the human intellect earlier—is a mental screen, mirror, or better yet mental video player on which thoughts and images from nobody knows really where are ceaselessly passing at a faster speed than most of us are aware of—I would like to say from the heart of Great Silence (others maybe say God or Supreme Source, according to their belief; I just prefer a different name) in its effort to influence man's Free Will and the evolution of life in our dimension of existence.

While we cannot control the source of mental images and thoughts, we have the power to choose which thoughts or images will display longer than others on our mental screens and at what speed. Like a physical video player, we have the ability and the power to wind and rewind the tape recorder. We can rewind backward, fast-forward, or just play it normally,

www.makanologos.com

Exalted Secrets of Brilliant Minds   395

and most of all, we have the power to play it in slow motion so as to allow us to clearly observe all the lines of the images, to hear the sounds of the words distinctively, and to pause or freeze the image for better observation. Unfortunately for most of us, our mental video players are always either in fast-forward or backward motion. For a lucky few, the mental video player is always playing normally; for a rarer few, the mental video plays controllably slow enough to a point of hearing the sounds, distinctively distinguishing the vowels and syllables that compose the words and see the dots that make up the pixels and lines of the images.

Try for a minute with your video player to fast-forward the tape, and then rewind backward before you play it normally. If you have never seen the pictures or heard the lyrics, can you really comfortably see what the movie is about? If before you take a final exam you are shown in fast-forward or backward mode a three-hour documentary in five minutes, can you really pass the test? If you can, then you are an exception; this rule does not apply to you. Many of us are always fast-forwarding our mental images. I hate to say this again, but I must to underscore the seriousness of what keeps the vast majority of the people from climbing the mountain of greatness. While the majority of people are always either rapidly fast-forwarding or rewinding their mental video players, a good portion of the population play theirs quite customarily. But this is not a book about being an average person, but rather a brilliant one.

While the minds of most of us can be compared to video players, the minds of brilliant ones can and should be compared to a microscope. This is not to mean that brilliant people have very slow minds—quite the contrary. It simply means that whatever the speed they let thoughts and images display on their mental screens, they can see like a microscope. They penetrate underneath the surface, they see what a naked eye cannot possibly see; "hear" inaudible sounds of silence; feel what the unaided mouth, hand, or nose cannot. Their

www.makanologos.com

observation of thoughts and images is so meticulous that they have the power to grasp the minutest details of whatever their mind, intellect, and hands are occupied with. While the minds of most of us cannot observe just one thing long enough to really understand it thoroughly, the minds of brilliant people are always occupied by one thing at a given time. By so doing, they know that one thing in detail to the point of rising above it and observing it from higher realms. Talking of the importance of keeping the mind occupied by one thing, in his small book *Meditation*, Sri Swami Satchidananda writes:

The technique of meditation is to keep the mind fully occupied on one thing. When the mind is fully occupied on one thing, it is kept away from many things and it becomes quiet...So that sticking to one thing, concentration on one thing will slowly make you rise above that one thing also. From many things get into one thing, and that one thing will become nothing (no-thing). Then you will realize everything by realizing yourself (page 4).

Before moving forward, I feel it necessary to make this point as clear as I can. When I say that the human mind is like a mental screen on which thoughts from the heart of silence are displayed, and the slower the thoughts display on that screen the better, by no means am I suggesting, cultivating, or fostering slow-mindedness—far from that. What I am suggesting is to keep thoughts and images of whatever is on the mind as long as possible for better observation, for the longer you keep a thought on the mind, the clearer will it illumine the intellect, and the better will it reveal itself to you.

All things being equal, who do you think will have a more delicious meal between two men, the one having grilled his steak for 20 seconds or the other for 20 minutes? All things being equal, whose mind do you think will do more microscopic work between the two fellows, the one having entertained an idea for 20 seconds or the other having entertained the same idea for 20 minutes? This does not mean that you should keep only one idea on your mind all the time—not at all. A brilliant mind works like a filter. Yes, it still is a human mind. Yes, it still is subject to human error. But what distinguishes it from the rest is that it works not only like a filter, but (and mostly) it gives importance to the minutest details of the structure before putting it back together. It is more analytical before synthesizing the information. It does not entertain all thoughts that come into its province. It chooses carefully the important from the unimportant, gold from the rubbish, and concentrates only on the gold and the important at the expense of the rubbish and the unimportant. If your mind is always entertaining any thought that finds its way to your mental screen, you must give up the quest of greatness and arousing your intelligence unless you reverse course.

Attention is not said to be the most important faculty because it has more power than others. It is so because it is the only ways and means that all other qualities, virtues, or faculties give us the best of themselves. A man of little attention will have little love, little truth, little silence power, little patience, and little determination — in short, little of anything that makes a brilliant mind brilliant and arouses the intelligence. Attention is that power that stimulates all dormant powers of man, the power that makes the Gods be and see everywhere and everything. Attention is basically what is known by relentless seekers of light as the All-Seeing Eye of God; it is the Holiest of all Holy Grails. Once man has mastery of the power of attention, the sky is the only imaginable limit for him.

Didn't the Master say, "*All things I do, even greater thing shall ye do?*" Was He hypocritical? I do not think so. The orthodox world can spin the truth however it wants, but the truth is always changeless. The Master knew that if we only wake up all our dormant power of attention, we can do anything we desire as long as it is constructive. What do you think wakes up all the potential powers of man? Should I answer this question for you? Well, with your permission, I will. It is attention.

www.makanologos.com

There is no magical or medical pill to awaken divine powers that are in man unless we learn to give attention, and I mean sufficient attention to whatever it is we want to understand before we act on it. Persistence is also one of those most powerful virtues, as we will see in a later chapter, but unless you persist by giving sufficient attention to something first, your effort will be vain and pointless. Success is never determined by physical strength, but rather by the ability to contemplate an idea or thought until it generates light sufficiently enough to allow it to reveal itself and all its secrets to us. Attention is basically the power that renders everything transparent to a conscientious observer. If your mind is like a pendulum, swinging left and right, or a monkey jumping from one branch of the tree to another, you may as well give up your search for greatness because you will never achieve it. An unstable mind is not a characteristic of the great minds; attention-powered stability, patience, and persistence are.

Like the rest of us, brilliant minds are always invaded by hundreds, maybe thousands of thoughts every day. But unlike most of us, brilliant minds are quick to flush out the unnecessary thoughts like a high-pressure pump. They choose their battles carefully and resolutely. Thoughts of all kinds come to brilliant minds, just as they come to all of us, but brilliant minds choose consciously — I repeat and spell out the key word c-o-n-s-c-i-o-u-s-l-y — very quickly in order to avoid cluttering up the ongoing examination of the wanted thought. Consciousness is such an important element of brilliant minds because it gives them authority to control their attention, to choose which thought will stay and which one will go, and go fast. If you remember what was said above, positive consciousness is illumination, illumination is light, light is God, and God is light. Thus a positively conscious person is always in the vicinity of God. The moment one loses the ability to control his attention, his chance of climbing the mountain of greatness or arousing his intelligence fades, and fades fast.

www.makanologos.com

"Thou shall not have any gods before Me" is the First Commandment according to Moses. Nothing could be truer. Why so? Let's first write that statement a little bit differently but with the same idea in mind. "Thou shall not give your attention to several things at the same time." When you have many gods or give your attention to several things, you commit the same "sin" — you diffuse your energy, you weaken not just the object of your attention but yourself as well, and literally not just the mind but all the body feels exhausted. By having so many gods, you scatter the power that would enable you to deserve the favors of the Great Architect of the Universe, and so it is with attention. When you disperse your attention to so many things, not only will you end up losing control of those things, but you will lose your power over them as well. This is the major reason why polygamy has been forbidden in so many cultures. When you are married to several spouses, you cannot possible give equal attention to them all. Even the Qur'an, which allows Muslims to marry more than one wife, does it under one condition: you give equal love to all of them. Is it possible? I will leave that to you.

Brilliant minds are so because of one and only one secret. Don't you scratch your head sometimes when you see those advertisements where they show that everything in nature is math, chemistry, and physics? They show how everything is math, physics, or chemistry by showing how from a tree, for instance, come all kinds of math, chemistry, or physical formulas. It is sometimes too good to be true, and that is because it is. You think so? Life around us everywhere is a cluster of formulas, but I prefer to say codes. The smartest among us, the most brilliant minds among us, are those who know how to decipher the codes that silently fill the universe around us. But only those who know how to utilize their attention are empowered to understand the codes of life.

Sometimes people spend fortunes rather than just paying attention to what their bodies are trying to tell them. For years,

www.makanologos.com

I suffered from an ear infection; in fact, many members of my family have. This may sound like an exaggeration, but it is not, for in a space of 17 years, I visited many doctors to no avail. They all gave me similar or slightly different medicine with little or no success at all. At one point, I gave up and expected to lose the power of hearing, but then I decided to pay attention to what my body was trying to tell me and I could not comprehend. As I paid more and more attention to the inner language of the body, I decided one day to fill cotton in my ear canals when taking shower. At one point, I was seeing doctors three to five times a month. But after a few weeks of keeping water away from my ear canals, I felt extremely well, better than ever before. As time went on, my hearing ability started to improve as the pain diminished. Then all of a sudden, I felt cured. I have never seen a doctor or had an ear infection since.

You see, if you pay attention sufficiently to things that are important to you, life will reveal itself to you. All the codes that fill the universe around you will decode themselves before your eyes, many times unexpectedly. All it takes is attention. As long as you serve one master at a time, on time and at the right time and in the right way, no secret of life shall be hidden from you. There is only one way to force the door of heaven open, and that is through the power of attention. Nothing else will open it. Nobody will open it for you but you. That is the great secret of brilliant minds. In fact, it is not a secret. It so easy, we simply do not think it is a great piece of knowledge. We think that to be a secret, it has to be some superstitious kind of thing, but it is not so.

So simple, it is indeed.

No high office, privilege, success or happiness in general is obtained in any other way.

To be a king, just give your full attention to royalty; to be president, give your full attention to the presidency;

To be a minister, give your full attention to ministry;

To be an athlete, give your full attention to athletics;

www.makanologos.com

To be wealthy, give your full attention to wealth;

To be healthy, give your full attention to health;

To be a musician, give your full attention to music;

To be pope, give your full attention to papacy;

To be beautiful, give your full attention to beauty, etc.

Ask presidents, popes, the wealthy, and all successful people, and they will tell you that attention is what got them where they are. While education is helpful, it is not a prerequisite, for attention is its teacher, and when education is required, it is required as a part of attention but not as a substitute.

Remember the words of the Master and John in Revelation:

"I am the way, the truth and the life" (John 14:5)

"And to the angel of the church in Philadelphia write; These things saith he that is holy, he that is true, he that hath the key of David, he that openeth, and no man shutteth; and shutteth, and no man openeth. I know thy works: behold, I have set before thee an open door, and no man can shut it: for thou hast a little strength, and hast kept my word, and hast not denied my name. " (Rev 3:7-8, KJV)

You will never go wrong whenever you substitute the words *way, truth, life, the key of David,* and *door* with the word *attention*. Attention is the way, the truth, the life, the key of David, and the door no man can shut if you decide to open it. Many times, people will travel or walk away from home, deceiving themselves that if they distance themselves from the environment, their troubles will go away. What silliness! You cannot possibly walk away from trouble as long as your attention is on them, but you can distance yourself from your troubles by taking your attention off them. Attention is a magnetic power; wherever we send it, there it pulls us. If you put your attention on something, it will pull you onto that thing. If you put attention on the distant stars, it will pull you there. If you put it on the activity at hand, it will put your mind in whatever you are doing. Wherever you put it, there will it pull you. Shouldn't you put your attention on something you love

www.makanologos.com

and crave rather than dividing it among different things you may or may not love? Make your choice, but this I want you to know: the moment you put your attention on something you really love and crave, your journey to the peak of the mountain of greatness starts right there and then. You probably do not need me to tell you that wherever your attention is, there you are, and whatever your attention is on, you become.

A man who gives his attention to dozens, hundreds, or thousands of things all day long achieves very little, but the one who gives his attention to one thing for a long time is as powerful as dynamite. He is the one who reaches the mountaintop of greatness during the early hours of the dawn, as the sun at high noon tests the will of the soul of man. Attention is the ultimate. When all the powers grow, they become attention. Haven't you noticed that when you truly love someone or something, you give him, her, or it your full attention? Or when you truly know something, you start paying attention to all its details? Attention is the binding power, the silver cord between all virtues.

Just as the sunlights up the valleys, the mountains and the flat terrain, attention illumines the mind, the intellect, and the feelings. In the history of mankind, there has never been a single human being who has achieved greatness—be it in religion, science, philosophy, military warfare, or sports—without heavily relying on the power of attention. The mind is the storeroom of divine knowledge that comes to us from higher realms of life through super-conscious ways of attention. The mind is basically the mirror that is between the Divine world and ours. All knowledge that man acquires consciously or otherwise is stored in the mind. Knowledge comes to the intellect from the mind like sunlight through the reflection of the mirror. Unfortunately, the mind (the inner mirror) is a very unstable resource for most of us. Only attention has the power to hold the mind steady while the intellect absorbs the light from higher sources.

www.makanologos.com

Brilliant minds are what they are because they succeed in holding steady their minds through the power of attention; therefore, they are able to depend on them by extracting any knowledge they need with a slight command. The majority of the people in the world lives in misery; not necessarily because of government policies or the lack of same, but because it has very little control of their minds. Attention steadies the mind, strengthens the intellect, invigorates the nerves, and energizes enthusiasm of the body.

A man whose attention is steady is like a rock. He is not just literally his own master and that of his fellow men; he is a master over the powers of nature. His eyes generate blinding light that can frighten a lion, leopard, or killer tiger; his commanding voice can demand rain to fall where and when needed and hold it where and when it is not needed. All great seers, kings, philosophers, artists, scientists, or high priests in history have relied heavily on their power of attention. Only an attentive person has the power to remove at will the veil that stands between the visible and the invisible. There is no mystery to a person of great attention, for he is capable of stepping at will into the world of limitless power and supply, invisible to the world, while the rest of us wonder how in the world he does it.

The secrets of success or the destiny of man is not inside the walls of the libraries of prestigious universities such as Harvard, Yale, Cambridge, Oxford, the Sorbonne, or Princeton, but in the mind. The race of life, if there is one, is not won by he who reads the most books or by he who has the highest education, the most money, or strongest physique; rather, it is won by he who knows how to steady his own mind and read it competently. The secrets of life are not in the books but in the minds of men. There you find all the formulas to unleash the powers of life and nature, to fulfill the needs of man, but only he who steadies his mind through the power of attention gains the know-how to do it. Those who interrupt their minds or those whose minds swing freely like a pendulum experience a

www.makanologos.com

life full of uncertainties, whereas those whose minds are stable experience a life of more certainty.

The expression *peace of mind* is a product of the highest wisdom indeed, and only fools ridicule it. There is not wealth above and below worthier than a peaceful mind. A man of a peaceful mind has the ability to bring both visible and invisible power to his service, just as a beautiful and aromatic flower inspires admiration and love in the hearts of men. A man who controls the power of his attention will have few obstacles in submitting external powers to his ability to direct his attention willingly. A person of stable mind acquires the power to subdue his emotions and passions, the two major hurdles to greatness.

If you know how fire and wind interrelate, then you should be able to know how inattention and the mind work together. *"Wind fans fire,"* said Swami Sivananda, and so the lack of attention agitates the mind. If your mind is like a forest fire at the mercy of the wind, you will run in all directions like a fool, but if your mind is like a kindled flame protected by glass around it, you will bring in the hearts of men in adoration of the highest good, the light. The secret is, thus, calming attention. A calm, stable, or steady mind is the highest treasure one can have. Attention calms the nerves, and *"he who has calm nerves, has a calm mind also,"* Sivananda is quoted to have said.

A calm mind does not only shine confidence but also, and most importantly, shines knowledge, without which climbing the mountain of greatness is absolutely impossible. Attention — which is a reorientation toward or a command to the mind to focus and display or entertain only desired thoughts or images — therefore removes the obstacles that prevent the mind from functioning efficiently. And in the words of Sivananda:

The mind will be quite steady like a flame in a windless place as disturbing energy has been removed...Steady practice arouses inner spiritual light, happiness and peace of mind...The mind of a man can be made to transcend ordinary experience and exist on a plane higher than that of reason known as super conscious state

www.makanologos.com

of concentration and get beyond the limit of concentration. He comes face to face with facts which ordinary consciousness cannot comprehend.

This ought to be achieved by proper training and manipulation of the subtle forces of the body so as to cause them to give, as it were, an upward push to the mind into the higher regions. When the mind is so raised into the super conscious state of perception, it begins to act from there and experiences higher facts and higher knowledge...the kindling of the fire of supreme knowledge, the realization of the Self...The mind gets one-pointed after practice... You will be at once filled with vigor, energy and strength. You will be elevated, renovated and filled with joy. (The Science of Pranayama, pages 90, 94)

It is the law of nature — those who have a one-pointed mind, those whose power of attention is fully developed, must not only govern but subdue those whose attention swings like the flames of a forest fire. In fact, a country that is ruled by a person of physical strength and little attention is a country of miseries indeed. Most dictatorships are ruled by these kinds of people. Hitler once thought his oratorical power coupled with the power of guns could make him the king of the world; patient and more attentive powers of the Allies proved him otherwise. As above, so below, taught the Egyptian Master Hermes Trismegistus. A cultured, civilized, and peaceful society must be governed by calm minds, for Heaven is no different. Up there, if you believe in it as I do, is not governed by confused and disturbed minds, but rather by attentive and one-pointed minds. Just as an attentive mind is a prerequisite to success in school and elsewhere in the physical world, it is also a prerequisite to the entrance through the *gates of Heaven*.

There are so many books out there telling readers how to succeed, but unfortunately very few of them focus on the power of attention. That is why I make no apology here for emphasizing this point. It is really impossible for a man to climb the mountain of greatness unless his attention is one-pointedly

www.makanologos.com

focused on the study or work at hand, because this is one of the best-kept secrets of brilliant minds, this is how intelligence is aroused, and this is the ELIXIR OF INTELLIGENCE, because light is its own defense and inspiration is its own revelation. This is how you watch and look within the light. Seeing all within it, you make joy live in you and others, for there is nothing hidden that is not revealed to a constructive seeker who needs to know it so long as he/she stands for the Highest Ideal in the universe and honor to life is the motive for which you do everything. This is the end of the road, for this is how the great ones gained their immortality and a place of honor in the hearts of all generations to come, and so can you, so long as you stand for the Highest Ideal in the universe and honor to life is the motive for which you do everything. A man of wavering attention is never master of himself and must never be the ruler of his fellow men.

You have heard those advertisements on television or elsewhere where people say something like, "When I was a kid, I wanted to be so and so." That is a big lie because they never wanted it; they just wished to be so and so. Had they really wanted, they could have ended up being what they wanted to be. When you want something you pay or give your whole attention to it, and when you give your whole attention to something, there is only one outcome—success. It is one thing to want something and another to wish for something. When you really want something, you give it your undivided attention, but when you wish, which most of us do, you occasionally give it attention, but you are disturbed by fear and doubt about your own abilities and, of course, discouragement. A steadfast attention will ultimately release desired results despite obstacles, but a wavering mind not only will have extraordinary difficulty achieving a desired result, it may also not even know when results are even produced.

Brilliant minds do not climb the mountain of greatness because they are the chosen few but because they are the self-

www.makanologos.com

tested few, and consequently they test themselves to the limit of human power and succeed by staying firm and steadfast to their goal regardless of the pain and suffering they may endure along the way. It is a law of nature — "no pain, no gain." As they run from pain, weak minds run like a forest fire in all directions. On the other hand, calm minds sustain pain in protecting their flames as they self-illumine while illumining the environment as well. Those who seek excuses everywhere to justify their lack of attention never realized much in life and are forgotten as soon as their flames of life withdraw from their bodily dwellings. A steady and unyielding attention is a treasure beyond description, and only a fool can suggest otherwise.

The forces and secrets of nature yield to man not necessarily because man has been given power over them by his creator, as the writings of sages suggest, but rather because they obey the firm and steady command that man sends through his power of attention. It may take time. It may take an hour, a day, a month, a year, or a lifetime or generations, but one thing is certain — when man relentlessly concentrates on an object, gives it all his attention, in the final analysis he comes out the victor. How many maladies that have savagely and mercilessly killed people for centuries that are now eradicated by man from the face of the Earth? How many age-old myths or beliefs has man proved wrong? Is the Earth still believed to be flat? Has not man annihilated, or nearly so, the notion of time and space since it is now possible to wake up in one continent, eat breakfast, and then eat lunch and dinner on two, three, or four different continents? Those wonders have been brought to us through the courtesy of the power of attention.

The mind is the warehouse of codes of knowledge, a stockroom of knowledge if you will, and if man's intellect will ever be able to decipher all the codes found therein, it will have to do it through a steady, calm, and focused attitude, aka attention. Many have heard of a "photographic memory." Well,

www.makanologos.com

memory cannot possibly be photographic, for it is only storage of knowledge. Memory is storage, just like a photo album. It is a folder that keeps photos while attention is the camera that supplies the album or memory with the contents to protect. As storage, memory does not travel long distances, and whenever it does, it loses the battle to time and space, whereas attention can travel millions of miles in time and space and conquer both quite easily. You can be on Earth and send your attention to any star, planet, or galaxy in space, and take pictures with your mental camera of your attention that will illumine generations. Attention has a naturally powerful built-in zoom technology. It can rapidly travel like a bullet to the edges of the universe and bring images to your location in a matter of seconds. Astronomers usually build telescopes to confirm or verify their suspicions. They may discover something along the way, but it is usually to confirm what their mental zoom had been shown before.

As attention travels in space, so does it travel in time as well. You can focus your attention on hundreds and thousands of years in the past or the future and predict events or shed light on ancient civilizations, solving what contemporaries consider mysteries of the past or the future. Attention is like light; once it is sincerely let out; it goes until it reaches its object. It is thanks to attention that historians rebuild or translate olden times and that scientists foresee future incidents. Locomotives, cars, ships, airplanes, telephones, and even the Internet of today were all accurately predicted hundreds of years before they were even built. While it is great to have a good memory to save pictures trusted to that mental storage, it must be recognized that attention is the camera of the mind that photographs the images and other information that are in the knowledge store. So if your attention is swaying all the time, you can tell with certainty the quality of the images in your mind. In short, the quality of images in your mind is determined by the quality of your attention.

www.makanologos.com

Scientists have spent decades of research and development since the first invention of the photo camera on coming up with a technology that can stabilize a camera as it takes a picture. While great things have been happening, ours are still far from perfection; thus it is still a work in progress, because for more than a decade in the twenty-first century, there still are many cameras that will not take quality images if the operator does not stabilize the apparatus. Fortunately for us human beings, our cameras have a natural built-in stabilizer. All that is required from us is to practice, and as you may well be aware of, practice makes perfect if you are patient and persistent. And of course, patience and persistence are some of the qualities of brilliant minds, as you will see in a later chapter.

Brilliant minds do not rush results. They are not naïve, either. They just work wisely to get outcomes on time, at the right time, and in the right way. What makes their minds brilliant is what most of us neglect to consider as an essential element of greatness. Little or poor minds think that to reach the mountaintop of greatness, one must be born with special qualities or surrounded by an incredible environment. I do not dispute the advantage of being born with special qualities or the impact of environment in the achievement of success in life if well used, but what I want my readers to understand is that if innate qualities and impact on the environment are the determining factors of greatness, then most of the people born in New York, London, Tokyo, Paris, and Los Angeles would reach greatness faster and more often in comparison to those in the so-called Third World, but we all know that is not the case.

Of course, innate qualities and friendly environments are helpful, but they are not decisive elements. You do not need to be born in London or be a member of the British royal family to have a photographic attention capacity. All it takes is the willingness to train and discipline your attention. And as I said above, practice makes perfect if it is subdued to patience and persistence. In fact, members of the royal family and privileged

www.makanologos.com

families in general spend a lot of time learning these same qualities. This cannot be emphasized strongly enough, and I believe there is no human being who cannot develop the power of patience and persistence if driven by sincere willpower. The first lesson Mother Nature teaches us is that of patience and persistence. It takes nine months in our mother's womb before we are born. And we do not walk on the very same day we are born.

While it takes us nine to twelve months to walk, we do not walk just because it is time to walk. No! We walk because of our persistent effort. Many times we try, and we fall time and again. But do we give up walking just because we got hurt while trying? Of course we do not. If we can all train our attention abilities with the same persistence we had as toddlers when learning to walk, it would not take us much time before we acquired a photographic attention, and by this I mean a calm and steady mind. Life will always bring numerous things to our attention, but unless we know how to sort out and demand our attention to do only the things we need and desire, we cannot climb the mountain of greatness, our intelligence cannot arise, and we cannot acquire the exalted secrets of brilliant minds. Every time you give attention to whatever crosses your mind, you are actually doing so at your own expense, and you are weakening the power of your attention. Knowing how to choose a few things to give attention to is the beginning of greatness. How much power or pressure do you think a water pipeline with several holes along the way has compared to the one of the same size that has only two, one hole on both ends of the tube?

The law of nature is never broken, at least not without dire consequences. Only humans break the law. We have been paying for that for centuries, and we will keep paying until the law is obeyed in its entirety. The law does not break or bend itself to accommodate human desires or to prove itself by pleasing human curiosity. That law of nature says, *"Thou shall*

www.makanologos.com

decree a thing, and it shall be established unto you. Seek, and ye shall find; ask, and it shall be give you; knock, and it shall be open to you." Sages of all cultures, all religions, and all time have taught this wisdom to mankind. When you give genuine attention to a thing, that thing will come to you as a matter of law. Why? Because when you give attention to something, you open yourself to that thing, and consequently it will reveal itself to you, or in simpler language, when you invite a guest into your house, you open the door and that guest will come in. Whether your guest will be friendly to you is all up to the nature of your relationship.

Can you really imagine Archimedes, Newton, Einstein, or any other great mathematician or physician you know to be what they were by simply wishing? The universe is full of guests, be they ideas or entities that want to be your loving and joyous visitors. Unless we give them our undivided attention, they cannot possibly come to us. Scientists have discovered many inventions and theories intuitively, but intuition does not simply come to man for the sake of it. It does so because man has given it sufficiently genuine attention. Attention is the torchlight that attracts all we have or are, and all we will ever hope to be or have. It is called intuition because it comes unexpectedly, not because it is not sought or not given attention to. If you do not give sufficient attention to a thing, it will never reveal itself to you intuitively, and if it does, you may never know its value or even what it is. It is that simple, for attention is the door that no man can open but you. It does not shut just because you are dealing with some matter of life on your other time.

Brilliant minds are nothing but doors through which mankind receives its blessings, the doors through which the Earth receives its initiation in wisdom, love, and power, or liberty, equality, and brotherhood among its children. Buddhism, Judaism, Christianity, and Islam were given to us through the attention that Masters Siddhartha Gautama

www.makanologos.com

(Buddha), Moses (prophets), Jesus the Christ, and Mohammed gave to the Source of Light, just as electricity, trains, planes, steamboats, and other marvelous inventions, as well as many other scientific breakthroughs, came to us through different individuals who pulled them from the All-Knowing Mind of God thanks to the magnetic powers of their attention. That is the law of life; all must come to us by the power of attention. The steadier the mind, the faster we draw things to us by the control of the attention that we give to our desires.

Satisfaction of man's desires is as certain as the extent to which he focuses his attention on what he wants. The sooner we take our attention off a thing, the faster the thing disappears from our mental radar. It is that simple. Through the power of attention, we live in a heaven or hell created by ourselves. All the nightmarish, depressing, saddening moments we live in life are moments we give our attention to, things we do not want, but we open doors to them anyway. You cannot possibly give your attention to happiness and be sad or experience anxiety of some sort. It is practically impossible. It is like plunging into a swimming pool with your clothes on, hoping they will not get wet.

When you give your attention to misery, you must experience misery. When you give your attention to happiness, you must experience happiness. When you give your attention to poverty, you must experience poverty, or if to wealth, you must experience that. This is not this author's imagination; it is the law. Rich people report that they are always thinking about wealth; their attention is always on the ways and means of making more of it; whereas poor people are always licking their wounds suffered in the battles of life, and the more their attention is on their wounds, the more wounds they will suffer. Those who take their attention off their wounds and place it on remedies find themselves cured much sooner than they expected. Attention to things we do not want gives them the power to torture us, but as soon as we take it off the unwanted

www.makanologos.com

Exalted Secrets of Brilliant Minds **413**

things, immediately they stop torturing us. Attention to things that we want brings us closer to them.

Try to stop thinking and talking about something that annoys you if you want to test the truthfulness of what I am telling you. Take it out of your mind and feelings, and you will be freer. Attention alone ties us to misery or happiness, depending on where we direct it. Those who are always thinking and talking about crime are either criminals, victims of crime, or crime fighters. Whether it is conscious or otherwise, giving attention to something is inviting that thing into your life, be it good or bad. There is no exception to this law; like begets like is the law, and no one is exempted from it. Wisdom is the ability to give attention to virtues, while foolishness is giving attention to vices. Knowledge is giving attention to facts, and ignorance is giving attention to nothingness. Power is giving attention to knowledge, and weakness is giving attention to mistakes. And so Shakespeare said, *"Knowledge is* [potential] *power."* "Potential" is in brackets because true power is not necessarily mere knowledge but knowledge in action. In mathematical reasoning, it will look something like this: "knowledge = power, but power is not necessarily equal to mere knowledge but knowledge in action." You may have a gun, but if you do not know how to use it correctly, you have no power. It is that simple.

Matthew 7:7-8: *"Ask and it shall be given you; seek, and ye shall find; knock, and it shall be opened unto you. For everyone that asketh receiveth; and he that seeketh findeth; to him that knocketh, it shall be opened,"* is one of the simplest, neatest, most pleasant, yet most philosophical and misunderstood verses in the whole Bible. It really sounds easy, doesn't it? Ask and bingo! You receive, right? Seek and bingo! You find. Knock and bingo! The door opens! Why bother to work hard if all you need to do is ask, seek, and knock to live a comfortable life? Indeed, it is that simple, except you must not simply ask with your physical mouth, seek with your physical eye, and knock with your physical hand. *"Before*

www.makanologos.com

Abraham was, I AM," we were told in John 8:58. Before physical action, there must be spiritual and mental fabric of the physical manifestation, and unless there is first this spiritual and mental fabric, you can ask until your mouth is dry, you can seek until you go blind and your legs crippled, you can knock until your hands are numb, and still you will never be given, find, or have the door opened to you.

As heartbreaking as it sounds, not all who ask are given; not all who seek find, and not all who knock are admitted. Physical action is just as important; it was not meant to precede spiritual and mental processes. Why? Because when sages of old — in fact in all cultures and civilizations, not just from the Bible — said to ask, seek, and knock in order to get what we want, they basically meant to give all our attention to the things we desire, and with efficient action afterward, we shall be given, find, or be admitted into the pleasure of our giver or host. Brilliant minds, somehow, for some reason, seem to know this secret early in life or learn about it quickly and put it into practice faster than most of us can comprehend. Attention is the magnetic power. They used to say, seek and knock in order for them to be given, to find, or to be admitted at the table of the chosen few.

Attention is what they use to draw whatever they desire, tangible or intangible, and the stronger the attention, the stronger the magnetic power, the sooner they fulfill their desires. Attention is the key, and as Mary Bailey writes of the Tibetan Master, Djwahl Khul, telling Alice A. Bailey, *"A key is here. Turn it as far as you can. The key needs dipping in the oil of the intuition"* (page 55). Most things that make life pleasant are not physical or tangible; therefore, they cannot possibly be given in any other way but spiritually or mentally, at the very least. Things such as courage, joy, hope, love, wisdom, strength, or faith cannot be given or found except spiritually or mentally.

You can travel the world over, and you will never find the magic pill for any of those qualities, even if you were unwise enough to believe so. Anyone who can discover a pill for true

www.makanologos.com

joy, love, or courage will be the richest person in the world overnight. Rich and poor, men and women, young and old, we all crave high-quality feelings such as joy, love, happiness, courage, hope, confidence, and fearlessness. Because we believe something from the outside can provide us those feelings, and because we do not know where to find the source of those things in the outside world, we surrender our lives to fate. "*Adviene que poura,*" say the French (or "come what may" in English), lifting their hands up in the air in a sign of total surrender to the unknown. But life would not be that way if we could only give our undivided attention to what we know and feel would take us to the peak of the mountain of greatness.

The mountain of greatness is never overcome by destructive desires, and hence brilliant minds have their spiritual and mental eyes and ears on constructive desires. That is how they climb so high on the mountain of greatness even when the peak is hidden in the clouds—it is there to those who dare to know where it is, and it is totally invisible to the crying babies of the masses. When attention is undividedly given to a constructive desire; when we adamantly ask, seek, and knock inside before we actively ask, seek, and knock on the outside; as Djwahl Khul put it to Bailey, "*It develops the intuition, gives play to the reasoning faculty...for...in the heart of every man lies hid the flower of the intuition,*" (pages 62, 69). This, of course, is not child's play. It is the most difficult yet the most rewarding thing to do. It requires discipline, and discipline means doing the right thing regardless of whether there is someone watching over our actions or not. It is easy to oppose your friends, parents, school authorities, government, or any other outside influence—in other words, opposing oneself sometimes. What is very difficult to most of us is to oppose ourselves, and of course not opposition for its own sake, but in the name of Good with a big G. When a man is able to oppose his own fears, doubts, selfishness, discouragement, inclinations, cravings, etc., that man is about to enter the door that no other man can shut.

www.makanologos.com

If only man forgave his fellow men as he forgives himself, the world would be one of the most peaceful places in the universe. But because man does not as easily forgive others as he forgives himself, well, the world is a better place for only the fittest. Man constantly commits evil against himself and against the world, but he constantly forgives himself. A man of iron will, a will strong enough to oppose himself against his weaknesses, is a man whose aura shines with discipline and confidence not only in him but in his fellow men as well. And the two most important qualities required in order to have a strong or undivided attention are discipline and confidence. Discipline and confidence foster an indomitable spirit and an invisible courage that are prerequisites to the development of a brilliant mind.

It takes courage and confidence to see and seize opportunity. I am not laughing; I am dead serious. Let me say it again — it takes courage and confidence to see and seize opportunity. Where many see danger, brilliant minds see opportunity. Not that they see different things, but they just see them through different lenses. Life is full of illustrations that show how a danger for one is but an opportunity to another person. I will let the reader find examples in his own life experiences for a better understanding, but let me lay these illuminating words of Mary Bailey here:

> Constructive change is part of growth, and even where reasons and trends are not clear at first, it is essential to make the best and the most of the opportunities change presents, for indeed "obstacles (or crises) are opportunities!" Sometimes one can turn a potential harmful or negative situation into positive channels because at the heart, or root, of every negative force lies the germ or seed of a positive energy (page 83).

How is it possible for an inattentive mind to see the energy, the electricity harvestable from a mighty river? Where many of us will throw our hearts to sharks, an attentive surfer will ride on the crest of waves to safety and enjoyment. Unless you have

www.makanologos.com

a disciplined attention, you cannot possibly see opportunities life throws your way in different shapes and forms. I shall, of course, say more about discipline and confidence in a later chapter, but while on the subject of attention, I felt it necessary to anticipate a little bit here, so it does not seem naïve or seem to be suggesting that attention is acquired effortlessly. As you will see in upcoming chapters, I feel deeply that it is important to reiterate time and again to the reader and all who care to foster a brilliant mind that this incredible magnetic power, attention, is not gained without a price.

A thing of great value comes to man through one unique pathway, and that is attention. While life is a web of interdependencies among man, his fellow men, the environment, and the Unseen Helpers, the only person who comes closer to total independence is the man who has a very attentive mind. Communists can preach what they will, but the truth of the matter is that society is nothing but a true pyramid with the inattentive masses on the bottom, the fairly attentive in the middle according to the strength of their attention, and the most attentive on the top of the edifice. Talk about the fairness of life — well, it is indeed unfair to life to be portrayed as unfair, because not only do we choose our place as the social pyramid erects itself, but we choose our own place by the choice we make (or not) to develop and strengthen our attention to constructive desires.

The more attention we give to constructive desires, the faster we pull ourselves to the peak of that mighty mountain of greatness where only the brave dare to reach. I know no secret of brilliant minds greater than attention to constructive desires. Yes! Action will always be required before anything is manifested on the physical plane. But it is worth mentioning here that — not to encourage laziness in any way, shape, or form, but to underscore the importance of attention — brilliant minds do not physically work hard. They are confined to mental work, and physical work is done for them one way or

www.makanologos.com

another. This is not fantasy but fact. Brilliant minds, attentive minds, are purposely excluded from the noise of the clueless masses just so they can calibrate their attention to a desired end. We have been told to *"know the truth and truth shall set you free,"* and what is the truth? A lot has been said about the truth in this book, but let me say one more thing here: only the attentive mind will find the truth; therefore, only the attentive mind will be genuinely free. True? Yes! Fair? You be the judge!

The man who employs his attention rather being employed by it has the potential of employing his fellow men as well. There is no mountain of greatness that a man who makes his attention his best servant cannot climb. An attention that does not serve its master is as good as a very sharp sword in the hands of a fool or fire in the hands of a child. Either he will destroy himself with it, or he will destroy the world. But there is no better servant than a trained attention that is taught obedience so when it is sent out, it comes back with something that is positive and constructive on its return current. More than anything else, brilliance of the mind depends on the power of attention to the right places from where it brings clarity and understanding of desired objectives. To understand the nature of things and affairs, attention must be fixed on them like a blazing torchlight in a dark cave.

I feel the urge here to restrain my human passions on this subject. I am so passionate about it that I am tempted to keep writing almost endlessly. By the law of nature, human imagination can fly to any height, but sooner or later it must, literally, come down to Earth where its work ought to be materialized. Likewise, human passions can probably make the Earth tremble, but they will never shake the sky. A lot of substance has already been packaged in here; therefore, the reader's imagination must be allowed to leave the room to fly, while, as all human imagination must, mine must now come down to earth. The most important goal of this work is to enable it to make it more substance-packed, not just to add to

www.makanologos.com

the literature but to improve the minds of the masses for the better.

Much can be said about attention. Would I were the master of time and space, I could go on almost indefinitely talking about attention alone. As I am listening to the voices of teachers of the past on this topic through the bookish heritage they left mankind, I feel humbled and empowered to write a book on attention. I learned so much about attention and its mysteries that I was practically unable to squeeze the analysis of every idea in these pages. As I did at the end of previous chapters and as I will do in the other chapters to come, I choose to summarize the vast inspirational ideas in a poem for the benefit of the reader. What is important, after all, is not what I wrote in this book or elsewhere; what is important is the inspiration that the reader gets to write not necessarily another book in his own life, but the feelings, thoughts, and actions that will translate the content of his life in the minds and lives of others. The life of each one of us is a book in itself and must be made to inspire good feelings, thoughts, and deeds in others. The content I choose to deal with in my book of life, as well as the style with which I present it, is what I am judged by in this world and elsewhere. Attention cannot be dealt with wholly here; the mammoth task that it is, it has to be tried in our books of life. And if I have been able to ignite even a small flash of light to enable someone to see better, my heart will humbly join yours in the joy sparked by the accomplishment of your desire, so long it is a constructive one.

Attention

The Storehouse of Wisdom
The Teacher of All Intelligence
The Filter of Knowledge
The Radiator of Understanding
The Dominion of the Gods

www.makanologos.com

The Dwelling of the Masters
The Egg of the Consuming Fire
The Food of a Pure Life
The Holy Grail of sincere Truth Seekers
The Immaculate Womb of Finest Creations
The Searchlight of Happiness and Joy
The Bridge into the Land of Endless Possibilities
The Wings of the Immortal Beings
The Magic Pill of Comprehension
The Virgin Mother of Illumination
The Brush of Creative Imagination
The Jewel in the Heart of All Virtues
The Priestess in the Temple of Silence
The Central Pillar in the House of the Sun
The Vessel of the Seeds of Wisdom, Strength, and Beauty
The Garden of Flowers of Purest Fragrance
The Glorious Armor of Crystal Light and the Cloak of Invincibility
The Royal Road and the Tower of the Truth of all Truths
In thee the man of free-willed obedience to Higher Self
Finds the Cup of Crystal Liquid Light
That transmutes him into the Genuine
Magnificent effect of the Causeless Cause.
By the author, Wisdom J.O.Y. Makano

CHAPTER XVIII

The Self-Confidence Pillar

Let's kick off this chapter with a quotation from Mary Bailey's book *A Learning Experience*, a quotation you just read in the previous chapter. I repeat it here to take the reader deeper into the understanding of what man views as obstacles, expressed in this work as the mountain of greatness, and that quotation is this:

> *Constructive change is part of growth, and even where reasons and trends are not clear at first, it is essential to make the best and the most of the opportunities change presents, for indeed "obstacles (or crises) are oppo\rtunities!" Sometimes one can turn a potential harmful or negative situation into positive channels because at the heart, or root, of every negative force lies the germ or seed of a positive energy* (page 83).

For the vast majority of people, when life suddenly hits an iceberg, the first reaction is usually negative. In a sense, they intend to lament, cry, worry, or surrender. "Oh my God! Not again! Why me?" are the typical first reactions of many, and the weakest ones go to the extent of self-inflicting bodily injuries that can cause death or permanent disability.

Well, the human mind is a mystery to all of us, but this much I know — duality is the most basic law of nature. There are always going to be left and right, good and bad, up and down, life and death, male and female, positive and negative, etc. — opposite, of course; not mixed up or disconnected but eternally inseparable and joined at the hip. One is always in the vicinity of the other, forever. As one falls, the other stands. That is not a mystery. It is a fact that even the newly conceived fetus understands that there are moments of happiness and those of sadness, time to sleep and time to awaken, or at least that much of this law. What is the point here? Well! The point here is exactly what Bailey said above: *"at the heart, or root, of every negative force lies the germ or seed of a positive energy."* The same is true for positive force. Love can be as destructive as hate, and wisdom can be as destructive as foolishness if used blindly. Illustrations of this point abound in real life everywhere. I will let you find your own.

Understandably, it is never easy to find a germ or seed of positive energy when the sky is falling over your head and the earth is melting under your feet at great speed. Of course, the ability to see the blessings that come in disguise is not given to many. Those who see blessings in disguise are called self-confident people. Their quality of self-confidence is so indispensable that it is one of the most important qualities that distinguishes brilliant minds from the rest of the pack, since it melts obstacles like oil on fire and makes intelligence increase like a balloon on fire. It is a quality without which it is practically impossible to climb the mountain of greatness or arouse intelligence. No man or woman who ever walked here on this green Earth ever achieved greatness without self-confidence. Every great person in the past, present, or future had, has, or will have this quality, for without it, there is no intelligence arousal, brilliant mind, or greatness, for that matter—case closed.

It has happened in the experience of all of us almost without exception—suddenly we are confronted with an unwanted situation, and we become panic-stricken, fearful, or out of control. With almost uncontrolled speed, it develops from worse to worst and never looks back. And the more fearful we become, the harder and faster the sky collapses over our head, and the earth under our feet, for its part, melts like ice cream on a summer day in the Sahara Desert. On the other hand, if you take a different attitude—let's say, that of coolness, calm, and serenity—like a boomerang, that same situation changes direction, many times, with the same speed or faster. When you adopt an attitude of stillness in front of what could be a

www.makanologos.com

perilous situation, you not only see your exit from it, but you also see all the constructive ways and means, all the positive forces and outcomes that can come out of the situation, whereas the terrified mind sees peril. *"Succeed in not fearing the lion and it will run away from you with all the speed of its power,"* wrote one author.

That is the power of self-confidence or self-control. It works like magic; in fact, it is magic in itself. It is the power that brilliant minds learn to cultivate early on in life. It empowers man to be the master of self. People do not admire a person who does not have confidence in his own self. Just as men believe in God, so does God believe in those men who believe in themselves. The *"talisman of Napoleon – absolute confidence in himself,"* writes Robert Collier. He goes on to say:

The world loves leaders. All over the world, in every walk of life, people are eagerly looking for someone to follow. They want someone else to do their thinking for them; they need someone to hearten them to action; they like to have someone else on whom to lay the blame when things go wrong; they want someone big enough to share the glory with them when success crowns his efforts. But to instill confidence in them that leader must have confidence in himself. A Caesar or a Napoleon who did not believe in himself would have been inconceivable. It is that which makes men invincible – the Consciousness of their own power. They put no limit upon their own capacities – therefore they have no limit. For Universal Mind sees all, knows all, and can do all, and we share in this absolute power to the exact extent to which we permit ourselves. Our mental attitude is the magnet that attracts from Universal Mind everything we need to bring our desires into being. We make that magnet strong or weak as we have confidence in or doubt of our abilities. We draw to ourselves unlimited power or limit ourselves to humble positions according to our own belief (The Secret of the Ages, pages, 239-240).

Self-confidence is the conquering power of all obstacles, and just as behind every physical engine there is energy, behind

www.makanologos.com

every brilliant mind there is self-confidence. Regardless of the brilliance of the mind, no great accomplishment is achievable by a single individual. All great men in history had supporters in one way or another to assist them in accomplishing exploits that make us and future generations know of them. What would Master Jesus have been without His fishermen friends? Could we even have known anything about Socrates without the pen of his student Plato? One thing is clear — people do not like to support a cowardly person, but no matter how smart or wise you are, people will not know about it unless you attract them with self-confidence. Did Jesus just confidently tell fishermen, "Follow me!" and they unquestioningly left their boats, nets, fish, and families, never minding where they were going as long as they were shielded by the shadow of a very confident man?

No word is more synonymous with victory than self-confidence. A person who thinks that greatness will just come on its own without some real evidence of self-confidence must not know what greatness is all about. Yes, of course, we are all entitled to dream, but it is important to understand that not all dreams are dreams; some of them are hallucinations, and we are still entitled to them as well. A good dreamer is the one who seeks victory by testing his own self-confidence unceasingly, fearing no death or human suffering, as he or she considers them inescapable parts of the earthly experience called mortal life. There is no greater waste of time and energy than seeking or trying to climb a mountain of greatness without self-confidence. Man can be as powerful as lightning or electricity, he may have the power to burn everything that stands in his way, but if he does not believe in his own ability to conquer those obstacles, his power is like an unsecured loaded gun in the hands of a child.

History is full of illustrations of larger armies that were defeated by meager yet very self-confident enemies; weak, barbarian, yet confident invaders have conquered powerful

www.makanologos.com

Exalted Secrets of Brilliant Minds   425

and civilized empires. Even angels come to the rescue of a constructively self-confident person. This statement may sound outlandish, but Joseph Campbell wrote:

At Medina, as Professor H. A. R. Gibb has pointed out, Mohammed sat astride Mecca's vital trade route to the north, and for seven years made brilliant use of this advantage to break the resistance of the oligarchy of this city. First operating as a mere brigand, he captured caravans and enriched the new community of God with booty taken from its neighbors. Next, as a brilliant generalissimo, he met and defeated (often with angelic aid)* larger than his own, sent against him by desperate merchants of his native place. And finally, having won to his side a number of the Bedouin tribes, returned to Mecca unopposed, in the year 630, and with a grand symbolic sweep established the new order by destroying every idol in the city (The Masks of God: Occidental Mythology, page 429). [In the footnotes Joseph Campbell writes, **As Constantine and his army had seen the "Shining Cross" before the crucial defeat of Maximian* (supra, pp. 385-386), *so Mohammed and his army, during the crucial battle at Badr, saw the angels giving them aid. The turbans of all except Gabriel were white, whereas his, according to eyewitnesses was yellow.* (A.A. Bevan, "Mohomet and Islam" in *The Cambridge Medieval History, Vol. II, page 318, note 1, citing Ibn Hisham*).

Lack of confidence not only guarantees defeat in any enterprise, but it makes an already bad situation even worse. When you are trying to get rid of a negative situation, the attitude to display to the outside as well as inside is optimism, not pessimism. Optimism inspires joy of accomplishment, makes you anticipate the happiness to come. It shows you the prize to be won in no uncertain way. It makes you feel the worthiness, the beauty, and the glory that your effort will win for you. The lack of optimism and self-confidence inspires fear and acceptance of defeat. Self-confidence is the power of not only the conquerors but of the lords of life as well. Self-confidence does not only empower the victories over empires and material things, but it enables the overpowering of negative qualities such as fear, doubt, greed, and anger under the masterful control of a confident man.

Greatness is very strict and uncompromising when it comes to self-confidence. You either have self-confidence and attain greatness or you lack it and will never arouse your intelligence or climb the mountain of greatness. The world is not necessarily ruled by wise or smart people, but make no mistake, we are ruled by the self-possessed or those who have more confidence in themselves than we do. Some of them know how to use wise and smart people, but many of them go to the extreme and screw up everything. And so life is what it is, a web of endless conflicts of interest, which is of course unfortunate. (Later on, I talk about how to balance self-confidence with other virtues to avoid this kind of outcome.)

The easiest thing in life that most of us do many times is to lay the blame on someone else or find a scapegoat for our trouble. Not so with brilliant minds — they find the cause of their trouble in themselves, and usually they find it to be the lack of more self-confidence. And so brilliant minds continuously work on their self-confidence because life is endlessly testing us to the last breath. Just because you earned millions of dollars at one point of your life, you cannot simply relax, thinking that it may never go away — not at all. Rich people are not rich because they have millions but because they work hard to keep and multiply what they have won; otherwise, the ever-vigilant law of gravity will pull them back to the bottom of the social ladder.

If we could all learn to blame our lack of self-confidence, the lives of many of us would be a different story. The first thing many people do when a problem stands in their way is to blame George, Jack, Mary, Paul, or Christine. But in fact, there is a reason why life sends all kinds of troubles our way, and the most important of them all is the opportunity to measure ourselves or measure our strengths against them. And nothing enables man to measure himself better than self-confidence.

www.makanologos.com

Self-confidence itself is the gold standard unit of measurement of achievement. Man can easily tell whether he will succeed or fail in a venture by the feeling of self-confidence or lack of it.

People who believe in their abilities, people who have confidence in themselves, tend to welcome challenges regardless of difficulties even if they do not know much, for they believe the challenge itself is the best teacher, and by standing up to it, it will reveal itself and surrender its secrets. And so they go from challenge to challenge, one step at a time, until they climb the mountain of greatness that appeared utterly impossible at the beginning. There is no better teacher than the challenge itself; it speaks a language audible to the ear and comprehensible to the mind of self-confident people only.

In man, there are all the powers needed to surmount any mountain or to simply cast it in the sea if need be. It is said that "God (Mother Nature if you like) does not give us more than we can handle," and so we are given lands, mountains, seas, skies, etc. If it is true that He does not give us more than we can handle, aren't we given lands to explore, mountains to climb, seas to sail, and skies to fly? Don't we have powers to do all these things? Those powers, of course, are latent in all of us. They lie deep down in us like those many treasures we pass by at night, not because we have no eyes to see but because of the nature of the night, darkness. Just as the light of the sun brings everything into plain sight for every seeing eye, self-confidence reveals to man the path to the power of wisdom, intelligence, humility, patience, persistence, courage, and all the other virtues that are dormant inside, like a fountain of potable water waiting to be tapped. By itself, of course, like any other virtue, self-confidence can be blinding. As French writer Pierre Corneille, once said, *"Danger breeds best on too much confidence."* But it is one of those virtues that can be balanced with any other virtues to produce marvels.

As the sun shines over all on the surface of the Earth, self-confidence shines over everything inside the man who is

www.makanologos.com

unafraid of facing life's challenges head on. You have heard people saying, "You never know until you try." What do you think they mean? Well, this is not a revelation to anyone but simply a reminder. Most people do discover their calling or fortune only when they stand up to a challenge. Why? Because when people face a sort of make-or-break situation or do-or-die challenge, they go deep inside themselves and discover that all the tools or powers to perform amazing things were there all along; they just did not know it or thought that only Harry or Paul could do it for them. And now that they know it or took Harry or Paul out of their minds, they use those infinite powers for as long as they can, and most of the time to their most astonishing shock. And because they are using inner powers, they become independent; they depend on themselves as the rest of the mass is willing to depend on those whom we call our rulers. We yield our lives to their use in the misguided fear of losing ours if we believe in ourselves.

That is the paradox of life. People refuse to put confidence in themselves, refuse to believe in their own ability, only to have confidence in a person who believes in himself. *"Whether you think you can or cannot, you are right either way,"* said the master industrialist Henry Ford. It is by believing right or wrong that we do right or wrong; it is by thinking that we can or cannot that we do or do not. How do you think those fellow men who pioneered vocations achieved greatness? Today the world is full of physicists, chemists, and mathematicians who know far more than Newton, Archimedes, or Lavoisier could ever have dreamed of. But why do we hold up these men who may not even compare to modern high school students? Because they were pioneers, they laid down the basis of our knowledge, and how did they know the basis? They self-confidently pursued their dreams, and their dreams taught them what they needed to know according to their times and needs.

Self-confidence is by itself a teacher; in fact, it the best teacher. It taught pioneers throughout history, it taught all those brilliant

www.makanologos.com

minds what they needed to know, and it can teach anyone who dares to try to confidently trust himself. Self-confidence is not a choice if you really want to climb the mountain; it is an absolutely imperative need for anyone who wants to follow in the footsteps of brilliant minds. Brilliant minds themselves are not brilliant because they are more intelligent or wiser than the rest of us; they are brilliant because they wisely and intelligently have confidence in themselves. They believe their abilities to achieve whatever is on their minds and trust in the proficiency of challenges to teach them by revealing themselves as they have taught all brilliants minds throughout history.

People will hardly ever bend to your will because you love them. They will not necessarily come to your rescue because of how much you may know. While love, knowledge, and many other qualities are indispensable puzzles of life, they are not as magnetic as self-confidence. One of the most important qualities of a brilliant mind is the ability to attract and wisely utilize other brilliant minds, and unless you have a highly sensitive self-confidence, how can brilliant minds be attracted to you? The foundation of religions, great nations, big businesses, sports teams, or anything else of great importance has always been a work of collaboration of several minds. If you want to climb the mountain of greatness, you must be able to attract useful people, and this is done only through the power of self-confidence. There are very few people who will waste their time or risk their lives to save yours out of sympathy, but if you display an unmistakable aura of self-confidence, many people will gladly give up their time or even risk their lives for your cause and life.

It is literally amazing to what extent people will go to serve you and your cause if you do not give them a conflicting message of hope and fear. The reason why most of us are constantly looking up to a leader or a hope-giver is that the future is unknown to all of us; therefore, the person who displays or even pretends self-confidence by giving us some assurance in what is to come

www.makanologos.com

gets most of our attention as well as our support. It is quite frankly naïve to think or believe that some people have it easy. Life is indiscriminately tough on all living beings, animals, vegetables, and minerals included. If you think minerals have it the easy way, just read on. Thomas Carlyle is quoted to have said, *"No pressure, no diamond,"* and Malcolm Forbes is quoted as saying, *"Diamonds are nothing more than chunks of coal that stuck to their jobs."* It takes not only sacrifice but also tremendous effort for a bird to build a nest and find food, just as it is so for humans and other creatures. People sometimes wish they were someone else, thinking that someone else was having it the easy way. That is totally ridiculous. No human being on Earth ever had it the easy way. Just because someone does not broadcast his troubles does not mean he/she does have not any. Humans may favor association by race, gender, or origin, but not so with life; it favors association only with those who take the pains of governing their feelings, thoughts, speech, and actions with the power of self-confidence.

Self-confidence — or the spirit of victory, invincibleness, and relentless courage — is a key ingredient in the mastery of life. Those who at the very least pretend or appear to display self-confidence reach the peak of the pyramid by simply stepping on the shoulders of the inferiority-complex-minded ones. If there is a case when a virtue can be faked, a case when pretense of a virtue is better than nothing at all, then it is in the case of self-confidence. God forgive me! But in this case, I allow myself to go as far as encouraging those who sincerely feel depleted of self-confidence to sincerely fake it if that is the only way they can scare away the monsters of fear, hate, discouragement, anger, greed, or selfishness. I say this because I know fake self-confidence fosters genuine self-confidence in the long run, or at least it gives one breathing room, at least momentarily, to fend off the attack of nefarious forces while fostering genuine self-confidence that will effectively seal one's destiny. In no country, group, or family, for that matter, has a person with an inferiority complex ever been tolerated as a leader, and whenever that happens, that country, group, or family usually is doomed. Prosperity or peace does not come except through self-confidence, and a country, group, or family that wants to welcome peace and prosperity must do it by opening its door widely to self-confidence. As man conquers fears, hate, doubt, irritation, and greed through the acquisition of self-confidence, so do peace and prosperity enter his world.

A person who radiates self-confidence does not simply impress fellow men; he also impresses the forces of nature, and Invisible Helpers and even Gods come in droves to assist him or her. Writing on the mysterious, almost supernatural assistance that comes to some of the most self-confident children on Earth, commonly known in all cultures as heroes, the prolific Joseph Campbell says in his book *The Hero with a Thousand Faces*:

Furthermore, we have not even to risk the adventure alone; for the heroes of all time have gone before us; the labyrinth is thoroughly known; we have only to follow the thread of the hero-path. And where we had thought to find an abomination, we shall find a god; where we had thought to slay another, we shall slay ourselves; where we had thought to travel outward, we shall come to the center of our own existence; where we had thought to be alone, we shall be with all the world (page 25).

…a promise that the peace of paradise, which was known first in the mother womb, is not to be lost; that it supports the present and stands in the future as well as in the past…though omnipotence may seem to be endangered by the threshold passages and life awakening, protective power is always and ever present within the sanctuary of the heart and even immanent within, or just behind, the unfamiliar features of the world. One has only to know and trust and ageless guardians will appear. Having responded to his call, and continuing to follow courageously as the consequences unfold, the hero finds all the forces of the unconscious at his side. Mother Nature herself supports the mighty task. And in so far as the hero's act coincides with that for which his society itself is ready, he seems

www.makanologos.com

*to ride on the great rhythm of the historical process. "I feel myself,"
said Napoleon at the opening of the Russian campaign, "driven
towards an end I do not know. As soon as I shall have reached it, as
soon as I shall become unnecessary, an atom will suffice to shatter
me. Till then not all the forces of mankind can do anything against
me,"* (pages, 71-72).

What we call luck or chance many times is not chance at
all but a mental attitude of dealing with defeat inwardly
while publishing victories, therefore giving to weak-minded
ones the image of a "chosen one." Many people we generally
think are living a peaceful life, many times are not in actuality.
They have serious problems hidden inside such that the day
those problems come to light, people scarcely believe them
to be true. Consequently they become disillusioned, angry,
and disgusted, especially those who invested all their hopes
in them. That is what happens when instead of placing your
confidence in yourself, you place it in others who may just be
very good actors.

The only person under the sun who will never play with
your life is you; everybody else is a potential actor. Therefore,
when you place your trust in others rather than in yourself,
you must entertain the possibility of great sorrow. I am not
suggesting that you should not trust your fellow men or should
not work with others—far from that. What I am advising is to
trust your feelings first before trusting someone else's, because
your feelings are the only thing that can tell you the right
thing to do and the right person to work with. And again, in
the name of the Good Lord, how is it possible to trust another
person when you do not have confidence in yourself? You can
neither feel nor hear the feelings and thoughts of other persons.
Your feelings are the only thing that can prompt you if you are
dealing with a player or a serious person. If you do not have
self-confidence and go ahead and place your confidence in
someone anyway, you may be deceiving yourself and therefore
be taken for an easy ride. You may become prey, that is. To have

www.makanologos.com

confidence in your fellow men, you must have self-confidence first; otherwise, you will never be capable of controlling the situation when negative events start to unfold. It may help to remember these words of Oprah Winfrey: *"Often we don't even realize who we're meant to be because we're so busy trying to live out someone else's ideas. But other people and their opinions hold no power in defining our destiny."*

What do you do in the middle of sea with a fairly good ship under attack from the raging waters? Do you rush to control the storm, or do you put your faith in yourself and control the ship, the only thing that can save your life? Unless you have a strong grip on the ship, you can never control the waves of the ocean, for it is true that an uncontrolled ship is vulnerable even to the slightest wind, whereas a well-controlled one can withstand a mighty storm. So it is with life. Self-confidence must precede confidence in your fellow men; otherwise, the trust you put in others will be nothing but naiveté as even your fellow men will never trust you if you do not trust yourself.

I have said this before about other qualities of brilliant minds, and I will say it again about self-confidence, and that is that it has no substitute. You simply cannot have other qualities and hope that they will fill the gap of self-confidence. No other quality can take its place; either you have it and let its magic unfold, or you do not and live a second-class life. Self-confidence is an incredible master key that opens all sorts of doors of greatness. Those who have wisely used it have left indelible marks in the hearts of generations. In fact, they have immortalized themselves, and among them some we call sons of God, some prophets, some geniuses, some saints, some great explorers, some skillful statesmen, some gifted writers, poets, artists, industrialists, etc. Self-confidence arouses intelligence as very few virtues can.

If you have taken exams and you are reading this book, as I must assume you have, self-confidence is by far the most frequent advice students get from teachers or administrators.

www.makanologos.com

On multiple choice exams, students are often advised, "Do not leave a question unanswered; make a guess if you do not know the answer." But guess who makes the best guesses most of the time? The one who trusts himself the most.

Self-confidence is not a matter of choice. The goal is to imitate brilliant minds if the venture of climbing the mountain of greatness is to be achieved. In fact, if you are somewhat undecided as to which quality you should start nurturing, I would suggest that before you breed any other quality, you should start with self-confidence. I cannot possibly stretch this long enough to emphasize that self-confidence is imperative if one wants to arouse his or her intelligence and climb the mountain of greatness. It works with all other qualities, but no other quality takes its place. *"In the heart of every man lies hid the flower of intuition,"* writes Mary Bailey. But through which channel does intuition come? How do you think pioneers get training in the field never before undertaken by man? How do you think geniuses sharpen their reasoning faculties? How do you think a child dares to stand and walk? I certainly leave those questions unanswered for your own exercise, but if you need a hint from me as to where to start, I will give you some initials, then you do the rest — and those initials are S.C.

Nature does befriend and trust its secrets to one and one person only, and that is a self-confident man. How many times have you heard people going hundreds or thousands of miles in search of wealth and happiness when in fact they basically leave it behind hidden in their own backyards? Ralph Waldo Emerson once said, *"If I have lost confidence in myself, I have the universe against me."* There you have it. The battle of winning confidence of self is like a battle against the universe. You know you are on the winning side when your self-confidence is growing, and the more doubtful and fearful you are of yourself, the more evident that your inner powers are threatened with serious exhaustion.

www.makanologos.com

"The kingdom of heaven is within," said the Good Master. All that man has, material or otherwise, comes from within. Maybe you think I am out of my mind. How can money, cars, clothes, friends, etc. come from inside? Yes, they do. Just think about it. Everything you see, touch, or feel was first invisible in our dormant thoughts and feelings inside us, including yourself. Then man started actively feeling and thinking about them until action was taken, then bingo! There is a car, airplane, clothing, etc. Our parents had to think and feel the need to conceive us, one way or another, before we became visible to the eyes of the world. There is one thing that makes man operate *miracles*, if you will, and that is energy. Energy is the fire of everything one can possibly think of, be it love, courage, intelligence, wisdom, silence, self-confidence, money, family, material possessions, etc. Again, energy comes from within. With energy, man can do anything: he can live longer, and he can acquire wisdom, intelligence, wealth, peace, happiness, friends, etc. In fact, energy is life and does not come from any magic pill without but from beyond man's eye, in the world within us. The moment we run out of energy within us, everything is lost, including the physical body, for life will have nothing to do with it since it will instantly become the food of the worms.

People with self-confidence tend to unconsciously draw energy from a mysterious source from the Infinite Magnetizing Field (IMF) we spoke about in previous chapters, in order to enable them to fend off negative forces that would paralyze most people in a matter of seconds. They have some inexplicable ability to transform that energy into what they desire, whereas those with less self-confidence tend to have less energy, as they need barely enough to make the next achievement if they have any at all. This is probably due to the fact that Supernatural Helpers or Invisible Teachers of mankind, who ceaselessly walk the Earth in search of worthy channels through which to express their desires more beautifully, usually take over when a person unfailingly demonstrates his or her power of self-confidence or dauntless dependability. Thus, cultivation of self-confidence will force Mother Nature to pour into you more energy, and by energy I do not mean merely health but the ability and wisdom to transform the laws of nature into things that soften life—now mark you, not for the purpose of abolishing life's challenges, for these will always be with us as *garde-fous* of our inner evolution. A strong, firm, and rational self-confidence is indispensable for any person who wants to arouse intelligence and climb the mountain of greatness. It is to a brilliant mind in particular and greatness in general what air is to life or water is to fish. Self-confidence is in fact the mother of all human achievements.

It is virtually impossible to exaggerate the significance of a balanced self-confidence. No man comes closer to achieving self-knowledge than a self-confident person. Self-confidence is indeed the true expression of self-knowledge, the only knowledge needed for great achievements in life. With self-confidence, man grades himself with actual grades, the grades that matter in life, not the ones labeled on us in school or elsewhere by the external world. Actually, it is these external labels that suffocate self-confidence in many people, and those who dare to rationally defy them develop an incredible self-confidence that enables them to break any glass ceiling that society sets for them. There are countless C-grade students out there who perform in real life incredibly far better than A-grade students. If you refuse to accept whatever grade the school system places on you and you wisely stick with your self-grade according to your performance in life, you can reach any height of greatness that you set for yourself. *"Attitudes are more important than facts,"* wrote Norman Vincent Pearle, quoting Dr. Karl Menninger.

It would be a disservice to my readers to just praise self-confidence without suggesting some ways and means to develop it. I am mindful that if you have read this book this far, chances are you must have read similar books, and you

www.makanologos.com

can bet that I have read many of them as well. Therefore, I will try to give you a prescription for self-confidence that I strongly believe has not been recommended by many authors in the details I tend to prescribe here. But before I press forward, let me try to define self-confidence one more time so that you can probably see the other side of the river from here before daring to swim across it. Self-confidence is a feeling that drives out the feelings of self-doubt, fear, impatience, and anger while inspiring, for instance, the four cardinal virtues of the Christian tradition: Prudence, Justice, Restraint, and Temperance. I include courage and fortitude as well, as well as virtues such as coherence, composure, and fitness of thought, speech, and actions. All of these are qualified by the Eightfold Path of Buddhist illumination: Right Belief, Right Intentions, Right Speech, Right Action, Right Livelihood, Right Endeavoring, Right Mindfulness, and Right Concentration. Now, wait a minute! Did I say self-confidence is the absence of fear or doubt? Pardon me if that is the impression you got. *"Courage is not the absence of fear, but rather the judgment that something else is more important than fear,"* Ambrose Redmoon is quoted to have said. Self-confidence is the desire to live your life confidently despite the existence of negative forces around us, and the willingness to inspire fellow men with the higher and better feelings.

You can bet that if there were a pill that would magically turn self-doubt and misestimating people to self-confidence at once, that pill would be given free or required like a vaccine around the world, despite its cost. I say this to give you an idea of how important self-confident is to life in general. Forget about personal problems for a minute. By itself, self-confidence, fully expressed in all of us, would solve overnight all the problems governments around the world have been dealing with since God only knows when. Thus, if by way of this writing I can ignite a small fire of self-confidence in my readers, the meaning of my humble life would be more than fulfilled beyond my wildest imagination. Jack Welch, the former CEO of General

www.makanologos.com

Electric, once said, *"Giving people self-confidence is by far the most important thing that I can do. Because then they will act."* And before Welch, the English poet Samuel Johnson said: *"Self confidence is the first requisite to great undertakings."* Now you understand why I take the task of inspiring self-confidence very seriously. And because of its importance to me, I will go as far as I can in history and dig through ancient records of wisdom, not necessarily to show you how I see it through my lenses, but more importantly to enable you to look at it through your own lenses.

Ancient records of wisdom, of course, have many archeological sites where the truth may be or has been found in different forms yet identical in substance to the Vedas of ancient India, which tell, *"Truth is one; the sages speak of it by many names."* I simply prefer to dive deep into the ocean of a more ancient source of wisdom, the cradle of civilization on the banks of the Nile River, the land of the Great Pyramid of Giza, and that is ancient Egypt, the mother of all civilizations, in the deep interior of the very heart of the Egyptian pyramid where some of the most outstanding Masters of wisdom the world has ever known—including Enoch, Thoth, Hermes Trismegistus, Zarathustra, Abraham, Moses, Pythagoras, Plato, the Good Lord, the Magnificent Comte de Saint Germain, Francis Bacon, and many more great souls unnamed by human tongue throughout the ages from the four corners of the world, the East, West, North and South—are said to have had their initiation under the guidance of Fantastic Teachers from the Wonderful Temples of Light of the Planet Venus and the Sun Itself. As a Masonic writer, John R. Bennett wrote in the earlier-mentioned publication:

Egypt has always been considered the birthplace of the Mysteries. It was there the ceremonies of initiation were first established. It was there that truth was first veiled in allegory and the dogmas of religion were first imparted under symbolic forms. From Egypt this system of symbols was disseminated through Greece and Rome

Exalted Secrets of Brilliant Minds **439**

and other countries of Europe and Asia, giving origin, through many immediate steps, to that mysterious association which is now represented by the Freemasonry (page 4).

I will explore just a *"FLASH"* of what was taught there, known as the Four Words or Activities, which bring Faith and Reason or science to the complement and acceptance of each other, and were used by the Ancient Sages as tools to ignite the Fire of self-confidence in their students. They are: ***"To know, to dare; to will, and to keep silent."*** As a source of self-confidence, of these four words, Levi writes:

Boldness united to intelligence is the mother of all success in this world. To undertake, one must know; to accomplish, one must will; to will really, one must dare; and in order to gather in peace the fruits of one's audacity, one must keep silent. TO KNOW, TO WILL, TO DARE, TO KEEP SILENT, are, as we have said elsewhere, the four kabalistic words which correspond to the four letters of the tetragrammaton and to the four hieroglyphic forms of the sphinx. To know, is the human head; to dare, the claws of the lion; to will, the mighty flanks of the bull; to keep silent, the mystical wings of the eagle. He only maintains his position above other men who does not prostitute the secrets of his intelligence to their commentary and their laughter.

All men who are really strong are magnetizers, and the universal agent obeys their will. It is thus that they work marvels. They make themselves believed, they make themselves followed, and when they say: This is thus, "Nature changes (in a sense) to the eyes of the vulgar, and becomes what the great man wished. This is my flesh and this is my blood," said a Man who had make himself God by His virtues; and eighteen centuries, in the presence of a piece of bread and a little wine, have seen, touched, tasted and adored flesh and blood made divine by martyrdom! Say now human will not accomplish miracles, (The Key of the Mysteries, pages, 150-151).

The attentive reader must have detected thus far that these rules of conduct to unleash the volcano of self-confidence—

www.makanologos.com

to know, to will, to dare, and to be silent—are basically the principal object of this work, for this is one the best-kept secrets of brilliant minds, this is how intelligence is aroused, and this is the ELIXIR OF INTELLIGENCE, because light is its own defense, and inspiration is its own revelation. This is how you watch and look within the light. Seeing all within it, you make joy live in you and others, for there is nothing hidden that is not revealed to a constructive seeker who needs to know it so long as he/she stands for the Highest Ideal in the universe and honor to life is the motive for which you do everything. This is the end of the road, for this is how the great ones of old gained their immortality and a place of honor in the hearts of all generations to come, and so can you. For that reason alone, I will to a great extent restrain myself from going deep and wide here, as many germs of this section have already been conveniently used in previous chapters, and if repeated here, they would be for decorative purposes only, which I very much believe would be a waste of the precious time of the reader as well as the space where some other useful ideas could be slipped in. If the reader feels the need for better clarification, he or she will benefit greatly by going back to the appropriate chapter, reread it, and ponder the material. In fact, it is my conviction that to get the most out of this book, the reader should read it at least more than once, and if possible, the reader should keep it in a reference library where he or she has trouble-free access for easy and frequent consultations. Not to look boastful, but I can almost guarantee that this is not a book you read just once and comprehend what is herein discussed. Casual reading will not do it, either. A wiser reader will do himself a great favor by keeping this book as a true treasure, because it is. Let's now briefly explore each of these rules.

I. TO KNOW

"Knowledge is the food of the soul," said Plato. Just as the sun is indispensable to life, so is knowledge to the achievement

www.makanologos.com

of greatness. A brilliant mind is itself a synonym for acquisition of knowledge. It is basically impossible to imagine a person who has climbed the mountain of greatness without sufficiently arming him- or herself with knowledge. Knowledge is not just a bulwark against the devil of ignorance; it is indeed one of the best weapons of success. Of knowledge, Benjamin Franklin said that it is an investment that pays the best interest, and contrasting knowledge with ignorance, William Shakespeare said, *"Ignorance is the curse of God; knowledge is the wing wherewith we fly to heaven."* It is much easier to be self-confident when you know something or more than when you are totally ignorant of a thing or situation.

Just as every edifice that is hoped to last or at least sustain some of the challenges of nature must have a solid foundation, a brilliant mind must rest on knowledge more than anything else. Nothing is more naïve than a mind that consoles itself with ignorance or inadequate knowledge while hoping to attain greatness at the same time. There is a reason why there is a proverb that says, *"Hope is not a method."* Can you imagine a person who has no knowledge of what he wants, even a bare minimum, becoming victorious in the battle of life? *"Knowledge is power,"* said Shakespeare, and to that Peter Drucker added, *"Today knowledge has power. It controls access to opportunity and advancement."* Of course, I do not take all these quotations at face value. Here I will show that knowledge unused not only passes from the mind, but it is no power at all.

How many times in life have opportunities come to an ignorant man and gone unnoticed? To be able to turn metals of life into gold, ideas into fortune, sweat into happiness, one must seek and possess knowledge or risk the possibility of not only failing to climb the mountain of greatness but also of becoming a doormat of fellow men. By nature, people are either too cold or too hot to an ignorant person, and when people are too cold or too hot toward you, that means they either want nothing to do with you or want to misuse and abuse you as their needs dictate.

www.makanologos.com

"We all need someone to lean on," says a famous lyric. But that someone is not just anyone, and most definitely not an ignorant person. That someone is a knowledgeable person. To climb the mountain, you will need to lean on others. For those others to support you, you must attract them with your knowledge first and foremost. When you have knowledge, people do not voluntarily come to you to be leaned on; in fact, they come with a strong desire to lean on you for their own purposes. And because of your knowledge, not only will you be able to attract them, but you will be able to lean on them at their own pleasure as long as you are wise enough to produce a win-win outcome in the relationship. That is the power of knowledge, and that is how the great ones aroused their intelligence and got to the top of the mountain of greatness.

But knowledge, of course, can be innate or learned. We all have used both sorts of knowledge to get where we are today, but the knowledge that gets man to the peak of the mountain of greatness is rarely inborn. There are few people, if any at all, who acquired a brilliant mind solely by the power of their innate knowledge. Even prophets had to go through some sort of education, visibly or otherwise. In a previous chapter, I indicated that Jesus was in *invisible colleges* when his father, Joseph, passed away, according to the Aquarium Gospel. Not only did Jesus attend college, before that he had to learn the value of working for a living as a carpenter under the tutelage of his father, Joseph. So you see, we all have to learn somehow. The knowledge that brilliant minds utilize to get to the finish line is learned or acquired knowledge. A truly brilliant mind, a mind that climbs the mountain of greatness, is always enlightened by vigorous study. Nothing propels man into the sky more than a vigorous study, and by study I mean not general studies but the study of yourself, your profession, your interests, or more specifically your bliss.

Knowledge can be a very confusing thing. Having a brilliant mind or climbing the mountain of greatness does not mean

www.makanologos.com

knowing or learning everything—not at all. It simply means knowing well what interests you, your line of work, to the best of your ability, what makes you happy regardless of financial reward. Therefore, in the school of life, in the journey to the mountaintop of greatness, one must not just know what will enable him to get there, but also what he may need to know in order to be victorious. When you tend to learn everything that comes your way, not only do you waste time, but more importantly, you run the risk of confusion and chaos. Information is not knowledge by design; thus, stay well informed in as many aspects of life as possible in order to recognize the world you live in and to acquaint yourself with your fellow men. But relentlessly study and seek understanding, knowledge, and wisdom in your line of work. Hence will you be lifted up and with you, your fellow men. Thus will you do it like the Master in John 12:32, who said, *"And I, if I be lifted up from the earth, will draw all men unto me."* This is one the best-kept secrets of brilliant minds, this is how intelligence is aroused, and this is the ELIXIR OF INTELLIGENCE, because light is its own defense, and inspiration is its own revelation. This is how you watch and look within the light; seeing all within it, you make joy live in you and others, for there is nothing hidden that is not revealed to a constructive seeker who needs to know it so long as he/she stands for the Highest Ideal in the universe and honor to life is the motive for which you do everything. This is the end of the road, for this is how the great ones of old gained their immortality and a place of honor in the hearts of all generations to come, and so can you, so long as you stand for the Highest Ideal in the universe and honor to life is the motive for which you do everything. Thus will you leave the world a better place than you found it as you perform those feats that will almost magically transport you simultaneously both to the top of and in the heart of the mountain of greatness!

An intellect that is enlightened by study must be able to acquire knowledge and understanding as a sponge would absorb water, hot or cold. Understanding and wisdom must be obtained one through the other and vice versa. As the Jewish *Sefer Yetzirah* puts it, "*Understanding through wisdom and wisdom through understanding*" is the first step on the journey toward the mountaintop of greatness. No man, of course, is wise and knowledgeable enough to illumine the world by himself. If you are a seeker of knowledge and wisdom, ponder this question from the Talmud and reflect on its answers: "*Who is wise? He who learns from everyman.*" You must, therefore, seek knowledge and wisdom from every available avenue, and the more wisely you use your knowledge and understanding, the higher will you rise to the mountaintop of greatness. Thus will you acquire an intellect enlightened by study.

Now that you have acquired knowledge, what should you do with it? Knowledge can sometimes be a double-edged sword. It can destroy you as well as destroy others. By itself, unused knowledge only passes from the mind; it serves you very little if at all. But you have it now. What should you do with it? Read on.

II. TO DARE

I have dedicated a whole chapter to courage in this book, filled with tremendous substance and designed to inspire the reader to the limits of his or her own imagination and ability. Thus, I will focus on giving the reader brief but vital counsel on how he or she can acquire courage, which nothing can check except integrity, thus igniting the dormant fire of self-confidence that may be dwelling in him or her at the present time. This, of course, I will do by describing some of the most important impediments to courage, different from the traditional ones such as fear and doubt that many writers have talked about so eloquently.

Let's start with self-pity. Before moving on, let me say that in my previous book, *The Best Kept Secrets of Personal Magnetism*, I

www.makanologos.com

discussed self-pity at great length; thus, I will be a bit cautious here not to repeat myself. Inside all of us, there is truly and literally a fire that can light our dwellings or burn them to ashes. That fire is there, but for most of us, it is not only covered by fear and doubt but mostly by the feelings of pity that we have for ourselves. Personally, I do not know any feeling that is more dangerous than the feeling of self-pity. No feeling sends man to suicide faster than self-pity. It is so dangerous that it can send man to physical death as well as "to second death or death after physical death," if you will. It is the toxic and the most poisonous of all negative feelings. The sole outcome of self-pity is self-destruction. Here is what an authority says about self-pity:

Self-pity is such an innocent looking little attitude, a baby-faced bandit...It is more dangerous than it looks. Self-pity never leads us to God, never improves the situation, and never improves us. It only makes us want to give up, crawl into a hole, and bury ourselves.

Self-pity can lead to self-destruction. It whispers, "End it all. Escape the pain and shame." For some people self-destruction means a suicide attempt. Others would never take their own life in one deadly moment but they kill themselves by degrees. They stop caring for themselves. They overeat, consume alcohol, stop exercising, and become careless about their appearance. They isolate themselves, sending signals that warn away anyone who would come close. (www.intermin.org/en/more, accessed Oct. 11, 2010)

A person who frequently has feelings of self-pity is dangerously drinking low but lethal doses of poison. These types of people can never face the truth, and because they are unable to face the truth, they can never possibly ignite the fire of self-confidence that is imperative in the achievement of greatness, a brilliant mind, and the arousal of intelligence. Truth is not always made to make man happy, but the strength to stand tall without blaming or judging oneself is the fastest

www.makanologos.com

way to flare up the fire of self-confidence. One cannot possibly be conquered by the feeling of self-pity and expect to have the audacity that nothing can check. Thus, to have the courage that stimulates the fire of self-confidence, one must eradicate the feelings of self-pity with all the power of his or her being and mind. Then and then only can he or she expect to dare to look and attempt to arouse his or her intelligence and climb the mountain of greatness.

Life is tough to all of us, as I said earlier. Believe it or not, life is as tough to commoners as it is to kings and lords. In fact, kings are not kings because they are immune to the tortures of life. They are kings because they have spinal cords stronger than those of most of us, to lift and carry the heaviest loads of pain life inflicts on us all. This is not a fantasy from the imagination of the author. Ask those who closely watch politically and economically powerful people, and they will tell you that what we see in public does not come close to the real-life political leaders' lives. Indeed, the smile and the happiness they project outside is many times mere make-believe.

Briefly, life is pitiless, or more accurately unfair, to all of us. Do not waste your time pitying yourself because it will never get you anywhere and will earn you nothing. Self-pity destroys personality, and it is one of the most stifling things that hamper individual development. It is the strongest disintegrating force of anyone's attributes, and it should not be allowed to take hold within someone's feelings or thoughts. Just because you feel pity for yourself does not mean the world will come to your rescue—not at all. Indeed, very few people like to associate themselves with self-pitying fellows.

A second element that I want to explain in the analysis of courage is the element of self-forgiveness. While the past is praised for its ability to shed light on the future, it must not be an adhesive substance to hold us back. Why do I bring self-forgiveness into this discussion? Well, many people fail to reach the mountaintop of greatness simply because they

www.makanologos.com

keep thinking of bad things, or they just cannot stop counting failures they, their role models, or their loved ones endured in the past. It is utterly impossible to climb the mountain of greatness and brilliant minds would never be brilliant minds by thinking about past failures in the most negative way.

I am not suggesting that past failures should be entirely eradicated from the mind — not at all. What I am suggesting is that if they should be thought of, it must be as teaching materials, and not discouraging ones. *"To err is human,"* we are told. For as long as man is human, he will always make errors, knowingly or otherwise, that may cause him to fail. The tragedy, of course, is to avoid facing life challenges for fear of failing. I am a strong advocate of carefully looking in the rearview mirror whenever needed while driving on the highways of life.

Life can be overwhelming sometimes; let's face it. Looking on the past in a negative way all the times is never helpful at all. Those who are not capable of facing what they may consider a tragic past are often helped by counting their benedictions, which means recalling the pleasure of past success. The flame of self-confidence is, of course, extinguished by negatively recalling past failures, when many times it is ignited by the memory of happy and successful moments. Think about it. Whenever we think of the joy and happiness we had from a past accomplishment, we tend to relive the moment by engineering another triumph in the present through any daring and rational risk; but whenever we think of a sad moment that resulted in a failure, we tend to be too cautious to the point of even giving up what would be a worthy adventure.

I will close this section by saying a word or two on the impact of perfection or the lack of development of self-confidence. As glorious as perfection is, if it were a real measurement of human greatness, there would never be any great man in the history of mankind. The *Oxford American Desk Dictionary and Thesaurus* defines *perfection* as "faultlessness." Imagine for just a moment what this world would be if there were among us some mortals

www.makanologos.com

who could never possibly make a mistake. If that were possible, man would have found the elixir of immortality, or at least we could have found cures for some of the most incurable diseases, including maladies and many other despicable diseases that have inflicted pain on man for centuries.

Unfortunately, perfection is not possible for any member of the human race. Now, what should we do? Should we close our hands just because we cannot do things faultlessly? Audacity that nothing can check is never achieved by avoiding mistakes but rather by learning from them. Nothing teaches better than past experience. For centuries, man has been learning and doing through one and one way only, and that is by trial and error. All the man-made marvels you can think of have come to us through that same method of trial and error. Therefore, if you are dead serious about kindling the dormant flame of self-confidence in you, you should never be afraid of testing the tool of achievement that has stood the test of time. Do not aim at perfection just as you do not want to aim at error. While perfection is a very noble goal, greatness is not about achieving perfection; it is about breaking through; it is about making life better, not perfect. Take your flame of self-confidence to the mountaintop one step at the time and you will light all the valleys, plateaus, and plains below.

III. TO WILL

Much in this section will be elaborated in the next chapter, yet we are here, so I will treat it as it works to ignite and strengthen self-confidence and as the Egyptians and other ancient schools of wisdom characterized the utmost manifestation of this tremendous power as *"the will nothing can conquer."* The will that in some instances is interpreted as action or desire is one of the most important ideal concepts or qualities humans can acquire. In the study of Jewish mysticism, or Kabbalah, in the arrangement of the *Ten Ineffable Sefirot*, or Divine Emanations,

www.makanologos.com

that are the subjects of kabbalistic study, the WILL, which is represented by what is called *keter* in Hebrew, is placed at the very top of the *Tree of Life*, or the Cosmic Tree, as well as the tree of knowledge, making it of all Divine Emanations' qualities the closest to God, and in some instances it is interpreted as God Himself.

Of the Will, in the *Sefer Yetzicah: The book of creation in theory and practice*, Rabbi Aryeh Kaplan writes, "*Will is even higher than wisdom, since it is the impulse that gives rise to all things, even thought. In kabalistic terms, will is designated as Crown (keter). Just as the crown is above the head, so is the Will above and outside all mental process*" (page 19). Thus it is that when the human will has grown to its fullest stature, man enters the kingdom of God by becoming Master of the energy within himself and in the world around him.

In the duality of the law of nature, the law of cause and effect, good and evil, above and below, etc. is said to be the cause of all action as opposed to effect, of good as opposed to evil, of above as opposed to below. It may seem naïve to say that will is greater than wisdom or love, but if you look at it with an independent mind-set, you will basically agree because will is in fact the cause of wisdom and love and any other quality or virtue you may think of. In his description of the will, Rabbi Kaplan, in the same work, goes on saying:

The highest faculty in man is will. This corresponds to the first of the Siferot, Keter (Crown). If one were to attempt to describe God, it would be tempting to say that He is pure Will. This would be very much like saying that God is "Spirit," or that He is "Love," since all such descriptions attempt to depict God in terms of human traits. If any human trait were to be used, however, it should be will since this is the highest of all human faculties... Keter (will) is said to be "good" since it is the Sefirah closest to God (pages 38, 45).

In English, there is an adage that says, "*Where there is a will, there is a way.*" It is truly amazing what man can achieve when

www.makanologos.com

he is really determined to keep his will in an unconquerable mood in everything he faces regardless of the nature of difficult or opposing forces. Ocean, land, and space have all been conquered by, more than anyone else, a man of strong will alone. A man of a strong will, incapable of giving up to any obstacle regardless of its magnitude, does not have the word *impossible* in his vocabulary, much less an image of it in his mind. He goes from conquest to conquest, from victory to victory like a hungry tiger in the midst of a herd of gazelles.

Only he who sees the seed of good in everything and the germs of triumph even in evil acquires this type of will. Wait a minute; I can feel some readers scratching their heads, asking themselves, *How can there be a seed of good in evil?* Yes there is, just as there is a seed of evil in good, depending, of course, on how you see and use it. I will show you how. Remember the quotation of Mary Bailey that opened this chapter? Let's just put a portion of it here to refresh your memory: "*Sometimes one can turn a potential harmful or negative situation into positive channels because at the heart, or root, of every negative force lies the germ or seed of a positive energy.*" Misused love, wisdom, or power can easily become destructive, not because love, wisdom, and power are bad things, but because their misuse can germinate an evil seed at the expense of the good one. So a man of strong will, the will that nothing can conquer, always sees and seeks the constructiveness in every challenge that life throws at him and deals with it accordingly, without lamentation or quitting.

A person who faces every life challenge with resolute positive and constructive feelings and thoughts, regardless of hardship, almost magically ends up finding solutions to all his problems. Will, as mentioned above, is also desire, and the origin of the word *desire* in Latin says it all: "*from Latin desiderare 'await what the stars will bring,' from the phrase de sidere 'from the stars,' from sidus (gen. sideris) 'heavenly body, star, constellation'*" (www.etmonlive.com/index.php?term=desire, accessed Oct. 11, 2010).

Well, men of strong and constructive will get inspiration that can be granted only by Invisible Helpers and the wisdom that only human experience can teach. *"The difference between a successful person and others is not a lack of strength, not a lack of knowledge, but rather a lack of will,"* says Vince Lombardi. **And Norman Vincent Peale adds:**

> *The feelings of confidence depend upon the types of thoughts that habitually occupy the mind. Think defeat and you are bound to feel defeated. But practice thinking confident thoughts, make it a dominating habit, and you will develop such a strong sense of capacity that regardless of what difficulties arise you will be able to overcome them. Feelings of confidence actually induce increased strength...The secret is to fill your mind with thoughts of faith, confidence, and security. This will expel all thoughts of doubt, all lack of confidence* (pages, 27, 28).

This is the Will that nothing can conquer, but no one can really prove that to you. Reading the best books ever written by the best writers ever born will not prove it to you. Counsel from the best teachers and education from the best schools on the face of the Earth will not do it for you. You can only prove or disprove it by learning yourself through your own experience of actions. Then will you taste the magic of that holiest of all human qualities, the "WILL" that nothing can conquer. The Will is so sacred that even Gods do not intrude in the will of men; if they did, the world would be perfect by now, but of course they (Gods) would fall to earth as they would have tampered with the Law that is not broken without penalties. The unconditional respect of the Free Will of men is the very covenant between God and man; thus, when you will something with all your strength, you will obtain it; even Invisible Helpers will find a way to bring it to you. That is the power of the true WILL.

www.makanologos.com

IV. TO BE SILENT

Like all the above three addendums, a topic on silence has already been dealt with in this work, and while I have been passionate to the best of my ability with every theme in this work, I believe nowhere have I been more so as I was with the subject of silence. I had to, because the nature of the concept and the reality or meaning of silence itself compel a writer who wishes the best to his readers to dig, like a goldsmith, deep in the Earth through rocks and soil to bring to light the most precious of all metals, gold, which not only enriches its discoverer but excites the eyes and souls of whoever sees or touches it. Everything visible came out of silence, and so everything is destined to go back to the source of its life, silence.

That is the power of silence, which is why it captivated my heart so strongly that, rather than referring my readers to the chapter about silence itself, I feel compelled to say a few more words about it. While I strongly believe it would be in the best interests of the reader to reread the Silence Principle chapter as many times as possible, I will explain some reasons that may have prompted ancient Egyptians to inscribe "to be silent" on the Sphinx and how you can use that same philosophy to arouse your intelligence to climb the mountain of greatness as all brilliant minds do.

I mentioned above that everything came of silence; therefore, everything is bound to return to silence so the proclamation of the ancients, "as above, so below," can be fulfilled. Well, if you take these words literally, you will surely get it wrong. What is meant is that silence is the source of all inspiration, and as the source of all inspiration, silence shapes all thoughts and clothes them with feelings that enable them to successfully come to life and enhance the human experience in whatever perspective of life he is heading. The thoughts and feelings that are inspired by a genuine silence are so clear and unmistakable, like sun at high noon, that they engrave themselves in the faith and reason

www.makanologos.com

of a person; they become a set of a principled life philosophy that nothing can corrupt or intoxicate.

When man has reached the point where silence becomes a mantle of fragrance to his mind and body, that person has reached or is at the point of no return to the pinnacle of the highest power any human can reach while yet moving in the physical body. Our spatial bodies allow us to move in any direction in our environment; our temporal bodies allow us to move in one and only one direction, toward the future; while our spatial and temporal bodies drag each other, causing the physical body to grind against time and space. Evidently the body tires and retires from life much faster than it would otherwise do. Silence brings the spatial and the temporal bodies harmoniously together and allows them to move through space and time not only peacefully, but most importantly effectively, therefore annihilating the notion of both time and space and making the ascension to the mountaintop of greatness not only possible but enjoyable.

That is the power of being incorruptibly silent and unimpressed by the dreams of the physical senses. There are countless things that can easily make man reach to the lowest point of character in life, but among the few that enable man to reach up high to success, nothing empowers man to reach up to the mountaintop of greatness like the power of silence. When man silently endeavors to reach up to his Higher Self, nature, as a matter of law, comes to his assistance and reveals itself to him with gifts that come beyond the reach of physical senses and surpass the understanding of the human mind. Man is just like a bird. In fact, unlike that natural bird that flies just several yards above the Earth, man is a better bird with better wings that can take him to the heart of infinity. Our traditions have rendered the wings of man obsolete. We erroneously believed that the airplane, automobile, trains, or boats would transport us faster than we can transport ourselves. We have forgotten that with the wings of silence and desire, we can reach any

www.makanologos.com

distance in space and any point in time and discover the necessary wisdom and understanding that can take us to the mountaintop of greatness.

If life is a sky and silence is the sun, they illumine anyone who dares to get out of the shadow. Great things have never been apprehended in the mayhem but always in the light of silence. Just as the light comes from above, only from silence comes inspiration, which lifts man to greatness and strength from action. A man who is enfolded in the mantle of silence is similar to a mysterious power that makes the enemy tremble like a leaf of a plant before a storm. The power of silence is many times inadequately described by the human vocabulary, for it is really multi-dimensional. It is like that of the soil when given a high-quality seed; it gives back manifold what it was initially given.

When you sow a few grains of rice, nature gives you in return countless grains of rice. Likewise, take one idea, go with it in the great silence, and before your inner eyes, your idea will reveal itself in every dimension possible. Let me close by reminding you that all powers of nature find their inexhaustible source in the realm of silence. Water, air, fire, electricity, gravitation, art, science, mind, etc.—all charge and recharge themselves from the almighty battery known as silence. There is no power as potent as the power of silence, and a man who solemnly acts in silence is the one who governs all petty souls whose peace is troubled by the winds of life, like the water of the ocean that is troubled by the wind of the air above it. Silence is golden, we are told, so learn to frequently enter into your temple of silence, and the world will forsake theirs and come worship in yours, making you the high priest and the point of contact with the Most High.

Silence is the real book of life, written in a language understandable only to disciplined and consciously hushed minds and intellects, a powerhouse of great and unthinkable treasures of wisdom with understanding and understanding

www.makanologos.com

with wisdom. Silence is the great treasure house of the universe, where all of everything that has ever been imagined by a human mind or will ever be thought by a human intellect is. In the silence is where both the human mind and the intellect lock on to the problem at hand until a lasting and effective solution is found. As Rabbi Kaplan puts it:

When one is locked on to a problem, there is tremendous, almost sensual joy in solving it. It is possible to go without food and sleep, to dismiss all fatigue, until the problem is solved. Beyond this, it appears that one can call forth intellectual resources of which one is usually unaware. Being locked on to a problem also brings a problem into a state of consciousness different from his normal state. A much greater portion of the mind seems to be involved in solving the problem than in normal mental state. It could therefore be considered a "problem solving" state of consciousness (Jewish Meditation, pages, 28-29).

Hundreds and thousands of generations later, the world still marvels at the work of the Egyptians and Babylonians, of geniuses such as Moses, Confucius, Plato, Alexander the Great, Jesus, Buddha, Isaac Newton, Galileo, Joan of Arc, and Columbus, to name a few. In fact, we still believe their works are beyond our reach to the point that we have surrendered and find comfort in simply worshiping many of them as if these people were humans of a different breed, which of course is not true, since they themselves were stunned with the outcome of their own feats as most of them were simply the results of unintended consequences. It may help you to remember this—you have everything the geniuses of old we worship today had. We were all created out of the same fabric, dirt, and were animated with the same breath, except our genius brothers and sisters were or are capable of locking on their desires in the silence of their inner chambers until their minds and intellects appeared godlike to themselves, to most of their contemporaries, and to generations afterwards.

www.makanologos.com

On the imperativeness of relaxing both the mind and the intellect in the "temple of silence" in order to stimulate a creative or solution-oriented attitude toward any problem, Rabbi Kaplan expands his reasoning quite effectively in these words:

It may be that the secret of geniuses is the ability to lock on to problems or creative efforts on a much deeper level than most people ordinarily attain. This lock-on state of consciousness appears to be associated with physical energy...It seems that the mind has two modes in which it possesses abnormal ability to solve problems. One is the lock-on mode, in which the energy of both mind and body is increased. The other is when a person is completely relaxed and mind drifts to the problem on its own. I think of the lock-on mode as a "hot" mode of thought and the relaxed mode as a "cool" mode of thought. In both cases, one's problem-solving ability is tremendously expanded. In hot mode concentration, the entire body is brought into play and, as it were, the adrenaline is made of flow. In cool concentration, body and mind are quieted down as much as possible, so that the mind is able to focus on the problem like a laser beam. (Jewish Meditation, pages, 29-30)

Now, as a final point on this ancient motto—to know, to dare, to will, and to be silent—this I wish you to anchor deep in your heart: if you ever wonder how in the world the pyramids of Egypt were built, how the Hanging Gardens of Babylon were suspended in the air (allegorically, of course), and how the Tower of Babel was erected, or if you ever wanted to build your own pyramid equal to or stronger than those of Egypt, suspend your garden as well as or better than that of Babylon, or erect your own tower as stunning as or taller than that of Babel, you must get wise through the understanding and understanding through the wisdom, power through persistence and persistence through power, strength through action and action through strength, by observing this ancient motto, for it is the holiest of the holy prescriptions of greatness. Man has never known a better one and probably never will

www.makanologos.com

Exalted Secrets of Brilliant Minds **457**

discover a better tool that will lead him to acquisition of pure divine powers, the manipulation of forces, or constructive energy than through positive feelings, thoughts, spoken words, and actions. And speaking of action, let's now go into the next chapter and see how the action principle plays a role in the fabric of greatness as we enjoy this poem of self-confidence.

Self Confidence

Self-confidence
What art thou?
Thou art
The bread and wine of the strong minds
The central power of the being,
Feeling of higher vibration little known to man
Anchor of balance and strength
Impregnating seed of all virtues,

In the majesty of thy presence
No storm dares to approach
All fears melt,
All doubts bow,
All greed vanishes,
All irritation transmutes,
But
Music is seen,
Joy lives,
Silence sings,
Action triumphs
Faith deepens,
Hope radiates,
Charity blossoms,
Like a flower on the banks of a soothing river

www.makanologos.com

Thy eyes like a sunbeam
Thy ears to all true seekers' voice listen
Thy mouth sacred tongue speaks
Thy hands a golden shield and flaming spear hold
Thy feet onward victory forever march
Thy shadow cloak of invincibility is

Unknown to the weak
Mystery to the wicked
Worthless to the fools
Priceless to the wise thou art.

May earnest students of wisdom cherish thee!
May the brave always in thy shadow live!
May the great share thy fruits!
May every wise mother from
The womb shower every child of thee
Thy absolute magnificence and magnitude teach.
Then and then only
Will ours be a world of the brave?
Bright and true brothers and sisters,
In peace and prosperity thereafter live.
By Wisdom J.O.Y. Makano, the author

www.makanologos.com

CHAPTER XIX

The Action Pillar

If we patiently and deliberately work toward our goal, then, the mystics say, we are more likely to receive inspiration. This flash of ingenuity and brilliance is facilitated by consistently working toward a goal...the armor and wisdom we develop when we fail. It is an understanding that we fail many times, and that our greatest glories occur when we try after each failure...reminds us that true genius is the result of painful exertion, that practice and failure bring us closer to our goal. (Daniel I. Schwartz, Finding Joy, page 94)

Ladies and gentlemen, let's start by saying that we hold this truth to be self-evident that Mother Nature is not blind, deaf, or senseless, for It knows when to rain and when to shine, when to plant, when to grow and when to kill, when and who to supply and when and who to deplete from, when to reward and when to punish, when to sunrise and when to sunset. We hold this truth to be self-evident that nature never misses its target by an inch or a second. We hold this truth to be self-evident that Mother Nature rewards or punishes every cause with a corresponding effect with perfect precision. We hold this truth to be self-evident that we humans are not here to fix a thing, for nothing is broken despite all the trumpets of the mortal minds of the scientific world. We are here to simply live by the Laws of Mother Nature and harvest accordingly.

We hold this truth to be self-evident that we are here to fix neither land nor air, neither water nor fire, neither life nor death, neither good nor bad. We are here to live a constructive life to the best of our abilities. Is there anyone among my venerable readers who thinks otherwise? Well, whether you agree or disagree, I ask you to hold your verdict until at least you come to the conclusion of the chapter, but the most appropriate time would be after you have analyzed everything in this declaration under meticulous scrutiny of your own life experience, of those around you, and especially of those who have really practically lived these principles in the eyes of honest observers.

There is, of course, a reason why I felt strongly to open this chapter with emulation of the famous Declaration of Independence of the United States of America—not to make a political point, of course, but to capture your attention more strongly so as to make you, the reader, think seriously on the points I am trying to make here so that you impress whatever you take from these pages more strongly on your mind and intellect. I hope, of course, it will help set off a mechanism of change or improvement for the better in your own life and that of those in your environment, as well as the world in general. And here we go. There will be nothing new here. I will not tell you that what I am about to state will be something that has never been said or thought by any human before. In fact, everything I have said so far and what I still have to say has been thought and said billions of times, and that is why I have quoted other authors. The difference, of course, is that these things seem so obvious to many of us that we disregard their powers because we think they should be said in an extraordinary way. Here I strive to say them in the simplest manner possible.

What I hope to achieve here is to remind my readers that the era of prophets is probably over, and if it is not, the truth is that most of us are more likely to be hit by lightning than to see a universally accepted prophet or clairvoyant in our lifetime. That said, remember this: the truth is ageless, self-proving, and, as the Vedas were quoted earlier as saying, *"Truth is one; the sages speak of it by many names."* Truth does not need a prophet or a mystic to say it in order for it to work its miracles. And one of those truths is this: life is always in perpetual motion, and anyone who tries, even slightly, to obstruct its movement pays a very high price, indeed. Life never slumbers, rests, or sleeps,

www.makanologos.com

even when man seems to sleep or rest. It moves constantly on all fronts, physically and mentally, as feelings, thoughts, and actions rotate in endless circles, and any attempt to stop that motion can only prove catastrophic. There is no prayer or cave that can save a person who is attempting to stop the motion of life because motion is action, action is God, and anyone who fights God always loses.

Either you move along, you cooperate with the movement of life, or you pay a horrible price, and the only way one can comply with this inescapable demand of life is the observance of the Action Principle. Life is energy, and energy is always expending at the expense of anything that is motionless and to the benefit of everything that expands or moves along with it. Here lies one of the most sacred secrets of life. There is not a more damning curse to life than inactivity. If our home planet, the Earth, itself must work hard 24 hours per day, 7 days per week, 365 days per year by revolving around the sun over and over while rotating around its axis to give us seconds, minutes, hours, days, weeks, months, seasons, years, decades, centuries, etc. in order to allow everything on it to come in existence, live, and leave room for the cycle to continue, why should you and I be exempted from activity? Everything else is possibly forgivable, but a person who stands still in the middle of life gets pitilessly crushed by a hundred-billion-pound train of life, while the one who cooperates with the law of activity may either be spared, given a second chance, or flown on the wings of ecstasy, depending on the level and quality of his or her cooperation. Life does not put up with lethargy. The unforgivable sin, which is much talked about in sacred scripture, is probably the attempt to live inactively. Work is the truest prayer, and anyone who works prays to God, whether you are an atheist or not, whether you know it or not. It does not matter; the law does not change because of your ignorance or knowledge of it. When you are working, especially when you are working for a noble cause, you are in touch with God.

www.makanologos.com

Christians like to talk about the antichrist. If there is such a thing as the antichrist, I would not be surprised that indolence or inactivity would be it. An idle mind is not only anti-progress; it is above all a destructive force against its possessor and society in general. Life fights with all teeth and nails against inactivity because action is such an integral part of life. Without it, the world would precipitously spin to a crashing disintegration. The thing to remember is that actions we take are not always for ourselves alone. Even though we are the ones who benefit from them the most, our actions are for the world we live in as well, hence the need to take every action or activity as a privileged responsibility and trust given by life. Therefore, every action must be performed with utmost care and humility. If there is a great fight worth fighting for, it is the fight against apathy, for it destroys life in all its dimensions, slowly but surely.

Inaction is not only a destructive force; it is self-destructive as well. Inactivity is always a direct result of feelings of apathy; the feeling of action always stimulates a brilliant mind. Because this (action) is one of the best-kept secrets of brilliant minds, this is how **intelligence is aroused**, and this is the ELIXIR OF INTELLIGENCE, because light is its own defense, and inspiration is its own revelation through action and action alone. This is how you watch and look within the light; seeing all within it, you make joy live in you and others, for there is nothing hidden that is not revealed to a constructive seeker who needs to know it so long as he/she stands for the Highest Ideal in the universe and honor to life is the motive for which he/she does everything. This is the end of the road, for this is how the great ones of old gained their immortality and a place of honor in the hearts of all generations to come, and so can you, so long as you stand for the Highest Ideal in the universe and honor to life is the motive for which you do everything.

Just as the feelings of inactivity lead to apathy, the feelings of constructive actions lead to achievement and greatness. If there is a single most important thing that climbing the mountain

www.makanologos.com

of greatness needs most, it is a constructive action. Action is where the rubber meets the road, where the virtues become visible to the human eye. I do not know how else I can make this clear; the scream from the bottom of my lungs may not travel through space and time as I would like; perhaps spelling the word **A-C-T-I-O-N** in both caps and bold will help. All the principles of greatness discussed in the book are nothing or useless unless they are acted upon. Here a point must be made quickly. This work is for use by those who are still in this world of duality and polarity, the world of cause and effect, high and low, left and right, positive and negative, good and evil, male and female, life and death, etc. I want to make clear that I am well aware that not all actions are beneficial. Thus I want the reader to know and understand that when I say *action* or *activity*, I mean only constructive actions or actions that are well intended and that eventually lead to the achievement of the goal despite mistakes and setbacks along the way. Destructive action is as much antichrist as inaction, if not worse, and I do not know what is worse than antichrist. More light on this point will come later in this chapter.

Action is really the bottom line; it is what matters most. A power plant can be greatly, smartly, wisely, or mightily built, but unless there is a light bulb, it can never light even a small room. Action is the light bulb; it is what people appreciate. When enjoying the light that comes in our houses and places of employment, people do not even think of electrical dams, generators, or the wire that travels hundreds or thousands of miles underground or over our heads. They think mostly of the light bulb, and so it is with action. Of course, there is a web of feelings and thoughts that crisscross each other before an action is produced, but fair or not, rightly or wrongly, only on rare occasions do people think about what is behind an action. They care and judge the action first and most of all. Action alone is the light bulb of all principles of greatness.

www.makanologos.com

No one knows what you feel or think until you act; thus our feelings and thoughts are externalized or materialized to the world by way of actions. One can be the wisest, the smartest, or the most perfect man under the sun, but if that is only so in his inner world, no one will pay attention to that particular individual. People are judged by their actions because they are the only thing that make the wheel of the planet roll, that make the world a fair and livable place, and more than that, that make our Earth a surprisingly "brighter star" in the cosmos than we like to give it credit for. "I am tired; I am hungry; I am sleepy; I do not have this or I do not have that" can all be good excuses for inactivity, but a brilliant mind, a mind destined to climb the mountain of greatness, always finds excuses for activity, not for inactivity. When hungry, he eats so he can be active. When tired, he rests so he can act better. When sleepy, he sleeps so he can acquire more energy in order to act both better and longer. When ignorant, he learns so he can act wisely. When sick, he seeks medical attention so he can act powerfully. When lonely, he seeks company so he can empower others. When clueless, he seeks inspiration so he can lead others into action, and so on.

Ours is still a physical world of physical life, and it works well when acted on physically. Even spiritual forces, the Invisible Helpers, depend on our physical actions in order to do for us what they can do only through us. God, if you believe in Him as I do, loves and blesses those who blend mental prayer with physical prayer or work more than those who find excuses for physical inaction in mental prayers. In fact, it is believed that work is the best of all prayers, for it is answered most of the time; it is usually answered on a timely basis. Even the best mental or verbal prayer will produce nothing unless it is backed up by appropriate action or work.

Action is the magic wand in the hands of every workingman. It operates miracles continuously, and it rarely fails. Action is actually the philosopher stone, the royal secret, and the real elixir of life long sought by medieval alchemists. God is

Himself wisdom and intelligence beyond our understanding. He does not side with the indolent who use prayer as an excuse for inaction. He answers almost instantaneously a call made to Him through proper action. A miracle is not necessarily making manna fall from heaven but rather transforming or multiplying what is already here on Earth, and nothing does it better, and almost unfailingly, than a proper action. While nature always shows us its beauty, splendor, and power, it is through action that it really reveals and hands to us the secrets of its magic.

In case you need a reminder, through action alone can man multiply a few grains of corn, rice, peanuts, etc. into countless grains. Through action, men can record thoughts and feelings as well as communicate through space, time, or generations, if you will. Through action, man has transformed himself into a bird (airplane) that can fly and walk on three or four continents in a space of twenty-four hours. Through action, man has walked on the moon. Through action, we all perform miracles in our own right every day. All the power of nature is revealed to us through action. Thus a wise man, a brilliant mind, a man willing to do all it takes to climb the mountain of greatness knows there is no alternative to action. The buck stops with action and nothing else. Wisdom, intelligence, and understanding grow positively through right actions, as a matter of fact. There is no greatness without right action. Can you imagine a Jesus who never preached, a Plato or Shakespeare who never wrote, a Ford who never built cars?

Imagine a Thomas Edison explaining a light bulb without actually building it. Imagine a farmer who tells of harvesting huge amounts of crops without actually planting them. Imagine a schoolboy who praises his own intelligence while failing to perform his homework or schoolwork in general. Imagine a parent who praises his or her family without providing for the needs of his or her children and spouse. Proving the laws of nature through action is the best way of understanding and teaching others and the only way to arouse intelligence and

www.makanologos.com

climb the mountain of greatness. Instinctively, people admire and coalesce around a man of right actions more than anything else. To climb a mountain of greatness, you will always need a helping hand along the way, and thus it can only make your life a little bit easier to prove your credibility through the power and wisdom of your action on your way to the mountaintop of greatness.

One of the most poetic stories of the Bible is the dream that Jacob had when he left Beersheba. He came to a place where he decided to spend the night, and as the day came to nightfall, using a stone as his pillow, he slept. In his sleep, he had a dream in which he saw a ladder set up on the Earth, the top of it reaching to heaven; and there were angels of God ascending and descending on it, according to the book of Genesis 28:11-19. A Jewish *midrash* (according to Wikipedia, the word means a way of interpreting biblical stories that goes beyond simple distillation of religious, legal, or moral teaching), in the words of Rabbi Kaplan, *"teaches that this ladder had four steps. According to great Jewish mystics, they represent the four steps one must climb to reach the highest level of spiritual domain…The first level is that of action, where we are still involved with our bodies."*

Whether you see it in the eyes of great Jewish teachers or through any lens of your choice, the truth is that action alone determines our fate or destiny here and now in this world. Forget for just a little while the acquisition of material things. A man who does not act halts the development of his own physical and mental body in one way or another. All the knowledge we acquire in school or elsewhere serves us nothing unless we put it into right action. Recall what I said earlier: knowledge is power, but knowledge that is not acted on not only passes from the mind, it is no power at all. It is practically impossible for someone who is not in any activity to develop his mental power. Learning is a progressive process, one action at a time. Man cannot suddenly become a mathematician, physician, farmer, teacher, etc. All the books or academic degrees in the world will

www.makanologos.com

not suddenly make you a lawyer, doctor, accountant, scientist, etc. unless you have been taking steps progressively and acting accordingly. While education is a very helpful tool, the bad news for college graduates is that employers favor experience (know-how) over a diploma (theories). And in his famous book *The Greatest Thing in the World,* Henry Drummond wrote on page 53, *"No man can become a saint in his sleep."* Without action, there is no progress; there is no greatness or brilliant mind.

In part of this work, I mentioned that there is no greatness without an underlying pursuit of divine power, which is itself the philosopher stone. I would like to state here once again, as I said above, that nothing sets man in pursuit of divine power better than work or right action. Through work, we pray to God as well as thank Him, and we give back to the community, especially to Mother Nature, for all the precious gifts we receive for free such as the air we breathe, thoughts that come to us unceasingly, the blood that circulates in our bodies, the heartbeats that require no effort on our part, etc.

It is okay to be a good talker or thinker, but people do not believe things because you think or say so; people believe action more than anything else in the world. As far as the power of conviction is concerned, thoughts and speech, if they have any power of conviction at all, cannot possibly have more than twenty-five percent, but actions retain seventy-five percent or more of the power of conviction. Feelings, thoughts, and speech bridge the world though actions. With all their glittering theories, all true prophets mix their speech with miracles (right actions) in order to fortify the conviction of their followers. That is why Mother Nature and society give people of action more responsibilities. A man who does not act is not responsible; a person who has no responsibility does not grow; a man who does not have responsibility cannot acquire a brilliant mind; and a person who does not have a brilliant mind cannot climb the mountain of greatness. Mother Nature makes

www.makanologos.com

sure that an inactive man does not grow spiritually, mentally, and even healthwise.

It is, of course, misleading to give the impression that every action leads to greatness when it is a well-known fact that is not to be the case. This book is about enlightening the minds and intellects of my readers and not propaganda. I expect to be judged for what I put down in this work not only by my contemporaries but by future generations as well. Therefore, I have gone to great lengths to make sure every word in here stands the scrutiny of the most rigorous standards of integrity to ensure my peace of mind now and throughout time and space. Its sole major or ultimate goal is to stimulate a wise and intelligent way of doing great things for the betterment of life in general anywhere here on our home planet.

That said, it would be disingenuous to praise the majesty of action in the search for greatness without suggesting the types of action that lead to that end. The truth is that it would be an insult to the masses of people to give an impression that most people do not climb the mountain of greatness because they do not act. It is a known fact that life without action of some sort is practically impossible. The fact that rich people are rich and poor people are poor does not mean that rich people act more than poor people; they simply happen to act differently, and the quality of action is what makes all the difference in the world. Sometimes, greatness is not attained by acting better than your fellow men, but by acting at the right time and the right place. Sometimes, all it takes is to be there and maybe no action at all, except the action of taking your physical and mental bodies there, and that is it. But the fact is that unless you have a certain state of mind before taking action, your stars may never line themselves up for you to find yourself at the right place at the right time to make you successful despite your smart or hard work. Exemplars are countless. We have seen over and again very smart people working for the less so; we have seen MBAs from Ivy League colleges and universities taking their orders

www.makanologos.com

from far less educated people than themselves. This book is full of these kinds of illustrations. In the next few pages, I will try to explore how you can increase the likelihood of being in the right place at the right time, and of course, after the conquest of the principles of masterful action.

While the understanding of the principles of mastery of action is not foolproof, it is believed that it greatly improves your power of acting the best possible way you can, as well as your odds of being in the right place at the right time. Before I put forward what are believed to be the ingredients of a masterful action, an action that leads to greatness, I want to make sure the reader understands that sometimes a good action performed at the wrong place and wrong time can be as bad as a bad action performed at the right time at the right place.

That said, the question arises, when do you know the right time and right place? This is honestly a very tough question. I do not think there is someone other than yourself who can answer it correctly. How? By checking and carefully examining the message sent to you by your inner feelings or Higher Self. This is true for all of us. Usually before we decide to take a specific action, there is a deliberation inside ourselves between our positive and negative feelings. I am not talking about a mental process that goes on inside our brains for a better understanding of the action we are about to take, but rather the inexplicable mood we feel about moving forward or otherwise with a situation which we may or may not clearly comprehend. The mood that overrides both the reason and emotions is what I am talking about. Paying attention to that inexplicable mood of our inner selves makes a big difference not only between success and failure but also between the possibilities of climbing the mountain of greatness or even getting a clue of where in the world the mountain of greatness is.

Thus, when all the advice in the world either from friends, relatives, experts, or books seems confusing or makes no sense

www.makanologos.com

at all, rely on your feelings. Talk to them if need be. Ask the questions as if you were asking the most trusted friend or expert in the world. Ask your feelings rhetorical and hypothetical questions if necessary, but just do not expect the answer to come in the same language you used. The answers, I am sure, will come, and they will come within you in one of these three ways: you will feel more harmonious with the position you favor the most, you will become more confused and doubtful about everything, or you will be prompted to wait. My own advice is to never act when you have mixed feelings. Of course, we are not all good readers of books of life, let alone our own feelings. Once you have given time to listen to your feelings, you should move at once with a sense of confidence, or with the spirit of risk-taking if your sixth sense impels you to act or drop the plan altogether and move on to the next challenge that life presents you. Meditation on the matter or a time in solitary silence usually clears the cloud that keeps you from seeing the plain view.

After you have decided to take an action, it is important to understand that the single most important thing that will cause your action to reward you with greatness is the motive behind it. The motive of your action, not its outcome, will be the most decisive element of your greatness. Let's cut through the meat and go straight to the bone: there are many noble motives out there that life presents, but none comes close to the motive of acting in the name of the greatest good. A poem in the chapter of courage was written for this purpose. A person who is on a quest for greatness must know one thing, and that is taking action in the name of the greatest good is the shortest way to the mountaintop of greatness.

Actions that are taken in the name of the greatest good are the only ones that have a constructive impact on life in general. The opposite of the action taken in the name of the greatest good would be an action that is taken for selfish reasons. It may seem silly to say that all actions must be taken in the name of the greatest good in order to climb the mountain of greatness. Let me explain this with an illustration of something we all do for selfish reasons yet could have been done for the greatest good (for the sake of goodness and not merely for any probable future compensation). Most of us eat and drink for the most selfish of reasons. We go out to buy food or drink just so we can satisfy ourselves. We eat and drink because we are hungry or thirsty, and we want to satisfy our appetite or quench our thirst for our own survival. Nothing is wrong with satisfying hunger or quenching thirst. It is quite all right. We need it for our physiological functions, but doing it for biological demands is purely selfish and cannot lead to greatness.

On the other hand, when a person eats and drinks in the name of the greatest good, he thinks something like this before finding food or drink to satisfy his appetite or quenching his thirst: "I am hungry or thirsty," he murmurs inside before continuing with his reasoning. "It is important that I eat so I can be healthy, because when I am healthy, I will be able to work. Work will enable me to provide for my family, and because I am able to provide my family, I will be a good parent and spouse. Being a good parent and spouse will cause me to contribute to society by raising good children so they can be good members of society." You can think about work the same way. Let's assume that you are a janitor or that anything in your line of work can lead to greatness. If you just work for the paycheck, even if you are the president of a big bank or a corporation, or even president of a country, you will never climb the mountain of greatness, even if you try in million years.

But if you do your job in the name of the greatest good as a janitor, your climb may be slow, but you will eventually reach the peak as long as you do not reverse course. How? "Okay, I am a janitor," one would think. "My job may be a janitor, but it is an important one. If I don't do it right, I may cause germs to spread and with it an outbreak of diseases and other financial and psychological injuries that may have destructive

www.makanologos.com

consequences to society. But if I do my job right, I will shield people from getting unnecessary illnesses. Thus I will help in keeping people healthy, and if people are healthy, they will work. Work will lead to prosperity and prosperity to peace, etc." You can think likewise of any action, be it of a cook, CEO, journalist, teacher, doctor, lawyer, athlete, mother, father, student, etc. And you will find that behind every action or profession, there is a greatest good that, if pursued with passion, sincerity, and determination, leads to greatness. This is one of the best-kept secrets of brilliant minds, this is how intelligence is aroused, and this is the ELIXIR OF INTELLIGENCE, because light is its own defense and inspiration is its own revelation. This is how you watch and look within the light; seeing all within it, you make joy live in you and others, for there is nothing hidden that is not revealed to a constructive seeker who needs to know it so long as he/she stands for the Highest Ideal in the universe and honor to life is the motive for which he/she does everything. This is the end of the road, for this is how the great ones gained their immortality and a place of honor in the hearts of all generations to come, and so can you, so long as you stand for the Highest Ideal in the universe and honor to life is the motive for which you do everything. Study every action before you act, give it your all, think through it, find the noblest motive for doing it, then go for it. If you are unable to find the noblest motive of an action, or if you are not comfortable with its noblest motive, that should be a good indication of its worthlessness.

The universe is the biggest school of all, and the Earth is one of its best classrooms. We are here to act, act responsibly and constructively, and thus through responsible and constructive actions, we grow in all dimensions of life. Responsibility is the real measure of an effective action, for those who do not act responsibly not only do not grow, but they also do not expand their knowledge, wisdom, and self-confidence, the real engines of progress and greatness itself. Now, having said that, it is

www.makanologos.com

important to mention that as easy as it is to lecture about the need for action and all the rewards that come with it, it is equally important to note that taking an action is not always an easy thing for most of us to do, and I mean action that leads to greatness. That is for a very simple and basic reason: taking a truly rewarding action is a risk, a risk whose light is so bright to the point of blinding many people.

Whether it is better to be blinded by light or darkness, I am wholly unqualified to counsel anyone here. However, what I think I am capable of is suggesting to my readers here is how to fend off the blindness in the first place, be it of the light or the darkness, when it comes to taking action. Actions that facilitate the brightness of the mind can either be common or uncommon, but the reason many of us do not see how we can climb the mountain of greatness through them is that our first reaction to them is usually "I do not know," and then we move on. Of course, if your feelings are not completely harmonious with a thing before taking an action, you may as well forget about greatness.

Regardless of all methods of "doing" things that science advises, the only method that nature has armed us with in our struggle against the outside forces is *trial and error*. It would be good to know everything before doing anything, but that is not always realistic, and most of the time, it is an expectation that does not square with the nature of man. Brilliant minds use the method of trial and error to the fullest extent of their abilities. When we are born, we are born with very little knowledge of our own, so we rely on our parents, teachers, and community to fill the almost empty vase we carry in our minds. While it is not entirely a bad thing to rely on external help in order to move forward in life, a complete reliance on external forces rarely takes someone to the mountaintop of greatness, for greatness is, for the most part, a result of internal strengths. With external forces, we can probably get somewhere, but without internal strengths, we can definitely not get anywhere.

www.makanologos.com

Thus, when facing an action that must be taken when you know very little or nothing about how to move forward, the first attitude must be the desire to learn through the action itself. That way, you dispel any feelings of fear and doubt, and once the monster of fear and doubt is defeated, the desire and ability to learn will grow almost instantaneously.

"Know thyself" is the secret ancient sages of Greece learned from Egyptian priests. *"Teach thyself,"* however, is not only the attitude but also the secret of brilliant minds. When man is equipped with a "teach thyself" (not arrogantly but humbly) mind-set, not only does he learn better, but also great teachers come from all corners of the universe to reveal the truth to him. Some will be driven by a genuine interest to enlighten him, some will be driven by the desire to be a part of a great adventure, and many others will be driven by the desire to make a living in a worthwhile activity, but all will be helpful. A quick recollection of Joseph Campbell's quotation in the last chapter on the help the hero gets from unexpected sources may be a good refresher here. This is the most important reason why some less-educated people climb the mountain of greatness on the shoulders of the more educated folks, and thus you see a small company that started in someone's garage or backyard become a giant global or national player.

With the "teach thyself" attitude, knowledge either unequivocally or painfully, perhaps, but surely reveals itself to us or through our fellow men who admire our courage to take on difficult tasks. Speaking of self-teaching, Rabbi Areyh Kaplan in *Meditation and the Bible*, quoting Rabbi Moshe Chaim Luzzatto (1707-1747), a master kabbalist and philosopher, wrote:

> *God ordained that man should naturally be able to teach himself, understand, and reason with intellect, and thus gain knowledge of things and their properties. On the basis of this knowledge, man is able to infer and deduce things that are not immediately apparent, and he can thus gain a more complete understanding of things.*

www.makanologos.com

This is the natural process of human reason...In this manner, one can gain knowledge of things otherwise accessible to human reason, but in a much clearer manner...This is the level of true prophecy. This is a degree of inspiration in which the individual reaches a level where he literally binds himself to God in such a way that he actually feels this attachment. He then clearly realizes that the One to whom he is bound is God (pages, 22, 23, 24).

I concur, however, that life experiences compel us to not hastily accept, but if you look at your own life, you will find out that those things that you have learned the best are things that you have learned as a result of self-motivation to teach yourself or learn by way of others, but only after a strong suppression of your own obstructive ego.

Yes, action is the ultimate greatness. However, according to the U.S. Census Bureau, there are 6,880,115,098 people (as of November 7, 2010,) when this page was being written (http://www.census.gov/main/www/popclock.html). All these people act in one way or another. Put together, the actions of all people on Earth taken in just one day can range in the trillions. The question is, how many of those actions lead to successful outcomes? Of course, no one can tell how many of those actions potentially lead to greatness, but what we can tell is the quality of actions that lead to greatness.

An attentive reader must by now have concluded that this work is a product of some very serious study. I do not claim everything in this book is an artifact of my intellect alone. I have learned most of the lessons in this book from many teachers, dead and alive, and I am grateful to them all and happy to be their humble student. Thus, the rest of this chapter will be constituted of something of a list of qualities that are thought to impregnate an action with the power of greatness. While the list may seem somewhat long, it is important to note that it is in no specific order. The reader is welcome to appreciate the items according to his or her own taste and circumstances. As a matter of personal choice, I will start with some pearls

www.makanologos.com

of wisdom in regard to action taken from *The Empty Chair* by Rebbe Nachman of Breslov:

- ❖ *"Seek the sacred within the ordinary. Seek the remarkable with the commonplace"* (page 59). Here, I really want to reiterate what I said above. Men and women take trillions of actions, big and small, every single day, yet not even a thousandth of a percent of them come even close to ennobling those who commit them. For an action to ennoble a person, it does not have to be an extraordinary action performed at an uncommon place. It does not have to be big or small. In fact, actions that ennoble men are usually ordinary actions that are intended to produce an extraordinary objective, and whether that action is done at the center of the city or the farthest corner of the country matters not. As long as you seek the greatest good in your action, everything else is just secondary.

- ❖ *"Know! A person walks in life on a very narrow bridge. The most important thing is not to be afraid"* (page 15). Whether it is sad news or breaking news, I do not know. All I know is that there is no guarantee in life. We all wish everything came to us on a silver platter. Unfortunately, that is not the case for all of us, kings and princes included. Tomorrow, the surprises that come with it are always everyone's guess. Not even a venture capitalist with the most connections and capital is guaranteed success in life. Many begin with huge advantages and fail miserably, while others begin with meager means and succeed tremendously. Therefore, where you start and what you start with should not be the point. The point should be the ability of your inner strength to repel fear of failure and doubt in your abilities. The bridge of life is narrow and precarious; walk on it with your head confidently high. Fear no fear, and fear will not only fear you, it will run away from you.

www.makanologos.com

Exalted Secrets of Brilliant Minds **477**

❖ *"You are wherever your thoughts are. Make sure your thoughts are where you want to be." "Thou shall have no other gods before me,"* says the First Commandment in the Bible. Am I blaspheming here? I hope you do not see it that way, but if you look at it clearly, you will find that the First Commandment really applies here. We are told we cannot have two opposing masters and love and obey them equally. What is the point here, then? The point is that when you want to take action that will take you to the mountaintop of greatness, you must give it your undivided attention. You must put your thoughts in it; then, despite its commonness, it will give you uncommon greatness. The reason most of us do not see the greatest goodness in small and common actions is that we do not give them the fullness of our attention, love, and care. Nachman goes on, adding, *"Is there something you really want or something you wish would happen? Focus every ounce of your concentration on that thing or event. Visualize it in fine detail. If your desire is strong and your concentration intense enough, you can make it come true"* (page 21).

❖ *"I will ignore tomorrow and all future tomorrows – today is all there is...Then, once you are already on the road, the real work begins. Keep at it and inspiration will come from within,"page, 40-41.* Many times, the greatest enemy of success is not lack of knowledge or resources; it is belief in the friendliness of tomorrow. What we can do today we postpone for tomorrow as if tomorrow existed, and because tomorrow is one of the worst illusions nature has sold us or we buy from nature, we end up putting off our actions forever, and consequently we do not climb the mountain of greatness. Brilliant minds understand quite well the potential dangers of relying on the next time. Once they have decided to carry on with a certain action, they carry it on to the end, regardless of the shortage of resources they may have had at the beginning. They

www.makanologos.com

understand that inspiration comes with work, and opportunities come to prepared or acting minds, not those who stand on the sidelines waiting. God knows how and when they act.

* *"Stay on course. Don't give up. In time, all barriers will disappear...Take comfort in the knowledge that the way down is only preparation for the way up"* (page 42). Many times, people fail not because things are difficult or complicated but because they are simply incapable, impatient, unwilling, or unmotivated to see their venture through to the very end. They forget that a farmer harvests not because he labored on land and planted the seeds, but because in addition to that, he removed the weeds, watered the soil (perhaps on a daily basis), and fought infectious plant diseases. Successful action lies in staying the course and never giving up once you are on the right course. Even if you fail numerous times, something is always gained. One of the biggest advantages of the "teach thyself" mind-set is that it teaches humility by understanding that things do not always go exactly your way, and when they do not, you must adjust. It teaches patience that you could not have learned otherwise, while at the same time you comprehend that none of your effort has been wasted, including the moment you spent fixing the mistake or the seeming failure.

* *"Don't be frustrated by the obstacles you encounter on your... journey. They are there by design, to increase your desire for the goal you seek. Because the greater the goal, the greater the yearning you'll need to achieve it...Never despair! Never! It is forbidden to give up hope"* (pages 47 and 110). If I could say only three words here and move on to another section, those three words would be persistence, persistence, and persistence. I strongly believe those three words are enough to convey what I mean to the reader. An entire chapter is coming up on persistence, but because

I feel the urge to say a little bit more here, let me say this: the mountain of greatness is conquered only by strong-willed and persistent minds, and brilliant minds are nothing more than just strong-willed and persistent minds. They understand and always remember that no obstacle is accidental, and there is no obstacle that comes their way that they cannot overcome. Thus, they sharpen and grow their minds brighter and brighter as they overcome one obstacle at a time with nothing but the sword and machine gun of persistence.

❖ *"If you don't feel happy, pretend to be. Even if you are downright depressed, put on a smile. Act happily. Genuine happiness will follow. Always wear a smile. The gift of life will then be yours to give…Avoid depression at all costs. It is the root of all illness and disease"* (pages 103, 105, 109). Have you ever heard of the thing spelled i-n-s-p-i-r-a-t-i-o-n? I know you know what it is, but do you know to whom it comes? Let's start by telling you that it does not come to sad, angry, depressed, or unhappy people. Brilliant minds, more than anything else, depend on inspiration to arouse their intelligence and climb the mountain of greatness, and nothing obstructs inspiration more than unhappiness. If there is any inspiration that an unhappy person gets, it is a destructive one such as suicide, selfishness, fear, doubt, and the like, whereas happy people get constructive inspirations of hope, faith, charity, courage, devotion, hard work, and the like. Action may not always guarantee success, but performing actions with a feeling of happiness improves your chances of success compared to doing it with a broken heart.

❖ *"Remember: Things can go from the very worst to the very best…in just the blink of an eye"* (page 113). Great feats rarely come without great frustrations. The *"Eureka! Eureka! Eureka!"* *"I have found it! I have found it! I have found it!"* exclamation says it all. Usually when we are

www.makanologos.com

frustrated the most, when we are at the point of giving in, that is when things turn from worse to unthinkable success. I will not say much here, as the wisdom is self-explanatory, and I believe your own intellect will shine even more light on it than I possibly can.

❖ Let's end these words of wisdom from Nachman with same insight that started this portion of the chapter as he said, "*Seek the sacred within the ordinary. Seek the remarkable within the commonplace.*" Here again, I will restrain from spilling too much ink, as I have a feeling that your mind would like to ponder it even better, but if my suggestion is needed, I will briefly repeat myself by recommending to always act for the interest of the greatest good if arousing intelligence and climbing the mountain of greatness is the goal you have in mind, for that is one of the best-kept secrets of brilliant minds.

Reaching the mountaintop of greatness is hardly ever a result of one single action or thought; in fact, it is a very complex business to the point that it is usually almost impossible to pinpoint with exact precision the most determining factor of success. While the above lamps from the Hasidic master may suffice in illuminating your mind, joining to them flashes of wisdom from other ancient knowledge can only make your mind even more effective and powerful. The works of some brilliant minds I examined for this purpose revealed the following and turned out to be major guiding lights of their success. I could not resist making them available to my readers:

• *Do not be bogged down by meeting, reading, and planning:* No question about it; the importance of meeting, reading, and planning cannot possibly be overstated, but brilliant minds learn their best lessons from Mother Nature. They understand that time is divided, at the very least by days and night and to a large extent by seasons, and there is good reason for that. They understand that a successful farmer is the one who knows when to plow his land, when to plant, when to water plants, and when to harvest, and that plowing all year long is not only unproductive, it is almost insane. Thus meeting, reading, and planning must be given ample time, but they should not stand in the course of action.

- *Always do it with love; do it with joy:* As we have stated above, inspiration rarely comes when man is sad, angry, or depressed. There is a good reason why there is hospital or at least medical treatment for depression, anger, or sadness, but there is hospital for treatment of neither genuine love nor happiness. In fact, happiness and joy are expressions of health and thus ultimate goals of life anywhere in the universe. Reaching the mountaintop of greatness is not an honor given to everyone; it is in fact a privilege and honor given to the very few, and those few are not chosen based on any specific criteria, but by an indescribable love and unbelievable joy with which they perform their duties. Love and joy alone set them apart from the rest of us and take them to the peak of any mountain that stands in their way. Let the outcome be your biggest motivation.

- *The peril of overthinking:* No one gets to the mountaintop of greatness without thinking, and thinking seriously. Brilliant minds certainly understand this, but what they understand even more is that taking all the time in the world before acting does not bring all the answers hoped for; some answers just come along the way. Therefore, it is important to do serious thinking before taking action, but it is naïve to the greatest extent to avoid risks by overthinking. Brilliant minds let experience be their best teacher. In other words, where they have no answer, they learn as the work goes on. They categorically avoid writing their plans in stone, as they are subject to change

www.makanologos.com

and improvement along the way, for work reveals new knowledge and experience teaches new wisdom.

- *Count your blessings:* One of the biggest obstacles that keep commoners in the common class is that they look down at themselves, causing the outside world to look down on them as well. *"To believe your thought, to believe that what is true in your private heart is true to all men — that is genius,"* said Ralph W. Emerson. This, of course, does not mean you should be arrogant or inflexible, but simply avoid the destructiveness of self-condemnation. When you keep counting your victories rather than your defeats, you are more likely to reach the mountain of greatness faster and easier than if you keep counting your defeats every time life slaps you with a new challenge. Brilliant minds gain new energy with victories as well as with defeats. They deny giving seeming defeat or temporary setbacks the power to suck any amount of energy out of them. They always look to the upside of life more than the downside.

- *Avoid sophistication:* In the age of high tech, who would not think that the highway is the road that leads to the mountaintop of greatness? Many times, all it takes to make great things happen is to just put old wine in a new bottle. The laws of nature have been here ever since the dawn of time. No one invented them, because they could not possibly have been invented by a human mind or brain. Just because there was no electricity two hundred or two thousand ago does not mean that the law of electricity did not exist. Just because computers, cellular phones, e-mail, and other novelties of the last few decades did not exist back then does not mean that the laws that make them possible today are new. Not at all — laws are always there, and those who create fame or greatness out of these laws are those who make them easily usable and understandable by the commonest among us. I am sure you can agree with me that no primary school diploma

www.makanologos.com

is required to make a call using a traditional phone or a cellular phone, for that matter, as long as one knows how to read numbers and the alphabet. So let common sense be your best guide, and your road to the mountaintop of greatness may not be as hard as you may think.

- *Commit no suicide, but fear no death:* Action is the ultimate fact of greatness. Quoting Drummond here again, I want to remind you, *"no one becomes a saint in his sleep."* You have got to act if you want to arouse your intelligence and climb the mountain of greatness. And this you must know: your worst enemy will be negative thoughts, for negative thoughts from others or yourself are thoughts against your best interests; thus, fight them with all your might. Act as wisely as you possibly can, but never let fear of consequences hold you down, and remember that every action, even the smallest, one is a risk; the greater the action, the higher the risk. For your information, bear in mind that brilliant minds go after the most rewarding risk—not the hardest or the easiest, but the most rewarding, regardless of where it is situated on the spectrum of effort.

www.makanologos.com

CHAPTER XX

The Humility Pillar

Humility is the solid foundation of all virtues. Kong Fu Zi

Humility is that low, sweet root, from which all heavenly virtues shoot. Thomas Moore

I have always suspected that the greatest desire of any writer is to leave no stone unturned on a subject. This, of course, is a very monumental task, and I believe few have accomplished it. But when writing on an epic topic like greatness, one wants to turn as many stones as he can in order to illumine as many paths of insight as possible that will show the reader the road to true wisdom, understanding, and knowledge, and will hopefully lead to him or her to a dedicated and triumphant application. This work was not designed with the intent to be a bible or spiritual guide, but mostly to humbly contribute to the human effort of illumining our minds and intellects for the purpose of a more harmonious, peaceful, and prosperous world.

Outright here and now, due the limited time, space, and power of the human mind and intellect, I confess my inability to turn every stone that makes up the mountain of greatness, and if this disappoints some of my readers, my only hope is that they will forgive my shortcomings after they put themselves in my shoes. Having said that, let's also add this: as this work is slowly coming to a close, as it should, I cannot, with all calm consciousness, live peacefully with myself by bringing it to closure without addressing what in my view is one of the greatest qualities of greatness and one of the best-kept secrets of brilliant minds. To do so would not only be self-deception on my part, but mostly it would be like inviting a guest of honor to sleep in the most expensively furnished and beautiful building without a roof on a cold and snowy winter night. While humility by itself does not constitute a synopsis of greatness (no virtue alone does), it is indeed one of the most important cornerstones of greatness and one of the most treasured secrets of brilliant minds. Therefore, concluding a book on greatness without seriously talking about humility, regardless of how brilliantly other topics may have been addressed, is like celebrating a wedding, birthday, or any happy moment in an uncovered edifice on a cold winter day or night. It just isn't funny or even rational at all. In here, I have discussed some tools of greatness that, if taken to extremes, may lead to lethargy or catastrophic injuries to mankind. But all of these virtues, watered with humility, can only produce great wonders.

No other quality wins man more rewards than humility. Authors of the Bible in both the Old and New Testaments tell us that God promises a humble person everything, including the Earth and the Kingdom of Heaven. *"Blessed are the meek for they shall inherit the earth,"* says Matthew 5:5. The reason for such enormous rewards to the humble may not be hard to discern if you look at it through the lenses of Helen E. Middleton when she says, *"Humility is the root, mother nurse, foundation and bond of all virtues."* Why? Let's ask the teacher, and here she (Middleton) goes on: *"The show of the sun is largest when its beams are lowest. Likewise, man becomes the greatest when he humbles himself to the lowest."*

Anymore questions to ask the teacher? Yes, but rather than answering the question herself, she will leave the podium to a much more respected and ancient sage by the name of Saint Augustine, who added, *"Humility is the foundation of all other virtues hence, in the soul in which this virtue does not exist there cannot be any other virtue except in mere appearance...It was pride that changed angels in to devils; it is humility that makes men as angels."* Still do not understand? Let's ask the good old Christian Saint again. Yes! The Saint answered, and with an instructive

www.makanologos.com

look, the old fellow signaled John Ruskin, a leading English art critic of the Victorian era, to put it in plain English:

I believe that the first test of a truly great man is his humility. I do not mean by humility, doubt of his powers. But really great men have a curious feeling that the greatness is not in them, but through them. And they see something divine in every other man, and are endlessly, foolishly and incredibly merciful…The greatest friend of truth is time, her greatest enemy is prejudice, and her constant companion is humility.

Was that not clear enough for you? asked the master. The words are clear, but the lesson is not so easy to grasp. Well! Maybe a little further dose from the *Sunshine Magazine* will help? Yes! nodded the student. Okay! Here it is: *"Humility leads to strength. It is the highest form of self-respect to admit mistakes and make amends for them."*

This imaginary conversation should not, of course, be tried at home by someone who is not seriously seeking to understand the secrets of brilliant minds and what really enables them to climb the mountain of greatness; otherwise, he will think greatness to be craziness, as awakening below causes awakening above, that one has to bow to the law in order to stand tall in the eyes of fellow men. The purpose here is to show the reader the scale of the power that humility wields and the importance of investing whatever effort possible in acquiring this incredible virtue if the mind has to be sharpened and the mountain of greatness to be conquered. A French philosopher, Christian mystic, and social activist, Simone Weil, who was described by her biographer, Gabriella Fiori, as *"a moral genius in the orbit of ethics, a genius of immense revolutionary range,"* of humility once wrote, *"Real genius is nothing else but the supernatural virtue of humility in the domain of thought."*

Most people early on in life do not apprehend the virtue of humility. A few lucky ones discover it in middle age or late in life. Those who do not discover it at all go to their graves as miserable creatures, but those who discover it early on in life live a very content life within themselves. Regardless of what outer appearances may suggest, they have peaceful, illumined, and free minds that go beyond the understanding of an average person. It is practically impossible to imagine the name of a great man registered in the memory of time and space who had no humility as the cornerstone of his character.

Why is it so? Because nothing really better reminds us of both our human and divine natures as humility does. Humility teaches us that there is always a higher power called the HIGHER SELF, or God, within all of us, even in a newborn, and that all human beings must bow to It whether a king, high priest, lord, or commoner. In addition, humility teaches that no man makes it to the mountaintop by his own effort alone; there is always help (visible or invisible) along the way; thus we owe gratitude, respect, and credit to all men. Let's put it in a very simple and clear way. When we are born, we came into this world naked, powerless, and above all, extremely vulnerable. Just to get to sit down, crawl, or stand up on our own feet takes an extremely concerted effort, not only of our parents but also from the community at large. *"It takes a village to raise a child"* is a very prominent African adage that has been translated in public policies in many countries around the world. Humility not only expresses the deepest heartfelt gratitude to those who, literally, made us what we are so proud to have become, but it is the best reminder of our potential weaknesses as well.

Being humble even as a child is not a sign of weakness but rather of strength. *"A baby fish will eventually become a big fish someday,"* it is said. No realistic teacher can ever think of his students as being always inferior to him or her. They go on to gain more wisdom, understanding, and knowledge than many of their former teachers, and with their acquisition, they grow in power and prestige greater than many of their teachers could possibly imagine. But should the acquisition of more knowledge, power, and prestige make a former student look

www.makanologos.com

down on or even equal to his or her former teacher? Yes, the student should indeed, but only if he/she is foolish.

Brilliant minds know and understand this principle. They understand that they are what they are because so many close or distant people helped them along the way as they stumbled on their journey up to the mountaintop of greatness. They never forget that their newfound happiness is a handiwork of so many people; therefore, they humble themselves to those who helped them along the way. And because it takes a village to raise a child, they bow to the community at large and respect all individuals they encounter everywhere. That is the reverence brilliant minds pay to the Good Samaritans who treated their wounds as rocks, and other obstacles hurt them inside and outside as they marched to the highest point of their greatness. After all, why should a California Silicon Valley millionaire not be grateful to a factory worker in Mississippi or a farmer in Kentucky who worked to pay taxes that financed the federal government that built roads, research, and other infrastructure that enabled the existence of Silicon Valley in the first place? Or deposited his or her hard-earned money in the banks that financed Silicon Valley ventures to begin with? You can look at it from so many angles.

Brilliant minds understand that true greatness is nothing but winning fellow men's admiration and support. If you go back again and take a look at how we are all born, as I said above, we come into this world with nothing as far as material is concerned. All we bring with us is a breath, a shell of flesh and bones, and even the breath and bones we cannot claim to be ours. They are so fragile that they cannot survive without the assistance of others. Now, where do we get money, clothes, knowledge, etc.? They do not fall from the sky into our hands. They come from the hands and mouths of others, and that is absolutely true for everything. Even the flesh and breath seem to come from the union of our parents. Thus everything we are born with or gain afterwards comes from other people. That is the truth, and arrogance is basically a violation of the law of nature. And thank heaven ignorance does not go unpunished sooner or later. Brilliant minds are brilliant primarily because they know and obey this law to the slightest command.

Arrogance is a tragic mistake that, unfortunately, many people still make, knowingly or otherwise. Arrogance is trying to force or dictate life to get what you want by your way or the highway. Humility, on the other hand, is cooperation with the most basic laws of life. Many people make the mistake of thinking that arrogance or stubbornness is a sign of strength and humility is a sign of weakness, but nothing could be further from the truth. Here is what a Hindu spiritual teacher, Swami Sivananda, said addressing the seeming weakness of humility: *"Humility is not cowardice. Meekness is not weakness. Humility and meekness are indeed spiritual powers."* A man can be humble yet firm and unyielding to fear, doubt, and anxiety. Humble folks are usually calm within and selflessly committed to the greater good, and by so doing; they become the favorites of the powers of nature, the Invisible Helpers. And the more they are favored by these powers, the more they become their channels to the outer world, and the more the road on their journey to the mountaintop of greatness is paved with fewer hindrances.

I do not mean to be humble or that one should feel unimportant—far from that. But one of the things that obstruct the feeling of humility in many people is a strong feeling of self-importance that they have carried for a very long time and may be unwilling to discard. The feeling that undervalues selfhood is destructive and undesirable at all costs, but the feeling of self-importance at the expense of others is suicidal and detrimental to the quest for greatness. *"I am so glad that I never feel important; it does complicate life,"* said the former U.S. first lady Eleanor Roosevelt—not to mean she was not important, but she just was not more so than any other human being, in her mind. And if a former first lady of the United States of America should snub the feeling of self-importance, what should many of us do, we

www.makanologos.com

whose idea of greatness is not close to being president of the United States of America?

Indeed, Eleanor Roosevelt, one of the most revered first ladies of the United States, might have been aware of this great secret of brilliant minds. As Malcolm Forbes would write, *"People who matter most are most aware that everyone else does too!"* It is those people who either do not know the path to greatness or know very little about greatness itself that think they matter more than anyone else. Those who are born with the quality of humility are usually in their own class, usually at the top of the food chain. They are admired from birth to death by their fellow men. Take a picture of a lion, the so-called king of all animals, or go to a zoo and look a lion in the eyes; you will notice that its eyes reflect or radiate humility, not arrogance. Now, would you say that lion is a weak creature? If you think so, go ahead and challenge it, if you are a dirty and ugly hyena. Most of us were not born with humility. Thus, if we are ever going to achieve greatness, we must achieve it through learning this incredible power. *"Some are born great, some achieve greatness, and some have greatness thrust upon them,"* said Shakespeare. So if you are not one of those lucky ones who were born with this inestimable gift and you want to achieve greatness, you will have to achieve it through learning the rules of humility. And if you want your fellow men to propel you to greatness, you must expect them to do it through your humble personality; otherwise, forget it.

Humility is one of the highest ideal principles of life, for it enables man to honor the life of his fellow men, and nothing attracts people to one's cause more than showing respect for their individualities. If you are going to want people to clothe, feed, or respect you or contribute to your cause, it is going to be incumbent upon you to show them your genuine respect for their lives—and I repeat *genuine* because you can only fake humility for so long. It really has to be bona fide and heartfelt; otherwise, your rise to the mountain of greatness will be only a temporary thing, and your downfall will only be a matter of time, and when that time comes, the crash will be disastrous. If there is a power of powers, it is humility, for as it was said above; it is the virtue of virtues, the mother and foundation of them all.

Fame, wealth, and power sometimes cause people to get puffed up, thinking everyone who is less famous, wealthy, or powerful is therefore less important. This is one of the biggest mistakes made on the way to the mountaintop of greatness. But if you think that very few people are born famous, wealthy, or powerful, you are probably not one of them. And even if you are, you are just one member of the human family; thus, if you are famous, you must bow before your fans and give them a special place in your heart. If you are rich, you must pay those who work for you their fair dues. If you are powerful, you must thank those who defend you. You must go the extra mile and thank the whole community near and dear to you, as well as all those who contributed directly and indirectly to your fortune. If you do this, your greatness will never decrease, regardless of whether you are dead or alive.

Life is sometimes paradoxical, and there is nothing you and I can do about it. The assumption that many people have is that arrogant people are knowledgeable, but the truth is that the arrogant folks are usually ignorant of what they pretend to know. Those who know best, on the other hand, are humble and more grateful for their knowledge because they know its consequences and benefits, mostly because they have gained it the not-so-easy way. When the atomic bomb was created, arrogant and ill-advised politicians were eager to use it to show their muscles and strength to the adamant opposition of the humble yet wiser and smarter scientists who had thought out the fabrication of that *man-made beast* in the first place. Politicians, of course, may have gotten away with murder and crimes against humanity, but in the end, they bowed to the

www.makanologos.com

wise advice of scientists by severely restricting its fabrication and banning its use in conventional military conflicts.

Power is not gained through arrogance, for it is a very destructive force that sooner or later ends up by backfiring. But the power gained through humility grows like a forest fire on a dry summer day, burning to ashes all evil intents in its way. The greater the power, the humbler brilliant minds become, and the higher and faster they climb the mountain of greatness. There absolutely must be a very good reason why some of the most illuminated minds who ever walked the face of the Earth advised us to behave as little children, and only an idiot can think that to be foolishness. Remaining humble and grateful to those who helped you along the way to the mountaintop of greatness is the most effective way of amassing even more power than one can possibly imagine. If you have taken time to read or inquire about visions and dreams of angels that appeared to men throughout time, it has been reported that all of them were magnificent yet humble beyond the understanding of the human mind.

The best politicians on Earth are those who bow to the will of the people whose voice holds their fate, and the most successful merchants are those who serve the satisfaction of their customers; otherwise, they will not stay in business a day longer. A smart politician bows lower as his powers grow higher, and a wise merchant serves the satisfaction of his customers more humbly as his business grows bigger. There is a reason why smart and wise banks and corporations invest more of their resources in customer service than in any other unit of their enterprise, and those that resist doing so do not stay operational for a long time. The greater the power to climb the mountain of greatness, the humbler, more unselfish, and respectful to others is the attitude of a brilliant mind.

Brilliant minds understand this because they know that everything that they have, including power, riches, and life, came from someone else. They created nothing. All they did was accumulate more of what was already there before they were even born, and basically they were mere recipients of the gifts of society at large and specifically their communities. An arrogant person cannot possibly think it is this way, because he/she thinks, erroneously of course, that members of community did not rush to him at birth or at any time with those terrific gifts to make him rich. The truth is that if members of a community or society in general do not do their fair share of service to life, no one can possibly fulfill his or her goal.

Brilliant minds understand that their victory is just a result of social effort. They know that no matter how skillful Pelé, Maradona, Michael Jordan, Kobe Bryant, Muhammad Ali, Michael Jackson, or any other athlete or artist was, he or she could not have won his or her group or teams' championships and glory without a dedicated participation of the team members, coaches, and staff, as well as fans. All those gifts come in an invisible form to human sight, as all great powers are always invisible. The humble and the wise men are able to see that, but the arrogant are blinded by their ignorance. There is nothing so great as a firm and strong humility to those who assisted you in climbing the mountain of greatness, because if you are honest with yourself, you will realize that you did not do it by yourself but with the help of countless people, many of whom you cannot possibly know until the day you dwell in the higher realms of life. If you have been paying attention, you must have noticed that even the most talented sports team is always weaker away than at home. Why? Because away, there are few fans cheering to stimulate the mental powers that are the true source of victory. Now, you tell me that community does not matter!

Until the day I dwell in the higher realms of life? Yes! Then and only then will the true powers of greatness flow flawlessly in, through and around you as water flows from the mountain into the valleys to the oceans, and your star shines, like a sun, at the top of the mountain with an unhindered, clear view to

www.makanologos.com

the masses. Your star, of course, will not shine because of your power but because of the gratitude people will send back to you and the happiness of counting you as one of them. Thus will the great law of life fulfill itself through you — "*as you sow, so shall you reap.*" When you give life, life gives back to you manifold, not because you sought it but because it is the law. You can ignore it at your own expense or obey it to your own amazement. The law is always independent of human will. It applies whether we like it or not, and this case will not be an exception. The actions and deeds of the person are always repaid in kind. Humility will gain you power and knowledge while arrogance will pay ignorance.

No matter how daunting the circumstances may appear to be, those who stand firm and steadfast with humility will find their fearless hearts rewarded with power to arouse their intelligence and to climb the mountain of greatness, and their minds will be filled with energy to take on even more challenging, yet climbable, mountains of greatness. This is how we are chosen by the Invisible Helpers or constructive powers of nature whose business it is to illumine mankind and inspire a constructive way of life here on the green Earth. These Invisible Helpers are not blind; instead, they use the All-seeing Eye of God, for they are the all-knowing mind of God. They know and feel all the good men do; that is how they only work through a few people who stand for the Highest Ideal in the universe, whose honor to life is the sole motive for which they do everything. It is said that "*except you become as little children you shall not enter the kingdom of heaven.*" We may as well say, "Except you become like little children, you will not be chosen to bring down heaven on Earth or climb the mountain of greatness." Think about it.

Thus, if you want to close the door through which your blessings will come, well, there is no reason to seek further; just wear the shroud of arrogance, and the door will be closed behind you with the speed of your thought. But if you want to

www.makanologos.com

keep it open, you must wear a cloak of humility and resolve. There is no middle ground when it comes to humility. You are either humble or you are not. A life lived with dignity is a life that is humble and firm. Accumulation of power should not be used as a tool to look down on others but rather as a tool to bring one safely down below to live among fellow men in order to surmount the common challenges of humanity. Humility, almost by itself, has taken people of the lower classes to the highest peak of their greatness.

A wise man always seeks more ways of humbling himself, not because he does not want to accumulate power, but because he wants to grow the one he already has, and because growth of power, not accumulation, is the best method of gaining more of it. In fact, true and long-lived power is exercised through humility rather than arrogance, as this may be poisonous to power. An attitude of humility can only gain you more power, energy, understanding, and knowledge that will completely disarm even the strongest enemy life sends your way. How do you think flies and mosquitoes bring down kings of animals, namely lions and elephants? Well, they start by scratching their backs until the big beasts accept them as useful guests. Then flies enter the beast's nostrils, and by the time the elephant or the lion realizes it, misery is inevitable. This does not mean that humility is synonymous with deception—not at all. But it means that when you have a humble attitude, you can turn your enemy into a friend if he/she is a reasonable person, or wipe him out if he is detrimental to the common good.

To a small extent, we all climb mountains every day of our lives as we fearlessly face and overcome challenges that we face in life. But the reason why, for the most part, only a few people climb mountains of greatness is simple. Rather than taking credit for their achievements, few people or brilliant minds give credit to those who helped them reach their goal. Believe it or not, it is not easy to reach the most glorious point

www.makanologos.com

of your life and then give credit to others, yet it is the strategy only brilliant minds know how to utilize impeccably.

Ask yourself this question: do you know a single individual, regardless of the high qualities of his or her skills, who can win soccer's World Cup, an NBA championship, a presidential election, or even a prophecy without the overwhelming help of others? So, thinking that the meal we ate today was due to our own effort is the most deceptive thing all of us are guilty of. At the very least, the most we did was either buy or cook the food before eating it, but someone else had to plow the land on which the food was grown or build the boat that went to fish it from the water. Someone had to grow it, to harvest it, to process it, to transport it to your local grocery store, to display it on the shelf, to even help you find it in the store, and so on. So why not give credit to all those people who worked so hard so that you could have the easiest part of picking up, cooking, and enjoying the food in the comfort of your home?

Giving credit to others is one of the most effective ways of humbling oneself. And when you give credit to others, you are giving credit directly to God. As the foremost English historian of the 12th century, William of Malmesbury, would say, *"The voice of the people is the voice of God."* This is how one is truly grateful, humble, and worthy of all accomplishments, rather than boosting yourself for something that really had very little to do with your own effort. Those who have a clear understanding of the mysteries of humility — brilliant minds — go from success to success, and their power grows greater and greater every moment of their lives as they never fail to remain humble in the eyes of those who assist them even to the slightest extent.

The downfall of the greatest empires that ever lived was triggered by one and one mistake only, and that is arrogance. A quick look into the pages of a number of history textbooks can easily prove this to you. The study of historical events is absolutely beyond the scope of this work, but this is what I

Exalted Secrets of Brilliant Minds **497**

would like to convey: the misconception that misguided people have is that arrogance elevates while humility lowers. Nothing could be further from the truth. Indeed, they both bring one up and down, except like a stone, arrogance brings you down to a disastrous end while like a massive glass, humility brings you down like a bouncing ball or an airplane, always landing safely and every time back up again and again to higher elevations.

That is the power of sincere humility. It gives you not only power to surge more quickly but also to regain whatever is lost fast enough to make you a magnet of your fellow men. This law may be clothed in simple words, but this is one of the most powerful secrets of brilliant minds, and only unwise minds dare to circumvent it, obviously to their own regret. Brilliant minds joyously bow to the powers of the many who directly or indirectly assisted them while at the same time they grow their own power by using and riding on the powers of the many. They do not let their fame, fortune, or success get into their heads to confuse them.

History is full of countless examples of people who went from lowly beginnings to the top of the mountains of greatness but were brought down crushingly by the ignorance of arrogance as they thought or felt themselves to be more important than the rest of mankind. In school, we study these sorry souls as footnotes of regretful past accounts of mankind and warnings that they are not to be repeated at all costs. Whereas monuments are built in the hearts of men as well as in the choicest locations of cities, glories and emulations are reserved to those who have reached the mountaintop of greatness and humbly bowed by giving credit to the masses and anyone else whose assistance was instrumental to their success.

Brilliant minds understand that, regardless of the power and success they have at the top or on their way to the mountaintop of greatness, their real power and success are fortified and built to last by humbly and sincerely bowing and thanking the masses and their close aids, for without them, they couldn't

www.makanologos.com

possibly have attained greatness. Throughout the history of mankind, it has not been done yet and probably will never be done by one person—climb the mountain of greatness without assistance of fellow men, directly or indirectly. Even God blesses man through his fellow men, so why not humbly give credit of your success to those who are its true architects and erectors?

Truly brilliant minds whose footprints have by no means been washed out by the power of time and space never failed to give all acknowledgement, praise, and credit to those who were instrumental in their achievements. Humility in feelings and deeds can only bless you with harmony and joy, the two most important states of mind, without which achievement can only be short lived. I have no illusion about thinking or suggesting that humility is an easy thing to do. No, because it is not. But this is important to remember—as you strive to humble yourself, the humbler you are, the more your success can only expand and never dwindle, unless you confuse humility with weakness. Those great ones who lower themselves as children before their fellow men get all the help in the world to stay at the top of the mountain. Like the flame of a candle, their minds brighten even more as they shine and light the candles in the minds and hearts of others.

As this chapter is coming to its end, I want to stress one more thing, and that is that humility is by no means synonymous with fear, weakness, or timidity, for these are characteristics of selfishness. The humility I am talking about here is selflessness powerfully charged with courage, firmness, and actions, which are the true foundation of real and lasting success in all human enterprises. When absolute fearlessness is combined with humility, man becomes a really magnetic power of genuine achievement and greatness, while at the same time he becomes a generator of strength and courage to those around him. His journey to the mountaintop of greatness may be slow, but it

www.makanologos.com

surely goes on, for his humility will motivate the energy of fellow men.

Regardless of the type of business you are in, humility, kindness, and determination will unlock almost any door of success at the right time, in the right place, and in the right way. Again, power gained on the way to the mountaintop of greatness but not used with humility will eventually turn against you in one way or another, sooner or later. As wonderful as power is, when not used correctly and without humility, it becomes destructive. Just as the missile makes a hole at the location from where it was launched, so too with arrogant power, which starts by destroying you first before it destroys your target. Feeding your ego will never get you anywhere on the path of greatness, but humility will certainly carry you not only to the top of the mountain of greatness, it will not only brighten you mind, but it will carry you beyond your fondest imagination, which only your experience can give you a gleam of an idea of what it is.

Shun pride and arrogance, and the world will gladly bestow the gifts of love, wisdom, and power upon you as you seek them through gratitude, humility, and determination and never through arrogance, pride, fear, or weakness. The tragedy of the man at the top of the mountain comes as he loses humility and gratitude to those whose hands hold his fate. The understanding of the Humility Principle is one of the most potent keys of greatness and the brilliant mind. Humility is the real golden platter from which great souls receive their power, as it is the key that opens all the necessary channels of success on the way to the mountaintop of greatness. This is one of the best-kept secrets of brilliant minds, this is how intelligence is aroused, and this is the ELIXIR OF INTELLIGENCE, because light is its own defense, and inspiration is its own revelation. This is how you watch and look within the light; seeing all within it, you make joy live in you and others, for there is nothing hidden that is not revealed to a constructive seeker

www.makanologos.com

who needs to know it so long as he/she stands for the Highest Ideal in the universe and honor to life is the motive for which he/she does everything. This is the end of the road, for this is how the great ones gained their immortality and a place of honor in the hearts of all generations to come, and so can you, so long as you stand for the Highest Ideal in the universe and honor to life is the motive for which you do everything.

www.makanologos.com

CHAPTER XXI

The Philanthropy (Charity) Pillar

"Giving is the expanding power of the universe."
Beloved Master Helios, Ascendant Master Dictations (lecture)
CD #02120 Part two,
"I AM" Activity of Saint Germain Foundation

"What's love got to do with it?" A silly question it seems like, except in the mind of the singer Tina Turner and those who shared her emotions. Silly! Yes, because love has got to do with everything in life and death. *"What's Love Got to Do With It?"* became Tina Turner's most successful single; that is how far we will go with this question of love. Now let's get to the real question we are obligated to answer in this work. What does charity got to do with greatness? Just as an average mind sees water as an element good for quenching thirst, preparing meals, cleaning the body, moistening plants, and other obvious utilizations, a brilliant mind sees in water more than just its natural uses; it sees electricity that can light cities, run machinery, and so on. So to the question of what charity has got to do with greatness, an average mind might confidently say nothing or very little, but to brilliant minds, charity has a tremendous lot to do with greatness. Like love in life and death, charity has to do with every piece of the puzzle known as greatness. It is an instrument through which brilliant minds expand their powers. It is by giving a few healthy seeds to the soil that the farmer harvests countless of them. The sun becomes even more self-luminous by ceaselessly illumining the system of worlds. Energy becomes power by giving of itself; thus through use, energy becomes power. The law of nature can be beautifully synthesized in three simple words: give and take. Through charity, brilliant minds see more than just

the fulfillment of a social imperative of lovingly, joyfully, and courteously lifting up a fallen brother, sister, comrade, fellow countryman, or total stranger during a rough time, but rather the ultimate opportunity to reach into the heart of infinity for the inner glorious power and the unique chance to smash the noxious serpent of selfishness, arrogance, and self-indulgence right on its head, thus debilitating it as much as they possibly can.

No book that I know of has more eloquently spoken about charity than the Holy Bible, in both the Old and New Testaments. As quoted earlier, in 1 Corinthians 13:1 and 13:13, Paul writes:

Though I speak with the tongues of men and angels, and have not charity, I am become as sounding brass, or a tinkling cymbal. And though I have the gift of prophesy and understand all mysteries, and all knowledge; and though I have all faith, so that I could remove mountains, and have not charity, I am nothing. And though I bestow all my good to feed the poor, and though I give my body to be burned, and have not charity, it profiteth me nothing...And now abideth Faith, Hope and Charity, but the greatest of these is charity.

In another translation, *charity* is translated as *love*. Thus in the New International Version, 2010, of the Bible, in its online version, speaking of love as charity in 1 Corinthians 13:4, it is written, *"Love is patient, love is kind. It does not envy, it does not boast, it is not proud. It does not dishonor others, it is not self-seeking, it is not easily angered, it keeps no record of wrongs."* And in his book *The Key of the Mysteries*, French occult author and ceremonial magician Eliphas Levi writes, **"To conquer love is to triumph over the whole nature and to understand the Spirit of Charity is to understand all mysteries."** Like Paul in Chapter 13 of his first epistle to the Corinthians, Levi was more passionate and poignant about charity in part 1 of *Religious Mysteries* in his book.

www.makanologos.com

Exalted Secrets of Brilliant Minds   503

A true seeker of greatness, a person who is seeking to brighten his mind in the likeness of the chosen few cannot possibly do himself a greater favor than studying the words of this extraordinary man, Levi, and I am sure the benefits that he/she will reap will be one of his most inestimable treasures securely guarded in the depths of his breast. Of the splendor of charity, Levi writes:

The word CHARITY and the spirit of which we speak is the Spirit of Charity. Before Charity, faith prostrates itself, and conquered science bows. There is here evidently something greater than humanity; Charity proves by its works that it is not a dream. It is stronger than all the passions; it triumphs over suffering and over death; it makes God understood by every heart, and seems already to fill eternity by the begun realization of its legitimate hopes...Then will there come the humblest and the simplest of all Sisters of Charity — the world will leave there all its follies, and all its crimes and all its dreams, to bow before this sublime reality.

Charity! Word divine, sole word which makes God understood, word which contains universal revelation! Spirit of Charity, alliance of the two words which are a complete solution and a complete promise! To that question, in fine, do these two words not find an answer? What is God for us, if not the Spirit of Charity?... It is by charity that twelve Galileans conquered the world; they loved truth more than life, and they went without followers to speak it to people and to kings, tested by torture, they were found faithful. They showed to the multitude a living immortality in their death, and they watered the earth with a blood whose heat could not be extinguished, because they were burning with ardor of Charity...

God can only be defined by faith; science can neither deny nor affirm that He exists. God is the absolute object of human faith. In the infinite, He is the Supreme and creative intelligence of order. In the world, He is the Spirit of Charity (pages 17-20).

In all fairness, let's ask this question: do we really need to add anything to that to make it clearer? I prefer to answer it

www.makanologos.com

silently, but I hope you send me a thought about what you think should be added here in a heart-to-heart conversation with me that you are more than welcome to initiate.

Charity is an incredible pillar of wisdom that most ordinary people do not understand, and only very few enlightened and brilliant minds have a slight idea of what it really is. It is through charity that great people acquire the magical power of carving their names in the hearts of their fellow men in the way that blocks time's ability to erase the deeds of man. Of all the people who have walked this Earth, the most memorable are those whose lives were motivated by the spirit of charity. Many poor heroes of the past who had nothing material to give gave their own blood and life as human sacrifices so that others could have the freedom to live in dignity.

Many powerful men have erected monuments for themselves during their lifetimes with their hands or money, but only the monuments of those who were wise enough to do it with truly loving, selfless, and humbling acts of charity still stand today, not at the top of any mountain or revered park, but in the hearts of the generations that followed. *"What we have done for ourselves alone dies with us; what we have done for others and the world remains and is immortal,"* said Albert Pike, the great Masonic master and the only Confederate military officer or figure to be honored with an outdoor statue in Washington, DC. Of course, Pike did not erect the statue but rather those who benefited from the life he generously gave in service to his brethren.

The medieval Catholic monk and author of *The Imitation of Christ*, a book that for centuries was the most-read book, second only to the Bible, Thomas á Kempis, speaking of greatness and charity, said, *"He is truly great who hath a great charity,"* and to that the hilarious Bob Hope added, *"If you haven't got any charity in your heart, you have the worst kind of heart trouble."* The world is a very delicate playground. Winning the game of life is the thing that makes it worthwhile. Concentrating on changing the

www.makanologos.com

playground so it suits you and your needs may be a waste of time at best, but adjusting to it so that you are squared away with it may be one of the wisest means of winning the game of life. We are compelled to play this game wisely by our own existence if life is to be enjoyed rather than played foolishly at our own risk.

Striving to change the world is a very dull idea and a very unrealistic undertaking; it is only possible if we start by self-changing. *"Everyone thinks of changing the world,"* said Leo N. Tolstoy, *"but no one thinks of changing himself."* How then do you think man acquires the power to transform himself into the engine that changes the world? Through the spirit of charity not only is man capable of changing himself to mirror the world he wants to live in, but he is also capable of changing the world along with him. Great people did not reach the mountaintop of greatness by climbing on a handmade ladder. There is no more perilous business than the business of daring to climb the mountain of greatness.

Both nature and man have placed fatal traps along the way to the mountaintop of greatness to purposely eliminate the weak and wicked, or more correctly to test whoever dares to try. Brilliant minds, of course, are fully aware of this threat; thus they do not use handmade or any man-made tools, for that matter, to climb the mountain of greatness. They defeat mountain lions, rolling stones, and cold winds of the mountain by riding on the shoulders of others, while at the same time hiding in the hearts of joyous fellow men. Nothing lifts one to the shoulders of companions while making his way in their hearts more quickly and safely than the spirit of charity. Charity that is done without arrogance or intention of payback is absolutely magical. As the former British Prime Minister Winston Churchill would say, *"We make a living by what we get, but we make a life by what we give."*

When you treat people with kindness, they may not treat you likewise. In fact, there is no guarantee they will ever do so,

www.makanologos.com

but the one guarantee you can count on is that life will sooner or later pay you in the same currency. There is a proverb that says, *"Kindness, like a boomerang, always returns."* Kindness or charity does not have to be a monumental achievement or something that attracts the attention of the public, but it can be a collection of those small acts of generosity. A charitable person does not seek praise, recognition, or payback rewards whatsoever. In fact, the most pleasurable acts of charity are those that are done anonymously, and the world will reward you publicly as it happily carries you to the mountaintop of greatness. Giving as action is a prayer. It has to be done privately. The Good Lord once said, as this online version of the Bible puts it:

"Watch out! Don't do your good deeds publicly, to be admired by others, for you will lose the reward from your Father in heaven. When you give to someone in need, don't do as hypocrites do — blowing trumpets in the synagogues and streets to call attention to their act of charity...But when you give to someone in need, don't let your left hand know what your right hand is doing. So that your giving may be in secret. Then your Father, who sees what is done in secret, will reward you publicly." (http://bible.logos. com/passage/NTL, accessed July 10, 2011)

This is one the best-kept secrets of brilliant minds, this is how intelligence is aroused, and this is the ELIXIR OF INTELLIGENCE, because light is its own defense and inspiration is its own revelation. This is how you watch and look within the light; seeing all within it, you make joy live in you and others, for there is nothing hidden that is not revealed to a constructive seeker who needs to know it so long as he/she stands for the Highest Ideal in the universe and honor to life is the motive for which you do everything. This is the end of the road, for this is how the great ones gained their immortality and a place of honor in the hearts of all generations to come, and so can you, so long as you stand for the Highest Ideal in the universe and honor to life is the motive for which you do everything.

www.makanologos.com

That is the secret of brilliant minds. That is what keeps them standing where many have fallen. That is what lights their eyes in darkness. That is what makes their ears hear the voice of silence. That is what makes them understand the least prompt that comes to their hearts and minds from Invisible Helpers. That is the source of greatness that surpasses the understanding of the mind of an average person. That is one of the most cherished lessons of the greatness of brilliant minds.

For the magic of charity to happen, it is fundamental to clearly understand what an act of charity is and what it is not, for nothing is more harmful, misleading, and poisonous than the misunderstanding of charity. A well-intentioned act of charity done the wrong way may well be a disaster to both the giver and the receiver. In his small book titled *The Secret*, Michael Berg outlines some questions that the giver must always ask deep in his own heart to make sure that a charitable act is what it ought to be, an act of charity. I will not transpose those questions here, but I will analyze some of their elements in order to bring the reader to the strategic edge of a springboard of imagination to better jump to the higher heights of his ability, and to return back to Earth safely and beautifully without splashing water needlessly or crashing, while at the same time, obviously, enjoying the game to the fullest.

a. *First, an act of charity must not contain a hidden agenda:* There is a reason why society has classified not-for-profit and for-profit activities. Spilling too much ink is not necessary to make this point clear. If your intent is to receive something back from your charitable action, it is by far wiser to invest a "donation" in a for-profit business than pretend to give it to charity. Charity was intended to give happiness to both the giver and the receiver. When you pretend to do charity while your genuine intention is to receive something back, you may have the material payback, but you will never receive the genuine joy that naturally emanates from charity. To

www.makanologos.com

this, a prolific Swedish scientist, philosopher, theologian, and revelator, Emanuel Swedenborg, added, *"True charity is the desire to be useful to others without thought of recompense."*

b. Over and over, it has been said, sung, or written in so many ways and in all languages of the world that money or any material thing cannot buy love. You probably do not need me to tell you this. While marriage works better for the rich than for the poor, the level of divorce is higher for the rich than for the poor. Money cannot buy happiness or love. An effort to buy love or happiness is certainly highly unwise. Anyone who practices charity so that others can love him or her is performing self-deception of the highest level. There are better things one can do with money than buy sympathy.

c. While morality is one of the most enriching qualities of the human heart, charity should not be performed based on moral convictions. As you will see later on in this chapter, morality-based charity can be very destructive or counterproductive at best. While the best charitable actions are those that help fulfill our own deepest interests and true destiny, any personal motive of charity must always be overridden by a social good. A true act of charity must not just change or impact the lives of those who will be physically touched by it in the short term, but it must have some long-term impact on society as well.

d. Let's present this point in the form of a "no-brainer" question. What is really an act of charity between a billionaire who gives $10,000,000 to a wealthy Ivy League university and a retired laundry worker woman who gives her $10,000 life savings to a local impoverished school? While you are pondering your answer, here is the point I want to make. Just as common sense would tell us that the person who shares his only daily meal from

www.makanologos.com

the get-go with others, regardless of the quantity, is more charitable than the person who gives the leftovers of his meal to others no matter the quantity, you must know that being charitable is not about making easy choices but hard yet good ones. Anyone who performs charitable acts because of their easiness must stop kidding him/herself. Of course, I am not implying that to be charitable, one must cause him/herself a physical or material injury — far from that — but it must be a purposely good choice made without necessarily an injury of any type. Nevertheless, it must be a consequential choice, not an easy one.

Having said that, I would like to underline one thing, and I call the attention of the reader to know that the point I will make from here to the end of this chapter is so vital to the whole concept of charity that it cannot possibly be stressed strongly enough. Charity can be a seed of harmony and tranquility as well as a poisonous fruit to both the giver and the receiver, but especially to the receiver. An act of charity that encourages lethargy, dependency, and apathy of human mind, intentionally or otherwise; an act of charity that leaves an able person always wanting without self-effort whatsoever; an act of charity that does not inspire man to depend on own abilities to break the shell of misery; is nothing but a poison of the worst kind and must be fought against with all the powers available to man by both society and the individual who is apparently benefiting from it.

When charity is done for the sake of giving rather than for the sake of society or the receiver, it becomes a tool to degrade others, a tool of arrogance for the giver, and it stops being a charitable act altogether. This is what the French writer George Sand had in mind when she said, "*Charity degrades those who receive it and hardens those who dispense it.*" Thinking that any human being can cure the ills of the world, much less poverty, through charity is arrogance, pure and simple, and ignorance at best. This kind of charity is very destructive. As Henry Ford

www.makanologos.com

once said, *"Capital punishment is as fundamentally wrong as a cure for crime as charity is wrong as a cure of poverty."*

It is indescribably wrong for a person to think that because of his or her wealth, he or she can remedy poverty by simply distributing his or her fortune. Like all other ills of the world, if they are going to be cured at all, individuals themselves must cure poverty. No single person has either the right or the power to solve all the problems of others. You can lend a hand, you can inspire, you can pull up a fallen brother, you can bring temporal relief to a heartbroken fellow, but that is as far as you can go. It is up to the individual to use his/her own God-given hands, his/her own brain, and his/her own mind to think, his/her own feet to walk, his/her own hands to work, his/her own faculties to transform his environment, lest he/she become a load to society. *"The greatest good you can do for another,"* Benjamin Disraeli once said, *"is not just to share your riches but to reveal to him his own."*

When you perform the kind of charity that enables others to recover their independence and pride and to gain the power to form a chain of constructive charity by pulling up a fallen fellow man next to them, then you can realistically attempt to eradicate poverty and all other human ills. No matter the goodness of your heart that seeks to eradicate poverty from the face of the Earth, the reality is that you are not always going to be there when people need to tackle their own problems. As well, the problems of life are not temporary like men who come and go. Problems are here to stay. In fact, they rise and fall with every breath of air we inhale or exhale. This lyric from *"Life's Climb"* by the young singer Miley Cyrus puts it in better words:

There's always gonna be another mountain.
I'm always gonna wanna make it move
Always gonna be an uphill battle
Sometimes I'm gonna have to lose
Ain't about how fast I get there
Ain't about what's waitin' on the other side
It's a climb.

www.makanologos.com

Exalted Secrets of Brilliant Minds **511**

You see, when one problem is solved, another arises almost instantaneously because that is just how life operates, and that is how we grow physically, mentally, and spiritually. Pretending to be the solver of all people's troubles is an illusion of the grandest proportions. As Oscar Wilde put it, *"Charity creates a multitude of sins."* Charity that leads people to not take charge of the responsibility for their own lives is unwise, unwarranted, and detrimental at best. No one put it more clearly than the American business magnate and philanthropist John D. Rockefeller when he said, *"Charity is injurious unless it helps the recipient to become independent of it."* Pretending to solve people's problems is to deny them an opportunity to grow, and denying someone the opportunity to grow is the worst crime we can commit on our fellow men. It is to be avoided at all costs because otherwise it will cause an unnecessary arrested development. Even God, whose wealth is unimaginably boundless, does not give all things to all people all the time without effort.

The question arises here as to how to make charity non-injurious to the recipient and more profitable to society. The answer to this question will, of course, lead us to the conclusion of this chapter, but what concerns me most is that it may stir an unintended controversy. The description of the unintended controversy that concerns me here is beyond the scope of this book; thus, I will let the reader ponder it for him/herself, and if he/she cares, he/she may make it the subject of his own work to keep the chain of illumination unbroken and going in time and space.

The answer, to that question I want to present my readers, comes from *The Sefer Yetzicah: the book of creation* and *The Bahir: The Book of Illumination*, both translation and commentaries of these ancient books of Kabbalah by Aryeh Kaplan. In chapter six 6:4, *The Sefer Yetzicah* says:

Also God made one opposite the other (Ecclesiastes 7:14)
Good opposite the evil
　　Evil opposite good

www.makanologos.com

Good from good
Evil from evil
Good defines evil
And evil defines good
Good is kept for the good ones
And evil is kept for the evil.

I want to caution the reader not to try to understand Hebrew literature literally, because letters are meant to mean several things since they can be permutated and are intentionally written without vowels just so the reader can deduce his/her own word and meaning as he/she sees fit. The original Hebrew text of this poem is in transcription right above it in the book, and it is intentionally left out of this work; the reader can consult the bibliography if interested in knowing more.

The point here is that the translator and commentator comments on only four phrases or sentences: *"one opposite the other," "good from good," "good defines evil,"* and *"good is kept for the good ones."* Everything else is not commented on. Fortunately for us, our interest is only in the comments he made on the last sentence, *"Good is kept for the good ones."* Remarkably, while the first two rhymes are commented on in only one short paragraph each, and the third rhyme is commented on in three fairly short paragraphs, this one — *"Good is kept for the good ones"* — is commented on in more than two pages. But only this part here grabs the attention of this work, as the author writes:

First of all, we must realize that any good that God gives must be the ultimate good that His creation can accept. The Psalmist said, "How great is Your good, stored up for those who fear You" (Psalms 31:20). Our sages interpret this to say that God bestows good in the greatest possible abundance. In another place, they teach us that this verse means that God is telling us, "You according to your strength, and Me according to Mine" (page 246).

The point I really want the reader to hold his headlight on is the very last one: *"You according to your strength, and Me according to Mine."* Philosophical volumes can be written on

www.makanologos.com

the meaning of that short sentence alone. This work is winding down, and there is neither time nor space to take on the challenge, but to avoid the risk of making charity destructive rather than constructive as it should be, let's say this: people must be helped or given to according to their strengths rather than their weaknesses. In other words, charity must be given to a deserving person, one who is really in need and worthy of it by all accounts. This simply means that when a person has a lack of something, all the help he should be given is to aid him to be able to obtain that by his own efforts.

One of the most popular quotations of Chinese wisdom attributed to Lao Tzu says, *"Give a man a fish, you have fed him for a day; teach a man to fish, you have fed him for a lifetime."* Charity that aims to empower people rather than diminish their abilities is the true pillar of the intelligence and wisdom of brilliant minds. It is one the best-kept secrets of brilliant minds. This is how intelligence is aroused, and this is the ELIXIR OF INTELLIGENCE, because light is its own defense, and inspiration is its own revelation. This is how you watch and look within the light; seeing all within it, you make joy live in you and others, for there is nothing hidden that is not revealed to a constructive seeker who needs to know it so long as he/she stands for the Highest Ideal in the universe and honor to life is the motive for which he/she does everything. This is the end of the road, for this is how the great ones gained their immortality and a place of honor in the hearts of all generations to come, and so can you.

Despite the brilliance of someone's mind, no human being can perform everything by himself. Brilliant minds understand that the magic of their power resides in their ability to tap into the minds of others, and what benefit is there in tapping into a weak mind? Thus, brilliant minds start by empowering others, through charity or otherwise. By so doing, they become the focus of admiration of many people around them. This enables them to easily tap into the minds of others, performing

www.makanologos.com

what average folks call the extraordinary. Charity that aims at working on people's weaknesses has very little constructive outcome, but charity that aims at strengthening and rewarding people according to their strengths is truly a laboratory of magic and alchemy.

We are in this world to conquer all challenges that life throws at us, and if Mother Nature were to do everything for us, life itself would not be enjoyable. We do not enjoy life when someone has solved our problems or has kept us out of trouble, but we enjoy it when, by our own effort, we have overcome or sustained a tough challenge. Civilization depends on the effort of every one of us, and brilliant minds understand this. Thus in order to roll the wheel of civilization forward, brilliant minds empower others, not by handing them free lunches but by enabling the arousal of their inner powers to make lunches for themselves as well as for others.

In the commentary of *The Bahir*, Rabbi Aryeh Kaplan makes a very interesting point in regard to charity. He challenges the concept of charity as giving something freely without its being earned. To many people, the idea of charity being earned may seem heartless, but an unbiased look at Kaplan's argument provides a different, possibly unpopular, but mind-challenging point of view. He makes this point:

If God were to bestow His good freely without its being earned, it would not be a perfect good. For one thing, since it was not earned, it would be the "bread of shame." Furthermore, since the recipient is receiving without giving, he does not resemble God when he receives, and this itself is a concept of shame. Therefore in order that this good be perfect, it must be earned. This is the concept of "righteousness" where a fair reward is given for a fair job of earning it…The solution of this dichotomy is the concept of "righteousness" and fairness, which indicates that man must earn this good, (pages, 138-139)

The bread of shame indeed — not much needs to be said here if you look at the joy, dignity, self-confidence, and respect that

www.makanologos.com

one gains by earning his life, and at the shame, humiliation, and loss of self-esteem the other endures by being handed just enough to satisfy his or her needs. Man does not live by bread alone, we are told. When a person's life depends entirely on the charitable actions of others, he/she tends to lose the sense of his or her personhood. This society must not encourage or condone voluntary loss of personhood by anyone for any reason whatsoever.

Dependence is really counterproductive, for it is one fatal virus that not only grinds the wheels of civilization fairly quickly, but it takes civilization quickly and prematurely to its grave. To prevent this tragedy from happening, charity must be wise and intelligently practiced as a virtue free from all emotional and sentimental deliberations. Only an unwise and imprudent father will let his child play with a loaded gun, fire, or razor blade in order to keep him/her from crying.

Rather than enabling the destruction of personhood, brilliant people practice charity to aid its reinforcement. They help individuals only when they are convinced that the assistance will lead the person to self-sufficiency, independence, or recovery of dignity as he/she seeks to become an asset to society at large and the community in particular. Thus, brilliant people provide scholarships to the needy who have shown the potential of becoming contributing members of society; they help the sick to recover their health so they can gain their self-dependency; they assist the unfortunate ones who cannot possibly help themselves due to severe innate, accidental, or other types of handicaps that keep them from fully expressing their will. Other than that, the favorite beneficiaries of charity of brilliant minds are causes that are competent in making an effective list of deserving individuals and spreading the benefits more fairly.

In closing this chapter, I leave you with these verses from Psalm 133 for your own enjoyment and inspiration, for with these words opened at the altar in the heart of the sanctum sanctorum are neophytes accepted into the house of initiation, as the scent and the light of these words are let in to fill the room.

The Psalms 133

The Blessings of Brotherly Unity
A Song of Degrees of David

1. *Behold, how good and how pleasant it is for brethren to dwell together in unity!*
2. *It is like the precious ointment upon the head, that ran down upon the beard, even Aaron's beard: that went down to the skirts of his garments;*
3. *As the dew of Hermon, and as the dew that descended upon the mountains of Zion: for there the LORD commanded the blessing, even life for evermore.* (The Holy Bible: King James Version, 2000)

www.makanologos.com

CHAPTER XXII

The Persistence Pillar

"Nothing in this world can take the place of persistence. Talent will not: nothing is more common than unsuccessful men with talent. Genius will not; unrewarded genius is almost a proverb. Education will not: the world is full of educated derelicts. Persistence and determination alone are omnipotent."
Calvin Coolidge

"The voice that tells us to give up hope is never the voice of wisdom."
Philip S. Berg

"Rise and rise again until lambs become lions"
Robin Hood

"You may be the only person left who believes in you, but it's enough. It takes just one star to pierce a universe of darkness. Never give up."
Richelle E. Goodrich, Smile Anyway

"Do it again. Play it again. Sing it again. Read it again. Write it again. Sketch it again. Rehearse it again. Run it again. Try it again. Because again is practice, and practice is improvement, and improvement only leads to perfection."
Richelle E. Goodrich, Smile Anyway

"Success is the result of perfection, hard work, learning from failure, loyalty, and persistence."
Colin Powell

It is no accident that this book enters the realms of silence with the chapter on persistence, or determination. This point must be made clear to the reader: the author is well aware of the fact that no matter how the language may be rosy here or elsewhere, the topics dealt with in this work are by no means child's play in theory or in practice. For if they were easy, life would be an extremely sweet experience for all of us. The success of all the pillars thus far explained depends on one and one pillar only, and that is the Pillar of Persistence. You can acquire the mastery of all the pillars imaginable in the world, but if you have no ability to be persistent, your outcome will be very short-lived, if there is any outcome at all. Determination is basically the vessel that holds the engines that make the apparatus run. You can be an excellent pilot and your airplane or ship may have sophisticated engines, mechanical, and electronic systems, but if the boat or airplane has a hole in the bottom, nothing else will matter. Persistence is nothing but the sharpening of all the other pillars discussed thus far by the mere act of keeping on keeping on until there is a breakthrough or the action becomes second nature to you. That is exactly why the very beginning of this chapter is a quotation from Joseph Campbell's *The Hero with a Thousand Faces*, to give you an upfront image of what happens when one hangs on and keeps relentlessly trying despite the odds against success in the face of apparently mighty obstacles.

The motif of the difficult task as prerequisite to the bridal bed has spun the hero-deeds of all time and world. In stories of this pattern the parent is in the role of Holdfast; the dragon's artful solution of the task amounts to a slaying of the dragon. The tests imposed are difficult beyond measure. They seem to represent an absolute refusal, on the part of the present ogre, to permit life to go its way; nevertheless, when a fit candidate appears, no task in the world is beyond his skill. Unpredictable helpers, miracles of time and space, further his project; destiny itself (maiden) lends a hand and betrays a weak spot in the parental system. Barriers, fetters, chasms, fronts of every kind dissolve before the authoritative presence of the hero. The eye of the ordained victor immediately perceives the chink in every fortress of circumstance, and his blow can cleave it wide.

www.makanologos.com

The most eloquent and deep-driving of the traits in his colorful adventure of Cuchulainn is that of the unique, invisible path which was opened to the hero with the rolling of the wheel and the apple. This is to be read as symbolic and instructive of the miracle of destiny. To a man not led astray from himself by sentiment stemming from the surfaces of what he sees, but courageously responding to the dynamics of his own nature — to a man who is, as Nietzsche phrases it, "a wheel rolling on itself" — difficulties melt and the unpredictable highway opens as he goes, (pages, 344-345).

Before getting into the body of this chapter, I wish to take a few moments to put myself in the spotlight here. I think this to be the most appropriate moment to do so. As you already know, ours is a world of ups and downs, left and right, back and forth, east and west, south and north, plus and minus, beginnings and endings, etc., so despite the joy I encounter in doing something, life obliges me to come to an end and move on to some other life requirements. So regardless of the pleasure I enjoyed writing this book and the pleasure I hope my readers will enjoy in reading it, nonetheless, this work must come to an end. As you can see, I am almost there. I would like to confess here to my readers before moving on to the heart of the matter of this last chapter that the joy that I lived while researching and writing this book was incomparable to anything that I have ever known so far in my life, besides enjoying sucking the breast of my beloved mom in the earliest days of life. Every time I thought the fountain of ideas was about to dry up, just with a little bit of digging, to my surprise, a well of inspiration would surge, lovingly and delicately feeding me with better thoughts, like a child in his mother's arms, making this work much more than I hoped it to be in quality.

This, of course, is due to only one thing, and that is the subject of this chapter — persistence and determination. When I first decided to write this book, to be honest, I was a little scared not only with the work that stood before me, but

www.makanologos.com

mostly with the magnitude of explaining my points of view since I could see difficulties in the topic itself. Indeed, it was a nightmarish kind of experience. In my head, I could hear how some people would be calling me names, how others would simply be questioning my competence and my credentials for writing such a book. Other people would ask demeaning kinds of questions, not about the merit of the work, but about me. This of course, despite the delay it caused me to get work started, was a less important factor in my decision making, and instead of discouraging me, nevertheless, in the subconscious it was a kind of the stimulus I really needed, not just to prove the critics wrong but to prove myself that there is not a thing I cannot do so long as I am determined to do it, no matter what the outer world thinks of me.

On the other hand, while my critics' attitude was irritating, to say the least, the most important element that scared me most was the self-questioning of my ability to produce a proficient work that I would be happy to attach my name to and accept the judgment of not only my contemporaries but also of generations to come, let alone my own offspring. This fear was inspired not only by my ability or lack thereof to think or write, but by a less-than-perfect grip on the English language, English being my second language that I learned only when I was already a fully mature person. Yet, soon afterward, it came to my mind to think of at least one person who achieved some worthy accomplishment without some kind of obstacle. In the end, I found that, while my English language proficiency was not so great, many great and brilliant minds had much tougher impediments than mine. Armed with this self-assuring key that opened some other avenues of thought in my mind, I started trusting my ability to do the work. I found it comforting to trust that the law of nature called persistence or determination would eventually send me friends of mighty power to rescue, whether I was aware or not. And as my trust grew, letter by letter, word by word, sentence by sentence, paragraph by paragraph, and chapter by chapter, my book grew, as, of course, did trust in my own ability. I lived this same experience when I wrote my first book, *The Best Kept Secrets of Personal Magnetism*, so the second time around; I lived it again while writing this book. It was not as life threatening as it was back then. Thus I kept my cool, and here I am writing the last chapter of the book. With these few words about me, let's now move on to the heart of the matter.

Persistence is genius, and there is no genius without persistence anywhere, above or below. Let's say this from the outset. If we all only understood, appreciated, and put to work the power of this law of nature called persistence, ours would be a world of angelic intelligence, an intelligence of true genius. It is absolutely impossible to exaggerate the power of rational persistence; few words can accurately express the magic of persistence in the right direction of actions. Throughout this book, I tried hard to restrain myself from using superlatives, and this is not going to be a superlative; nevertheless, I want to make it clear here that the power of a rational persistence cannot possibly be exaggerated.

There are two wings of greatness that truly brilliant minds use to reach the mountaintop of glory. Those are, first, all the other qualities unveiled in this book up to this chapter on the one side, and second, on the other side, persistence. Why, you may ask? Because none of the other pillars works efficiently alone unless it is greatly backed by the power of persistence. Persistence develops in a person a certain kind of faith in the self that is basically stronger than you and I can imagine, the kind of faith with which the mountains of life are literally obliterated. Think of this for a moment: how many times did you fall down when you were learning to walk in your childhood? Now that you are walking, can you imagine a human being, regardless of his status, who can convince you that walking is as difficult as flying with bare hands? Can you ever question your power to walk for as long as you are healthy?

www.makanologos.com

Be it love, attention, silence, or any other quality of greatness, they are all strengthened and perfected by persistence, and without persistence, they will remain dormant and consequently useless. The formula for greatness is very simple and easy to put into words once this pillar of greatness, persistence, is clearly understood. To brighten one's mind is not rocket science. It is simply the understanding of your goal, and you keep on working and walking (linearly) toward it until you reach it, and the moment you allow yourself to be distracted or pulled hither and thither by anything that glitters, you are lost.

It is that simple, but the world has "many things that glitter," many distractions that easily pull even a person of strong character at an unguarded moment off the track of achievement. The only shield that safeguards us from these unwarranted influences is persistence. Unless one is firm and resolute in pursuing his/her goal, thinking about climbing the mountain of greatness is basically being in denial. You can call them unwarranted influences, if you choose, or obstacles, if you will, but this you must know: without unwarranted influences or obstacles, there is no greatness. Brilliant minds prefer to call obstacles stepping-stones because overcoming them with great calm and determination and not escaping them is what greatness is all about. Here is how one expert put it in terms of faith: *"Untested faith may be true faith, but it is sure to be small faith, and it is likely to remain little as long as it is without trials. Faith never prospers so well as when all things are against her: Tempests are her trainers, and bolts of lightning are her illuminators."* (http://alesiachristine.blogspot.com/2009/12/untested-faith.html, accessed July 10, 2012)

A man with a fired-up determination is like powerful dynamite intended to blow up rocks in the heart of a mighty mountain. When one is dynamically determined, everything being equal, there is almost no goal he cannot reach, no obstacle he cannot overcome, below and above, just as Joseph Campbell phrased it:

When a fit candidate appears, no task is beyond skill...To a man not led astray from himself by sentiment stemming from the surfaces of what he sees, but courageously responding to the dynamics of his own nature – to a man who is, as Nietzsche phrases it, "a wheel rolling on itself" – difficulties melt and the unpredictable highway opens as he goes (pages 344-345).

It is the acceptance of negative conditions such as discouragement, fatigue, and fear that keeps people from achieving their goal or brightening their minds. Those inner monsters are the real dangers that keep the majority of people from even locating the mountaintop of greatness. When man takes a stand and is determined to climb any mountain, sometimes, in fact many times, the mountain itself bends to the will, desire, or command of the person, only to lift him/her up without much confrontation.

A great deal of the time, people fail to climb the mountain of greatness not because the mountain is too high or slippery, but rather for the simple reason that they give in even before they come close to it. They try to cross the bridge way before they come to it, just to give in to it before even facing it. A brilliant mind is not brilliant because of its brainpower but because of the calmness of its mind and its patience to deal with problems only when they come up. A majority of the time, things that keep us from taking a stand are things that we fear, and ironically, over 99% of the things that we fear never happen in the first place. One online Facebook entry put it this way: *"99% of the things we FEAR & worry about are in the FUTURE of which 98% will never happen...Fear never solves tomorrow's problems; it only robs today's peace & sleep."* Elsewhere, another online writer says this:

*We worry about too many things. We panic too often. And, we let too many things **scare us**. Many of these things never happen. Or they turn out to be not as bad as we imagined. Truth be told, there are very few true emergencies in life. It is important to be*

www.makanologos.com

able to keep your bearings in the face of urgent and perceived emergencies.

Check your own life experience to verify the accuracy of these statements.

So, the easiest way to train your mind to take a stand or acquire the quality of persistence is to always be calm first. Never allow yourself to cross a bridge before you physically come to it, meaning never try to solve a problem before its time comes, that is, all or most criteria and circumstances being in place or pointing in that direction. A team that fears its opposing team long before they meet on the court has strong odds of losing the game regardless of skilled players on its roster. Persistence and determination stand on the hope of a brighter tomorrow, while fear and discouragement destroy hope not only of a better tomorrow, but also of your ability to overcome any obstacle life has placed in your way while climbing up to the mountaintop of greatness. And when hope is destroyed, as it often is by most of us, no further effort is made. Life is about growth, and conquered obstacles elevate man higher on the mountain of greatness. Dodging them is to suffocate growth.

Remember this: when one is without hope, he or she cannot possibly make any further effort to climb the mountains of life. Brilliant minds strengthen their determination by charging and sustaining it with hope. Hope alone is the battery of their persistence. *"Hope is not a method"* is a very well known saying, and of course, anyone who thinks that things will happen because he/she has a strong hope is indeed in deep trouble. Hope was never meant to make things happen; it is only a battery to keep the consuming fire of effort behind the action burning in order to sustain an inflexible persistence even in the face of overwhelming odds. This is the only way brilliant minds make it to the mountaintop of greatness. This is one the best-kept secrets of brilliant minds, this is how intelligence is aroused, and this is the ELIXIR OF INTELLIGENCE, because light is its own defense, and inspiration is its own revelation.

www.makanologos.com

This is how you watch and look within the light. Seeing all within it, you make joy live in you and others, for there is nothing hidden that is not revealed to a constructive seeker who needs to know it so long as he/she stands for the Highest Ideal in the universe and honor to life is the motive for which he/she does everything. This is the end of the road, for this is how the great ones gained their immortality and a place of honor in the hearts of all generations to come, and so can you, so long as you stand for the Highest Ideal in the universe and honor to life is the motive for which you do everything. In front of a humble yet firm and determined person, life's barriers sometimes quietly melt without pressure or a fight from the outside. Simply, as in the words of Joseph Campbell, *"difficulties melt and the unpredictable highway opens as he goes."* Greatness is the highest price life can bestow upon any soul; therefore, it is a privilege reserved for the few, not the chosen but rather the persistent ones. A Japanese proverb says, *"money grows on the tree of persistence."* How true is that for you? I will not guess your answer, but here is my point: the Gods will offer any amount of the most precious stones in exchange for your tree of persistence if you have one. Life rewards greatly those who sustain its blows, for they are friends and protégés of Gods and Goddesses. Why? you might ask, and rightly so. Achieving great things here on Earth is the business of Gods and Goddesses, and they achieve those great things through persistent people. Thus, one who desires to have Friends of mighty power in both the world of senses and the mental world must first of all refine his power of persistence.

One of the most unfortunate things that was either purposely indoctrinated by religion in the minds of the masses or simply misunderstood by them is that, if you pray, then God will do the rest. While I believe in the power of prayer, and I would never even slightly discourage anyone from praying, the truth of the matter is that God can do for a person only what He can do through that person, and that means man must

www.makanologos.com

be physically doing something before God can do anything physical through him. If praying alone were the solution to mankind's problems, I think God would have solved all of them long ago. For eons, man has been praying to God, and God has been waiting for man to rightly position himself so He can act through him. Mankind's problems must and will be solved by a persistent man in action because that is the only prayer that sings melodious music into the ears of God; the only prayer that turns His attention to us; the only prayer that opens His eye to see us; the only prayer that motivates God to sing and speak into our brains the songs and words of inspiration; the only prayer that prompts God to project into our minds visions of splendor; the only prayer that induces God to pump us with unlimited energy to conquer any obstruction standing in our way.

It is a little bit difficult for me to put in words how much I truly believe from the bottom of my heart that wisdom is the purpose of life and that persistence is the ways and means through which to acquire it. I so deeply believe in the splendor of wisdom and the power of persistence that I took on "Wisdom" as my pen name and passed it onto my son as his legal name while adding "Persistence" as his middle name, both of which were on his legal birth certificate more than two years before these words were put into writing. That is how much I believe in what I am talking about here. I am trying to convey the greatest secret I know of here, second only to the knowledge and understanding of God. I hope many of my readers will agree with me that the most sacred secret of success resides solely in the power of an individual's tenacity. Neither God nor men desire to work with an unreliable person, a person who may be ready to give in to an apparent obstacle.

No man who ever walked on the face of the Earth has ever had all the qualities to climb the mountain of greatness. If the possession of the best qualities were the prerequisite of greatness, there would never have been a great person. But you

www.makanologos.com

and I know very well that there have been men and women of almost divine greatness. These people became what they became not because they were truly the best at what they did, but because they persistently tried their best in everything they were engaged in. Thomas Edison, who is regarded as one of the most intelligent people of all time, himself credits his success to hanging on after many failures until at last success came knocking at his door by the command of his power of persistence.

Albert Einstein, himself a personification of intelligence, refused to attribute his success to intelligence but rather to his power of persistence *"It's not that I'm so smart; it's just because I stay with problems longer…I think and think for months and years. Ninety-nine percent, the conclusion is false. The hundredth time I am right,"* he once said. Marie Curie, another powerhouse of geniuses of the twentieth century, could not agree more. *"Life is not easy for any of us. But what of that? We must have perseverance and above all confidence in ourselves. We must believe that we are gifted for something and that thing must be attained,"* she once said. And before Einstein and Curie, revealing the secret of his success, Louis Pasteur, a French chemist and microbiologist known for remarkable breakthroughs in the causes and prevention of diseases, said, *"Let me tell you the secret that has led me to my goals; my strength lies in my tenacity."*

Pasteur, Edison, Curie, or Einstein—any of these names can be interchanged with the word *greatness* in any dictionary, and the world will easily understand what exactly is meant. Yet these people attribute their greatness not to their brainpower or anything else, but to the power of persistence. There are reasons why persistence is ranked high among powers that make greatness possible, and it is not too difficult to figure out why. Man is by nature an imperfect being with half-baked talents, and the only way he can improve himself and fully bake his talents is by practicing not just what is easy but whatever he sets his mind to regardless of the so-called difficulties.

www.makanologos.com

Practice makes perfect, we are told, and *"smooth seas do not make a skillful sailor,"* says an African proverb. Explaining *"practice makes perfect,"* the online *Free Dictionary* by Farlex says that it is *"something that you say which means if you do something many times you will learn to do it very well,"* and a Wikipedia entry says, *"Practice is the act of rehearsing a behavior over and over, or engaging in an activity again and again, for the purpose of improving or mastering it, as in the phrase 'practice makes perfect.'"*

Another thing that most of us do not realize is that life itself is a very fragile substance. Because we breathe almost effortlessly (when healthy) and because the very air we breathe is free, we tend to take life for granted until the time we are in serious danger of losing it. Tomorrow is one of the greatest mysteries of life, yet we usually go into it blindly, putting our faith in the unknown. Of course, there is not much we can do about it. The only thing we can do, it looks like, is put our faith in the hands of those who are the most persistent amongst us because, powered by hope, persistent folks tend to see far and anticipate solutions to potential problems. If you look closely, you will notice that religion, philosophy, and science, the three most important disciplines that have steered the ship of mankind up to this point, have been dominated by very persistent and determined individuals who succeeded when almost 99.99% of the odds were against them. If you think Moses, Socrates, Jesus, Mohammed, Copernicus, or Galileo, you will conclude that theirs are stories of self and world conquests, not coronations.

Throughout the history of mankind, man has always sought ways and means to discriminate against fellow men, sometimes based on physical appearance, wealth, religion, gender, etc. All these elements have been fought over and will forever be fought over as long as they are used by the shortsighted to divide society based on exterior characteristics. But the holiest element that divides the strong from the weak, the leaders from the followers, and the excellent from the mediocre is persistence, an interior characteristic. And this element will never be subject to a law of man as long as it is used to seek true joy rather than false joy, as we will see later on. Or as the *I Ching* puts it, *"One should act in consonance with the way of heaven and earth, which is enduring and eternal. The superior man perseveres long in his course, adapts to the times, but remains firm in his direction and correct in his goals."*

The magic of persistence is not merely its power of enabling greatness or discriminating the excellent from the mediocre, but its power of turning failure into success or mediocrity into excellence. It really gives power to the seemingly weak people and transforms poverty into wealth, chaos into order, and evil into good. A persistent person can go without it, but only temporarily. As Orison Swett Marden said, *"There is genius in persistence. It conquers all adversities. It gives confidence. It annihilates obstacles. Everybody believes in a determined man. People know that when he undertakes a thing, the battle is half won, for his rule is to accomplish whatever he sets out to do."* When a man is armed with rational persistence, he is armed with not only a weapon that can literally free him physically, but a weapon that can rid him of all the flaws that lead men to defeat in the battle of life. The fruits of persistence can hardly be put into words except to say that a persistent person acquires Friends of mighty powers and earns the trust, friendship, and company of the Gods and Goddesses, for anything he/she desires is given him, including health, happiness, and wealth in any shape or form as his flame of persistence blazes on.

Persistence is the only force of nature so associated with time. Time is eternity, for in the end, eternity always wins. Time knows no opponent because it persistently and tirelessly fights back. Civilizations come and go as they bow to the mighty power of time. Very hard and great rocks give in to gentle and weak yet persistent drops of water. The current of a river is unconquerable not only because of its power but because of its persistence in pushing on. Persistence knows no defeat. As John D. Rockefeller phrases it, *"I do not think that there is any other quality so essential to success of any kind as the quality of perseverance. It overcomes almost everything, even nature."*

A man who knows and practices persistence in everything he does knows and practices the highest wisdom of greatness. A farmer who does not know that first he has to plow the land, then bury the seeds underground, and let plants grow while taking care of them before harvesting; and a student who does not first listen alertly to the teacher and then attentively learn the lesson are both headed toward devastating defeat in their careers. Persistence is one of the most prevailing powers of Mother Nature. A man who starts with a mind-set of persistence in whatever he does has already won three-quarters of his battles. There is no single great achievement in the world that can be or has been accomplished without persistence.

There is no greater enemy of achievement than discouragement. A person can be the strongest and smartest person on the face of the Earth, but if he cannot defeat feelings and thoughts of discouragement, he is doomed to fail. Discouragement is a very destructive feeling. Throughout the history of man, it has defeated very talented, skilled, powerful, and intelligent people, and many of the miseries we live with today are simply consequences of our own discouragement and that of those generations that came before us. Discouragement is just like the wrong medicine that not only goes down badly but also causes many side effects, such as muscle pain, headache, stomach pain, nausea, eye irritation, memory loss, etc.

When discouragement is about to strike a person, there are very good reasons why one should not continue the task at hand. A vast majority of people buys the bogus excuses of discouragement and end up either failing or not even trying. A persistent person not only knows how to identify the enemy of discouragement by its name but also by its look; thus he pays no attention to discouraging feelings, thoughts, or external influences that may cause him or her to either revise or abandon everything he has thought or done so diligently up to that point. Rather than giving in to misguided feelings or thoughts of discouragement, a persistent man bases his conclusions on the results or development of the work along the way. He is not stubborn but rather determined in his search for the good and does not give in to temporary setbacks or fear and doubt over achieving his quest.

Having described persistence and determination the best way possible my humble mind could enable me to, I think it is very important that I help enlighten those readers who may not be inclined to read between the lines. If they don't, they may be prey to a blind persistence that may not only lead them to their failures but to their mental and physical deaths as well. Please do not get me wrong here; determination or persistence is a very great quality. Ninety-five percent of the time, persistence will perform wonders for you, but the five percent of the time that is left, persistence can be as deadly as anthrax or any deadly poison you know. Thus there is a need to shed some light here on this substance, to help those who may not consider deeper interpretations of words.

As invincible as the power embedded in persistence is, it was never meant to work alone and break or disregard the laws of nature, but rather was meant to manipulate them wisely and constructively. Yes, laws are meant to be broken or bent, some people may say. But I advise you to always be careful with the laws of nature because they are never tampered with without consequences, except in rare instances. And of course, greatness is not about breaking the laws either of nature or man, but rather about manipulating them constructively. Engineers building a dam do not dry out the river, but they momentarily displace it while they are building the structure. Attempting to blockade the river may not only result in failure, but it will certainly jeopardize lives and negatively affect the ecosystem.

Regardless of the power of the flame of persistence that breathes in you, if you insist on jumping off a fifty-story building unaided, you will certainly die, but if you insist on skydiving

www.makanologos.com

or parachuting from as high as the plane can take you, you may not be expert at it the first few times you try, but in the end, you will become an expert if you obey the laws of that discipline. Persistence arouses consciousness of a strong will, but it must be for a good cause and use appropriate means in order for it to bring out our best inner qualities to serve us as we strive to dignify our lives in all its dimensions. Unrestricted persistence can be destructive if led by desire to obtain false joy.

While persistence is one of the most significant prerequisites of greatness, it can be implemented in a negative way as well. Addiction is one the most deplorable misuses of the power of persistence. *"An addict,"* as Rabbi Philip S. Berg puts it, *"whether of drugs, alcohol, gambling, or sex is understood by contemporary psychotherapy as a failed seeker after true joy."* Addiction is gained by the power of persistence, but rather than persisting in something that is harmful to society and the body, it follows a purely selfish need with a very strong desire that lets loose the wheels of persistence at an uncontrollable speed. While persistence is not the cause of consequences that may have happened, the motives that triggered persistence, selfish needs, can be fatal when sought with a burning persistence.

To ensure that persistence bears genuine fulfillment of greatness, the motive and means behind it must not be selfish or wrong. It is perfectly okay to pursue strong desires or needs with determination, but if these needs or desires are intense yet misguided, they can result not only in self-destruction but also serious injury to society at large. Insane or selfish manipulation of the laws of nature or society can go unpunished for a while, but persistently violating them never continues without dire consequences. One can occasionally achieve his goals by breaking the laws of nature and society, but he or she will almost certainly never reach the mountain of greatness.

It is not by feeding or satisfying your ego that you climb the mountain of greatness but rather by serving yourself through your service to society, not serving society through self-service.

www.makanologos.com

Exalted Secrets of Brilliant Minds   533

The whole is the sum of its parts, or maybe I should say, the whole is greater than any of its parts. The good of society is greater than your good. When you persistently pursue something that will benefit the whole society, it will ultimately benefit you, and it will never lead you to a destructive addiction but to true greatness, for it is the service of greater good that makes brilliant minds bright.

With all its might, persistence is utterly incapable of brightening a mind or transporting a mind to the mountain of greatness if the person has negative motives or destructive goals. A person who wants to brighten his mind must gaze at a bright star, not a dark star. As long as you insist on gazing at a dark star, your mind will never see the light, much less see the way leading up to the mountaintop of greatness. There is no greater blessing than the power of persistence, and if you innately have it, count yourself among the blessed few, for you already have the foundation of greatness within you. But if you don't have the power of persistence, the good news is that you can always learn through meditation and other means that it can be easily found with little effort.

"The difference between a successful person and others is not a lack of strength, not a lack of knowledge, but rather a lack of will," said Vince Lombardi. But this will to keep on keeping on must not be the will to ignorance or negativity, but rather the will to the greater good. Persistence for the greater good is the best recipe for greatness, whereas persistence into selfishness is its antipode. Truly brilliant minds know and clearly understand instinctively that it is the persistent pursuit of magnificent goals that causes prominence, and that is why they run to the mountaintop of greatness as if they were running down the valley. A mind seeking to brighten itself must know this: when it bows to the greater good persistently, its trip to the mountaintop of greatness will take care of itself.

The purpose of this book is not to simply make readers feel good about themselves, but rather to question the genuineness

www.makanologos.com

of the motive of their feelings, whether it is a longing for self-knowledge, an intelligent path for the course of their actions, or simply a journey in the land of actions or illusions. It is for the reader to determine where he/she is now and where he/she is going, but one thing is certain, of course. This book can help you determine where you need to go from here and how you can get there from here by merely asking yourself and answering these simple questions: How would you be today if, as a child, you had given up trying to walk because of the many falls you endured? If you had given up learning to talk because of the unintelligibility of your first words? If in kindergarten or first grade you had given up learning because of the hardship of learning the alphabet and basic numbers for the first time, let alone the fear of facing the stranger, Mr. or Ms. First Teacher?

These may seem laughable or comic questions, but the truth of the matter is that our first and most important achievements are not necessarily products of brainpower but of persistence. It is when we forget this critical fact that later on in life our dreams become literally steep mountains, climbable only by the fittest amongst us, when in fact early on in our childhood, we overcame the most important obstacles that predetermined the success of everything else afterwards. Those who proceed confronting every adverse situation or dream with that childhood mentality of persistence — that determination to walk regardless of countless falls, or to talk at all costs despite the difficulties of putting words together — go on to acquire brilliant minds and reach any mountaintop they fix their eyes on. Ultimately but erroneously, they are called the *"chosen few,"* when in fact they are the persistent few.

In our childhood, we all persistently banged on the doors of fear and doubt until they opened. We triumphantly passed through them and left them behind us as we went on to acquiring and mastering one faculty after another. But as we grow older, we forget what helped us to walk, talk, or learn new things for the first time and succeed as children. Those among us who

www.makanologos.com

maintain their childhood tenacity of learning and doing things are our kings and lords, as they set the agenda of our lives. The feeble masses build their huts in the valleys of life while the persistent few build their castles on the mountaintops, for they are the lords, barons, high priests, kings, and princes of this world. Life can be lived anywhere, but if life can be consciously chosen to be lived at the edge or limit that inspires brilliant minds, the fulfillment of a high purpose is possible. All great men who ever lived made this choice deliberately and had to cling to their goals despite the difficulties and odds against them. About persistence, as quoted at the top of this chapter, President Calvin Coolidge said:

Nothing in this world can take the place of persistence. Talent will not; nothing is more common than unsuccessful people with talent. Genius will not; unrewarded genius is almost a proverb. Education will not; the world is full of educated derelicts. Persistence and determination alone are omnipotent. The slogan "press on" has solved and always will solve the problems of the human race.

Obviously, I feel the urge to recall the words of P. S. Berg here again: *"The Voice that tells us to give up hope is never the voice of wisdom."* It has never been a part of true wisdom at all to abruptly quit one's dream or desire due to difficulties or lack of time needed to accomplish it. Like a sun, wisdom comes forcefully around high noon or in the second half of the day after cutting through the morning clouds. Wise men, most of whom are very mature people, acquire wisdom not by quitting but by hanging on despite hardship, learning as they go and growing up in wisdom only after many trials and errors before earning the respect and admiration of their fellow men.

There is no royal road to any successful endeavor, let alone to the mountaintop of greatness or the acquisition of a brilliant mind. Before taking off to climb the mountain of greatness, you will have better odds if you teach yourself the art of not only patience but also picking yourself up, dusting off the dirt that

www.makanologos.com

will certainly mess up your clothes, and then proceeding not necessarily in the same direction and with the same means, but toward the same goal nevertheless. When you are capable of doing this, you will be equipped and enabled to face many dangers and difficulties that you are almost certain to encounter on your way up to the mountaintop of greatness.

It is sometimes easier to open the door than to close it. On the way to great achievements, there are doors of fear and doubt that will have to not only be opened but also closed behind you. In other words, you will have to tear down any barrier of fear and doubt before reaching the mountaintop of greatness, and that is the secret of brilliant minds. In fact, the brilliance of the mind is nothing more than relentless creativity as the search for trophies fearlessly and doubtlessly goes on. Fletcher describes persistence as follows:

It is for this reason that to sensitive souls, the souls awakened to the Presence of the Spirit, the immanence of the God-Presence becomes in all the secret haunts of nature an abiding fact ever present to their consciousness. Therefore, these enlightened ones see more, hear more, feel more, and receive more from intimate association with nature than those average folk whose chief characteristics are their gregariousness, their obtuseness to blatant noise, and their love of excitement – often indeed, their acute horror of being alone. They are afraid of the mystery of life which in silence knocks on the door of consciousness, – afraid because it has been clothed in terror when it should be radiant with beauty. (Ella A. Fletcher, *The Law of the Rhythmic Breath,* page 250)*

This is one the best-kept secrets of brilliant minds, this is how intelligence is aroused, and this is the ELIXIR OF INTELLIGENCE, because light is its own defense, and inspiration is its own revelation. This is how you watch and look within the light; seeing all within it, you make joy live in you and others, for there is nothing hidden that is not revealed to a constructive seeker who needs to know it so long as he/she stands for the Highest Ideal in the universe and honor to life is

www.makanologos.com

the motive for which he/she does everything. This is the end of the road, for this is how the great ones of old gained their immortality and a place of honor in the hearts of all generations to come, and so can you, so long as you stand for the Highest Ideal in the universe and honor to life is the motive for which you do everything. This is how you win Friends of mighty powers, the Invisible Helpers who use the All-seeing Eye of God, for they are the All-knowing mind of God. This is what brings illumination to the mind, illumination to the feelings, illumination to the thoughts, and illumination to the actions. This is how brilliant minds are acquired.

Parting words

What goes up must come down. While I am a deep believer in the notion that the end is always in the beginning and vice versa, as the plants or forests are always in the seeds and the seeds are in the plants or forests, and while the end of this work is embedded in its beginning, I am compelled to bring it to a visible end here and now. I have strived to show you how the trees that came out of the seeds enter back into the seeds whence they came, where it is invisible and silent. I feel it is the right time to bring my passions under the rule of reason here, but before I do, let me say a few words. This work is the product of tremendous, genuine, and most of all relentless study that led me to some of the very amazing schools of life that I could have hardly dreamed of when I first planned to embark on its undertaking. This was not simply a writing experience; it was a learning experience. Along the way, as I studied the materials of inspiration, I learned a lot, and I am grateful to all the teachers and masters I met along the way. I take off my hat and humbly and willingly bow to their greatness.

That said, despite my convictions about what is in this book, I neither invite anyone to nor hope anyone will believe any statement in this book thoughtlessly or fanatically. No one should feel compelled to take my word for it. Rather, it

www.makanologos.com

is my deepest hope, wish, and above all recommendation that my readers evaluate every single word in this work through persistent actions. They have to be proved first if they are to be believed and passed on to those we love. I believe that when you put them to the test, not only will your own experience prove their truthfulness, but you, your loved ones, and society in general will benefit tremendously, for that is the whole purpose of the pain I took to write this book in the first place. If the only two things that you gained from this work are seeing life through a more optimistic lens and feeling the courage to overcome any obstacle that may stand between you and your burning constructive desire, my goal has been achieved. But this cannot be possible unless the work has been subjected to deep study, serious thought, and sincere actions.

While the passion to write still weighs heavily on me, the desire to say one more thing is still burning in my heart. However, despite the beauty of the game, the referee must bring it to an end, the forest must reenter the seed, and the voice must find solace in the silence whence it came. I, like a player on a winning team, want the carnival to go on, as I can hardly contain myself. Thus, I will let the amazing teacher Ella A. Fletcher and the masterful mythologist Joseph Campbell blow the final whistle on my behalf. Let's have Ella A. Fletcher start:

It is only when we can attain the inward calm can we free ourselves from the tango of the common daily perplexities and avocations, that we gain a true perspective of things that absorb us; realize the pettiness of the most of them, separate the wheat from tares; and cultivate a judgment that will successfully guide us and bring order and peace. There can be no final word on this subject. Its profound importance has been made clear to all who are sufficiently interested to think. To such there will be no fruitless moments of thought and endeavor. Ever, as they seek, will the Path become more illuminated; and they and I must continue to learn

www.makanologos.com

as long as we strive for "More Light" (The Law of the Rhythmic Breath, page, 362).

But, as a departing point for pondering before I withdraw back into silence and invisibility whence everything that is came, I put on the menu these words of Joseph Campbell in *The Hero with a Thousand Faces,* as they must be digested and almost religiously absorbed to clearly and unwaveringly steer the feelings, thoughts, and actions of all aspirants and students of genuine greatness:

Man is that alien presence with whom the forces of egoism must come to terms, through whom the ego is to be crucified and resurrected, and in the whole image society is to be reformed. Man, understood however not as "I" but as "Thou": for the ideals and temporal institutions of no tribe, race, continent, social class, or century, can be the measure of the inexhaustible and multifariously wonderful divine existence that the life in all of us.

The modern hero [man dying to reach the mountaintop of greatness for the greatest good], *the modern individual who dares to heed the call and seek the mansion of that presence with whom it is our whole destiny to be atoned, cannot, indeed must not, wait for his community to cast off its slough of pride, fear, rationalized avarice, and sanctified misunderstanding. "Live," Nietzsche says, "as though the day were here." It is not society that is to guide and save the creative hero, but precisely the reverse. And so every one of us shares the supreme ordeal — carries the cross of the redeemer — not in the bright moments of his tribe's great victories, but in the silence of his personal despair* (page, 391).

This is not a final word, as water does not cease to be by evaporating into the atmosphere or a tree by concealing itself in the seed. We must begin learning; thus the school must continue, as we are forever students, even after we reach the mountaintop of greatness. To an astute reader, this has been a springboard of imagination or a gateway into the world of shortwave and higher-frequency wisdom that surpasses the understanding of the mind, intelligible only through the experience of one's own

www.makanologos.com

feelings, thoughts, and, of course, actions. The breeze is truly revitalizing at the mountaintop of greatness. Strive to reach it at all legitimate costs for the greatest good, for this is one the best-kept secrets of brilliant minds, this is how intelligence is aroused, and this is the ELIXIR OF INTELLIGENCE, because light is its own defense, and inspiration is its own revelation. This is how you watch and look within the light. Seeing all within it, you make joy live in you and others, for there is nothing hidden that is not revealed to a constructive seeker who needs to know it so long as he/she stands for the Highest Ideal in the universe and honor to life is the motive for which he/she does everything. This is the end of the road, for this is how the great ones gained their immortality and a place of honor in the hearts of all generations to come, and so can you, so long as you stand for the Highest Ideal in the universe and honor to life is the motive for which you do everything. This is how you win Friends of mighty powers. This is what brings illumination to the mind, illumination to the feelings, illumination to the thoughts, and illumination to the actions. This is how brilliant minds are acquired. Thank you, and see you in the heart of light and silence.

Praise for "Exalted Secrets of Brilliant Minds"
In the second book in his "Hints of Wisdom Series", Exalted Secrets of Brilliant Minds: How to Arouse Intelligence and Climb the Mountain of Greatness Like the "Chosen" Few, Wisdom J.O.Y. Makano shares the techniques the heroes of the world used to reach greatness. For generations these secrets have only been revealed to a select few that traveled to great lengths in the hopes of receiving them, but with today's technology and freedom of information more people are able to delve into the mysteries that had before only been revealed to the precious few. Makano takes the role of the guide and leads readers to the steps of greatness. It is within your reach and this book can help lead you there.

www.makanologos.com

Unlike many self-help books that only reach a target audience or specific niche subject, Makano's Exalted Secrets of Brilliant Minds is for any mind hoping to attain greatness. Whether the reader wishes for scholarly, political, spiritual, or financial greatness this book will help them get there. Whatever your career pursuits are this book will help give you the advice needed to be the best in your field. No matter your dreams, greatness is possible.

Makano is a prolific reader and scholar of both ancient and current teachings and his education make this a highly diversified book. His expertise in the subject is certainly not a matter of question after reading this wise tome. The teachers and realms of wisdom within this text range from spiritual documents, such as the Bible and the Quran, scholarly works, such as those by the likes of Joseph Campbell, and even pop culture works. With so many teachers agreeing on the traits that lead to success, such as love, persistence, humility, self-confidence, and truth, readers can rest assured that Makano's beliefs are trusted, and with the footwork the author has done, readers can easily delve into the teachings without the struggles of past seekers of knowledge.

However, this is not a book to be read quickly and then cast aside. Makano stresses that this is simply the first step to greatness; while reading grants wisdom it is useless without taking action. This book requires readers to immerse themselves into it and spend time with the text...What is the joy of reaching a destination without the accompanying journey to get there? Whatever the initial purpose, it is undeniable that there is a wealth of valuable information for anyone wishing to begin their trek to greatness.

While this book is not a bit of light reading, the author's conversational style is sure to be a welcoming voice for readers who have struggled through less approachable teachings. Wisdom J.O.Y Makano is both a well learned and likeable teacher which makes learning enjoyable. This book will be a

www.makanologos.com

welcome for anyone struggling to find their way in life or those wanting to climb the ranks into greatness. I recommend Exalted Secrets of Brilliants Minds to anyone willing to keep an open mind and to put in some hard work in order to reach success.

By Tania Staley, Maryville, Tennessee; for Pacific Book Review.

ABOUT THE AUTHOR

Wisdom J.O.Y Makano is a philosopher, a poet, and a lifelong student of creative and esoteric mythologies, learning along the way what impels those immovable seeds of the human race to go for the perilous "quest for the road that leads to the place all wish to find."* He lives in the Pacific Northwest of the United States of America with his lovely wife and five children. *Exalted Secrets of Brilliant Minds* is Makano's second book. He is also the author of *The Best Kept Secrets of Personal Magnetism*, his first book, and two forthcoming books, namely, *The Central Mountain* (manuscript under review) and *Emancipated Intelligence* (manuscript in progress). Makano holds a bachelor of arts, a Master of Public Administration, and a Master of Arts in Teaching from Washington State University, Portland State University, and Lewis and Clark College, respectively. You can reach Makano by e-mail at makanologos@yahoo.com or visit his website at **www.makanologos.com**.

THE END!

*Joseph Campbell's *The Masks of God: Creative Mythology*, page 159.

Full credit to my TEACHERS

BIBLIOGRAPY

Aaron, David: *Endless Light: The Ancient Path of the Kabbalah to Love, Spiritual Growth and Personal Power.*

Alcone, Krishnamurti: *At the Feet of the Master.*

Bailey, Alice A.: *From Intellect to Intuition.*

Bailey, Mary: *A Learning Experience.*

Behrend, Genevieve: *Your Invisible Power: The Mental Science of Tomas Troward.*

Bennett, John R.: *The Origin of Freemasonry and Knights Templar.*

Berg, Michael: *The Secret: Unlocking the Source of Joy and Fulfillment.*

Berg, Dr. Rav Philip S.: *The Essential Zohar.*

Berg, Dr. Philip S.: *Education of a Kabbalist.*

Berg, Yehuda: *God Does Not Create Miracles, You Do!*

Braude, William G., translator: *The Book of Legends/Sefer Ha-Aggadah (Legends from the Talmud and Midrash)*, edited by H. N. Bialik and Y. H. Ravnitzky.

Brunton, Paul: *Discover Yourself.*

Brunton, Paul: *Hermit in the Himalayas.*

Brunton, Paul: *The Secret Path.*

Burroughs, Tony: *The Code: 10 Intentions for a Better World.*

Campbell, Joseph: *The Hero with a Thousand Faces.*

Campbell, Joseph: *The Masks of God: Occidental Mythology.*

Campbell, Joseph: *Myths to Live By.*

Campbell, Joseph: *The Power of Myth.*

CNN's Fareed Zakaria's GPS (Sunday, October 18, 2009).

Codd, Clara M.: *The Technique of the Spiritual Life.*

Codd, Clara M.: *The Way of the Disciple.*

Collier, Robert: *The God in You.*

Cooper-Oakley, Isabel: *The Comte de Saint Germain: The Secret of the Kings.*

De Hoyos, Arturo: *Scottish Rite Ritual, Monitor and Guide; 2nd Edition.*

Dumont, Theron Q.: *The Solar Plexus or Abdominal Brain.*

Drummond, Henry: *The Greatest Thing in the World.*

Emerson, Ralph Waldo: *"Self-Reliance": The Wisdom of Ralph Waldo Emerson for Inspirational Daily Living;* edited and with an introduction by Richard Whelan.

Epstein, Perle: *Kabbalah: The Way of Jewish Mistic.*

Fletcher, Ella Adelia: *The Law of the Rhythmic Breath: Teaching the generation, conservation and control of Vital force.*

Goddard, David: *Tree of Sapphires.*

Gonzalez-Wippler, Migene: *Kabbalah for the Modern World.*

Gospel of John 12:32.

Gospel of Luke 17:21.

Gospel of Matthew 6:33 KJV.

Graham, Lloyd M.: *Deceptions and Myths of the Bible.*

Haanel, Charles: *The New Psychology.*

Haddock, Frank Channing: *Power of Will.*

Haggard, H. Rider: *She.*

Halevi, Z'ev Shimon: *The Work of the Kabbalist.*

Holmes, Ernest: *The Art of Life.*

Kaplan, Aryeh (translation, intro., & commentary): *The Bahir: The Book of Illumination.*

Kaplan, Aryeh: *Jewish Meditation.*

Kaplan, Aryeh (revised edition): *Sefer Yetzicah: The book of creation in theory and practice.*

Kidder, David, and Noah D. Oppenheim: *The Intellectual Devotional.*

Levi, Eliphas: *The Key of the Mysteries* (translated from French by Aleister Crowley).

MacGregor Mathers, S. L.: *The Kabbalah Unveiled.*

Matt, Daniel C.: *The Essential Kabbalah.*

Nachman of Breslov, Rebbe: *The Empty Chair.*

Peale, Norman Vincent: *The Power of Positive Thinking.*

Ray, James Arthur: *Harmonic Wealth.*

www.makanologos.com

Rieker, Hans-Ulrich: *The Secret of Meditation*.

Satchidananda, Sri Swami: *Meditation*.

Schwartz, Daniel I.: *Finding Joy: A practical spiritual guide to happiness*.

Shinn, Florence S.: *The Game of Life and How to Play*.

Sivananda, Swami: *The Science of Pranayama*.

Spalding, Baird T.: *Life and Teaching of the Masters of the Far East, Volumes I, II, III, IV, V, and VI*.

Steiner, Rudolf: *Selections from the Works of Rudolf Steiner: The Mysteries, Teachings and Mission of a Master Christian Rosenkreutz*.

Towne, Elizabeth: *The Wisdom of Elizabeth Towne (Just how to wake the Solar Plexus), 3-in-1 Omnibus Edition*.

The Voice of the "I AM" #8, August 1950, published by the Saint Germain Press, Inc., Chicago, Illinois.

Wolf, Rabbi Laibl: *Practical Kabbalah*.

http://www.britannica.com/EBchecked/topic/510019/Rosicrucian

http://en.wikipedia.org/wiki/Socrates

www.truegospelpeace.com/thyself.htm

http://www.etymonline.com/index.php?term=desire

http://www.biblegateway.com/passage/?search=Matthew+18%3A1-6&version=KJV

http://en.wikipedia.org/wiki/virtue

http://www.latimes.com/news/nationworld/world/la-fgw-skorea-cloning27-2009oct26,0,5787969.story

http://en.wikipedia.org/wiki/Impeachment_of_Bill_Clinton.

www.washingtonpost.com/wp-srv/national/longterm/watergate/articles/080974-3.htm

http://www.ftrain.com/franklin_improving_self.html

www.deadlysins.com/sins/

http://www.flamebright.com/PTPages/Benjamin.asp

http://en.wikipedia.org/wiki/virtue

*http://www.biblegateway.com/passage/?search=Matthew+18%3A1-6&version=KJV*Matthew 18:1-6 (King James Version)

http://ploticus.sourceforge.net/stevepages/moralvirtues.html

http://victorian.fortunecity.com/duchamp/410/bsamurai.html

CPSIA information can be obtained
at www.ICGtesting.com
Printed in the USA
FFOW02n0952140514
5391FF